"If there were no debt in our money system, there would be no money."

—Marriner Eccles
7th Chair of the Board of Governors of the Federal Reserve System

"Following the war the Federal government ran a heavy [budget] surplus. It could not pay off its debt, retire its securities, because to do so meant there would be no bonds to back the national bank notes. To pay off the debt was to destroy the money supply."

—John Kenneth Galbraith, Economist

"Commercial banks create checkbook money whenever they grant a loan, simply by adding new deposit dollars in accounts on their books in exchange for borrower IOUs."

—Federal Reserve Memorandum

"Banks lend by creating credit. They create the means of payment out of nothing."

—Ralph Hawtrey, Economist

```
FEDWIRE
Federal Reserve Wire Network
Real Time Gross Settlement Funds Transfer System

Account: AIG_INSURANCE
Amount on deposit: -$63,541,992,914

User BEN_SHALOM_BERNANKE, are you sure you
wish to create $70,000,000,000 and credit it
to the account of AIG_INSURANCE? Y

WARNING! User BEN_SHALOM_BERNANKE, you are
about to create $70,000,000,000 of additional
reserves. Commercial banks may create
$630,000,000,000 of additional deposits from
these reserves, meaning $720,000,000,000
may be created. Are you sure you wish to
proceed? Y

WARNING! User BEN_SHALOM_BERNANKE,
$720,000,000,000 is 9.25% of the
$7,787,962,318,571 M2 money supply. If all
newly created money circulates, prices will
increase 9.25%. Are you sure you wish to
proceed? Y

Creating money and crediting account of
AIG_INSURANCE. Please wait. . .

Account: AIG_INSURANCE
Amount on deposit: $6,458,007,086

This money creation must be confirmed by 2
other Federal Reserve Governors. AIG_INSURANCE
will not have access to funds until this
verification protocol is completed.

Account: CITTGROUP
Amount on Deposit: -$21,998,306,741

User BEN_SHALOM_BERNANKE, are you sure you
wish to create $25,000,000,000 and credit it
to the account of CITIGROUP? ■
```

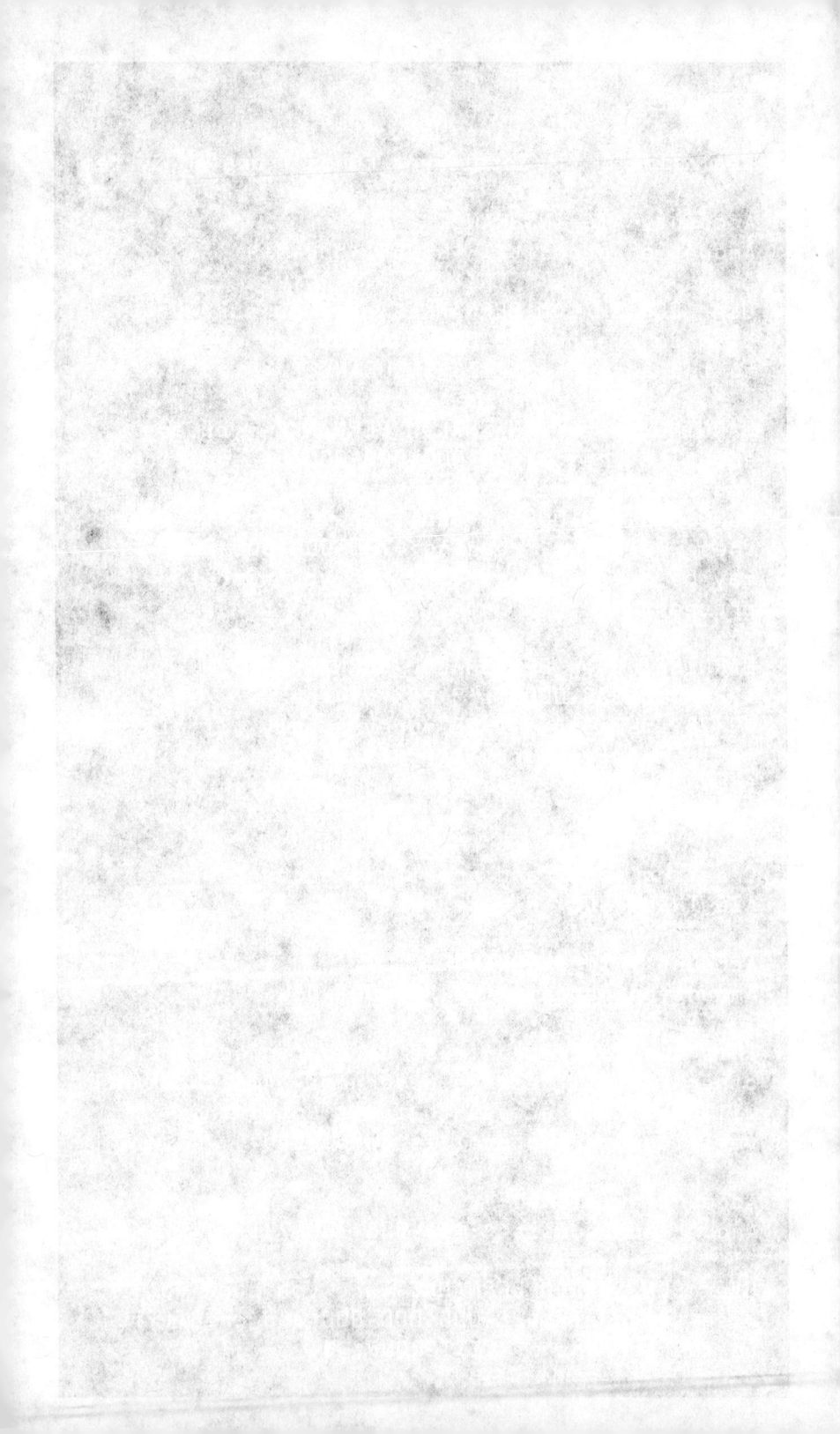

BUBBLENOMICS 2

BOOKS BY LAWRENCE ROWE

FICTION

The Founding Fathers Return

The Tesla Paradox

NONFICTION

Bubblenomics

SATIRE

Another Modest Proposal

VISIT LAWRENCE ONLINE

LawrenceRowe.com

This is the black & white version of *Bubblenomics 2*.

BUBBLENOMICS 2

Lawrence Rowe

MR

New York

ISBN-13: 978-0976766827

LCCN: 2011937775

Bubblenomics 2 may be purchased at special bulk quantity discounts for educational or promotional use. For information, e-mail: specialmarkets@lawrencerowe.com.

First paperback printing: May, 2016.

10 9 8 7 6 5 4 3 2 1

For my Mother

Who sacrificed everything for me

"So you think that money is the root of all evil. Have you ever asked what is the root of money?"

—Ayn Rand

"The study of money, above all other fields in economics, is the one in which complexity is used to disguise truth or to evade truth, not to reveal it. ... The process by which banks create money is so simple that the mind is repelled."

—John Kenneth Galbraith

"If all bank loans were paid, no one would have a bank deposit, and there would not be a dollar of coin or currency in circulation. This is a staggering thought. We are completely dependent on the commercial banks. Someone has to borrow every dollar we have in circulation, cash or credit. If the banks create ample synthetic money we are prosperous; if not, we starve. We are absolutely without a permanent money system. When one gets a complete grasp upon this picture, the tragic absurdity of our helpless position is almost incredible—but there it is. ... It is the most important subject intelligent persons can investigate and reflect upon. It is so important that our present civilization may collapse unless it becomes widely understood and the defects remedied. ... Somehow, the intelligent public of this nation must learn the fundamentals of this question."

—Robert Hemphill
Former Credit Manager at the Federal Reserve Bank of Atlanta

TABLE OF CONTENTS

INTRODUCTION

I wrote *Bubblenomics* and *Bubblenomics 2* to explain the most fundamental problem facing our civilization, the one problem which underlies most other political and economic problems. As banker Robert Hemphill noted in the epigraph, our banking & money system are "the most important subject intelligent persons can investigate and reflect upon."

This book is the sequel to *Bubblenomics*. It can be understood without having read *Bubblenomics*, but most readers without formal economic training find that having read *Bubblenomics* makes this book much easier to understand.

The more I learned about our banking system, the more repugnant it became. Economist John Kenneth Galbraith said, "The process by which banks create money is so simple that the mind is repelled." Most people who learn that banks simply create money are not just repelled but horrified.

Psychologists call this reaction "cognitive dissonance." Cognitive dissonance is mental inconsistency. It is an uncomfortable feeling caused by holding conflicting ideas simultaneously. In most people, cognitive dissonance about money creation results because they sense that it is unjust for a cabal of bankers to create money while everyone else must work for money. These conflicting ideas highlight the evil of our banking system and create unease in moral individuals. Many times during this book you will probably feel this unease.

Most money is not physical, but rather exists only on bank ledgers. Rules govern the way banks create and uncreate money on ledgers, and banks govern economies via their money creation and uncreation power. A person who doesn't understand the process of money creation and uncreation can never understand why economies collapse, why Depressions result, and why depressed economies stagnate and don't recover.

Money uncreation is especially counter intuitive to those who work for money. Banks uncreate vast sums of money on ledgers. No one who labors for money destroys it, as they would be squandering their labor.

Cognitive dissonance, indeed.

If banks have been extremely greedy and created gargantuan sums of money for loans, ledger-money rules eventually require them to uncreate gargantuan sums of money. Uncreating gargantuan sums of money would destroy the economy. Banks therefore scheme to avoid uncreating gargantuan sums of money. This can be done, but preventing money uncreation creates prolonged economic stagnation. This is the true story of America's economic woes during Depression v8.1929-1942, Depression v9.2006-201x, and most other Depressions in American and world history.

No matter how many times I ponder our fraudulent money system, I remain stunned by the audacity of the robbery which Speculatos perpetrate. Speculatos are the super-powerful speculating bankers introduced in *Bubblenomics*. Speculatos rule civilization by maintaining the exclusive prerogative to create money and forcing everyone else to work for money. Speculatos' audacity is flabbergasting, yet the most flabbergasting fact of all is that so few people understand our money system. Propaganda which sheeple are Fed about Depressions makes them angry, but they are not told even a fraction of the truth about what is happening—and will happen.

I am aware that the term "sheeple" alienates readers. Sheeple is a combination of the words sheep and people. It is a derogatory term used by Speculatos to describe the working class, which they consider a mindless herd that is meek, docile, and easy to exploit. Speculatos are confident that sheeple are too dumb and lazy to learn bubblenomics, especially the more detailed aspects contained in this book. I don't use the word sheeple to demean readers, but rather to drive home the point that we are being exploited.

I have read most books on money and monetary policy written since the late 1600s, when modern Central Banks were first created and rampant money creation and uncreation was institutionalized. Many of these books are excellent, but none truly took me inside the bowels of the banking beast and provided a vivisection of its money excretion. *Bubblenomics 2* does so. No other book teaches this critical information.

Pondering the way money is computed and uncomputered, the way money is created and uncreated on computer ledgers, can really bend your brain into a pretzel! What truly makes *Bubblenomics 2* unique is its exceptional clarity in explaining the tricky concepts that are the backbone of our monetary system. Having a vague sense that banks create and uncreate money out of thin air is different than understanding the precise money creation (and money uncreation) mechanisms they utilize.

Sheeple spend their lives slaving to avoid a scarcity of money, but have no interest in understanding the money system which enslaves them via the creation of excessive amounts of money. This is a strange and pitiful dichotomy. Also a disheartening one. As this book goes to press in May 2016, Depression v9.2006-201x persists and the economy continues to stagnate, but this econolypse no longer interests sheeple. Sheeple's view is that Speculatos already got away with it, nothing will change, and hearing about the mongo cornholing which the working class has taken is depressing. Why learn bubblenomics now, after Speculatos made a clean getaway?

Speculatos are still getting away with it. They have been getting away with it for centuries, and they will get away with it for centuries more unless sheeple educate themselves. Unless the banking & money system are reformed, human history will remain a hymn of sorrow, an endless series of Depressions and wars.

Depressions can only be eradicated by an enlightened populace. Ignorance is a choice. Sheeple who remain ignorant about our banking & money system abet Speculatos, and are essentially accessories after the fact in Speculato crimes.

Bubblenomics 2 follows the same format as *Bubblenomics*, short chapters that explain basic concepts, and outlined picture pages at the end of chapters that provide more detail. Readers can choose the level of detail they want by reading only the picture pages that interest them.

Bubblenomics ended with the completion of a Bachelor's in Bubblenomics, and *Bubblenomics 2* begins a Master's in Bubblenomics. A Master's Degree is an advanced degree which requires commitment and effort. *Bubblenomics 2* is grueling at times. Banking is not *American Idol*. To understand the machinations of genius financial criminals, some very boring, complicated information must be learned. There is no other way. If you think real solutions to corruption can be obtained in a fun and easy way without any real work, please put this book down, return to the herd, and enjoy your servitude.

Over the years I have met many people who flounder trying to understand our fraudulent banking system. Often these individuals have read dozens of books on the topic but are still perplexed and have elementary misconceptions. People have often asked me to recommend a book that explains our fraudulent banking system, but they usually complain that the books I suggest are boring or confusing. *Bubblenomics 2* is the book I always wished I could hand them.

LR
May 2016

MASTER'S

IN

BUBBLENOMICS

LIE-ABILITIES

"Our national circulating medium [money supply] is now at the mercy of loan transactions of banks; and our thousands of checking banks are, in effect, so many irresponsible private mints. What makes the trouble is the fact that the bank lends not money but merely a promise to furnish money on demand—money it doesn't possess."
—Irving Fisher, Economist

In *Bubblenomics*, rampant money creation by commercial banks was shown. Commercial banks accept deposits, provide savings and checking accounts, and issue loans. Commercial banks create money out of thin air anytime they issue a loan, but can be bank-rupted if too much of this conjured money is demanded or withdrawn. This seems paradoxical. How can a commercial bank with the power to create money go broke? Can't it just computer enough money to cover any losses?

No.

Let's start a commercial bank: Fifth Fleece Bank. Banks are licensed by the government. To get a license to fleece, you need CAPITAL, a.k.a. assets or startup cash. No cash, no license. No license, no bank. You have to have money to create money.

To keep its license to fleece, Fifth Fleece Bank must maintain a BALANCE SHEET which shows its ASSETS & LIABILITIES. Assets are items of value that Fifth Fleece Bank owns or is owed. Liabilities are what it owes. Liabilities can't exceed assets. Never, ever, ever.

Fifth Fleece Bank opens with $50 in investment capital. It has no customers yet. Its balance sheet:

```
Capital       Assets              Liabilities
$50           $0                  $0
```

The computer font is used because these transactions occur digitally. The computer font indicates fraudulent banking in which money is computered (created on a computer) and uncomputered (uncreated on a computer).

Those new to accounting sometimes confuse capital and assets. Capital is the money invested and can be thought of as profit. Assets & liabilities are the way banks record internal transactions like deposits and loans. A profitable bank accumulates assets that greatly exceed liabilities and transfers some of these assets to capital.

Customers open accounts with Fifth Fleece Bank. They are not told about fractional-reserve lending, or most wouldn't deposit money. What if a customer asks about fractional-reserve lending? Tellers are not lying when they claim to have

no idea, and the bank Capo—the Captain or manager of the fraudulent operation—bombards them with so many soothing 5-syllable words that they are duped.
The Capo seems way smarter than the customer, is enthroned in an opulent office,
and has an aroma of legitimacy.

Capos make fractional-reserve lending sound not just natural, but inevitable.
How could banks pay interest on deposits if they weren't lending those deposits
out? Fractional-reserve lending is implied by the act of paying interest. If banks
didn't fractional-reserve lend, they would have to charge depositors to store money and greatly increase fees for other services, and no one wants that. Without
fractional-reserve lending, any saved and unlent deposit would be a contraction of
the circulating money supply, which would hurt the economy. Fractional-reserve
lending isn't fraud, but a blessing, because it gets dormant deposits circulating in
the economy, generating prosperity. Half-truths at best, but sheeple are duped.

Customers deposit $100 of reserves at Fifth Fleece Bank. They give $100 of
reserves to Fifth Fleece Bank:

Capital	Assets	Liabilities
$50	$100 (Reserves)	

Reserves are ledger cash. The fact that these transactions are conducted on
ledgers doesn't change the fact that reserves are cash. You should always think of
reserves as cash.

Reserves can be physical cash, but they don't have to be physical cash. One
simple analogue which will suffice for now is a deposited check. A customer depositing a $100 check at a bank has transferred cash reserves to the bank without
giving physical cash to the bank. The transaction is conducted on computer ledgers
using non-physical, accounting-entry reserves.

Cash is an asset, something with value. Cash can be spent to buy goods &
services. The cash reserves which depositors entrust to Fifth Fleece Bank are therefore entered into its books as an asset.

Fifth Fleece Bank has accepted reserves from depositors, but must now give
the depositors something in return. Fifth Fleece Bank can't just take the money
and run (though it can just take the money and lend, as we'll see). Fifth Fleece
Bank opens accounts for depositors. These deposit accounts are promises to redeem
the reserves which were deposited. Fifth Fleece must give the depositors their
reserves back anytime the depositors demand them. The updated ledger showing
the deposit accounts:

Capital	Assets	Liabilities
$50	$100 (Reserves)	$100 (Deposits)
$50	$100	$100

To a depositor, a deposit is an asset that they can spend, which is good from their viewpoint. To a bank, a deposit is a liability which it may have to pay out, which is not good from its viewpoint. Fifth Fleece Bank thus enters the deposit in its ledger as a liability.

We are examining bank ledgers which show deposits and transactions from banks' perspective, not depositors' perspective. Depositors' perspective is different than banks, and depositor ledgers are therefore different than banks, as we'll see later when depositor ledgers are shown.

Fifth Fleece Bank accepted the reserve asset before creating the deposit liability. No competent banker assumes liabilities without first acquiring assets to honor or offset those liabilities, or they go broke fast.

The $100 of reserves that Fifth Fleece Bank possesses are an asset, and the $100 deposit that customers can demand at any time are a liability. Assets & liabilities are equal. Liabilities can't exceed assets, and don't.

This use of two ledger entries for a single deposit can confuse those unfamiliar with accounting. How can one deposit be both an asset and liability? Shouldn't a single deposit have a single accounting entry?

No.

The use of assets & liabilities is standard accounting practice, and is not fraudulent. Every new deposit or loan will result in an asset and a liability of equal value—even at an honest bank.

Those unfamiliar with accounting and banking also tend to muddle reserves and deposits. In an absolute sense, the reserve is the deposit, but in terms of accounting, on ledgers, the reserve and the deposit are two separate entities. Reserves are cash which has been set aside or reserved to honor deposits. Reserves back deposits and are used to redeem deposits. Deposits are promises to redeem reserves. Deposits are a claim to reserves. You will become hopelessly perplexed if you don't maintain this distinction.

So Fifth Fleece Bank has accepted $100 of cash reserves from customers, and created $100 of deposit accounting entries which are promises to redeem those reserves. $100 of reserves back $100 of deposits. Deposits are 100% backed by reserves. The RESERVE RATIO, the ratio of reserves to deposits, is 100%:

$$\text{Reserve Ratio} = \frac{\text{Reserves}}{\text{Deposits}} = \frac{\$100}{\$100} = 1.00 \text{ or } 100\%$$

This initial moment right after Fifth Fleece Bank opens and accepts its first deposits will be the only time it has a 100% reserve ratio and can honor simultaneous withdrawal demands by all customers. This is the only time it is solvent and can simultaneously honor all deposits.

Now the fun begins. Additional deposits are created. In *Bubblenomics*, we learned that America has three types of banks: a Central Bank, commercial banks, and investment banks. The Central Bank is the supreme bank, and exercises centralized control over commercial banks and investment banks. The FEDERAL RESERVE or FED is America's central bank. The Federal Reserve Bank has decreed a STATUTORY RESERVE RATIO REQUIREMENT of 10%. Commercial banks only have to keep an amount of reserves equal to 10% of deposits. This amount of reserves is the STATUTORY RESERVE BALANCE REQUIREMENT. 10% or $10 of Fifth Fleece Bank's reserves must be kept to back the $100 of deposits, 90% or $90 of its reserves are recategorized as "excess" reserves which can be used for loans:

Capital	Assets	Liabilities
$50	$10 (Reserves)	$100 (Deposits)
	$90 ("Excess" Reserves)	
$50	$100	$100
		100% Reserve Ratio

The reserve ratio will be shown on the lower right hand side of all ledgers forevermore.

John Q. Debtor wants a $90 mortgage, Fifth Fleece Bank issues the mortgage and writes Debtor a $90 check. "Excess" reserves are used for the loan and paid out to John Q. Debtor or his bank. Fifth Fleece Bank's updated balance sheet:

Capital	Assets	Liabilities
$50	$10 (Reserves)	$100 (Deposits)
$50	$10	$100
		10% Reserve Ratio

Fifth Fleece Bank has $100 of deposits, but only $10 of reserves. Fifth Fleece Bank has embezzled $90 of reserves and lent them out, but it doesn't subtract $90 from depositors' accounts. Depositors would notice this, freak out, and mob the bank demanding deposits. Depositors think they can demand $100 of deposits, but Fifth Fleece Bank's reserves—its money on hand to honor deposits—are only $10 or 10% of deposits. Fifth Fleece Bank's reserve ratio is now 10%:

$$\text{Reserve Ratio} = \frac{\text{Reserves}}{\text{Deposits}} = \frac{\$10}{\$100} = 0.10 \text{ or } 10\%$$

$90 of Fifth Fleece Bank's deposit liabilities are not backed by reserves and can't be honored. $90 of Fifth Fleece Bank's deposit liabilities are now lie-abilities:

> **lie•abil•i•ty**, noun, a liability which a bank can't honor because it has engaged in fraudulent fractional-reserve lending; a promise made by a bank to pay out reserves that it doesn't possess; any demand deposit not backed 100% by reserves.

Fifth Fleece Bank has created lie-abilities—liabilities not backed by reserves—and is bankrupt. Isn't it? Fifth Fleece Bank's liabilities exceed its assets. Don't they? No. The $90 loan is an asset because Fifth Fleece Bank expects John Q. Debtor to repay it:

Capital	Assets	Liabilities
$50	$10 (Reserves)	$100 (Deposits)
	$90 (Loan to be Repaid)	
$50	$100	$100
		10% Reserve Ratio

Liabilities don't exceed assets, but if depositors withdraw even $10.01, Fifth Fleece Bank is short reserves. Loans may be assets, but they are not reserves. Loans become reserves when they are repaid. Loan payments will be made over years, meaning reserves needed to honor deposits will trickle in over years. Honest books would show:

Assets	Liabilities
$10 (Reserves)	$100 (Deposits)
$90 (Reserves bank doesn't have and prays depositors don't demand)	
$10	$100
	10% Reserve Ratio

This is our banking system in a nutshell. Deposits are fractionally backed by reserves, or fractionally reserved. If depositors demand significant amounts of their reserves, banks don't have them and are bank-rupted.

If depositors withdraw $4, Fifth Fleece Bank has enough reserves to honor the demand:

```
Assets                          Liabilities
$10 (Reserves)                  $100 (Deposits)
$90 (Loan)
-$4 (Reserve payment)            -$4 (Deposit withdrawal)
```

```
$96                             $96
                                    6.3% Reserve Ratio
```

The new additions to the ledger are shown in red. As ledgers grow more complex, this will make them easier to read. In accounting, negative entries are sometimes colored red, but we will also color positive entries red. The red is an indication that an entry is new, and doesn't indicate anything else.

If you have the black & white printed version of this book, the red ledger entries are not colored but will appear in a more rounded font (for computer fonts) or in a bold font (for handwriting fonts used later). A color printed version of *Bubblenomics 2* is available. Some readers feel that the red ledger entries simplify and enhance learning and therefore prefer the color version of this book.

When the depositor withdraws $4 from their bank account, Fifth Fleece Bank gives them $4 of reserves to honor the demand. This $4 is subtracted from Fifth Fleece Bank's reserves. As the depositor has been given $4 of the cash which they previously deposited, they no longer have a claim to this $4, so it is subtracted from the balance in their deposit account. Fifth Fleece Bank's ledger after the deposit withdrawal is processed:

```
Assets                          Liabilities
 $6 (Reserves)                  $96 (Deposits)
$90 (Loan)
```

```
$96                             $96
                                    6.3% Reserve Ratio
```

Assets & liabilities both decreased by $4 on Fifth Fleece Bank's ledger. As mentioned, this is standard accounting procedure. Every addition or credit to bank ledgers should include two entries, one credit to assets and one credit to liabilities. Every subtraction or debit to bank ledgers should include two entries, one debit to assets and one debit to liabilities.

Before the deposit withdrawal, Fifth Fleece Bank had $10 of reserves backing $100 of deposits, which was a 10% reserve ratio. After the deposit withdrawal, Fifth Fleece Bank has $6 of reserves backing $96 of deposits, which is a 6.3% reserve ratio:

$$\text{Reserve Ratio} = \frac{\text{Reserves}}{\text{Deposits}} = \frac{\$6}{\$96} = 0.063 \text{ or } 6.3\%$$

Before the withdrawal Fifth Fleece Bank could honor 10% of deposits, after the withdrawal it can only honor 6.3% of deposits. Fifth Fleece Bank's lie-abilities—its deposits which are unbacked by reserves—were 90% of its total deposits before the withdrawal, but are 93.6% of total deposits after the withdrawal. As Fifth Fleece Bank's reserve ratio decreased, its lie-abilities increased. Its risk of defaulting on its deposit obligations increased.

Even honest banks want more deposits so that they can issue more loans and earn more interest income. No bank likes deposit withdrawals because less deposits mean less loans that can be issued. However, dishonest banks that fractional-reserve lend hate deposit withdrawals because they increase lie-ability exposure. Honest banks never have lie-ability exposure, as we will see.

Back to the beginning again, when Fifth Fleece Bank has $100 of deposits and has loaned out $90 of reserves. If depositors demand $10—a mere 10% of total deposits—Fifth Fleece Bank can honor these withdrawals, but has no more reserves to honor any other deposits:

```
Assets                          Liabilities
$10 (Reserves)                  $100 (Deposits)
$90 (Loan)
-$10 (Reserve payment)          -$10 (Deposit withdrawal)
_____
$90                             $90
                                     0% Reserve Ratio
```

The updated ledger after the deposit withdrawal is processed:

```
Assets                          Liabilities
 $0 (Reserves)                  $90 (Deposits)
$90 (Loan)
_____
$90                             $90
                                     0% Reserve Ratio
```

Fifth Fleece Bank is still solvent, but any deposit withdrawal bankrupts it because it has no reserves. As there are no reserves, reserves don't need to be shown on the ledger:

```
Assets                          Liabilities
$90 (Loan)                      $90 (Deposits)
_____
$90                             $90
                                     0% Reserve Ratio
```

The $90 deposit is backed only by a $90 loan, not by any reserves. Depositors who come to withdraw money want to be paid reserves, not loans. Banks are therefore not allowed to keep no reserves. There are statutory reserve ratio requirements which decree that reserves equal to some percentage of deposits must be kept by banks. It is easy to see that a bank with no reserves won't be in business long, but even if a bank were irresponsible enough to attempt to operate with no reserves, the law prevents such recklessness. The law doesn't prevent a similar form of recklessness that is paltry reserve levels close to zero, as we will see. The law prevents the absurd danger of a bank with no reserves, but not the absurdity of banks with dangerously low reserves.

If depositors had tried to demand $10.01, Fifth Fleece Bank expends all its reserves, and is still short reserves to honor the withdrawal. Its lie-abilities are exposed:

```
Assets                              Liabilities
$10.00 (Reserves)                   $100.00 (Deposits)
$90.00 (Loan)
-$10.01 (Reserve payment)           -$10.01 (Deposit withdrawal)
_____
$89.99                              $89.99
                                    -0.01% Reserve Ratio
```

The negative reserve ratio of -0.01% indicates that the bank is short an amount of reserves equal to 0.01% of deposits.

The ledger showing the deposit withdrawal broken up into the portion that can be honored and the portion that can't be honored:

```
Assets                              Liabilities
$10.00 (Reserves)                   $100.00 (Deposits)
$90.00 (Loan)
-$10.00 (Reserve payment)           -$10.00 (Deposit withdrawal)
-$0.01 (Reserve shortage)           -$0.01 (Lie-ability exposure)
_____
$89.99                              $89.99
                                    -0.01% Reserve Ratio
```

The loan is not reserves. The loan can't be used to honor a deposit. Only reserves can be used to honor a deposit. Fifth Fleece Bank only had $10 of reserves, so can only pay the depositor $10. The updated ledger after this $10 is paid:

```
Assets                          Liabilities
$90.00 (Loan)                   $90.00 (Deposits)
-$0.01 (Reserve shortage)       -$0.01 (Lie-ability exposure)
```
___

```
$89.99                          $89.99
                                     -0.01% Reserve Ratio
```

The reserve shortage and lie-ability exposure are the portion of the withdrawal that Fifth Fleece Bank can't honor, which in this case was $0.01 or 1¢. The same principle would have held for any withdrawal larger than $10.01, the only difference is that the reserve shortage and lie-ability exposure would have been larger. If the depositor tried to withdrawal $30, the final ledger would have been:

```
Assets                          Liabilities
$90 (Loan)                      $90 (Deposits)
-$20 (Reserve shortage)         -$20 (Lie-ability exposure)
```
___

```
$70                             $70
                                      -22% Reserve Ratio
```

There would have been $20 of lie-ability exposure rather than 1¢ of lie-ability exposure.

A depositor who discovers that their bank can't honor its contractual deposit commitments is not amused. The defrauded depositor tells other depositors that their bank is bank-rupt, and all depositors run to the bank and demand reserves that the bank doesn't have. This is a bank run.

As we begin viewing ledgers with larger numbers, the decimal points and commas of different sized numbers will be lined up to allow easy comparison. For those rusty at math, $1 thousand is $1,000, or a 1 followed by 3 zeroes. $1 million is $1,000,000, or a 1 followed by 6 zeroes. $1 billion is $1,000,000,000, or a 1 followed by 9 zeroes. $1 trillion is $1,000,000,000,000, or a 1 followed by 12 zeroes. Here are the different sized numbers in ledger form:

```
            $1,000 ($1 Thousand)
        $1,000,000 ($1 Million)
    $1,000,000,000 ($1 Billion)
$1,000,000,000,000 ($1 Trillion)
```
___

```
$1,001,001,001,000
```

In the previous example there is only $100 of deposits, but applied on a massive scale with billions or trillions of dollars of deposits, the simple fractional-reserve fraud can devastate an economy. And has. For example, here is Bank of America's balance sheet in September 2008, during Depression v9.2006-201x, just before "The Bailout" (The Emergency Economic Stabilization Act of 2008) passed:

```
Assets                              Liabilities
  $7,608,945,000 (Reserves)           $672,067,377,000 (Deposits)
$664,458,432,000 (Loans
                    a.k.a. reserves Bank of America doesn't have
                    and prays depositors don't demand)

$672,067,377,000                    $672,067,377,000
                                           1.1% Reserve Ratio
```

When explaining different concepts, it is useful to show real world money supply and banking data from a single point in time. That point in time will be September 2008, during Depression v9.2006-201x, just before The Bailout passed.

In September 2008 just before The Bailout passed, Bank of America had $664 billion of lie-abilities, $664 billion of deposits unbacked by reserves that it could not honor if they were demanded. Bank of America had $672 billion of deposits, but only kept $7 billion of reserves to honor them, which is a 1.1% reserve ratio:

$$\text{Reserve Ratio} = \frac{\text{Reserves}}{\text{Deposits}} = \frac{\$7,608,945,000}{\$672,067,377,000} = 0.011 \text{ or } 1.1\%$$

This 1.1% reserve ratio is less than the 10% Fed-decreed statutory reserve ratio requirement used in most examples of fractional-reserve banking. This discrepancy will be explained later, ignore it for now.

Bank of America only had enough reserves to honor 1.1% of its deposits. Each $1 of its reserves backed $88.33 of deposits. If depositors tried to withdraw just 2% of deposits, or $13 billion ($13,441,347,540), Bank of America couldn't have honored the demands:

```
Assets                              Liabilities
   $7,608,945,000 (Reserves)          $672,067,377,000 (Deposits)
 $664,458,432,000 (Loans)
 -$13,441,347,540 (Reserve            -$13,441,347,540 (Deposit
                    payment)                             withdrawal)

$658,626,029,460                    $658,626,029,460
                                      -0.89% Reserve Ratio
```

The ledger showing the deposit withdrawal broken up into the portion that can be honored and the portion that can't be honored:

Assets		Liabilities	
$7,608,945,000	(Reserves)	$672,067,377,000	(Deposits)
$664,458,432,000	(Loans)		
-$7,608,945,000	(Reserve payment)	-$7,608,945,000	(Deposit withdrawal)
-$5,832,402,540	(Reserve shortage)	-$5,832,402,540	(Lie-ability exposure)
$658,626,029,460		$658,626,029,460	
		-0.89% Reserve Ratio	

Loans are not reserves. Loans can't be used to honor deposits. Can you imagine going to Bank of America to withdraw $5,000, and the teller handing you someone's car loan? Or the teller asking you and the 86 people in line behind you if you'd accept a mortgage instead of cash? Negative, Ghostrider. Only reserves can be used to honor deposits. Bank of America only had $7,608,945,000 of reserves, so can only pay depositors $7,608,945,000. The updated ledger after this $7,608,945,000 is paid:

Assets		Liabilities	
$664,458,432,000	(Loans)	$664,458,432,000	(Deposits)
-$5,832,402,540	(Reserve shortage)	-$5,832,402,540	(Lie-ability exposure)
$658,626,029,460		$658,626,029,460	
		-0.89% Reserve Ratio	

Don't let the large numbers intimidate you. This is the same fraud from the $100 ledger. Bank of America depositors attempt to withdraw $13.4 billion—2% of Bank of America's $672 billion of deposits. Bank of America only has $7.6 billion of reserves to honor the $13.4 billion of deposit demands. The remaining $5.8 billion of deposit withdrawals ($13.4 billion - $7.6 billion = $5.8 billion) can't be honored. Bank of America has a $5.8 billion reserve shortage. That is a lot of defrauded depositors. These defrauded depositors tell others, and soon all Bank of America depositors run to Bank of America demanding reserves that it doesn't have. . .

Obtaining $5.8 billion of reserves is a bit harder than obtaining the $90 of reserves in the simplified teaching examples, but even $5.8 billion is a miniscule amount of Bank of America's lie-ability exposure. If 10% or $67 billion of Bank of America's deposits were withdrawn, it faced a $60 billion reserve shortage. If 20% or $134 billion of Bank of America's depositors demanded their money, it faced a

$127 billion reserve shortage. If 30% of Bank of America's depositors demanded their reserves, Bank of America faced a $194 billion reserve shortage...

Where could Bank of America obtain $60 billion of reserves? Or $127 billion of reserves? Only one place—but let's not get ahead of ourselves. Every bank in America practices fraudulent fractional-reserve lending and has lie-ability exposure similar to Bank of America's. When The Bailout passed in September 2008, only 8 U.S. banks had more than $100 billion of deposits, and these 8 huge banks held 40% of all U.S. bank deposits. Here are the actual reserve ratios of 7 of these huge banks at the time of The Bailout:

Bank	Domestic Deposits	Total Reserves	Reserve Ratio	Lie-abilities
Bank of America	$672,067,377,000	$7,608,945,000	1.1%	$664,458,432,000
J.P. Morgan Chase	$668,094,000,000	$30,055,000,000	4.5%	$638,039,000,000
Wachovia	$375,361,000,000	$13,577,000,000	3.6%	$361,784,000,000
Wells Fargo	$296,059,000,000	$4,408,000,000	1.5%	$291,651,000,000
Citibank	$272,398,986,000	$24,476,576,000	9.0%	$247,922,410,000
U.S. Bank	$128,591,505,000	$1,354,941,000	1.1%	$127,236,564,000
Suntrust	$111,375,100,000	$1,037,691,000	0.9%	$110,337,409,000

For those who still find large numbers daunting, here is the table in a more simplified form:

Bank	Domestic Deposits	Total Reserves	Reserve Ratio	Lie-abilities
Bank of America	$672 billion	$7.61 billion	1.1%	$664 billion
J.P. Morgan Chase	$668 billion	$30.1 billion	4.5%	$638 billion
Wachovia	$375 billion	$13.6 billion	3.6%	$361 billion
Wells Fargo	$296 billion	$4.41 billion	1.5%	$291 billion
Citibank	$272 billion	$24.5 billion	9.0%	$247 billion
U.S. Bank	$128 billion	$1.35 billion	1.1%	$127 billion
Suntrust	$111 billion	$1.04 billion	0.9%	$110 billion

In most cases, these reserve ratios are much higher than those which banks had maintained. This is because banks had already begun receiving significant amounts of Bailout money from the Federal Reserve. More on this later.

Washington Mutual Bank is not on this list. It had about $186 billion of deposits at the time of The Bailout, didn't keep sufficient reserves, couldn't honor depositor withdrawals, and went bank-rupt. Washington Mutual Bank was the 6th largest bank in America, and its bank-ruptcy was the largest bank failure in U.S. history at that time. The Federal Deposit Insurance Corporation (FDIC) and Federal Financial Institutions Examination Council (FFIEC) require all U.S. banks to submit quarterly financial statements or "call reports" which the public can access. The FDIC and FFIEC usually maintain archival reports of banks that fail, but Washington Mutual Bank's report at that time is no longer available. The author called the FDIC and FFIEC and both refused to provide the Washington Mutual Bank call report. Neither the FDIC nor the FFIEC would give a reason why the report would not be provided. Thus there is no definitive primary source from which Washington Mutual Bank's reserves or reserve ratio can be determined. This is why it was excluded from the list of the 8 largest banks.

In September 2008 just before The Bailout passed, J.P. Morgan Chase Bank had $668 billion in deposit liabilities, only had enough reserve assets to honor $30 billion or 4.5% of deposits, and therefore had $638 billion of deposit lie-abilities it couldn't honor. Wachovia Bank had $375 billion in deposit liabilities, only had enough reserve assets to honor $13 billion or 3.6% of deposits, and therefore had $361 billion of deposit lie-abilities it couldn't honor. Wells Fargo Bank had $296 billion in deposit liabilities, only had enough reserve assets to honor $4 billion or 1.5% of deposits, and therefore had $291 billion of deposit lie-abilities it couldn't honor...

Et cetera, et cetera, ad nauseam, ad infinitum. The temptation to write a hundred page paragraph listing the paltry reserves and massive lie-abilities of every U.S. bank will be resisted.

The root cause of most bank failures is fraudulent fractional-reserve lending. There is a reason we don't say restaurant-rupt, pharmacy-rupt, or grocer-rupt. The word bank-rupt is apt:

> **bank-•rupt**, adjective, engaged in fraudulent fractional-reserve lending and has had lie-abilities exposed; can't honor depositor demands for reserves and is insolvent. Also: bank-rupted. Abbreviated: rupt, rupted, ruptcy.

Suppose no depositor withdraws money, but John Q. Debtor defaults on his $90 loan. His loan repayment asset must be zeroed out:

Capital	Assets	Liabilities
$50	$10 (Reserves)	$100 (Deposits)
	$0 (Defaulted Loan)	
$50	$10	$100

10% Reserve Ratio

Lie-abilities exceed assets by $90, and even if capital were liquidated to honor the deposit, there is not enough to make up the shortfall. Capital can't be liquidated quickly regardless, so the bank and its depositors are screwed.

Why can't Fifth Fleece Bank create another $90 of reserves when depositors demand their $100 or when the loan defaults? Accounting rules don't allow this.

Commercial banks can't create money anytime they please. A computered money supply without rigidly enforced accounting rules would be no different than a physical money supply in which everyone had a printing press in their basement. If Bank of America could simply create $60 billion of reserves out of thin air when its depositors attempted to withdraw money, and Citibank, Wells Fargo, J.P. Morgan Chase, and every other bank in America could also create reserves out of thin air when their depositors attempted to withdraw money, there would be money creation without limit, and hyperinflation would result.

Commercial banks are allowed to create deposits and embezzle reserves, but are not allowed to create reserves. Commercial banks are allowed to accept deposits of reserves, create deposit accounts which are a claim to the deposited reserves, lie and tell the depositor that they have a claim to the full amount of reserves, and then embezzle 90% (or more) of the reserves and lend them. Commercial banks are allowed to create deposits in excess of reserves, but they are not allowed to create reserves which back deposits and are needed to honor deposits.

Okay. Commercial banks can't create reserves. You get it. This statement was repeated multiple times because it is critical to understanding the fractional-reserve scam. You will become hopelessly confused if you are not emphatically clear about which banks can create reserves and which banks can't.

Fifth Fleece Bank is insolvent, but can keep operating as long as depositors with claims to $100 don't demand more than $10. Bank of America is insolvent, but can keep operating as long as depositors with claims to $672 billion don't demand more than $7 billion. J.P. Morgan Chase Bank is insolvent, but can keep operating as long as depositors with claims to $668 billion don't demand more than $30 billion. Wells Fargo Bank is insolvent, but can keep operating as long as depositors with claims to $296 billion don't demand more than $4 billion. Citibank is insolvent, but can keep operating as long as depositors with claims to $272 billion don't demand more than $24 billion...

Usually, depositors only demand significant percentages of deposits if word of loan defaults leaks out. If word of loan defaults doesn't leak, or loans are never defaulted, banks practicing fraudulent fractional-reserve lending can remain insolvent yet operational, without customers realizing their deposits are lie-abilities.

LIE-ABILITIES PICTURE PAGES

TO SKIP THE PICTURE PAGES AFTER THIS CHAPTER, PLEASE TURN TO PAGE 20

STATUTORY RESERVE RATIO AND RESERVE BALANCE REQUIREMENTS

Statutory reserve ratio requirements and reserve ratios will be discussed through-out this book, as will statutory reserve balance requirements and reserve balances. These terms often perplex people learning about fraudulent fractional-reserve lending for the first time, so they will be defined rigorously here to avoid confusion. If you are even a little bit confused about statutory reserve ratio requirements and statutory reserve balance requirements, it is critical that you read this section.

Let's begin by defining the four terms:

STATUTORY RESERVE RATIO REQUIREMENT: The portion of deposits, expressed as a percentage, that a bank is legally required to back with reserves.

STATUTORY RESERVE BALANCE REQUIREMENT: The amount of reserves, in dollars, that a bank is legally required to hold.

RESERVE RATIO: The portion of a bank's deposits, expressed as a percentage, that a bank backs with reserves.

RESERVE BALANCE: The amount of reserves, in dollars, that a bank holds. A bank's reserve balance is also called its reserves.

If the statutory reserve ratio requirement is 10%, and if First Fraud Bank has $100 of deposits, then its statutory reserve balance requirement is $10 (10% x $100 = $10). Stated another way, 10% of $100 is $10. First Fraud Bank must hold an amount of reserves equal to 10% of its deposits, and this amount of reserves is its statutory reserve balance requirement. The statutory reserve ratio requirement is used to compute the statutory reserve balance requirement.

The statutory reserve ratio requirement and statutory reserve balance requirement are the minimum levels that banks can maintain. Most banks maintain higher levels that are their reserve ratio and reserve balance. If the statutory reserve ratio requirement is 10% and First Fraud Bank has $100 of deposits, it has a $10 statutory reserve balance requirement, but suppose it holds $15 of reserves rather than $10 of reserves. In this case, First Fraud Bank's reserve balance is $15. With $15 of reserves backing $100 of deposits, First Fraud Bank's reserve ratio is 15%. Bankers would say that First Fraud Bank has $100 of deposits, a 10% statutory reserve ratio requirement, a $10 statutory reserve balance requirement, a reserve balance of $15, and a reserve ratio of 15%. Other bankers would know exactly what this means, that First Fraud Bank is legally required to hold reserves equal to 10% of deposits or $10, but has kept a larger amount of reserves equal to 15% of deposits or $15. There are statutory requirements that are the minimum legally allowable, and then the higher levels that banks actually maintain, and both must be enumerated to completely describe a bank's financial position.

In the previous example, First Fraud Bank can't have a reserve balance of $9, as its reserve ratio is then 9%. Its reserve ratio of 9% would be less than its statutory reserve ratio requirement of 10%, and its reserve balance of $9 would be less than its statutory reserve balance requirement of $10, neither of which is allowed. A bank's reserve ratio can be greater than its statutory reserve ratio requirement, but not less. A bank's reserve balance can be greater than its statutory reserve balance requirement, but not less.

These principles don't change when applied to multiple banks, or the entire banking system. The only difference is that the reserves and deposits of multiple banks, or all banks, would be summed, producing a resultant amount of reserves and deposits on which the same calculations can be performed.

These principles also don't change when applied to the banking systems of most other nations, though the currency changes, and some of the terminology is often a bit different.

Statute is a fancy word for law. It can also be a rule created by an organization or institution. Congress has passed banking statutes. It has also created an institution, The Federal Reserve System, with the power to create banking statutes. A statutory reserve ratio requirement or statutory reserve balance requirement is a reserve ratio or reserve balance required by statute, either by a law passed by Congress, or by the Federal Reserve Bank created by Congress. Congress generally specifies a range of statutory reserve ratio requirements, and then gives the Federal Reserve the power to choose a statutory reserve ratio requirement in this range.

In the real world, all of a bank's deposits are not subject to a single statutory reserve ratio requirement. In the real world, banks categorize deposits in various ways, and different statutory reserve ratio requirements are applied to each deposit category. The use of a single statutory reserve ratio requirement applied to all deposits is a simplification to aid learning.

Banks apply different statutory reserve ratio requirements to different categories of deposits, and then determine the total amount of reserves legally required to back all deposits, resulting in a single statutory reserve balance requirement. The statutory reserve balance requirement is what ultimately concerns banks, as it is the amount of reserves they are legally required to hold. Banks are careful not to let their reserve balance fall below their statutory reserve balance requirement. Banks generally don't do this by increasing their reserve balances, that is, by holding more reserves, but rather by utilizing legalized frauds to decrease their statutory reserve balance requirements far below their reserve balances. More on this later.

If all this seems hopelessly confusing, don't fret. These concepts and processes will all be explained in much greater detail as we proceed. For now, focus on the core concepts. Commercial banks have a certain amount of deposits. They back these deposits fractionally, with an amount of reserves which is less than the amount of deposits. This results in a reserve ratio, the ratio of reserves to deposits. Banks want the lowest reserve ratio possible, so they can maximize reserve embezzlement and loan issuance.

Outsiders think of commercial banks or the banking system as having a relatively fixed amount of deposits which must be backed by a certain amount of reserves, but this is incorrect. As we will see, commercial banks begin with a relatively fixed amount of reserves and create additional deposits, thereby decreasing their reserve ratios. Commercial banks want to create as many deposits as possible, as each new deposit is a loan that earns them interest. When commercial banks repeatedly create additional deposits, they repeatedly decrease their reserve ratios, their ratio of reserves to deposits, until they reach the lowest levels allowable. If this confuses you, don't worry, as deposit creation and its effects will be described rigorously as we proceed. For now the main thing to understand is that there are statutory reserve ratio requirements and statutory reserve balance requirements that are the minimums allowed, and banks usually maintain reserve ratios and reserve balances higher than these minimums.

CYBERSMITHS

"Our national circulating medium [money supply] is now at the mercy of loan transactions of banks; and our thousands of checking banks are, in effect, so many irresponsible private mints. What makes the trouble is the fact that the bank lends not money but merely a promise to furnish money on demand—money it doesn't possess. The banks can build upon their meager cash reserves an inverted pyramid of such 'credit,' that is, checkbook money, the volume of which can be inflated and deflated."
—Irving Fisher

"Checkable liabilities of banks are money. These liabilities are customers' accounts. They increase when customers deposit currency and checks and when the proceeds of loans made by the banks are credited to borrowers' accounts."
—*Modern Money Mechanics*, Federal Reserve Publication

"Commercial banks create checkbook money whenever they grant a loan, simply by adding new deposit dollars in accounts on their books in exchange for a borrower's IOU."
—*I Bet You Thought*, Federal Reserve Pamphlet

"Banks lend by creating credit. They create the means of payment out of nothing."
—Ralph Hawtrey, Economist

Most people think that banks loan pre-existing money. This is incorrect. Each bank is a private mint that creates the money it loans. Bank loans are made with money conjured out of thin air. Most people are completely ignorant of this fundamental fraud at the heart of our banking system.

Many writers criticize bank money creation without documenting the nuts and bolts of the actual money creation, which makes it difficult to accept the validity of their claims. The author adheres to the scientific method and demands proof of claims before accepting their validity. As Carl Sagan noted, extraordinary claims require extraordinary evidence. The claim that trillions of dollars of mortgages and loans are simply conjured out of thin air by commercial banks is extraordinary. To accept the validity of this extraordinary claim, extraordinary proof is required Unfortunately, most people criticizing banks provide paltry proof. This was a significant problem that the author encountered when first researching our banking & money system. Vague claims about money creation were not sufficient evidence for the author. The author wanted a precise enumeration of the methodology banks use to create money and the rules that govern their money creation. Sharing this extraordinary evidence is the reason the author wrote this book and especially this chapter.

To limber the mind for the fraud that follows, it may be helpful to restate the goldsmith scam which was explained in *Bubblenomics*. A goldsmith—a medieval banker—accepted a deposit of gold, stored the gold deposit in his vault, and issued a paper promissory note, which was a promise to redeem the gold anytime the depositor demanded it. Gold was money. People trusted the goldsmith, so the goldsmith's paper promissory notes were considered as good as gold, accepted in lieu of gold as payment for goods & services, and became the first modern paper money.

Goldsmiths realized that only about 10% of deposits were ever redeemed. That is, only 10% of depositors ever showed up at the goldsmith's vault, handed him a paper promissory note, and demanded their gold. If a goldsmith accepted 100 ounces of gold deposits, and issued 100 one-ounce promissory notes, he knew that only 10% of those notes or 10 one-ounce promissory notes would be redeemed.

Everyone knew that the goldsmith was wealthy, so many people asked him for loans. The 10% redemption rate meant that the goldsmith could create 900 additional one-ounce promissory notes, lend them out, and charge interest on these loans. 1,000 paper promissory notes would then be circulating, each supposedly representing an ounce of gold in the goldsmith's vault. There were only 100 ounces of gold in the goldsmith's vault. Thus 100 ounces of gold reserves backed 1,000 paper promises to redeem an ounce of gold, which is a 10% reserve ratio (100 ÷ 1,000 = 0.10 = 10%). At this 10% reserve ratio, 90% of paper promissory notes could not be honored. 900 of the 1,000 circulating promissory notes could not be honored.

Usually, less than 10% of the 1,000 one-ounce promissory notes were redeemed, so the goldsmith's 100 ounces of gold were sufficient to honor these redemption demands. The goldsmith was therefore able to run his scam indefinitely as long as he didn't get greedy and circulate too many promissory notes. If he got greedy and circulated too many promissory notes, prices increased, people grew suspicious, redemption demands exceeded his gold reserves, and his fraud was discovered. The goldsmith had to be careful.

The goldsmith produced no honest goods & services, but the promissory notes he received as interest payments on his loans could be used to buy goods & services. The goldsmith was a parasite who scammed members of the community that accepted his promissory notes as money. By creating fraudulent deposit claims which exceeded reserves, the goldsmith was able to earn something for nothing and bilk an entire community.

All things evolve. With the advent of computers and the information age, goldsmiths became cybersmiths. A cybersmith—a modern banker—holds ledger reserves for a depositor and creates a ledger deposit which is a promise to redeem

GOLDSMITHS VS. CYBERSMITHS

GOLDSMITH (Medieval Banker)	CYBERSMITH (Modern Banker)

Accepts a Deposit of 1 Ounce of Gold	Accepts a Deposit of $100 of Ledger Reserves

```
Assets            Liabilities
$100 (Reserves)
```

Creates 10 Paper Promissory Notes Each Which is a Promise To Redeem 1 Ounce of Gold	Creates $1,000 of Deposits Which are a Promise To Redeem $1,000 of Reserves

```
Assets            Liabilities
                  $100 (Deposits)

Assets            Liabilities
                  $100 (Deposits)

Assets            Liabilities
                  $100 (Deposits)

Assets            Liabilities
                  $100 (Deposits)

Assets            Liabilities
                  $100 (Deposits)

Assets            Liabilities
                  $100 (Deposits)

Assets            Liabilities
                  $100 (Deposits)

Assets            Liabilities
                  $100 (Deposits)

Assets            Liabilities
                  $100 (Deposits)

Assets            Liabilities
                  $100 (Deposits)
```

9 Paper Promissory Notes Are Not Backed by Gold And Therefore Cannot Be Honored	$900 of Deposits Are Not Backed By Reserves And Therefore Cannot Be Honored

those ledger reserves. By creating fraudulent deposit claims which exceed reserves, cybersmiths are able to earn something for nothing and bilk an entire civilization. Cybersmiths run the same scam as goldsmiths, but they substitute ledger reserves and paper-currency reserves for gold reserves, and ledger deposit accounts for paper promissory notes.

The previous chapter simplified the loan process to make learning easier. "Excess" reserves were shown leaving Fifth Fleece Bank's books, but their destination was not shown. The loan creation and issuance was also not shown in detail. These processes will now be described rigorously. To prevent confusion, capital won't be shown, and we'll start at the very beginning.

First Fraud Bank accepts a $100 deposit of reserves, creates a $100 deposit that is a promise to redeem the $100 reserves upon demand, and initially keeps $100 of reserves backing the $100 deposit, which is a 100% reserve ratio:

Assets	Liabilities
$100 (Reserves)	$100 (Deposits)
$100	$100
	100% Reserve Ratio

First Fraud Bank practices fraudulent fractional-reserve lending and has a 10% statutory reserve ratio requirement. 10% or $10 of reserves must be kept to back the $100 deposit, 90% or $90 of reserves are recategorized as "excess" reserves which can be used for loans:

Assets	Liabilities
$10 (Reserves)	$100 (Deposits)
$90 ("Excess" Reserves)	
$100	$100
	100% Reserve Ratio

First Fraud Bank now has $90 of "excess" reserves it can lend. It creates a $90 mortgage for John Q. Debtor:

Assets	Liabilities
$10 (Reserves)	$100 (Deposits)
$90 ("Excess" Reserves)	
$90 (Loan to be Repaid)	
$190	$100
	100% Reserve Ratio

John Q. Debtor signs the mortgage and agrees to make payments to First Fraud Bank for 30 years. The loan asset is created before the loan liability. Only after John Q. Debtor has signed the mortgage and agreed to make payments does First Fraud Bank issue him a $90 loan check:

```
Assets                          Liabilities
 $10 (Reserves)                  $100 (Deposits)
 $90 ("Excess" Reserves)
 $90 (Loan to be Repaid)          $90 (Loan Check)


$190                            $190
                                    53% Reserve Ratio
```

John Q. Debtor can demand reserves from First Fraud Bank by cashing his loan check. John Q. Debtor can also deposit his loan check at another bank, and that other bank will demand reserves from First Fraud Bank. The loan check is therefore a liability to First Fraud Bank.

First Fraud Bank could have created a deposit for John Q. Debtor rather than a check, but the loan was shown as a check to differentiate it from deposits and minimize confusion. Most banks don't create deposit accounts when issuing loans to sheeple, rather they issue checks. This keeps borrowers from embezzling the loan money and spending it on something besides its intended purpose.

John Q. Debtor has not deposited or cashed the loan check yet, so it is still on First Fraud Bank's books. John Q. Debtor could deposit his loan check at First Fraud Bank, but ignore that possibility for now and assume that he deposits it at a second bank. In this case, Steal Second Bank:

```
            First Fraud Bank
    Assets                  Liabilities
     $10 (Reserves)          $100 (Deposit)
     $90 ("Excess" Reserves)
     $90 (Loan)               $90 (Loan Check) →» →»
    $190                     $190


            Steal Second Bank
    Assets                  Liabilities
                             $90 (Deposit) —« «
    $0                      $90
                                    53% Reserve Ratio
```

The 53% reserve ratio is for the entire banking system, not for any single bank. On any ledgers showing multiple banks, the reserve ratio shown at the lower right will always be for the entire banking system.

The line with arrows represents the transfer of the $90 check from First Fraud Bank to Steal Second Bank. After John Q. Debtor deposits the loan check at Steal Second Bank, the loan check is no longer on First Fraud Bank's ledger:

```
              First Fraud Bank
Assets                        Liabilities
 $10 (Reserves)                $100 (Deposit)
 $90 ("Excess" Reserves)
 $90 (Loan)
 ─────────────────────────────────────────
 $190                          $100


              Steal Second Bank
Assets                        Liabilities
                               $90 (Deposit)
 ─────────────────────────────────────────
 $0                            $90
                              53% Reserve Ratio
```

The $90 liability created by First Fraud Bank has been transferred to Steal Second Bank. It has been subtracted from First Fraud Bank's ledger, and added to Steal Second Bank's ledger. Bankers and accountants would say that First Fraud Bank's liabilities were debited (subtracted from or decreased), and that Steal Second Bank's liabilities were credited (added to or increased).

The "credit" is called credit because it is literally a credit to the bank's liability ledger. This is the origin of the term "issue credit."

When Steal Second Bank accepted the First Fraud Bank loan check and credited it to an account for John Q. Debtor, Steal Second Bank increased its liabilities. Steal Second Bank now has a deposit for John Q. Debtor that it may have to pay out. Steal Second Bank has no assets—no reserves or loans—that it can use to honor this deposit. Steal Second Bank contacts First Fraud Bank and requests payment for the loan check. It demands $90 of assets to offset the $90 liability it has incurred.

First Fraud Bank would love to pay Steal Second Bank the $90 loan and keep its $90 of "excess" reserves, as then it could immediately issue another loan. If Steal Second Bank accepts the loan asset as payment and John Q. Debtor tries to withdraw money from his account, Steal Second Bank has no reserves to honor his deposit and is rupted. Loans can also be defaulted upon, a risk that doesn't exist with cash reserves. Steal Second Bank will only accept reserves from First Fraud Bank as payment for the loan check. If First Fraud Bank can't pay reserves, Steal Second Bank will uncreate John Q. Debtor's deposit and refuse his check. First Fraud Bank can pay reserves, so transfers its $90 of "excess" reserves to Steal Second Bank to honor the loan check it issued:

```
                        First Fraud Bank
          Assets                        Liabilities
           $10 (Reserves)                $100 (Deposit)
    «—     $90 ("Excess" Reserves)
           $90 (Loan)
    ————————————————————————————————————————————————————
           $190                          $190


                        Steal Second Bank
          Assets                        Liabilities
    »—    $90 Reserves                   $90 (Deposit)
    ————————————————————————————————————————————————————
          $90                            $90

                                        53% Reserve Ratio
```

First Fraud Bank's "excess" reserves are categorized as mere reserves once they are transferred to Steal Second Bank. This is because Steal Second Bank hasn't engaged in fraudulent fractional-reserve lending yet, and therefore hasn't recategorized its reserves yet. The ledgers after First Fraud Bank pays reserves to Steal Second Bank:

```
                        First Fraud Bank
          Assets                        Liabilities
           $10 (Reserves)                $100 (Deposit)
           $90 (Loan)
    ————————————————————————————————————————————————————
           $100                          $100


                        Steal Second Bank
          Assets                        Liabilities
          $90 Reserves                   $90 (Deposit)
    ————————————————————————————————————————————————————
          $90                            $90

                                        53% Reserve Ratio
```

The "excess" reserves have been removed from First Fraud Bank's ledger because they were transferred to Steal Second Bank.

Steal Second Bank has a 10% statutory reserve ratio requirement. 10% or $9 of its reserves are set aside to honor the $90 deposit. 90% or $81 of its reserves are recategorized as "excess" reserves:

First Fraud Bank

Assets	Liabilities
$10 (Reserves)	$100 (Deposit)
$90 (Loan)	
$100	$100

Steal Second Bank

Assets	Liabilities
$9 (Reserves)	$90 (Deposit)
$81 ("Excess" Reserves)	
$90	$90

53% Reserve Ratio

First Fraud Bank has no "excess" reserves. All its "excess" reserves have been used to issue loans. First Fraud Bank is LOANED UP. Steal Second Bank has "excess" reserves which it can pay out to honor a loan check. Steal Second Bank can therefore issue a loan. It is not loaned up.

$100 was initially deposited at First Fraud Bank, yet there are now $190 of deposits, $100 at First Fraud Bank, $90 at Steal Second Bank. Deposits are money which depositors can spend. The money supply has increased by $90.

If we add up the reserves, "excess" reserves, and deposits of all banks, we obtain a master ledger for the economy. In this simple example there are only 2 banks, so the process is easy:

Assets	Liabilities
$10 (1st Fraud Reserves)	$100 (1st Fraud Deposits)
$90 (1st Fraud Loan)	$90 (Steal 2nd Deposits)
$9 (Steal 2nd Reserves)	
$81 (Steal 2nd "Excess" Reserves)	
$190	$190

53% Reserve Ratio

Combining like elements on the ledger, and adding them, we obtain:

Assets	Liabilities
$19 (Reserves)	$190 (Deposits)
$81 ("Excess" Reserves)	
$90 (Loans)	
$190	$190

53% Reserve Ratio

On this master ledger for all banks, total reserves are $100. Total reserves include reserves and "excess" reserves. $100 of reserves back $190 of deposits, a 53% reserve ratio (100 ÷ 190 = 0.53 = 53%). Reserves are 53% of deposits. If depositors withdraw more than 53% of deposits, all banks in the economy are rupt.

John Q. Debtor thinks his loan was issued with preexisting deposit money which other bank depositors surrendered, but no deposit money was subtracted from other depositors' accounts. This is a crucial observation. If physical money were being loaned rather than ledger money, a loan could never be made without surrendering money. A person with $100 of cash reserves in their pocket can't lend someone $90 of cash reserves and still have $100 of cash reserves in their pocket. The person lending the $90 of cash reserves has to give the person borrowing money $90 of cash reserves, and only has $10 of cash reserves in their pocket after issuing the loan. Loans utilizing physical cash reserves require someone to surrender physical cash reserves, but loans utilizing ledger deposits can be made without any depositor surrendering a ledger deposit. This is because the reserves backing ledger deposits can be embezzled without telling depositors, and additional claims to those embezzled reserves can simply be created. These additional claims to embezzled reserves are additional deposits that are literally money.

John Q. Debtor thinks he obtained preexisting loan money which other depositors surrendered, but in reality First Fraud Bank created a debt or promissory note, and then MONETIZED it. That is, First Fraud Bank accepted a borrower's promise to repay, calling it a loan asset on their ledger, and then monetized that loan asset by issuing "credit" to the borrower which is First Fraud Bank's deposit liability. As these transactions are virtual, performed on computer ledgers like your checkbook, this money is often called checkbook money. Checkbook money is just as real as physical money to sheeple who buy & sell goods & services with it using debit cards, credit cards, and checks.

This monetization concept confuses many, but is the core of the scam, so let's restate it. No deposit is surrendered or debited when a loan is monetized, rather the deposit used to issue the loan is created out of thin air. The promise to repay the loan is created before the deposit is created. The debt exists before the money being lent for it. Only after a borrower signs a contract agreeing to repay the loan does the bank hand them a loan check they can spend. The borrower's promise to repay is the bank's asset. The loan check or "credit" is the bank's liability. In handing a borrower a check that is newly created money, the bank has "monetized" the promise to repay, or MONETIZED A DEBT. It has converted a promise to repay money in the future into money which exists in the present. This is done by creating additional money.

Sheeple encounter the term monetize in the media, but usually have no idea what it means. This is amazing, as most banks worldwide monetize relentlessly. That is, most banks worldwide create money relentlessly. Tens of thousands of banks in every nation on Earth monetize debts perpetually with trillions of dollars, euros, yen, yuan, dinar, rupees, pesos, pounds, etc., all created out of thin air on ledgers.

Think of gold receipts. Each gold receipt such as a dollar was once backed by a fixed weight of gold, and this money system was called a gold standard. Gold money could be created without anyone incurring a debt by simply digging up gold. Our money is debt-backed, not gold-backed. Our money system is a debt standard, not a gold standard. A debt standard is governed by the un-golden rule: money is circulated *only* to monetize a debt. Under a debt standard, money and debt are tethered. Money can't be created without creating debt. Under a debt standard, if there were no debt, there would be no money.

Anyone can create a loan contract. The problem for most people is obtaining the money to honor the contract. That is, obtaining the money to lend. Bankers came up with an elegant and ingenious solution to this dilemma: create the money out of thin air. The process is so simple that the mind is repelled.

If an individual prints money for a loan, they are convicted of counterfeiting and jailed. If an individual writes a check for a loan which is not fully backed by cash reserves, they are convicted of check fraud and jailed. Money creation is criminalized for all individuals except bankers, and for all businesses besides banks. Banks are allowed to engage in money creation that is illegal for everyone else. They are allowed to create payment obligations which are literally bad deposits, which are not fully backed by the cash reserves needed to honor them. This ledger-kiting process is not criminalized, but rather legalized, and made to seem honest and respectable by referring to it as an economic principle called fractional-reserve lending.

Fractional-reserve lenders issue piles of loans, create money for those loans, and keep interest payments made by hordes of borrowers. There is no easier way to become obscenely rich.

First Fraud Bank embezzled $90 of reserves and used them to honor a $90 loan check which was deposited at Steal Second Bank. Steal Second Bank has a new $90 deposit which is fully backed by $90 of reserves. Steal Second Bank has recategorized $81 of its reserves as "excess" reserves. Steal Second Bank can now create an $81 loan. It issues an $81 mortgage to Jane R. Debtor:

```
                    First Fraud Bank
        Assets                    Liabilities
         $10 (Reserves)           $100 (Deposit)
         $90 (Loan)

        $100                      $100


                    Steal Second Bank
        Assets                    Liabilities
         $9 (Reserves)            $90 (Deposit)
         $81 ("Excess" Reserves)
         $81 (Loan)

        $171                      $90
                                      53% Reserve Ratio
```

Jane R. Debtor signs the mortgage, agreeing to make payments to Steal Second Bank for 30 years. Only then does Steal Second Bank issue her a loan check:

```
                    First Fraud Bank
        Assets                    Liabilities
         $10 (Reserves)           $100 (Deposit)
         $90 (Loan)

        $100                      $100


                    Steal Second Bank
        Assets                    Liabilities
         $9 (Reserves)            $90 (Deposit)
         $81 ("Excess" Reserves)
         $81 (Loan)               $81 (Loan Check)

        $171                      $171
                                      37% Reserve Ratio
```

Jane R. Debtor deposits her loan check at Third Thievery Bank:

```
              First Fraud Bank
Assets                      Liabilities
  $10 (Reserves)              $100 (Deposit)
  $90 (Loan)

  $100                        $100


             Steal Second Bank
Assets                      Liabilities
  $9 (Reserves)               $90 (Deposit)
  $81 ("Excess" Reserves)
  $81 (Loan)                  $81 (Loan Check) →» →»

  $171                        $171


            Third Thievery Bank
Assets                      Liabilities
                              $81 (Deposit) —« «

  $0                          $81
                              37% Reserve Ratio
```

After Jane R. Debtor deposits the loan check at Third Thievery Bank, the loan check is no longer on Steal Second Bank's ledger:

```
              First Fraud Bank
Assets                      Liabilities
  $10 (Reserves)              $100 (Deposit)
  $90 (Loan)

  $100                        $100


             Steal Second Bank
Assets                      Liabilities
  $9 (Reserves)               $90 (Deposit)
  $81 ("Excess" Reserves)
  $81 (Loan)

  $171                        $90


            Third Thievery Bank
Assets                      Liabilities
                              $81 (Deposit)

  $0                          $81
                              37% Reserve Ratio
```

Third Thievery Bank contacts Steal Second Bank and requests payment for the loan check. It demands $81 of assets to offset the $81 liability it has incurred. Steal Second Bank transfers its $81 of "excess" reserves to Third Thievery Bank to honor the loan check it issued:

First Fraud Bank

Assets	Liabilities
$10 (Reserves)	$100 (Deposit)
$90 (Loan)	
$100	$100

Steal Second Bank

Assets	Liabilities
$9 (Reserves)	$90 (Deposit)
$81 ("Excess" Reserves)	
$81 (Loan)	
$90	$90

Third Thievery Bank

Assets	Liabilities
$81 Reserves	$81 (Deposit)
$81	$81

37% Reserve Ratio

Steal Second Bank's "excess" reserves are categorized as mere reserves once they are transferred to Third Thievery Bank. This is because Third Thievery Bank hasn't engaged in fraudulent fractional-reserve lending yet, and therefore hasn't recategorized its reserves yet. The ledgers after Steal Second Bank pays reserves to Third Thievery Bank:

First Fraud Bank

Assets	Liabilities
$10 (Reserves)	$100 (Deposit)
$90 (Loan)	
$100	$100

Steal Second Bank

Assets	Liabilities
$9 (Reserves)	$90 (Deposit)
$81 (Loan)	
$90	$90

Third Thievery Bank

Assets	Liabilities
$81 Reserves	$81 (Deposit)
$81	$81

37% Reserve Ratio

The "excess" reserves have been removed from Steal Second Bank's ledger because they were transferred to Third Thievery Bank.

Steal Second Bank issued an $81 loan check which was deposited at Third Thievery Bank. Third Thievery Bank has a new $81 deposit which is fully backed by $81 of reserves. Third Thievery Bank has a 10% statutory reserve ratio requirement. 10% or $8.10 of its reserves are set aside to honor the $81 deposit. 90% or $72.90 of its reserves are recategorized as "excess" reserves:

```
                First Fraud Bank
Assets                      Liabilities
 $10 (Reserves)              $100 (Deposit)
 $90 (Loan)

 $100                        $100

                Steal Second Bank
Assets                      Liabilities
 $9 (Reserves)               $90 (Deposit)
 $81 (Loan)

 $90                         $90

                Third Thievery Bank
Assets                      Liabilities
 $8.10 (Reserves)            $81 (Deposit)
 $72.90 ("Excess" Reserves)

 $81.00                      $81

                            37% Reserve Ratio
```

First Fraud Bank and Steal Second Bank have no "excess" reserves. All their "excess" reserves have been used to issue loans. First Fraud Bank and Steal Second Bank are loaned up. Third Thievery Bank has "excess" reserves which it can pay out to honor a loan check. Third Thievery Bank can therefore issue a loan. It is not loaned up.

$100 was initially deposited at First Fraud Bank, yet there are now $271 of deposits, $100 at First Fraud Bank, $90 at Steal Second Bank, and $81 at Third Thievery Bank. Deposits are money which depositors can spend. The money supply has increased by $171.

If we add up the reserves, "excess" reserves, and deposits of all banks, we obtain a master ledger for the economy. In this simple example there are only 3 banks, so the process is still easy:

```
Assets                          Liabilities
 $10.00 (1st Fraud Reserves)     $100 (1st Fraud Deposits)
 $90.00 (1st Fraud Loan)          $90 (Steal 2nd Deposits)
  $9.00 (Steal 2nd Reserves)      $81 (3rd Thievery Deposits)
 $81.00 (Steal 2nd Loan)
  $8.10 (3rd Thievery Reserves)
 $72.90 (3rd Thievery "Excess" Reserves)
```

```
$271.00                         $271
```

37% Reserve Ratio

Combining like elements on the ledger, and adding them, we obtain:

```
Assets                          Liabilities
 $27.10 (Reserves)               $271 (Deposits)
 $72.90 ("Excess" Reserves)
$171.00 (Loans)
```

```
$271.00                         $271
```

37% Reserve Ratio

On this master ledger for all banks, total reserves are still $100. Total reserves include reserves and "excess" reserves. $100 of reserves backs $271 of deposits, a 37% reserve ratio. Reserves are 37% of deposits. If depositors withdraw more than 37% of deposits, all banks in the economy are rupt.

We began with a 100% reserve ratio, which existed when the initial $100 deposit was backed by $100 of reserves. When the $90 loan was issued, the total amount of deposits in the banking system increased from $100 to $190, but the amount of reserves stayed constant at $100 and did not increase. $100 of reserves backed $190 of deposits, and the reserve ratio decreased from 100% to 53%. When the $81 loan was issued, the total amount of deposits in the banking system increased from $190 to $271, but the amount of reserves stayed constant at $100 and did not increase. $100 of reserves backed $271 of deposits, and the reserve ratio decreased from 53% to 37%...

Third Thievery Bank has $72.90 of "excess" reserves, and can issue another loan, continuing the progression of deposit creation. Of money creation. Loans become deposits which become loans which become deposits which become loans which become deposits which become loans which become deposits...

As each bank decreases its reserve ratio from 100% to 10% by embezzling reserves and creating additional deposits, the reserve ratio of the banking system decreases. Initially, all banks have a reserve ratio of 100%, so the reserve ratio of the banking system is 100%. Eventually, all banks will have created the maximum amount of deposits allowable and have a reserve ratio of 10%, so the reserve ratio of the banking system will be 10%. At this point, all banks will be loaned up and none will have any "excess" reserves. The banking system will have created the maximum number of deposits allowable from the amount of reserves that exist.

In the simple examples shown, all reserves were initially deposited at a single bank, but in the real world reserves are initially deposited at many banks. These many banks commence fractional lending at the same time. In the simple examples shown, each loan check was transferred to a bank with no preexisting deposits, but in the real world loan checks are transferred to banks that already have deposits. Thus a more realistic example might involve $10 of reserves being deposited at 10 different original banks ($100 total), and those 10 original banks issuing loan checks that are deposited both at the 10 original banks and at new banks. Those banks receive reserve payments, embezzle reserves, issue additional loans, and continue the process of fraudulent fractional-reserve lending.

Let's return to the initial ledger. $100 of reserves are deposited into the banking system:

Assets	Liabilities
$100 (Reserves)	$100 (Deposits)
$100	$100
	100% Reserve Ratio

A statutory reserve ratio requirement of 10% is established, and the process of fractional-reserve deposit creation then proceeds. Deposit creation will be random and erratic, and vary depending where those with reserves deposit them initially and where those who receive loan checks deposit them. Deposits and loans could ping back and forth within one bank or between 7,000 banks. It doesn't matter which banks reserves and loans are deposited at, once all banks are loaned up the final master ledger for the entire banking system will be:

Assets	Liabilities
$100 (Reserves)	$1,000 (Deposits)
$900 (Loans)	
$1,000	$1,000
	10% Reserve Ratio

$100 of initial deposits have become $1,000 worth of deposits via fractional-reserve fraud. $100 of reserves backs $1,000 of deposits, a 10% reserve ratio. Banks as a whole only have enough reserves to honor 10% of deposits, no more. If depositors demand more than 10% of deposits, every bank in the economy is rupted, and the economy is vaporized in the process.

An initial deposit of reserves is made into the banking system. Initially, there is a single deposit 100% backed by reserves. Fractional-reserve lending is fundamentally a process of creating additional deposits which are backed not by reserves, but rather by loans. The total amount of loans in a system of fractional-reserve lending will be equal to the total amount of additional deposits created. This reality is shown more clearly on the revised ledger below. On this ledger, deposits are segregated into original deposits backed by reserves ($100) and conjured deposits backed by loans ($900):

Assets	Liabilities
$100 (Reserves)	$100 (Original Deposits)
$900 (Loans)	$900 (Conjured Deposits)
$1,000	$1,000
	10% Reserve Ratio

Deposit liabilities must be backed by some asset. Commercial banks can't create reserve assets, but they can create loan assets. Fractional-reserve lending is fundamentally a process in which commercial banks create additional deposit liabilities and create loan assets that back those deposit liabilities. The loans created are assets which enrich commercial banks. The deposits created are liabilities to commercial banks that can impoverish or even bank-rupt them if demanded. The loan assets that pay interest are what commercial banks desire, and deposit creation is simply a way to facilitate the issuance of as many loan assets as possible.

A common misconception is that First Fraud Bank could accept a $100 deposit of reserves and create a $900 loan. This would allow the $900 of additional deposits to be created in one shot by a single bank:

Assets	Liabilities
$10 (Reserves)	$100 (Deposits)
$90 ("Excess" Reserves)	
$900 (Loan)	$900 (Loan Check)
$1,000	$1,000
	10% Reserve Ratio

The problem is that First Fraud Bank doesn't have enough reserves to honor the $900 loan check if it is deposited at another bank such as Steal Second Bank. Steal Second Bank would demand $900 of reserves from First Fraud Bank as payment for the check, and First Fraud Bank only has $90 of reserves. This is why First Fraud Bank only issued a $90 loan in previous examples.

If the $900 loan check were deposited at First Fraud Bank rather than Steal Second Bank, then First Fraud Bank would not have to pay out reserves to any other bank. First Fraud Bank would simply convert the loan check into a deposit. First Fraud Bank's ledger would then be:

```
Assets                      Liabilities
  $100 (Reserves)             $1,000 (Deposits)
  $900 (Loans)
_____
$1,000                      $1,000
                                      10% Reserve Ratio
```

As no loan check was deposited at another bank, First Fraud Bank holds all bank deposits. In this case, the master ledger for all commercial banks in the economy is the master ledger for the only commercial bank in the economy.

Though this example illustrates important principles, it is unrealistic. Banks hold millions or billions of dollars of deposits and issue many loans rather just one. Some of the loans a bank issues are deposited at other banks. A single commercial bank never holds all deposits. Even if a single commercial bank did hold all deposits, it would never issue a single loan equal to 90% of the value of all deposits because no one could obtain a loan that large.

The fear of paying out reserves constrains commercial-bank deposit creation. First Fraud Bank isn't going to risk an $810 reserve shortage, so it won't create a $900 loan which exceeds its "excess" reserves by $810. $100 of deposits becomes $1,000 of deposits only through a succession of deposit creations by many banks, each one creating a new deposit equal to or less than its "excess" reserves (or only slightly larger than "excess" reserves, for reasons shown later). Deposit creation in a system of fractional-reserve lending is fundamentally an iterative process.

Suppose the economy has 100 apples, the initial $100 deposit of reserves is the entire money supply, apples have always cost $1, and everyone who possesses $1 thinks it represents a claim to 1 apple. If the money supply is increased to $1,000, then people holding $1,000 think there are 1,000 apples until prices adjust to the increased supply of money. Ye olde business cycle is now being manufactured. The malinvestment called the boom has begun, and it will be liquidated during the eventual bust. In creating additional deposits, fractional-reserve lenders also create the business cycle.

The goldsmith had 100 ounces of gold in his vault but issued 1,000 one-ounce gold receipts. Cybersmiths had $100 of reserves in their virtual vaults but issued $1,000 of deposits. The goldsmith accepted deposits of gold reserves, and created paper receipts which exceed gold reserves. Cybersmiths accept deposits of ledger reserves and create deposits which exceed ledger reserves. The goldsmith circulated 900 additional loan receipts by lending them. Cybersmiths circulated $900 of additional deposits by lending them. Cybersmiths perpetrate the exact same scam as goldsmiths, the cybersmith scam is just harder to follow because it takes place on ledgers.

Earlier the reader was cautioned not to muddle reserves and deposits. The reason why should now be apparent. Deposits and reserves both function as money, but reserves are more fundamental than deposits because they are scarcer than deposits and are what banks use to pay each other when settling transactions. Depositors like you and I pay each other with deposits, but banks pay each other with reserves. Commercial banks accept deposits of reserves, and transfer reserves between each other to settle transactions. Commercial banks can only create loans and deposits, not reserves which are needed to honor deposits and settle bank-to-bank transactions. A cybersmith can no more create reserves than a goldsmith could have snapped his fingers and conjured more gold.

Cybersmiths have the same motivation as the goldsmiths: interest. In this scam an initial $100 deposit has led to $900 in additional loans. The initial $100 deposit is now earning interest 9 times.

Goldsmiths—medieval bankers—created more gold receipts than gold, lent the additional receipts they created, received interest payments on these loans, and used these interest payments to buy goods & services from sheeple, thereby siphoning wealth from sheeple without producing wealth. Cybersmiths—modern bankers—create more deposits than reserves, lend the additional deposits they create, receive interest payments on these loans, and use these interest payments to buy goods & services from sheeple, thereby siphoning wealth from sheeple without producing wealth. Cybersmiths run the same scam that goldsmiths perpetrated with gold and promissory notes, but cybersmiths perpetrate the scam using computerized assets and lie-abilities.

Conventional descriptions of fractional-reserve lending make deposit creation sound innocuous, even beneficial. One can scour scores of mainstream textbooks, journals, encyclopedias, and newspapers and not find a single mention of the parasitism which fractional-reserve lending creates nor the economic havoc it wreaks. The true intentions and consequences of fractional-reserve lending are only taught to initiates who profit off it.

At its core, fractional-reserve lending is a system of recursive embezzlement. Banks embezzle reserves which back deposits, and use those embezzled reserves to issue loans. Banks can't admit their embezzlement to depositors by debiting depositors' accounts. Depositors would see money subtracted from their accounts, have a conniption, and run to banks demanding reserves that banks embezzled, lent, and no longer possess. To hide their embezzlement and avoid having to debit depositors' accounts, fractional-reserve bankers create new deposits. As no new reserves are created with new deposits, the new deposits are lie-abilities which can't be honored.

Viewed on an economy-wide scale, the scam is breathtaking. Here is the master ledger for the U.S. banking system in September 2008, just before The Bailout passed:

```
Assets                          Liabilities
  $102,736,000,000 (Reserves)   $7,052,700,000,000 (Deposits)
$6,949,964,000,000 (Loans
                    a.k.a. reserves banks don't have
                    and pray depositors don't demand)


$7,052,700,000,000              $7,052,700,000,000
                                     1.46% Reserve Ratio
```

$102 billion of initial reserve deposits became $7 trillion worth of deposits via fractional-reserve fraud. $102 billion of reserves backed $7 trillion of deposits, a 1.46% reserve ratio. Banks as a whole only had enough reserves to honor 1.46% of deposits. If depositors withdrew more than 1.46% of deposits, every bank in the economy would have been rupted, and the economy would have been vaporized.

If depositors demanded $550 billion which banks promised them but did not possess, banks had a $447 billion reserve shortage. Such bank runs could never happen, right? Wrong. Such bank runs did happen in September 2008, and preventing this lie-ability exposure from vaporizing the world economy is why The Bailout was passed. Fraudulent fractional-reserve banking made The Bailout necessary. Without fraudulent fractional-reserve lending, The Bailout would have been unnecessary and there would have been no Depression v9.2006-201x.

In our simple example, $100 was deposited at First Fraud Bank and banks created $900 of new deposits. These $900 of new deposits were created to facilitate $900 of new loans. In the real world, $102 billion was deposited at commercial banks and commercial banks created $6.95 trillion of new deposits. These $6.95 trillion of new deposits were created to facilitate $6.95 trillion of new loans.

Commercial banks created $6.95 trillion out of thin air and lent it! They did not work to obtain this loan money, nor was it deposited by someone who worked to obtain it. Commercial banks simply conjured this $6.95 trillion. If you could create $6.95 trillion out of thin air, lend it out to a bunch of stupid suckers, and get them to pay interest, do you think you might be able to etch out a living?

In all eras, the scam has the same end result: depositors demand reserves which banks have promised them but don't possess. Bank lie-abilities are eventually exposed, even if banks liquidate all their capital to make up reserve shortages. We all know what happens next: when banks are short of capital, they head to the Capitol.

CYBERSMITHS PICTURE PAGES

TO SKIP THE PICTURE PAGES AFTER THIS CHAPTER, PLEASE TURN TO PAGE 58

BANK OF AMERICA'S SEPTEMBER 2008 FDIC CALL REPORT

Board of Governors of the Federal Reserve System
Federal Deposit Insurance Corporation
Office of the Comptroller of the Currency

Federal Financial Institutions Examination Council

1

Consolidated Reports of Condition and Income for A Bank With Domestic and Foreign Offices - FFIEC 031

Institution Name	**BANK OF AMERICA, NATIONAL ASSOCIATION**
City	**CHARLOTTE**
State	**NC**
Zip Code	**28255**
Call Report Quarter End Date	**9/30/2008**
Report Type	**031**
RSSD-ID	**480228**
FDIC Certificate Number	**3510**
OCC Charter Number	**13044**
ABA Routing Number	**53000196**
Last updated on	**3/16/2009**

Board of Governors of the Federal Reserve System, Federal Deposit Insurance Corporation, Office of the Comptroller of the Currency
Legend: NR - Not Reported, CONF - Confidential

All commercial banks must submit "Consolidated Reports of Condition and Income" to regulators 4 times per year. These reports are also called "Call Reports." Sheeple shown the exorbitant deposit creation by commercial banks often refuse to accept its factuality, and dogmatically claim that criticisms of fraudulent fractional-reserve banking are a ridiculous conspiracy and that the data is a fabrication. As strange as this sounds, the author has encountered many such über skeptics. Bank of America's September 2008 Call Report is therefore shown on this page and the next 3 pages, so that readers can confirm the raw data used in calculations throughout this book. Other Call Reports are available at the Federal Financial Institutions Examination Council (FFIEC) website.

BANK OF AMERICA, NATIONAL ASSOCIATION   FFIEC 031
RSSD-ID 480228   Quarter End Date 9/30/2008
Last Updated on 3/16/2009   [10]

(TEXT4464) Intercompany Management Fees

(TEXT4467) Professional Fees

(TEXT4522) Foreign Currency Translation

(TEXT4769) Additional lines for RI.E Line 1 Other non interest income: Banker?s Acceptance and Lc Fees = $387MM, Other Credit Card Fees:$104MM, Other Servicing Earnings=$217MM. Additional Lines for RI.E Line 2 Other non interest Expense: Subscription Services=$36MM, Non-credit Losses and Recoveries=$483MM, B/D Commissions and Clearance=$347MM, Other Operating Expense=$247MM, Other Expense $244MM.

Schedule RC - Balance Sheet

Dollar amounts in thousands

1. Cash and balances due from depository institutions (from Schedule RC-A):			1.
a. Noninterest-bearing balances and currency and coin	RCFD0081	34,233,130	1.a.
b. Interest-bearing balances	RCFD0071	17,709,801	1.b.
2. Securities:			2.
a. Held-to-maturity securities (from Schedule RC-B, column A)	RCFD1754	1,246,557	2.a.
b. Available-for-sale securities (from Schedule RC-B, column D)	RCFD1773	235,300,608	2.b.
3. Federal funds sold and securities purchased under agreements to resell:			3.
a. Federal funds sold in domestic offices	RCONB987	92,241,553	3.a.
b. Securities purchased under agreements to resell	RCFDB989	48,400,256	3.b.
4. Loans and lease financing receivables (from Schedule RC-C):			4.
a. Loans and leases held for sale	RCFD5369	16,692,774	4.a.
b. Loans and leases, net of unearned income	RCFDB528	652,180,246	4.b.
c. Allowance for loan and lease losses	RCFD3123	9,247,050	4.c.
d. Loans and leases, net of unearned income and allowance	RCFDB529	642,933,196	4.d.
5. Trading assets (from Schedule RC-D)	RCFD3545	130,646,697	5.
6. Premises and fixed assets (including capitalized leases)	RCFD2145	9,469,782	6.
7. Other real estate owned (from Schedule RC-M)	RCFD2150	761,934	7.
8. Investments in unconsolidated subsidiaries and associated companies (from Schedule RC-M)	RCFD2130	5,779,048	8.
9. Not applicable			9.
10. Intangible assets:			10.
a. Goodwill	RCFD3163	42,459,131	10.a.
b. Other intangible assets (from Schedule RC-M)	RCFD0426	19,787,486	10.b.
11. Other assets (from Schedule RC-F)	RCFD2160	61,408,898	11.
12. Total assets	RCFD2170	1,359,070,851	12.
13. Deposits:			13.
a. In domestic offices	RCON2200	672,067,377	13.a.
1. Noninterest-bearing	RCON6631	192,205,413	13.a.1.
2. Interest-bearing	RCON6636	479,861,964	13.a.2.
b. In foreign offices, Edge and Agreement subsidiaries, and IBFs (from Schedule RC-E, part II)	RCFN2200	174,163,168	13.b.
1. Noninterest-bearing	RCFN6631	3,685,487	13.b.1.
2. Interest-bearing	RCFN6636	170,477,681	13.b.2.
14. Federal funds purchased and securities sold under agreements to repurchase:			14.
a. Federal funds purchased in domestic offices	RCONB993	24,049,729	14.a.
b. Securities sold under agreements to repurchase	RCFDB995	153,670,764	14.b.
15. Trading liabilities (from Schedule RC-D)	RCFD3548	79,003,513	15.
16. Other borrowed money (includes mortgage indebtedness and obligations under capitalized leases) (from Schedule RC-M)	RCFD3190	85,137,278	16.

The Call Report is an extremely detailed report that few laypersons can understand. The Call Report that Bank of America submitted to the FDIC in September 2008 just before The Bailout passed was 50 pages. Page 10 is shown here. Line item 13a is deposits in domestic offices. This item is highlighted yellow for easy identification. The highlighted amount is 672,067,377, but all amounts are in thousands of dollars, so the actual amount is $672,067,377,000, or $672 billion. Bank of America held $672 billion of domestic deposits in September 2008.

BANK OF AMERICA, NATIONAL ASSOCIATION

RSSD-ID 480228

Last Updated on 3/16/2009

FFIEC 031

Quarter End Date 9/30/2008

11

Dollar amounts in thousands

17. Not applicable			17.
18. Not applicable			18.
19. Subordinated notes and debentures.........	RCFD3200	22,563,133	19.
20. Other liabilities (from Schedule RC-G).........	RCFD2930	32,926,823	20.
21. Total liabilities.........	RCFD2948	1,243,581,785	21.
22. Minority interest in consolidated subsidiaries.........	RCFD3000	1,719,058	22.
23. Perpetual preferred stock and related surplus.........	RCFD3838	0	23.
24. Common stock.........	RCFD3230	2,893,890	24.
25. Surplus (exclude all surplus related to preferred stock).........	RCFD3839	91,230,199	25.
26. Not available			26.
a. Retained earnings.........	RCFD3632	29,707,039	26.a.
b. Accumulated other comprehensive income.........	RCFDB530	-10,061,120	26.b.
27. Other equity capital components.........	RCFDA130	0	27.
28. Total equity capital.........	RCFD3210	113,770,008	28.
29. Total liabilities, minority interest, and equity capital.........	RCFD3300	1,359,070,851	29.
1. Indicate in the box at the right the number of the statement below that best describes the most comprehensive level of auditing work performed for the bank by independent external auditors as of any date during 2007.........	RCFD6724	NR	M.1.

Schedule RC-A - Cash and Balances Due From Depository Institutions

	(Column A) Consolidated Bank		(Column B) Domestic Offices		
Dollar amounts in thousands					
1. Cash items in process of collection, unposted debits, and currency and coin.........	RCFD0022	30,006,605			1.
a. Cash items in process of collection and unposted debits.........			RCON0020	22,307,379	1.a.
b. Currency and coin.........			RCON0080	7,341,491	1.b.
2. Balances due from depository institutions in the U.S.........			RCON0082	2,153,068	2.
a. U.S. branches and agencies of foreign banks (including their IBFs).........	RCFD0083	16,336			2.a.
b. Other commercial banks in the U.S. and other depository institutions in the U.S. (including their IBFs).........	RCFD0085	13,450,425			2.b.
3. Balances due from banks in foreign countries and foreign central banks.........			RCON0070	350,793	3.
a. Foreign branches of other U.S. banks.........	RCFD0073	43,083			3.a.
b. Other banks in foreign countries and foreign central banks.........	RCFD0074	8,159,028			3.b.
4. Balances due from Federal Reserve Banks.........	RCFD0090	267,454	RCON0090	267,454	4.
5. Total.........	RCFD0010	51,942,931	RCON0010	32,420,185	5.

This is page 11 of the Call Report that Bank of America submitted to the FDIC in September 2008 just before The Bailout passed. In the section "Schedule RC-A - Cash and Balances Due From Depository Institutions," line item 1a is currency and coin. This is vault-cash reserves, which is also called physical-currency reserves. It is highlighted yellow for easy identification. Bank of America held $7,341,491,000 of vault-cash reserves, which is $7 billion of vault-cash reserves. Line item 4 is balances due from Federal Reserve Banks. This is Fed-account reserves. It is also highlighted yellow for easy identification. Bank of America held $267,464,000 of Fed-account reserves, which is $267 million of Fed-account reserves. $267 million of Fed-account reserves backing $672 billion of deposits is not enough Fed-account reserves, but Bank of America relied on its ability to run massive Daylight Overdrafts with the Federal Reserve, a topic which will be discussed much later. Adding vault-cash reserves and Fed-account reserves gives total reserves, which is $7,608,945,000, or $7.608 billion. Bank of America held $7.6 billion of domestic reserves which backed $672 billion of domestic deposits, which was a 1.1% reserve ratio.

A banker reading this might object strenuously to the claim that Bank of America only had $7.6 billion of reserves. They would claim that Bank of America had a larger amount of reserves, as much as $32 billion of reserves, which is the total in line item 5.

Even if Bank of America possessed $32 billion of reserves—which it did not—this was only 4.8% of its $672 billion of deposits, or a 4.8% reserve ratio. This is still an absurdly low reserve ratio, and is unacceptable.

As we will see later, to argue whether Bank of America's reserve ratio was 1.1% or 4.8% is to miss the point completely. Either reserve level is obscenely low. A 100% reserve ratio is the only acceptable reserve ratio.

Items in the process of collection have not been collected. All banks perpetually have large numbers of uncollected or unposted transactions, which is sometimes called FLOAT. Float can rightfully be called an asset, as it is an expected payment like a loan. Float is a payment expected over the extreme short term, within hours or days. Float can't rightfully be called a reserve, because it is a payment not possessed. If a depositor comes into Bank of America attempting to withdraw physical-currency reserves from their bank account, Bank of America can't pay the depositor with items in the process of collection. Bank of America can't honor deposits using float funds that have not been posted or collected. Bank of America must honor depositor withdrawals with vault-cash reserves that are the currency and coin in its vaults, or with Fed-account reserves that are the money in its Federal Reserve Bank account. Some of these concepts will confuse the reader for now, and they will be explained rigorously later, but for now the bottom line is that it is ridiculous to categorize float as reserves.

If I owe you $100, promise to pay you $100 when you demand it, and you do so, I can't simply tell you that Steve owes me $100 and I'll pay you when Steve pays me. I can't pay you with my float, I can only pay you with currency or coin in my possession. You may accept a check drawn on my bank account, but I must have funds in that account to write a check. I shouldn't write you a $100 check that you may cash immediately if I don't have $100 in my account. If Steve wrote me a $100 check that I deposited in my bank account, I shouldn't write you a $100 check until that check is posted to my account—until that check is no longer float, but is cash reserves.

It is preposterous for banks to claim that their float is reserves. Only cash possessed by banks is reserves, and this is what the author used for all reserve calculations shown in this book.

DIAGRAM OF FRACTIONAL-RESERVE DEPOSIT CREATION

0

First Fraud Bank (100%)

Assets	Liabilities
$10 (Reserves)	$100 (Deposit)
$90 ("Excess" Reserves)	
$90 (Loan) **1**	$90 (Loan Check)
——	——
$100	$100

3   **2**

Steal Second Bank (53%)

Assets	Liabilities
$9 (Reserves)	$90 (Deposit)
$81 ("Excess" Reserves)	
$81 (Loan) **4**	$81 (Loan Check)
——	——
$90	$90

6   **5**

Third Thievery Bank (37%)

Assets	Liabilities
$8.10 (Reserves)	$81.00 (Deposit)
$72.90 ("Excess" Reserves)	
$72.90 (Loan) **7**	$72.90 (Loan Check)
——	——
$81.00	$81.00

9   **8**

Fourth Filch Bank (29%)

Assets	Liabilities
$7.29 (Reserves)	$72.90 (Deposit)
$65.61 ("Excess" Reserves)	
$65.61 (Loan) **10**	$65.61 (Loan Check)
——	——
$72.90	$72.90

12   **11**

Fifth Fleece Bank (24%)

Assets	Liabilities
$6.56 (Reserves)	$65.61 (Deposit)
$59.05 ("Excess" Reserves)	
$59.05 (Loan) **13**	$59.05 (Loan Check)
——	——
$65.61	$65.61

15   **14**

Sixth Swindle Bank (21%)

Assets	Liabilities
$5.91 (Reserves)	$59.05 (Deposit)
$53.14 ("Excess" Reserves)	
$53.14 (Loan) **16**	$53.14 (Loan Check)
——	——
$59.05	$59.05

18   **17**

Loan issuance and deposit creation continue until all
"excess" reserves are exhausted and all banks are loaned up.

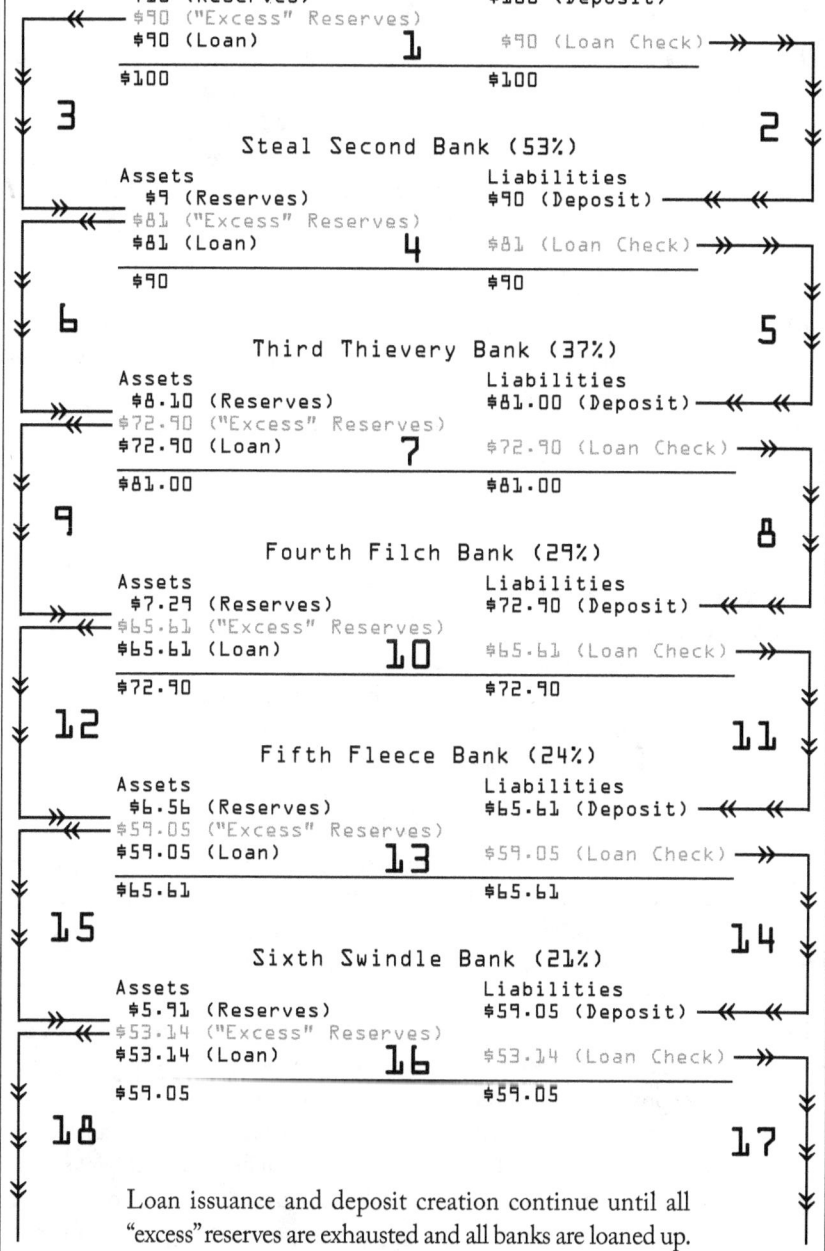

This diagram shows cascading deposit creation in a fractional-reserve banking system. Previous examples showed the process on multiple diagrams, here the process is shown on a single diagram. The large-sized numbers on the diagram show the order in which the transactions occur to aid visualization.

0

There are initially no deposits in the banking system. The first reserves injected into the banking system are deposited at First Fraud Bank. $100 of reserves are deposited. First Fraud Bank has $100 of deposits and $100 of reserves to honor the deposits. First Fraud Bank keeps 10% or $10 of reserves to honor deposits, and recategorizes 90% or $90 of reserves as "excess" reserves which can be loaned.

1

First Fraud Bank creates a $90 loan out of thin air. John Q. Debtor signs the loan contract and agrees to make payments on the loan. First Fraud Bank then creates a $90 loan check out of thin air and gives it to John Q. Debtor. A promise to pay money in the future (a loan asset) has been converted into money which exists in the present (a loan check liability). A loan has been monetized.

2

John Q. Debtor deposits his loan check at Steal Second Bank. Steal Second Bank "cashes" the loan check by opening an account for John Q. Debtor and crediting the account with a deposit in the amount of the loan check. A $90 deposit is thus created at Steal Second Bank. The loan check is no longer on the ledger of First Fraud Bank, and the loan check entry on First Fraud Bank's ledger is colored gray to reflect this fact. The loan liability has been removed from First Fraud Bank's ledger and transferred to Steal Second Bank's ledger. The loan liability is no longer a check; it is now a bank deposit.

3

John Q. Debtor's deposit is a liability to Steal Second Bank, as John Q. Debtor can withdraw it at any time. Steal Second Bank has no assets that it can use to honor this deposit liability. Steal Second Bank demands an asset payment from First Fraud Bank for the loan check so that it has assets to honor it.

Deposits are assets to depositors who can redeem deposits for reserves, but deposits are liabilities to banks, which may have to honor deposits by paying out reserves. A depositor transferring a deposit to another depositor is giving that depositor an asset. A bank transferring a deposit to another bank is transferring a liability to that bank. Depositors pay each other with deposits, but banks don't pay each other with deposits, as these are liabilities to banks. Depositors transfer deposits to other banks, and then banks demand payment from each other to honor these transfers of deposit liabilities. Banks pay each other with reserve assets, which can be used to honor deposit liabilities.

First Fraud Bank gives its $90 of "excess" reserves to Steal Second Bank to honor the loan check it issued. The $90 of reserves is removed from First Fraud Bank's ledger and transferred to Steal Second Bank's ledger. As the $90 of reserves is no longer on First Fraud Bank's ledger, they are grayed out on First Fraud Bank's ledger to reflect this fact. Steal Second Bank keeps 10% or $9 of reserves to honor deposits and recategorizes 90% or $81 of reserves as "excess" reserves, which can be loaned.

4

Steal Second Bank creates an $81 loan out of thin air. Jane R. Debtor signs the loan contract and agrees to make payments on the loan. Steal Second Bank then creates an $81 loan check liability out of thin air and gives it to Jane R. Debtor. A promise to pay money in the future (a loan asset) has been converted into money which exists in the present (a loan check liability). A loan has been monetized...

5-18

The process of loan and deposit creation proceeds in iterative fashion. Steps 1-3 are repeated cyclically at each new bank. Each bank keeps only 10% of reserves to back deposits, recategorizes the remaining 90% of reserves as "excess" reserves, creates a loan equal to its "excess" reserves, monetizes the loan by creating a check, has the check deposited at another bank, and pays that other bank reserves to honor the loan check it issued. Steps 1-3 are fractional-reserve lending and monetization by First Fraud Bank, steps 4-6 are fractional-reserve lending and monetization by Steal Second Bank, steps 7-9 are fractional-reserve lending and monetization by Third Thievery Bank, steps 10-12 are fractional-reserve lending and monetization by Fourth Filch Bank...

The limiting factor in this deposit creation process is reserves. Each bank accepts a deposit, obtains reserves equal to 100% of that deposit, keeps 10% of those reserves to honor the deposit, and then creates a new deposit equal to 90% of its reserves via the monetization of debt process. Each bank then transfers the newly-created deposit and the reserves needed to honor it to another bank. Each bank keeps a small portion of the reserves it is paid, and passes the majority of those reserves on to the next bank.

With each iteration of this process, more reserves have been kept by banks to back deposits, and fewer reserves are passed along to the next bank. With each iteration of this process, more deposits have been created, but more reserves have not been created, meaning the reserve ratio of the banking system as a whole steadily decreases. Each bank which has shuffled its "excess" reserves along to another bank has an amount of reserves equal to 10% of deposits, a 10% reserve ratio. Only the last bank which received reserves as payment for a new loan deposit has "excess" reserves. Though each individual bank (except the last bank) has a 10% reserve ratio, the banking system as a whole doesn't have a 10% reserve ratio. The reserve ratio of the banking system as a whole is calculated by summing all reserves, summing all deposits, and dividing total reserves by total deposits. As no new reserves are created, and reserves are simply shuffled between banks, reserves in this example will always be $100. The reserve ratio is initially 100% when First Fraud Bank accepts a $100 deposit, has $100 of reserves, and has not created loans or additional deposits. The reserve ratio decreases to 53% when the $90 deposit is created, 37% when the $81 deposit is created, 29% when the $72.90 deposit is created, 24% when the $65.61 deposit is created, 21% when the $59.05 deposit is created... These reserve ratios for the entire banking system are shown in parenthesis after the bank name on the diagram.

Fractional-reserve lending is inherently recursive. Recursive means that successive elements are dependent upon preceding elements. In fractional-reserve lending, the size of the deposit that Steal Second Bank can create is determined by the size of the deposit which First Fraud Bank created. The size of the deposit that Third Thievery Bank can create is determined by the size of deposit which Steal Second Bank created. Each iteration or step is constrained by money creation in the previous step, creating a house of cards.

A house of cards can be collapsed by reaching into the structure and removing the cards on the lower level which were placed first. The same is true of fraudulent fractional-reserve lending. If the initial $100 deposit is withdrawn from First Fraud Bank and is not re-deposited at another bank, then the house of cards collapses and a chain reaction of money uncreation is initiated. A house of cards can also be collapsed by removing cards from higher levels, and this is also true of the fractional-reserve lending house of cards. If deposits are withdrawn from Steal Second Bank, Third Thievery Bank, or Fifth Fleece Bank, and not redeposited at other banks, then the house of cards collapses and a chain reaction of money creation is initiated. This chain reaction of money uncreation will be shown later, and the way it destroys an economy will also be explained.

With each additional iteration of fraudulent fractional-reserve lending, the size of the new deposit created, and amount of "excess" reserves transferred to honor the new deposit, grows smaller. This is to be expected of any recursive, fractal process—any recursive process in which successive elements are a fraction of previous elements.

The fractional-reserve deposit creation process would proceed for dozens of iterations. By the 120th iteration, the newly created deposit would be less than a cent, as would the reserves transferred to honor that deposit. At this point, "excess" reserves utilized in an additional iteration of fractional-reserve lending would be less than a cent, and would therefore be effectively zero. Every bank would have a 10% reserve ratio, no banks would have any "excess" reserves, and the reserve ratio of the banking system would be 10%. The banking system would be loaned up, and the fractional-reserve process would have proceeded to its theoretical maximum—unless more reserves were created or payments were made on loans, two eventualities which will be covered later.

In our examples, every loan check was deposited at a new bank, every bank created a single loan equal to its "excess" reserves, and every bank paid out 100% of its "excess" reserves to honor loan checks. In the real world, some loan checks would be deposited at preexisting banks with deposits rather than at new banks without deposits, each bank would issue multiple loans rather than a single loan, and banks would not have to pay out reserves equal to the face value of all loan checks.

In the third iteration of our example, Third Thievery Bank's loan check was deposited at Fourth Filch Bank, but what if it had been deposited back at Steal Second Bank? Suppose you and I both have $100 in our pocket, I owe you $90, and you owe me $81. In theory I have to pay you $90 of cash reserves out of my pocket, and you have to pay me $81 of cash reserves out of your pocket, but the effective cash flow is the difference between the two loans, or $9. To settle both loans, only a single net transaction is required, me paying you $9.

This same principle applies with banks issuing loans, and becomes relevant when new loan checks are deposited at banks which have already issued loans rather than at new banks which have not issued loans. When many banks begin issuing large numbers of small loans (rather than a small number of large loans as in our examples), the reserve payments they must make to each other cancel out to a significant degree. Banks can therefore issue loan checks which exceed their "excess" reserves without having their lie-abilities exposed. This concept is addressed rigorously in the Three-Bank Monte chapter.

These factors make fractional-reserve deposit creation proceed more rapidly than in our examples, with fewer iterations. If the concepts in these last few paragraphs confused you, don't worry, they will be explained in more detail later. For now, the important thing to understand is that there are inaccuracies in the simplified fractional-reserve lending examples presented. In the real world, money can be created much more rapidly.

FRACTIONAL-RESERVE LENDING PROCEEDS UNTIL "EXCESS" RESERVES EXHAUSTED

	Deposit	Reserves	"Excess" Reserves		Deposit	Reserves	"Excess" Reserves
1	$100.000	$10.000	$90.000	46	$0.873	$0.087	$0.786
2	$90.000	$9.000	$81.000	47	$0.786	$0.079	$0.707
3	$81.000	$8.100	$72.900	48	$0.707	$0.071	$0.636
4	$72.900	$7.290	$65.610	49	$0.636	$0.064	$0.573
5	$65.610	$6.561	$59.049	50	$0.573	$0.057	$0.515
6	$59.049	$5.905	$53.144	51	$0.515	$0.052	$0.464
7	$53.144	$5.314	$47.830	52	$0.464	$0.046	$0.417
8	$47.830	$4.783	$43.047	53	$0.417	$0.042	$0.376
9	$43.047	$4.305	$38.742	54	$0.376	$0.038	$0.338
10	$38.742	$3.874	$34.868	55	$0.338	$0.034	$0.304
11	$34.868	$3.487	$31.381	56	$0.304	$0.030	$0.274
12	$31.381	$3.138	$28.243	57	$0.274	$0.027	$0.247
13	$28.243	$2.824	$25.419	58	$0.247	$0.025	$0.222
14	$25.419	$2.542	$22.877	59	$0.222	$0.022	$0.200
15	$22.877	$2.288	$20.589	60	$0.200	$0.020	$0.180
16	$20.589	$2.059	$18.530	61	$0.180	$0.018	$0.162
17	$18.530	$1.853	$16.677	62	$0.162	$0.016	$0.146
18	$16.677	$1.668	$15.009	63	$0.146	$0.015	$0.131
19	$15.009	$1.501	$13.509	64	$0.131	$0.013	$0.118
20	$13.509	$1.351	$12.158	65	$0.118	$0.012	$0.106
21	$12.158	$1.216	$10.942	66	$0.106	$0.011	$0.096
22	$10.942	$1.094	$9.848	67	$0.096	$0.010	$0.086
23	$9.848	$0.985	$8.863	68	$0.086	$0.009	$0.077
24	$8.863	$0.886	$7.977	69	$0.077	$0.008	$0.070
25	$7.977	$0.798	$7.179	70	$0.070	$0.007	$0.063
26	$7.179	$0.718	$6.461	71	$0.063	$0.0063	$0.056
27	$6.461	$0.646	$5.815	72	$0.056	$0.0056	$0.051
28	$5.815	$0.581	$5.233	73	$0.051	$0.0051	$0.046
29	$5.233	$0.523	$4.710	74	$0.046	$0.0046	$0.041
30	$4.710	$0.471	$4.239	75	$0.041	$0.0041	$0.037
31	$4.239	$0.424	$3.815	76	$0.037	$0.0037	$0.033
32	$3.815	$0.382	$3.434	77	$0.033	$0.0033	$0.030
33	$3.434	$0.343	$3.090	78	$0.030	$0.0030	$0.027
34	$3.090	$0.309	$2.781	79	$0.027	$0.0027	$0.024
35	$2.781	$0.278	$2.503	80	$0.024	$0.0024	$0.022
36	$2.503	$0.250	$2.253	81	$0.022	$0.0022	$0.020
37	$2.253	$0.225	$2.028	82	$0.020	$0.0020	$0.018
38	$2.028	$0.203	$1.825	83	$0.018	$0.0018	$0.016
39	$1.825	$0.182	$1.642	84	$0.016	$0.0016	$0.014
40	$1.642	$0.164	$1.478	85	$0.014	$0.0014	$0.013
41	$1.478	$0.148	$1.330	86	$0.013	$0.0013	$0.012
42	$1.330	$0.133	$1.197	87	$0.012	$0.0012	$0.010
43	$1.197	$0.120	$1.078	88	$0.010	$0.0010	$0.009
44	$1.078	$0.108	$0.970		$1000	$100	$900
45	$0.970	$0.097	$0.873				

This table on the previous page shows fractional-reserve lending in a more compact form, allowing a larger number of iterations of deposit creation to be observed. All banks in this example maintain a 10% reserve ratio, keeping enough reserves to honor 10% of deposits, and paying the remaining 90% of their reserves out to back a newly created deposit that is loaned.

In row 1, there are no reserves in the banking system, and a bank receives $100 of reserves as a deposit. These are the only reserves injected into the banking system for the entire example, and the total reserve supply therefore remains fixed at $100. 10% or $10 of reserves remain reserves, 90% or $90 of reserves are recategorized as "excess" reserves which are used to issue a $90 loan. When the $90 loan check is deposited at the next bank in row 2, it becomes a $90 deposit.

In row 2, the next bank demands $90 of reserves to back its loan-check deposit, and is paid $90 of reserves. 10% or $9 of reserves remain reserves and are kept to back the $90 deposit, 90% or $81 of reserves are recategorized as "excess" reserves which are used to issue an $81 loan. When the $81 loan check is deposited at the next bank in row 3, it becomes an $81 deposit...

In each row, "excess" reserves on the right column become additional deposits in the left column of the next row. The deposit supply steadily decreases with each new row. The middle "Reserves" column shows the reserves backing each deposit. The total amount of reserves used to back deposits increases with each row. Summing the deposits in all rows gives total deposit creation. Summing the reserves in all rows gives the total amount of reserves backing all deposits. As banks issue loans equal to the amount of their "excess" reserves, summing the "excess" reserves in all rows gives the total amount of loans issued. When all rows are summed, there are $100 of reserves backing $1,000 of deposits, and $900 of loans have been issued.

Again, it is important to remember the duality inherent in bank deposits. Deposits of reserves are made at banks. Banks create deposit-account ledger entries that are promises to redeem reserves, and then embezzle and lend out the reserves backing those deposits. Deposits are claims upon reserves, and fractional-reserve lending is the fraudulent process of creating deposit claims that exceed the supply of reserves.

The iterations shown on this table stop when the deposit amount reaches 1¢, as the next deposit in the iteration would be less than 1¢. Though a cent is the smallest physical monetary unit, ledger money transactions can involve fractions of cents. The 88 iterations of money creation shown in the table sum to slightly less than the totals shown in the table. Dozens of more iterations of money creation involving fractions of cents would be necessary to create an amount of money exactly equal to the theoretical maximum.

It would seem absurd to issue loans of a few cents or fractions of cents, but real banks deal with much larger sums than those in these simple examples. If the first bank in the progression accepts $100 million of deposits rather than a $100 deposit, row 50 in the table is a $573,000 of deposits rather than a 57¢ deposit, and row 88 is $10,000 of deposits rather than a 10¢ deposit. With $100 million of initial deposits, $547 is created in the 116th iteration, what would have been row 116 in the table if more rows had been shown. $547 is enough to issue a small credit card loan, but it would only have been 5% of 1¢ (0.05 of a cent) in our simplified example with a $100 initial deposit.

In the real world, it never takes this many iterations to reach the maximum money creation allowed. In the real world, every deposit is not made at a new bank, so deposit creation is accelerated. Though money creation proceeds much, much faster in the real world than in this example, it was included to help people visualize deposit creation and understand it better.

FRACTIONAL-RESERVE LENDING WITH LARGER INITIAL DEPOSIT

	Deposit	Reserves	Excess Reserves
1	$100,000,000	$10,000,000	$90,000,000
2	$90,000,000	$9,000,000	$81,000,000
3	$81,000,000	$8,100,000	$72,900,000
4	$72,900,000	$7,290,000	$65,610,000
5	$65,610,000	$6,561,000	$59,049,000
6	$59,049,000	$5,904,900	$53,144,100
7	$53,144,100	$5,314,410	$47,829,690
8	$47,829,690	$4,782,969	$43,046,721
88	$10,450	$1,045	$9,405
89	$9,405	$940	$8,464
90	$8,464	$846	$7,618
91	$7,618	$762	$6,856
92	$6,856	$686	$6,170
93	$6,170	$617	$5,553
94	$5,553	$555	$4,998
95	$4,998	$500	$4,498
145	$26	$2.58	$23.18
146	$23	$2.32	$20.86
147	$21	$2.09	$18.78
148	$19	$1.88	$16.90
149	$17	$1.69	$15.21
150	$15	$1.52	$13.69
151	$14	$1.37	$12.32
152	$12	$1.23	$11.09
213	$0.020	$0.002	$0.018
214	$0.018	$0.002	$0.016
215	$0.016	$0.002	$0.015
216	$0.015	$0.001	$0.013
217	$0.013	$0.001	$0.012
218	$0.012	$0.001	$0.011
219	$0.011	$0.001	$0.010
220	$0.010	$0.001	$0.009

This table shows an initial $100 million deposit. Black bars are portions of the table which are omitted. The table skips ahead to later iterations. Approaching the 100th iteration of money creation, thousands of dollars are still created with each iteration—easily enough for a car loan, credit card loan, or student loan. It takes more than 150 iterations for the loan size to shrink to $10, and 220 iterations for the loan size to shrink to 1¢. In the real world, this many iterations would never be required to create enough deposits for the whole banking system to be loaned up. In the real world, reserve payment cancellation allows banks to issue loans which exceed their "excess" reserves, accelerating the deposit creation process.

Most Deposit Creation Occurs in the First Few Iterations of Fractional-Reserve Lending

	Deposit	Reserves	Excess Reserves	Total Deposits Created	Percent of Deposit Creation Utilized	Reserve Ratio of Banking System
1	$100.000	$10.000	$90.000	$0.000	0.00%	100.00%
2	$90.000	$9.000	$81.000	$90.000	10.00%	52.63%
3	$81.000	$8.100	$72.900	$171.000	19.00%	36.90%
4	$72.900	$7.290	$65.610	$243.900	27.10%	29.08%
5	$65.610	$6.561	$59.049	$309.510	34.39%	24.42%
6	$59.049	$5.905	$53.144	$368.559	40.95%	21.34%
7	$53.144	$5.314	$47.830	$421.703	46.86%	19.17%
8	$47.830	$4.783	$43.047	$469.533	52.17%	17.56%
9	$43.047	$4.305	$38.742	$512.580	56.95%	16.32%
10	$38.742	$3.874	$34.868	$551.322	61.26%	15.35%
11	$34.868	$3.487	$31.381	$586.189	65.13%	14.57%
12	$31.381	$3.138	$28.243	$617.570	68.62%	13.94%
13	$28.243	$2.824	$25.419	$645.813	71.76%	13.41%
14	$25.419	$2.542	$22.877	$671.232	74.58%	12.97%
15	$22.877	$2.288	$20.589	$694.109	77.12%	12.59%
16	$20.589	$2.059	$18.530	$714.698	79.41%	12.27%
17	$18.530	$1.853	$16.677	$733.228	81.47%	12.00%
18	$16.677	$1.668	$15.009	$749.905	83.32%	11.77%
19	$15.009	$1.501	$13.509	$764.915	84.99%	11.56%
20	$13.509	$1.351	$12.158	$778.423	86.49%	11.38%
21	$12.158	$1.216	$10.942	$790.581	87.84%	11.23%
22	$10.942	$1.094	$9.848	$801.523	89.06%	11.09%
23	$9.848	$0.985	$8.863	$811.371	90.15%	10.97%
24	$8.863	$0.886	$7.977	$820.234	91.14%	10.87%
25	$7.977	$0.798	$7.179	$828.210	92.02%	10.77%
26	$7.179	$0.718	$6.461	$835.389	92.82%	10.69%
27	$6.461	$0.646	$5.815	$841.850	93.54%	10.62%
28	$5.815	$0.581	$5.233	$847.665	94.19%	10.55%
29	$5.233	$0.523	$4.710	$852.899	94.77%	10.49%
30	$4.710	$0.471	$4.239	$857.609	95.29%	10.44%
31	$4.239	$0.424	$3.815	$861.848	95.76%	10.40%
32	$3.815	$0.382	$3.434	$865.663	96.18%	10.36%
33	$3.434	$0.343	$3.090	$869.097	96.57%	10.32%
34	$3.090	$0.309	$2.781	$872.187	96.91%	10.29%
35	$2.781	$0.278	$2.503	$874.968	97.22%	10.26%
36	$2.503	$0.250	$2.253	$877.472	97.50%	10.23%
37	$2.253	$0.225	$2.028	$879.724	97.75%	10.21%
38	$2.028	$0.203	$1.825	$881.752	97.97%	10.19%
39	$1.825	$0.182	$1.642	$883.577	98.18%	10.17%
40	$1.642	$0.164	$1.478	$885.219	98.36%	10.15%
220	$0.01	$0.001	$0.009	$900.000	100.00%	10.00%

In the table on the previous page, the 5th column "Total Deposits Created" shows the total amount of additional deposits created from the initial $100 deposit of reserves. The total deposits created shown in the table doesn't include the initial $100 deposit of reserves, which was fully backed by reserves and not created by fraudulently embezzling reserves. The total deposits in the banking system would be total deposits created plus the initial $100 deposit. The reserve ratio of the banking system is shown in the rightmost 7th column. The reserve ratio of the banking system would be total reserves divided by total deposits. As commercial banks can create additional deposits but not additional reserves, total reserves in the banking system are always $100. The percentage of deposit creation utilized is shown in the 6th column "Percent of Deposit Creation Utilized." In row 1, when the initial $100 deposit of reserves is made and no new deposits have been created, 0% of the deposit creation capacity has been utilized.

Row 220 shows the end of the fraudulent fractional-reserve lending progression. $900 of new deposits have been created, 100% of the deposit creation capacity has been utilized, and the reserve ratio for the banking system as a whole is 10%. There is less than 1¢ of "excess" reserves—effectively none—and the entire banking system is loaned up.

Prior to row 220, less than $900 of new deposits have been created. For example, in row 2, $90 of new deposits have been created, which is 10% of the $900 maximum. In row 4, $243.90 of new deposits have been created, which is 27.1% of the $900 maximum.

By the 8th iteration of fractional-reserve lending, more than 50% of money creation has occurred. By the 15th iteration of fractional-reserve lending, more than 75% of money creation has occurred. By the 24th iteration of fractional-reserve lending, more than 90% of money creation has occurred.

By the 6th iteration of fractional-reserve lending, the reserve ratio of the banking system has decreased to almost 20%—$1/5^{th}$ its original level of 100%—and is only double its final value of 10%. By the 24th iteration of fractional-reserve lending, the reserve ratio of the banking system is less than 11%. There is not a huge difference between a 10% and an 11% reserve ratio.

After only 24 iterations of fraudulent fractional-reserve lending, more than 90% of money creation has occurred and the reserve ratio has decreased from 100% to 11%. The money creation and reserve ratio decreases after the 24th iteration of fractional-reserve lending are relatively inconsequential. A banking system doesn't need to proceed through hundreds of iterations of fractional-reserve lending to create enough deposits to loan itself up.

YOUSURY

Usury is usually defined as exorbitant interest rates charged by predatory lenders. Usury you pay is your usury, which we'll nickname "yousury." For sheeple, usury is a number rather than a concept. Sheeple consider interest rates above a certain arbitrary numerical threshold unjust. A more meaningful definition of usury is interest paid on loan money which is simply conjured out of thin air. Usury is interest paid on money which the lender didn't have to save, earn, or borrow, but merely created. To focus on the numerical interest rate paid on conjured loan money, rather than the origin of the conjured loan money, is to be duped and miss the point. Any interest rate is usurious if the loan money was conjured out of thin air rather than saved, earned, or borrowed.

To envision your usury, that is, yousury, imagine a bank with $100,000 of deposits. We'll call it Seventh Servitude Bank. Seventh Servitude Bank has a 10% statutory reserve ratio requirement. It has not made any loans yet, so has $10,000 of reserves and $90,000 of "excess" reserves.

```
Assets                        Liabilities
 $10,000 (Reserves)            $100,000 (Deposits)
 $90,000 ("Excess" Reserves)
```

```
$100,000                      $100,000
                                       100% Reserve Ratio
```

Seventh Servitude Bank computers your mortgage, your car loan, your student loan, your credit card loan. . . If you have no loans, play along, or imagine you are someone you know who is deeply in debt. It shouldn't be hard to think of someone deeply in debt, as most Americans and humans are deeply in debt in large part because of fractional-reserve lending. Seventh Servitude Bank's ledger:

```
Assets                          Liabilities
 $43,000 (Reserves)              $100,000 (Deposits)
 $57,000 ("Excess" Reserves)
$250,000 (Your Mortgage)         $250,000 (Your Mortgage Check)
 $25,000 (Your Car Loan)          $25,000 (Your Car Loan Check)
  $5,000 (Your Credit Card)        $5,000 (Your Credit Card)
 $50,000 (You or Your Child's     $50,000 (You or Your Child's
          Student Loans)                   Student Loan Checks)
```

```
$430,000                        $430,000
                                       23% Reserve Ratio
```

Seventh Servitude Bank created $330,000 out of thin air and lent it to you. Substitute the name of your bank, its actual deposit amounts, and your actual loan amounts, and you have an accurate picture of the way your loans were conjured.

Most sheeple who see a personalized ledger like this grow angry or disheartened. Some disbelieve. It can't really work this way! You can't really have spent decades breaking your back repaying loans which banks simply conjure. If this was all true, it would be ludicrous!

Our banking system is ludicrous, and sadly, this is the truth. Most Americans bust their asses for decades paying loans which are simply conjured out of thin air by commercial banks via the process just described. As explained in *Bubblenomics*, our civilization has two classes of people: serfs who work for money, and banking Lords who simply conjure money on ledgers.

BAILOUTVILLE

"These capitalists generally act harmoniously and in concert, to fleece the people, and now that they have got into a quarrel with themselves we are called upon to appropriate the people's money to settle the quarrel. ... [The legislature] proposes to spend thousands of the people's public treasure, for no other advantage to them than to make valueless in their pockets the reward of their industry [print money to fund government deficits and Bailout banks, thereby devaluing preexisting money that citizens hold]. Mr. Chairman, this work is exclusively the work of politicians; a set of men who have interests aside from the interests of the people, and who, to say the most of them, are, taken as a mass, at least one long step removed from honest men. I say this with the greater freedom, because, being a politician myself, none can regard it as personal."

—Abraham Lincoln
Speech to the Illinois Legislature opposing a bank Bailout

First Fraud Bank has its lie-abilities exposed when depositors demand reserves that it doesn't possess, or when borrowers default on loan assets that must be zeroed out causing liabilities to exceed assets. Guv'ment can take reserves from the people and give them to First Fraud Bank. This will provide reserve assets that First Fraud Bank needs to honor deposit withdrawals, or replace zeroed-out loan assets so that liabilities no longer exceed assets. First Fraud Bank can then continue defrauding the people.

What if guv'ment doesn't provide a Bailout? As with goldsmiths, some depositor doesn't get their money. First Fraud Bank's bank-ruptcy could lead to dangerous questions by defrauded depositors. A population that understands fraudulent fractional-reserve lending is a threat to all banks, not just First Fraud Bank.

Why?

All commercial banks practice fraudulent fractional-reserve lending and create lie-abilities, meaning none have the reserves to honor all deposits. Every commercial bank in America (and every commercial bank in most of the rest of the world) is bank-rupt all of the time. If a large percentage of sheeple realized this and tried to withdraw money, every commercial bank in America would be instantly rupt.

Banks are partners in crime with a relationship eerily similar to mob families. Mob families compete against each other ruthlessly, but also keep the peace and work together on certain key issues which transcend their differences. Banks have to attract depositors to obtain reserves so that they can embezzle those reserves and create additional deposits. In our simple example, the initial $100 deposit was made at First Fraud Bank because a customer preferred it over some other bank. Loan checks are also deposited at banks which holders of those loan checks prefer. Banks compete against other banks in trying to attract depositors and obtain scarce reserves. This competition is ruthless. However, all banks run the same fractional-reserve scam, and when it comes to protecting and perpetuating that fractional-reserve scam, banks are all for one and one for all.

Thus First Fraud Bank must be saved—and will be. If First Fraud Bank is puny it might be allowed to go under, as a local failure won't cause a ripple in the national pond, but large failures that would cause many people to question banking practices are not allowed.

Guv'ment tells sheeple that First Fraud Bank is "too big to fail" and poses a "systemic risk." Sheeple are not sure what that means, but it sounds good. Being sheeple, they don't reason it through. If a bank is "too big to fail," why not break it up into several banks which are small enough to fail, and then let them fail? Everyone accepts the premise of too big to fail, but no one can seem to enumerate exactly what too big to fail means. What about the concept of too big to bail—out that is. What about Bailouts so huge that they strain the capacity of taxpayers and the guv'ment itself? No one in power is concerned about that.

Guv'ment gives First Fraud Bank a Bailout and business proceeds as usual. First Fraud Bank embezzles reserves again, issues loans again, creates lie-abilities again, and gets bailed out again. Sheeple are ignorant of Bailouts past, but they happened. Savings & Loans and Keating's Five during the late 1980s and early 1990s, for example. And FDR's gold seizure.

Confident it will be bailed out any time it gets into trouble, First Fraud Bank makes insane loans that pay obscene interest rates. Bailouts are part of its business plan. This is MORAL HAZARD. If you have fire insurance, why buy extinguishers? If guv'ment covers your bad loans, why not roll the dice on lucrative ones?

Defenders of fraudulent fractional-reserve lending say that banks earn their profit because they are risking capital. Like most effective lies, this one has a hint of truth. Banks assume risk when they create deposits not fully backed by reserves and lend them—assuming they are not bailed out—but the wealth they lend is stolen from sheeple via the inflation tax. The assumption of lie-ability risk by banks is not a substitute for eliminating the inflation tax. Claiming otherwise is like saying a burglar should keep what he stole because breaking into your house was risky.

The interest which banks are paid on fractional-reserve loans increases their capital, providing a buffer against risk. Previous bank ledgers did not include interest payments on conjured loans. Let's reexamine bank ledgers with interest payments included. First Fraud Bank opens with $50 of capital, accepts $100 of deposits, and maintains a mere 10% reserve ratio. First Fraud Bank's balance sheet:

```
Capital                Assets                Liabilities
$50                      $10 (Reserves)     $100 (Deposits)
                         $90 ("Excess" Reserves)
_____

$50                    $100                 $100
                                            100% Reserve Ratio
```

In previous examples, First Fraud Bank issued a single $90 loan. This time it will issue 3 loans which total $90:

```
Capital                Assets                Liabilities
$50                      $10 (Reserves)     $100 (Deposits)
                         $90 ("Excess" Reserves)
                         $40 (Loan)            $40 (Loan Check)
                         $30 (Loan)            $30 (Loan Check)
                         $20 (Loan)            $20 (Loan Check)
_____

$50                    $190                 $190
                                            100% Reserve Ratio
```

The loan checks are deposited at other banks. Those other banks demand reserve payments. First Fraud Bank pays out all its "excess" reserves to honor the loan checks. The "excess" reserves and loan checks are no longer on its ledger:

```
Capital                Assets                Liabilities
$50                      $10 (Reserves)     $100 (Deposits)
                         $40 (Loan)
                         $30 (Loan)
                         $20 (Loan)
_____

$50                    $100                 $100
                                            10% Reserve Ratio
```

First Fraud Bank made three loans totaling $90. All loans are 30-year mortgages paying 6% interest per year. All borrowers make payments for the first year, paying $5.40 of interest (6% = 0.06, $90 x 0.06 = $5.40). These profits are added to existing capital on First Fraud Bank's ledger:

Capital	Assets	Liabilities
$50.00	$10 (Reserves)	$100 (Deposits)
$5.40 (Mortgage interest)	$40 (Loan)	
	$30 (Loan)	
	$20 (Loan)	

$55.40	$100	$100
		10% Reserve Ratio

This oversimplifies the accounting involved in loan payments, but the process will be described more rigorously in future chapters once other critical concepts have been explained.

In just one year, First Fraud Bank's capital has increased by $5.40, or 10.8%. This is just First Fraud Bank. $900 of loans can be created from an initial $100 deposit, but First Fraud Bank only created $90 of loans. Other banks can create an additional $810 of loans and earn interest on them. Assume that the additional $810 of loans are all 30-year mortgages paying 6% interest per year. Banks as a whole have created $900 of loans paying 6% interest per year. This $900 "earns" $54 of interest (6% = 0.06, $900 x 0.06 = $54), a 54% return rate on the original $100 deposit.

54%!

54%! Speculatos concocted fractional-reserve lending for a reason.

In these simple examples, capital is a much larger percentage of deposits than banks actually maintain. As will be shown later, capital need only be about 8% of assets, or about 8% of loans. This means the bank shown on the ledger above could have opened with about $8 of capital and accepted $100 of deposits. With $8 of capital, the $5.40 of interest would have been a 67.5% increase in capital, a much larger increase than the 10.8% increase which resulted with $50 of capital.

While no single bank earns a 54% interest rate, banks as a whole have earned $54 of interest on $100 of reserves, effectively charging a 54% interest rate on those $100 of reserves. Only $10 of reserves are shown on First Fraud Bank's ledger, but there are $100 of reserves in the banking system spread amongst all banks. The initial $100 deposit was reserves. Fractional-reserve lending is merely the process of creating more deposits than there are reserves, and lending unbacked deposits out at interest. Defenders of fraudulent fractional-reserve lending would use the $1,000 of deposits or $900 of loans rather than the $100 of reserves for the interest calculation, and call the 54% interest rate a mischaracterization, but it is not— as we will see when loans are repaid and deposits are uncomputered, and when honest 100% reserve banking is examined. Fractional-reserve lending exists to create a massive wealth transfer from sheeple to Speculatos via this 54% usury.

Few conventional descriptions of fractional-reserve lending mention the exorbitant interest profits which it generates. Exorbitant interest profit is fractional-reserve lending's true purpose, and not mentioning this true purpose in descriptions is dishonest. It is easy to make fractional-reserve lending sound reasonable and ethical when such a basic fact is ignored, and this is what all mainstream descriptions of fractional-reserve lending do.

Back to First Fraud Bank. Year two, sheeple make another $5.40 of interest payments on their loans:

Capital		Assets		Liabilities	
$55.40		$10	(Reserves)	$100	(Deposits)
$5.40	(Mortgage interest)	$40	(Loan)		
		$30	(Loan)		
		$20	(Loan)		
$60.80		$100		$100	
				10% Reserve Ratio	

In just two years, First Fraud Bank's capital has increased by $10.80, or 21.6%. Banks as a whole have "earned" $108 of interest on their $900 of conjured deposits. In just two years, interest payments to all banks exceed the original $100 deposit of reserves!

First Fraud Bank's ledger after 3 more years of loan payments:

Capital		Assets		Liabilities	
$60.80		$10	(Reserves)	$100	(Deposits)
$16.20	(Mortgage interest)	$40	(Loan)		
		$30	(Loan)		
		$20	(Loan)		
$77.00		$100		$100	
				10% Reserve Ratio	

Mortgage interest is $5.40 per year, 3 years of interest payments total $16.20. These are 30-year mortgages; payments have only been made for 5 years, or 17% of the life of the mortgage. First Fraud Bank has increased its capital by 54%. Over 5 years, banks as a whole have earned $270 of interest payments, almost 3 times the initial $100 deposit of reserves!

First Fraud Bank has earned $27 of interest profits, increasing its original $50 of capital to $77. If the $20 loan is defaulted upon, then 22% of loans have defaulted, but First Fraud Bank has earned enough interest profit to cover the loss without dipping into its original $50 of capital. Interest payments on the remaining $40 loan and $30 loan—and any other additional loans issued—will replenish First Fraud Bank's "losses" on the defaulted loan.

This example neglects the bank's operating costs, repayment of loan principal (principal would usually be kept constant by issuing new loans), dividends paid out to stockholders, and other factors, and is rough at best. Still, a well run bank that engages in fraudulent fractional-reserve lending can rapidly recoup its initial capital investment. Then it isn't risking anything.

A house is usually used as collateral for the mortgage used to buy it. Banks own the house until the mortgage is fully paid, and can sell the house if the borrower defaults. If the down payment was small, the house often can't be sold for enough to cover the mortgage—which is why banks make borrowers whose down payment is less than 20% take out a mortgage insurance derivative. If the borrower defaults, the mortgage is paid by the insurer. Banks take a similar approach on most other loans and forms of credit, demanding insurance or large down payments to mitigate their risk.

Not exactly going to Vegas, eh? It is the ultimate golden goose, but greedy bankers insist on feeding it steroids, and end up being bailed out by the very sheeple they robbed in the first place. Like shooting the burglar, and then being forced to pay his medical bills and nurse him back to health.

Again, the scam grows more appalling if viewed economy-wide. In September 2008 just before The Bailout passed, here is the master ledger for all U.S. commercial banks:

```
Assets                                    Liabilities

  $102,578,000,000 (Reserves)             $7,052,400,000,000 (Deposits)
$1,147,500,000,000 (T-debts)             $2,412,000,000,000 (Borrowings)
$1,363,700,000,000 (Other securities)      $86,600,000,000 (All other debt)
$1,434,800,000,000 (Home mortgages)
  $540,600,000,000 (Home equity loans)
$1,686,100,000,000 (Commercial mortgages)
$1,533,000,000,000 (Business loans)
  $362,600,000,000 (Credit cards)
  $491,300,000,000 (Other consumer credit)
  $888,822,000,000 (All other loans)
_____

$9,551,000,000,000                       $9,551,000,000,000
                                              1.45% Reserve Ratio
```

Red numbers on the ledger above are billions of dollars, black numbers are trillions of dollars. This oversimplified ledger doesn't include all commercial bank assets & liabilities, and therefore fudges the "All other loans" and "All other debts" entries a bit to balance itself, but is nonetheless generally accurate. The 1.45% reserve ratio is computed using only deposit liabilities, not "Borrowings" or "All other debt."

Everything on the left side of the ledger except reserves is commercial bank credit, money commercial banks created out of thin air, lent, and earned interest on. Borrowings on the right side of the ledger are money banks borrowed to re-loan. Borrowings are owed, but can't be demanded immediately like deposits, rather they are loans banks are making payments on. Banks go borrowing at low interest, and lend at high. There is nothing immoral about this if the money borrowed is preexisting and not conjured out of thin air—which it often isn't.

Banks told customers with $7.052 trillion of deposits that they could demand reserves at anytime, but lied and kept only $102 billion of reserves to honor deposits. Banks accepted $102 billion of deposits, created $6.95 trillion out of thin air and used this money to issue loans to governments, corporations, businesses, and sheeple. This fraud allowed banks to "earn" interest on $1.15 trillion of T-debts, $1.43 trillion of mortgages, $541 billion of home equity loans, $1.69 trillion of commercial mortgages, $1.53 trillion of business loans, $363 billion of credit card loans...

Despite all this interest income, and profits which often exceeded $100 billion per year after paying all expenses including taxes and dividends, banks still went rupt and wanted Bailouts.

It is a preposterous system, as we can see by examining an honest bank that doesn't have the luxury of fractional-reserve lending.

BAILOUTVILLE PICTURE PAGES

TO SKIP THE PICTURE PAGES AFTER THIS CHAPTER, PLEASE TURN TO PAGE **77**

FEDERAL RESERVE STATISTICAL RELEASE H.8: ASSETS & LIABILITIES OF COMMERCIAL BANKS IN THE U.S.

FEDERAL RESERVE statistical release

H.8 (510)
Assets and Liabilities of Commercial Banks in the United States[1]
Not seasonally adjusted, billions of dollars

Page 2
October 24, 2008

Account	2007 Sep	2008 Mar	2008 Apr	2008 May	2008 Jun	2008 Jul	2008 Aug	2008 Sep	Week ending Sep 24	Oct 1	Oct 8	Oct 15
ASSETS												
1 Bank credit:	8,939.5	9,470.5	9,400.8	9,385.9	9,341.1	9,329.0	9,348.1	9,551.0	9,533.8	9,840.9	9,880.9	9,916.7
2 Securities in bank credit	2,363.3	2,557.7	2,533.8	2,507.2	2,485.4	2,473.8	2,462.2	2,511.2	2,486.2	2,594.3	2,645.4	2,617.3
3 Treasury and Agency securities[2]	1,162.1	1,116.0	1,102.8	1,110.1	1,123.7	1,120.0	1,134.3	1,147.5	1,139.0	1,164.9	1,157.2	1,157.3
4 Other securities[3]	1,201.1	1,441.7	1,431.1	1,397.2	1,361.7	1,353.8	1,328.0	1,363.7	1,347.3	1,429.4	1,488.2	1,459.9
5 Loans and leases in bank credit[4]	6,576.2	6,912.8	6,866.9	6,878.6	6,855.6	6,855.2	6,885.8	7,039.9	7,047.5	7,246.7	7,235.5	7,299.4
6 Commercial and industrial	1,354.7	1,484.4	1,492.1	1,494.1	1,497.0	1,498.9	1,502.7	1,533.0	1,550.3	1,570.3	1,589.5	1,599.4
7 Real estate	3,505.4	3,640.0	3,630.2	3,627.8	3,616.5	3,610.8	3,615.1	3,661.5	3,620.0	3,811.1	3,819.8	3,825.3
8 Revolving home equity	472.4	496.8	502.4	508.4	514.4	521.6	526.0	540.6	534.3	575.8	578.0	580.4
9 Other residential	1,465.9	1,504.3	1,482.1	1,465.2	1,439.5	1,423.6	1,419.4	1,434.8	1,405.8	1,509.4	1,514.9	1,515.3
10 Commercial	1,567.0	1,639.0	1,645.8	1,654.2	1,662.6	1,665.5	1,669.6	1,686.1	1,679.9	1,726.0	1,726.8	1,729.7
11 Consumer	786.1	812.2	818.2	822.8	826.9	833.0	843.7	853.9	856.8	858.8	857.2	865.9
12 Credit cards and other revolving plans	333.2	338.8	339.7	340.8	342.8	347.5	355.4	362.6	364.9	369.4	367.9	377.3
13 Other	453.0	473.4	478.5	482.0	484.1	485.4	488.3	491.3	492.0	489.4	489.3	488.6
14 Security[5]	279.0	301.5	284.5	294.2	281.2	282.1	294.9	327.3	354.4	340.2	306.8	277.6
15 Fed funds and RPs with brokers	220.0	239.6	223.4	238.2	234.8	234.5	246.9	267.5	272.9	275.7	248.4	214.8
16 Other	59.0	61.9	61.1	56.0	46.3	47.6	48.0	59.7	81.5	64.5	58.5	62.7
17 Other loans and leases	651.0	674.7	641.8	639.8	634.0	630.5	629.5	664.2	666.1	666.3	662.1	731.3
18 Interbank loans	395.5	450.2	449.5	434.6	436.4	422.7	427.4	460.5	461.1	450.6	452.2	451.6
19 Fed funds and RPs with banks[6]	318.3	368.5	365.9	353.3	355.3	349.8	353.3	389.9	390.9	380.8	379.9	372.6
20 Other	77.6	81.6	83.6	81.3	81.0	72.9	74.1	70.6	70.1	69.9	72.2	79.0
21 Cash assets[7]	301.8	300.5	308.8	304.1	296.3	292.4	285.9	366.1	368.6	467.3	486.6	555.1
22 Other assets[8]	933.7	1,007.1	998.0	984.3	998.4	1,016.1	1,015.7	1,052.3	1,062.4	1,120.6	1,128.0	1,116.5
23 TOTAL ASSETS[9]	10,501.8	11,140.7	11,061.3	11,011.6	10,971.3	10,952.4	10,967.7	11,316.4	11,313.5	11,760.3	11,825.5	11,917.5

The Federal Reserve releases statistics about the entire banking system each week. One such release H.8 is shown on this page and the next page. The asset entries on the large ledger on page 63 are highlighted on this page, and the liability entries are highlighted on the next page.

FEDERAL RESERVE statistical release

H.8 (510)
Assets and Liabilities of Commercial Banks in the United States[1]
Not seasonally adjusted, billions of dollars

Page 2
October 24, 2008

Account	2007	2008	2008	2008	2008	2008	2008	2008	Week ending			
	Sep	Mar	Apr	May	Jun	Jul	Aug	Sep	Sep 24	Oct 1	Oct 8	Oct 15
LIABILITIES												
24 Deposits	6,439.9	6,864.3	6,893.4	6,862.6	6,865.6	6,831.4	6,844.3	7,052.4	7,045.6	7,258.7	7,186.7	7,218.4
25 Transaction	599.7	614.5	642.4	609.3	602.6	605.4	589.9	631.1	704.5	660.3	604.7	638.6
26 Nontransaction	5,840.3	6,249.8	6,250.9	6,253.3	6,263.0	6,226.0	6,254.4	6,421.4	6,341.1	6,598.3	6,582.0	6,579.9
27 Large time	1,867.6	2,109.4	2,108.9	2,131.3	2,127.4	2,094.5	2,103.5	2,148.6	2,156.2	2,151.8	2,092.2	2,075.1
28 Other	3,972.7	4,140.4	4,142.1	4,122.0	4,135.6	4,131.5	4,150.9	4,272.8	4,184.9	4,446.5	4,489.8	4,504.8
29 Borrowings	2,239.3	2,306.2	2,307.3	2,338.9	2,317.8	2,307.2	2,342.9	2,412.0	2,427.2	2,573.8	2,530.4	2,572.8
30 From banks in the U.S.	447.2	486.7	479.3	481.2	479.4	467.5	469.9	478.2	478.3	463.0	475.4	463.6
31 From others	1,792.1	1,819.5	1,828.0	1,857.7	1,838.5	1,839.7	1,873.0	1,933.8	1,948.8	2,110.5	2,055.0	2,109.4
32 Net due to related foreign offices	95.9	22.8	-37.5	-64.5	-52.3	-23.3	-66.3	-48.0	-29.3	-7.3	115.6	163.4
33 Other liabilities	603.2	763.5	728.0	698.4	666.4	665.3	671.5	712.7	678.1	752.0	800.8	782.3
34 TOTAL LIABILITIES	9,378.3	9,956.9	9,891.2	9,835.4	9,797.5	9,780.6	9,792.3	10,129.2	10,121.5	10,577.2	10,633.5	10,736.9
35 Residual (assets less liabilities)[10]	1,123.5	1,183.9	1,170.1	1,176.3	1,173.7	1,171.8	1,175.5	1,187.3	1,192.0	1,183.1	1,192.0	1,180.6

Footnotes appear on page 13.

This is Federal Reserve Statistical Release H.8 in 2008 around the time that The Bailout was passed. This release shows the total liabilities (this page) and total assets (previous page) of all U.S. commercial banks. Several months are shown, and the Fed also provides weekly data for the 4 weeks prior to the release. This H.8 was released in October 24, 2008, so it shows the 4 weeks prior to the week of October 24. Three data items are highlighted for the month of September 2008: total deposit liabilities for all commercial banks, total transaction deposit liabilities for all commercial banks, and total non-transaction deposits for all commercial banks. Total deposits are $7,052.4 billion ($7,052.4 trillion), total transaction deposits are $631.1 billion, and total non-transaction deposits are $6,421.4 billion ($6,4214 trillion). The sum of transaction deposits and non-transaction deposits is the total deposits ($631.1 billion + $6,421.4 billion = $7,0524 billion). Transaction and non-transaction deposits will be discussed later. The key statistic is the $7.05 trillion of deposits, which is total deposits held by commercial banks in 2008 when the economy imploded and The Bailout passed.

FEDERAL RESERVE STATISTICAL RELEASE H.3: AGGREGATE RESERVES OF DEPOSITORY INSTITUTIONS

FEDERAL RESERVE statistical release

H.3 (502)
Table 2

AGGREGATE RESERVES OF DEPOSITORY INSTITUTIONS AND THE MONETARY BASE

Not adjusted for changes in reserve requirements[1]
Not seasonally adjusted
Millions of dollars

Date	Reserves of depository institutions		Required	Monetary base[3]	Reserve balances with F.R. Banks[4]	Vault cash[5]		Surplus[7]	Net carryover of reserve balances[8]
	Total[2]	Nonborrowed				Total	Used to satisfy required reserves[6]		
Month[9]									
2008-Jan.	44065	-1595	42424	831104	8715	53163	35349	17813	
Feb.	42778	-17379	41053	828692	8147	53651	34631	19021	
Mar.	42706	-51817	39728	832358	9754	50446	32952	17494	
Apr.	43506	-91904	41661	830494	9254	49315	34252	15063	
May	45111	-110669	43100	833974	9688	48576	35423	13153	
June	43933	-127345	41660	839085	9181	49333	34752	14581	
July	44124	-121539	42147	846462	9343	49225	34781	14444	
Aug.	44134	-123944	42146	847302	9430	50142	34704	15438	
Sep.	102578	-187527	42535	908051	67167	50443	35411	15032	

This is Federal Reserve Statistical Release H.3 when The Bailout passed. For September 2008, total reserves and required reserves of all depository institutions are highlighted yellow. The statutory reserve requirement for all depository institutions was $42.535 billion, but they kept $102.578 billion of reserves. The red-highlighted negative values in the nonborrowed reserves column indicate that the banking system was bank-rupted by lie-ability exposure and was only able to honor deposits because the Fed conjured billions of dollars out of thin air and lent these reserves to banks. By September 2008, the Fed had conjured $187 billion of reserves to Bailout banks, but this was insufficient to cover their lie-abilities. The Bailout was therefore passed. It authorized the Fed to create more than $1 trillion of reserves to cover bank lie-abilities. The banking system was insolvent and kept solvent solely by reserves conjured by Fed.

COMMERCIAL BANKS ONLY KEPT $50 BILLION OF VAULT CASH TO HONOR $7,052 BILLION OF DEPOSITS!

FEDERAL RESERVE statistical release

H.8 (510)

Assets and Liabilities of Commercial Banks in the United States[1]
Not seasonally adjusted, billions of dollars

Page 2

October 24, 2008

LIABILITIES

Account	2007 Sep	2008 Mar	2008 Apr	2008 May	2008 Jun	2008 Jul	2008 Aug	2008 Sep	Week ending Sep 24	Oct 1	Oct 8	Oct 15
24 Deposits	6,439.9	6,864.3	6,893.4	6,862.6	6,865.6	6,831.4	6,844.3	7,052.4	7,045.6	7,258.7	7,186.7	7,218.4

FEDERAL RESERVE statistical release

H.3 (502)
Table 2

AGGREGATE RESERVES OF DEPOSITORY INSTITUTIONS AND THE MONETARY BASE

Not adjusted for changes in reserve requirements[1]
Not seasonally adjusted
Millions of dollars

Date	Reserves of depository institutions			Monetary base[3]	Reserve balances with F.R. Banks[4]	Vault cash[5]			Net carryover of reserve balances[8]
	Total[2]	Nonborrowed	Required			Total	Used to satisfy required reserves[6]	Surplus[7]	
Month[9]									
Aug.	44134	-123394	42146	847302	9430	50142	34704	15438	
Sep.	102578	-187527	42535	908051	67167	50443	35411	15032	

The fundamental fraud of fractional-reserve lending can be seen by juxtaposing Releases H.3 and H.8. These same two releases will be reproduced on the next 7 pages without any changes being made, except for what is highlighted. Total vault cash held by all depository institutions was $50.443 billion but they had issued at least $7,052.4 billion of promises to provide cash upon demand.

FEDERAL RESERVE statistical release

H.8 (510)
Assets and Liabilities of Commercial Banks in the United States[1]
Not seasonally adjusted, billions of dollars

October 24, 2008

Account	2007 Sep	2008 Mar	2008 Apr	2008 May	2008 Jun	2008 Jul	2008 Aug	2008 Sep	Week ending Sep 24	Oct 1	Oct 8	Oct 15
LIABILITIES												
24 Deposits	6,439.9	6,864.3	6,893.4	6,862.6	6,865.6	6,831.4	6,844.3	7,052.4	7,045.6	7,258.7	7,186.7	7,218.4

FEDERAL RESERVE statistical release

H.3 (502)
Table 2
AGGREGATE RESERVES OF DEPOSITORY INSTITUTIONS AND THE MONETARY BASE
Not adjusted for changes in reserve requirements[1]
Not seasonally adjusted
Millions of dollars

Date	Reserves of depository institutions			Monetary base[3]	Reserve balances with F.R. Banks[4]	Vault cash[5]		Surplus[7]	Net carryover of reserve balances[8]
	Total[2]	Nonborrowed	Required			Total	Used to satisfy required reserves[6]		
Month[9]									
Aug.	44134	-123944	42146	847302	9430	50142	34704	15438	
Sep.	102578	-187527	42535	908051	67167	50443	35411	15032	

With at least $7,052.4 billion of promises to provide cash on demand, but only $50,433 billion of vault cash on hand to honor these promises, banks had $7,001.967 billion of promises they could not honor. That is, $7,001.967 billion of deposits they could not redeem for cash even though this promise was made. Banks had $7,001.967 billion ($7.002 trillion) of lie-abilities, at least where vault cash was concerned. $7 trillion of fraudulent deposits that could not be honored and redeemed for cash!

FEDERAL RESERVE statistical release

H.8 (510)
Assets and Liabilities of Commercial Banks in the United States[1]
Not seasonally adjusted, billions of dollars

Account	2007 Sep	2008 Mar	2008 Apr	2008 May	2008 Jun	2008 Jul	2008 Aug	2008 Sep	Week ending Sep 24	Oct 1	Oct 8	Oct 15
LIABILITIES												
24 Deposits	6,439.9	6,864.3	6,893.4	6,862.6	6,865.6	6,831.4	6,844.3	7,052.4	7,045.6	7,258.7	7,186.7	7,218.4

FEDERAL RESERVE statistical release

H.3 (502)
Table 2
AGGREGATE RESERVES OF DEPOSITORY INSTITUTIONS AND THE MONETARY BASE

Not adjusted for changes in reserve requirements[1]
Not seasonally adjusted
Millions of dollars

Date	Reserves of depository institutions Total[2]	Nonborrowed	Required	Monetary base[3]	Reserve balances with F.R. Banks[4]	Vault cash[5] Total	Used to satisfy required reserves[6]	Surplus[7]	Net carryover of reserve balances[8]
Month[9]									
Aug.	44134	-123944	42146	847302	9430	50142	34704	15438	
Sep.	102578	-187527	42535	908051	67167	50443	35411	15032	

With $7,052.4 billion of deposits backed by only $50.443 billion of vault cash, there was only $1 of cash for every $140 of deposits! $139 out of every $140 of deposits could not be redeemed for cash! Amazingly, this paltry vault cash was deemed excessive by Fed, as required cash reserves were only $35.411 billion. "Regulations" allowed banks to issue $7.052 trillion of deposits and only keep $35.411 billion of vault cash to honor them, meaning $198 out of every $199 of deposits could not be redeemed for cash!

FEDERAL RESERVE statistical release

H.8 (510)
Page 2
Assets and Liabilities of Commercial Banks in the United States[1]
Not seasonally adjusted, billions of dollars

October 24, 2008

Account	2007 Sep	2008 Mar	2008 Apr	2008 May	2008 Jun	2008 Jul	2008 Aug	2008 Sep	Week ending Sep 24	Oct 1	Oct 8	Oct 15
LIABILITIES												
24 Deposits	6,439.9	6,864.3	6,893.4	6,862.6	6,865.6	6,831.4	6,844.3	7,052.4	7,045.6	7,258.7	7,186.7	7,218.4

FEDERAL RESERVE statistical release

H.3 (502)
Table 2
AGGREGATE RESERVES OF DEPOSITORY INSTITUTIONS AND THE MONETARY BASE
Not adjusted for changes in reserve requirements[1]
Not seasonally adjusted
Millions of dollars

Date	Reserves of depository institutions			Monetary base[3]	Reserve balances with F.R. Banks[4]	Vault cash[5]			Net carryover of reserve balances[8]
	Total[2]	Nonborrowed	Required			Total	Used to satisfy required reserves[6]	Surplus[7]	
Month[9]									
Aug.	44134	-123944	42146	847302	9430	50142	34704	15438	
Sep.	102578	-187527	42535	908051	67167	50443	35411	15032	

An honest person with $7,052.4 billion of commitments to provide cash immediately upon demand but only $50.443 billion of cash on hand to honor these commitments would reckon that they had a severe cash shortage. Not bankers. And certainly not bank "regulations" and "regulators." According to corrupt "regulations," banks with $7.002 trillion of deposits they could not redeem for cash did not have a vault-cash shortage, but rather had a $15.032 billion vault-cash surplus!

FEDERAL RESERVE statistical release

H.8 (510)
Assets and Liabilities of Commercial Banks in the United States[1]
Not seasonally adjusted, billions of dollars

Page 2
October 24, 2008

Account	2007 Sep	2008 Mar	2008 Apr	2008 May	2008 Jun	2008 Jul	2008 Aug	2008 Sep	Week ending Sep 24	Oct 1	Oct 8	Oct 15
LIABILITIES												
24 Deposits	6,439.9	6,864.3	6,893.4	6,862.6	6,865.6	6,831.4	6,844.3	7,052.4	7,045.6	7,258.7	7,186.7	7,218.4

FEDERAL RESERVE statistical release

H.3 (502)
Table 2
AGGREGATE RESERVES OF DEPOSITORY INSTITUTIONS AND THE MONETARY BASE

Not adjusted for changes in reserve requirements[1]
Not seasonally adjusted
Millions of dollars

Date	Reserves of depository institutions			Monetary base[3]	Reserve balances with F.R. Banks[4]	Vault cash[5]			Net carryover of reserve balances[8]
	Total[2]	Nonborrowed	Required			Total	Used to satisfy required reserves[6]	Surplus[7]	
Month[9]									
Aug.	44134	-123944	42146	847302	9430	50142	34704	15438	
Sep.	102578	-187527	42535	908051	67167	50443	35511	15032	

Many depositor withdrawals are payments to other banks rather than withdrawals of physical cash, and these are paid using Fed-account reserves or "Reserve balances with F.R. (Federal Reserve) Banks." September 2008 data shows $67.167 billion of Fed-account reserves, but this is deceptive, as most of it was bailout money Fed conjured out of thin air in that month to save commercial banks. In August 2008, commercial banks only held $9.430 billion of Fed-account reserves, and most months prior to this were similar.

FEDERAL RESERVE statistical release

H.8 (510)
Assets and Liabilities of[2] Commercial Banks in the United States[1]
Not seasonally adjusted, billions of dollars

Page 2
October 24, 2008

Account	2007 Sep	2008 Mar	2008 Apr	2008 May	2008 Jun	2008 Jul	2008 Aug	2008 Sep	Week ending Sep 24	Oct 1	Oct 8	Oct 15
LIABILITIES												
24 Deposits	6,439.9	6,864.3	6,893.4	6,862.6	6,865.6	6,831.4	6,844.3	7,052.4	7,045.6	7,258.7	7,186.7	7,218.4

FEDERAL RESERVE statistical release

H.3 (502)
Table 2
AGGREGATE RESERVES OF DEPOSITORY INSTITUTIONS AND THE MONETARY BASE
Not adjusted for changes in reserve requirements[1]
Not seasonally adjusted
Millions of dollars

Date	Reserves of depository institutions Total[2]	Nonborrowed	Required	Monetary base[3]	Reserve balances with F.R. Banks[4]	Vault cash[5] Total	Used to satisfy required reserves[6]	Surplus[7]	Net carryover of reserve balances[8]
Month[9]									
Aug.	44134	-123944	42146	847302	9430	50142	34704	15438	
Sep.	102578	-187527	42535	908051	67167	50443	35411	15032	

Commercial banks had lie-abilities fatally exposed in September 2008. Fed conjured $63.583 billion of reserves and lent them to banks, increasing "nonborrowed" (conjured and lent) reserves from −$123.944 billion to −$187.527 billion. When the banking system is solvent, nonborrowed reserves is positive, meaning banks have reserves even if they hadn't borrowed any from Fed. When negative nonborrowed reserves has a magnitude greater than total reserves, the banking system is rupt and surviving solely on Fed loans.

FEDERAL RESERVE statistical release

Page 2

October 24, 2008

H.8 (510)
Assets and Liabilities of Commercial Banks in the United States[1]
Not seasonally adjusted, billions of dollars

Account	2007 Sep	2008 Mar	2008 Apr	2008 May	2008 Jun	2008 Jul	2008 Aug	2008 Sep	Week ending Sep 24	Oct 1	Oct 8	Oct 15
LIABILITIES												
24 Deposits	6,439.9	6,864.3	6,893.4	6,862.6	6,865.6	6,831.4	6,844.3	7,052.4	7,045.6	7,258.7	7,186.7	7,218.4

FEDERAL RESERVE statistical release

H.3 (502)
Table 2
AGGREGATE RESERVES OF DEPOSITORY INSTITUTIONS AND THE MONETARY BASE
Not adjusted for changes in reserve requirements[1]
Not seasonally adjusted
Millions of dollars

Date	Reserves of depository institutions			Monetary base[3]	Reserve balances with F.R. Banks[4]	Vault cash[5]		Net carryover of reserve balances[8]	
	Total[2]	Nonborrowed	Required			Total	Used to satisfy required reserves[6]	Surplus[7]	Net carryover of reserve balances[8]
Month[9]									
Aug.	44134	-123944	42146	847302	9430	50142	34704	15438	
Sep.	102578	-187527	42535	908051	67167	50443	35411	15032	

Nonborrowed reserves of depository institutions increased by $63.583 billion from August to September of 2008. This is the total amount of reserves Fed conjured for commercial banks. Most of these reserves were non-physical, digital reserves in Fed-accounts of commercial banks, "Reserve balances with F.R. Banks," which increased by $57.737 billion. This greatly increased the total reserves in the banking system, by $58.344 billion, to $102.578 billion, more than double the previous level of $44.134 billion.

FEDERAL RESERVE statistical release

H.8 (510)   Page 2
Assets and Liabilities of Commercial Banks in the United States[1]
Not seasonally adjusted, billions of dollars

October 24, 2008

Account	2007 Sep	2008 Mar	2008 Apr	2008 May	2008 Jun	2008 Jul	2008 Aug	2008 Sep	Week ending			
									Sep 24	Oct 1	Oct 8	Oct 15
LIABILITIES												
24 Deposits	6,439.9	6,864.3	6,893.4	6,862.6	6,865.6	6,831.4	6,844.3	7,052.4	7,045.6	7,258.7	7,186.7	7,218.4

FEDERAL RESERVE statistical release

H.3 (502)
Table 2
AGGREGATE RESERVES OF DEPOSITORY INSTITUTIONS AND THE MONETARY BASE
Not adjusted for changes in reserve requirements[1]
Not seasonally adjusted
Millions of dollars

Date	Reserves of depository institutions			Monetary base[3]	Reserve balances with F.R. Banks[4]	Vault cash[5]		Surplus[7]	Net carryover of reserve balances[8]
	Total[2]	Nonborrowed	Required			Total	Used to satisfy required reserves[6]		
Month[9]									
Aug.	44134	-123944	42146	847302	9430	50142	34704	15438	
Sep.	102578	-187527	42535	908051	67167	50443	35411	15032	

Even $102.578 billion of reserves wasn't enough to save commercial banks when depositors withdrew $500 billion of deposits or roughly 8% of deposits, as this exceeded total reserves of the banking system by almost $400 billion. Severe reserve shortages and the resulting lie-ability exposure are the fundamental cause of all Depressions in modern history. All modern Depressions are caused by fractional-reserve lending which allows banks to fraudulently create deposits which exceed reserves.

DEFINITIVE STATISTICS FOR ENTIRE U.S. BANKING SYSTEM IN 2008

Compiling statistical aggregates for thousands of banks is cumbersome, and there is variation in values that Fed reports. If one checked the H.8 or H.3 releases a few weeks before or after the ones shown on the previous pages, or loaded them at a later time than the author did, the data might vary by a few billion dollars. There is also some variation between deposit supply data reported for commercial banks and the money supply data reported for the banking system as a whole, including savings banks, savings and loan associations, credit unions, and other depository institutions. As banks create and uncreate large amounts of deposits each day as loans are issued and paid, and there are some lags in reporting and corrections made to reported values, this variation in reported statistics is unsurprising.

To avoid any error, or at least minimize unavoidable uncertainty, the author contacted a Federal Reserve economist that compiles the Fed's statistical releases, and asked for definitive money supply and deposit information in September 2008 at the time that The Bailout passed. This economist provided the following statistics for the entire U.S. banking system:

Required Reserves:	$42.700 billion
Total Reserves:	$102.736 billion
Total Deposits:	$7,052.700 billion
Total Transaction Deposits:	$631.100 billion
Total Non-Transaction Deposits:	$6,421.600 billion

These statistics vary slightly from those shown on the previous pages, but as they came straight from the proverbial horse's mouth and are definitive, they will be used for all calculations for the entire U.S. banking system throughout this book.

Minor deviations between the two statistics are insignificant. For example, the $42.7 billion of required reserves (statutory reserve requirement) and $7,052.7 billion of deposits in the data above yield a statutory reserve ratio requirement of 0.6% ($42.7 billion ÷ $7,052.7 billion = 0.6%). The $42.535 billion of required reserves (statutory reserve requirement) and $7,052.4 billion of deposits from the statistical releases on the previous pages also yield a statutory reserve ratio requirement of 0.6% ($42.535 billion ÷ $7,052.4 billion = 0.6%).

HONEST BANKING

"[Commercial] Banks can't create money under 100% reserves [a 100% reserve banking system], and banks would earn their profit by financial intermediation only, lending savers' money for them (charging a loan rate higher than the rate paid to savings or "time-account" depositors) and charging for checking, safekeeping, and other services. With 100% reserves every dollar loaned to a borrower would be a dollar previously saved by a depositor (and not available to the depositor during the period of the loan), thereby re-establishing the classical balance between abstinence and investment. With credit limited by saving (abstinence from consumption) there will be less lending and borrowing and it will be done more carefully—no more easy credit to finance the leveraged purchase of "assets" that are nothing but bets on dodgy debts. ... With 100% reserves there is also no danger of a run on a bank."

—Herman Daly, former World Bank Economist

"No, but you... you... you're thinking of this place all wrong. As if I had the money back in a safe. The money's not here. Your money's in Joe's house, and in the Kennedy house, and Mrs. Macklin's house, and a hundred others. Why, you're lending them the money to build, and then, they're going to pay it back to you as best they can. Now what are you going to do? Foreclose on them?"

—George Bailey (Jimmy Stewart), during a bank run in *It's a Wonderful Life*

At an honest bank, depositors' reserves would always be "back in a safe," unless they gave the bank explicit permission to lend them. Let's open Infinite Integrity Bank and accept a $100 deposit of reserves. Infinite Integrity's balance sheet:

Assets	Liabilities
$100 (Reserves)	$100 (Demand Deposits)
	100% Reserve Ratio

The handwriting font indicates honest 100% reserve banking in which no money is computered or uncomputered. Honest 100% reserve banking is also referred to as full reserve banking, but we will use the term 100% reserve banking.

John Q. Debtor wants a $90 loan. As Infinite Integrity is an honest bank, we have a 100% reserve requirement. All deposits are set aside and reserved in their entirety, like coats in a coat check. There is no fraudulent fractional-reserve lending.

We can't lend the reserves which back customers' deposits without obtaining their explicit permission. We don't have any reserves to lend.

This sucks. What are we going to do? Lend our own capital, our own money? Are you nuts? We started a bank to risk other people's wealth.

To lend other people's money we must get their permission. John Q. Debtor wants a 1-year car loan. Jane R. Depositor agrees to surrender her deposited reserves for 1 year, but knows that we usually charge 6% interest on car loans, and demands half of the profit, or 3% interest. This means the bank only earns 3% profit on the loan.

3%? 3-freakin'-percent? Under fraudulent fractional-reserve lending, depositors weren't explicitly asked to surrender reserves. When depositors are asked to explicitly surrender reserves, they demand much higher interest rates. No more 0.3% savings accounts or 0.75% Certificates of Deposit (CDs).

We agree to Jane R. Depositor's demand. She surrenders her claim to $90 of her reserves, and we begin paying her 3% interest. We sign a contractual promise to return Jane R. Depositor's deposit—her claim to reserves—in 1 year. Our updated ledger:

Assets	Liabilities
$100 (Reserves)	**$10 (Demand Deposits)**
	$90 (1-Year Time Deposits)
$100	$100

100% Reserve Ratio

Honest banks only have two types of deposits, DEMAND DEPOSITS and TIME DEPOSITS. Demand deposits can be demanded at anytime, so must be backed 100% by reserves. Time deposits are explicitly surrendered by depositors for a period of time, can't be demanded by depositors for that period of time, and don't need to be backed by reserves for that period of time. The reserves backing time deposits can therefore be legitimately lent by the bank for the duration of the time deposit. The time deposits on Infinite Integrity Bank's ledger are colored grey to indicate the fact that they can't be demanded by the depositor. Greyed time deposits added to ledgers won't be colored red the way that other items added to ledgers are.

The $90 time deposit can't be demanded for a year, so for that time it is not a liability and doesn't have to be backed by reserves. Only the demand deposit has to be backed by reserves. After Infinite Integrity Bank sets $10 of reserves aside to honor its $10 of demand deposits, it has $90 of excess reserves:

Assets	Liabilities
$10 (Reserves)	*$10 (Demand Deposits)*
$90 (Excess Reserves)	*$90 (1 Year Time Deposits)*

$100	*$100*

100% Reserve Ratio

As Infinite Integrity Bank only has $10 of reserves to back demand deposits, its demand deposits were decreased to $10. This is a simple yet highly significant step that was not performed with fractional-reserve lending. With fraudulent fractional-reserve lending, reserves backing demand deposits were decreased, but the demand deposits were not decreased, which is how lie-abilities were created.

Infinite Integrity Bank's excess reserves are not embezzled as with fractional-reserve lending, so the "excess" is not enclosed in quotations as was done with fractional-reserve lending. In fraudulent fractional-reserve banking, "excess" reserves are not truly excess. In honest 100% reserve banking, excess reserves are truly excess. Reserves are not promised to one depositor while simultaneously being paid out to another party, as with fractional-reserve lending. Infinite Integrity Bank's excess reserves are reserves which Jane R. Depositor has voluntarily and explicitly surrendered.

This is a critical distinction. In honest 100% reserve banking, reserves are lent only if they are voluntarily and explicitly surrendered by the depositor. In honest 100% reserve banking, depositors' permission to lend their reserves is never presumed in an implicit or indirect manner. Any lending in which loan money is not voluntarily and explicitly surrendered by a depositor is fraudulent. Speculatos expend considerable effort muddling this critical distinction, as this is the only way they can perpetrate their fractional-reserve scam. Don't be duped.

Infinity Integrity Bank has $90 of excess reserves which were obtained honestly. It has $90 of reserves which it can use to honor a loan check if that check is deposited at another bank and that bank demands payment. Infinite Integrity Bank therefore issues a $90 loan to John Q. Debtor:

Assets	Liabilities
$10 (Reserves)	*$10 (Demand Deposits)*
$90 (Excess Reserves)	*$90 (1 Year Time Deposits)*
$90 (1 Year Loan)	

$190	*$100*

100% Reserve Ratio

John Q. Debtor signs the loan contract, agreeing to make payments to Infinite Integrity Bank for 1 year. Only after John Q. Debtor signs the loan does Infinite Integrity Bank issue him a loan check. Infinite Integrity Bank makes sure it has the loan asset on its books before it creates the liability which is the loan check. Infinite Integrity Bank's ledger after it issues the loan check:

Assets	Liabilities
$10 (Reserves)	$10 (Demand Deposits)
$90 (Excess Reserves)	$90 (1 Year Time Deposits)
$90 (1 Year Loan)	**$90 (Loan Check)**
$190	$190

100% Reserve Ratio

The excess reserves will be used to honor the loan check. The excess reserves back the loan check. We'll put the excess reserves on the same ledger row as the loan check to simplify visualization. The amounts on the ledger will be unchanged, the position of the excess reserves and 1-year loan will simply be swapped:

Assets	Liabilities
$10 (Reserves)	$10 (Demand Deposits)
$90 (1 Year Loan)	$90 (1 Year Time Deposits)
$90 (Excess Reserves)	$90 (Loan Check)
$190	$190

100% Reserve Ratio

The time deposit accounting entry confuses some, but this ledger reorganization can help eliminate that confusion. Earlier it was explained that every liability must be offset by an asset of equal value. The time deposit liability is the counterpart of the loan asset. The loan backs the time deposit in the same way that reserves back a demand deposit; a promise to repay deposit liabilities (time deposit) is backed by a promise to repay reserve assets (loan).

Both the loan and time deposit are IOUs. They are promises to supply reserves and deposits which are not possessed. The loan is a reserve asset that a borrower owes to the bank, the time deposit is a deposit liability which the bank owes to a depositor that lent the bank reserves. This would seem pretty basic, but on the fractional-reserve ledger there was no lender surrendering a deposit and the claim to reserves that it represented. How can you have a loan without someone surrendering money? You can't—not an honest loan anyway.

We colored time deposits grey because the depositor did not possess them. As loans are reserves not possessed by the bank, they will also be colored grey:

Assets	Liabilities
$10 (Reserves)	$10 (Demand Deposits)
$90 (1 Year Loan)	$90 (1 Year Time Deposits)
$90 (Excess Reserves)	$90 (Loan Check)
$190	$190

100% Reserve Ratio

This grey coloring makes it easy to identify time deposits and the loans which back them, which helps minimize confusion. The grey loan and grey time deposit are paired and shown on the same row, which is symbolic of the fact that every loan requires a time deposit which is surrendered money used for the loan.

Infinite Integrity Bank's assets & liabilities have increased from $100 to $190, but money has not been created. Jane R. Depositor's account balance is $10, not $100. She can't spend her 1-year time deposit. Though the time deposit is on the ledger, total liabilities which depositors can spend are only $100, the $10 demand deposit and $90 loan check. The money supply has not increased from its initial level of $100.

Contrast Infinite Integrity Bank's ledger with First Fraud Bank's ledger:

First Fraud Bank

Assets	Liabilities
$10 (Reserves)	$100 (Deposits)
$90 (Loan)	
$90 ("Excess" Reserves)	$90 (Loan Check)
$190	$190

10% Reserve Ratio

Infinite Integrity Bank

Assets	Liabilities
$10 (Reserves)	$10 (Demand Deposits)
$90 (1 Year Loan)	$90 (1 Year Time Deposits)
$90 (Excess Reserves)	$90 (Loan Check)
$190	$190

100% Reserve Ratio

At First Fraud Bank, no distinction is made between demand deposits and time deposits. By abandoning this distinction, First Fraud Bank evades the need to convert demand deposits into time deposits before issuing loans. If no time deposit is created, then no depositor has surrendered reserves for a loan. If a deposit (or check) is created for a loan, and no preexisting deposit is decreased in size or debited, then the net result is an increase in deposits which are literally the money supply. Thus when First Fraud Bank issues a loan, the deposit supply that is literally the money supply increases from $100 to $190.

Any ledgerized lending in which deposit money is not surrendered requires deposit creation. Forsaking the process of converting demand deposits into time deposits—of subtracting loaned money from a depositor account—necessitates deposit creation. It is impossible to let depositors retain their claim to reserves and to simultaneously lend those reserves out and give some other party a claim to those reserves, unless additional deposits are created.

When Infinite Integrity Bank issues a loan, a deposit for the loan exists before the loan is issued. Deposit money is not computed out of thin air to make the loan. No debt is magically "monetized." Infinite Integrity is able to issue a loan only because a depositor surrendered reserves and deposits which are used for the loan. The difference between First Fraud Bank's ledger and Infinite Integrity Bank's ledger is but a single entry, the $90 time deposit which is subtracted from the original $100 (demand) deposit. Though simple, this difference is paramount, and it is the cause of a significant portion of all human suffering.

To help visualize the difference between honest 100% reserve lending and fraudulent fractional-reserve lending, the following page shows them side by side.

John Q. Debtor obtains his loan check from Infinite Integrity Bank and deposits it at Totally Trustworthy Bank, which is also an honest 100% reserve bank:

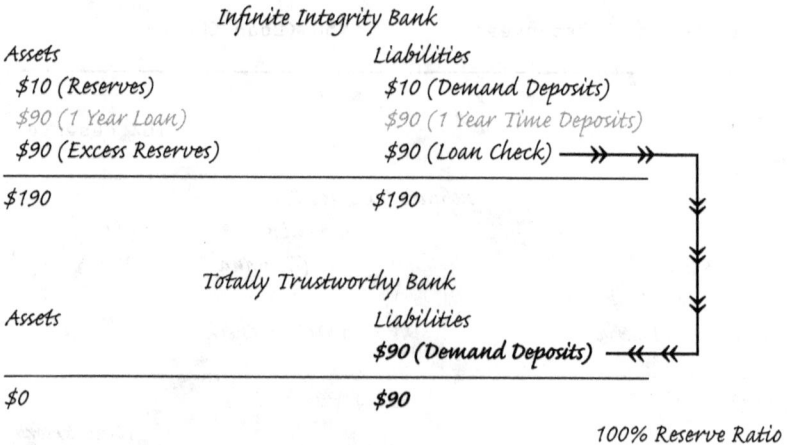

Infinite Integrity Bank

Assets	Liabilities
$10 (Reserves)	$10 (Demand Deposits)
$90 (1 Year Loan)	$90 (1 Year Time Deposits)
$90 (Excess Reserves)	$90 (Loan Check) ⟶ ≫ ≫
$190	$190

Totally Trustworthy Bank

Assets	Liabilities
	$90 (Demand Deposits) ⟵ ≪ ≪
$0	$90

100% Reserve Ratio

In the fractional-reserve lending examples, each successive bank had a number in its name to indicate the recursive nature of fractional-reserve deposit creation. 100% reserve lending is non-recursive, so these number names will be forsaken.

HONEST 100% RESERVE LENDING VS. FRAUDULENT FRACTIONAL-RESERVE LENDING

Honest 100% Reserve Lending

Infinite Integrity Bank

Assets	Liabilities
$10 (Reserves)	$10 (Demand Deposits)
$90 (1 Year Loan)	$90 (1 Year Time Deposits)
$100	$100

Totally Trustworthy Bank

Assets	Liabilities
$9 (Reserves)	$9 (Demand Deposits)
$81 (1 Year Loan)	$81 (1 Year Time Deposits)
$90	$90

Vast Virtue Bank

Assets	Liabilities
$8.10 (Reserves)	$8.10 (Demand Deposits)
$72.90 ("Excess" Reserves)	$72.90 (Time Deposits)
$81.00	$81.00

Initial Demand Deposits: $100 Final Demand Deposits: $100
Reserve Ratio: 100%

Fraudulent Fractional-Reserve Lending

First Fraud Bank

Assets	Liabilities
$10 (Reserves)	$100 (Deposits)
$90 (Loan)	
$100	$100

Steal Second Bank

Assets	Liabilities
$9 (Reserves)	$90 (Deposits)
$81 (Loan)	
$90	$90

Third Thievery Bank

Assets	Liabilities
$8.10 (Reserves)	$81 (Deposits)
$72.90 ("Excess" Reserves)	
$81.00	$81

Initial Deposits: $100 Final Deposits: $271
Reserve Ratio: 37%

$100 of reserves are deposited in both banking systems and both issue $171 of loans. In honest 100% reserve banking, depositors surrender money for loans, converting demand deposits into time deposits. In fraudulent fractional-reserve banking, depositors don't surrender money for loans so additional deposits are created for loans. Deposits not backed by reserves can't be honored. In fraudulent fractional-reserve banking, deposits exceed reserves, so only a fraction of deposits are backed by reserves and can be honored. In honest 100% reserve banking, demand deposits equal reserves, so all demand deposits are backed by reserves and can be honored.

After John Q. Debtor deposits the loan check at Totally Trustworthy Bank, the loan check is no longer on Infinite Integrity Bank's ledger:

Infinite Integrity Bank

Assets	Liabilities
$10 (Reserves)	$10 (Demand Deposits)
$90 (1 Year Loan)	**$90 (1 Year Time Deposits)**
$90 (Excess Reserves)	
$190	**$100**

Totally Trustworthy Bank

Assets	Liabilities
	$90 (Demand Deposits)
$0	$90

100% Reserve Ratio

$90 of demand deposit liabilities were transferred from Infinite Integrity Bank to Totally Trustworthy Bank. The transfer of money was not permanent, as with a purchase, but was a loan. Thus the depositor lending the money maintains an IOU (a UOI, actually) which is a promise of repayment. This IOU is the time deposit entry.

One depositor has not directly lent another depositor money, as this would just be a personal loan. Rather, Infinite Integrity Bank has acted as a FINANCIAL INTERMEDIARY. Financial intermediary is just a fancy word for middleman. Banks utilize money surrendered by depositors, and lend that money to borrowers. The borrower and lender in a loan transaction never deal with each other directly, they deal with the financial intermediary. The financial intermediary is responsible for repaying loan money to the depositor who surrendered it, and the borrower is responsible for repaying the loan to the financial intermediary. If the borrower doesn't repay the loan, the financial intermediary must nonetheless repay it to the lender. This makes being a financial intermediary risky—at least in an honest 100% reserve banking system.

A financial intermediary earns money on the spread between interest paid depositors to surrender deposits and interest earned on loans made with surrendered deposits. When a fractional-reserve banker conjures loan money out of thin air, no depositor is surrendering loan money and being paid interest, and there is thus no spread between the interest paid and interest earned. When loan money is simply conjured out of thin air, the money-surrendering process that should underlie lending, and which sheeple think underlies lending, has not occurred. When no money is surrendered for a loan, the banker which conjured loan money is acting as a counterfeiter or con artist, not a financial intermediary.

There is a tendency for those frustrated with fraudulent fractional-reserve banking to criticize all banking and lending. This is absurd. Banks and lending are vital to the successful functioning of a modern economy, and if you doubt this, try rounding up $100,000 for a mortgage or business by taking up a collection, obtaining numerous small personal loans, or posting an ad on Craigslist. Or visit a stagnant third-world Hutville with a primitive, underdeveloped banking system where loans are impossible to obtain. Lending is not inherently dishonest, nor is the act of charging interest, even high interest, on honest loans that don't utilize conjured money. Honest financial intermediaries assume risk, and should be free to earn a reasonable profit for that risk. The problem is dishonest bankers that earn exorbitant profits via fraudulent money creation and reckless risk taking, escape the consequences of this risk taking, and force sheeple to pay the cost of it via Bailouts and Central Banks.

Totally Trustworthy Bank contacts Infinite Integrity Bank and requests payment for the $90 loan check. It demands $90 of assets to offset the $90 liability it has incurred. Infinite Integrity Bank transfers its $90 of excess reserves to Totally Trustworthy Bank to honor the loan check it issued:

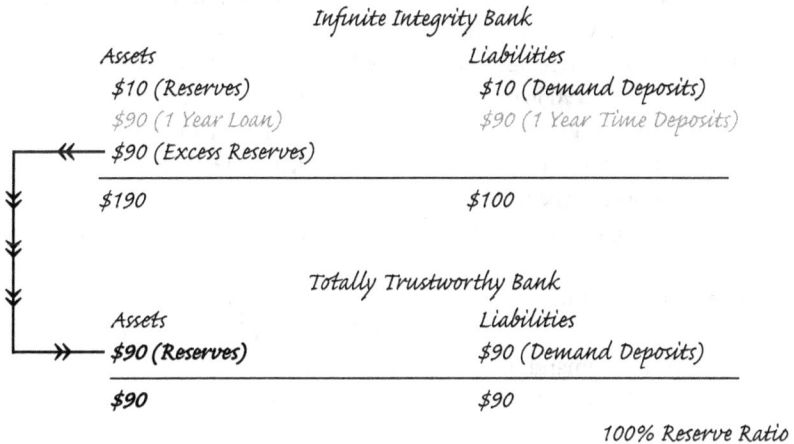

Infinite Integrity Bank

Assets	*Liabilities*
$10 (Reserves)	$10 (Demand Deposits)
$90 (1 Year Loan)	$90 (1 Year Time Deposits)
$90 (Excess Reserves)	
$190	$100

Totally Trustworthy Bank

Assets	*Liabilities*
$90 (Reserves)	$90 (Demand Deposits)
$90	$90

100% Reserve Ratio

On Totally Trustworthy Bank's ledger, the excess reserves are entered as reserves. This is because Totally Trustworthy Bank's $90 of deposits are demand deposits which must be 100% backed by reserves. Totally Trustworthy Bank can only obtain excess reserves by converting demand deposits into time deposits.

The $90 of excess reserves are removed from Infinite Integrity Bank's ledger because they were transferred to Totally Trustworthy Bank:

Infinite Integrity Bank

Assets	Liabilities
$10 (Reserves)	$10 (Demand Deposits)
$90 (1 Year Loan)	$90 (1 Year Time Deposits)
$100	$100

Totally Trustworthy Bank

Assets	Liabilities
$90 (Reserves)	$90 (Demand Deposits)
$90	$90

100% Reserve Ratio

Infinite Integrity Bank has no excess reserves. All its excess reserves have been used to issue loans. Infinite Integrity Bank is loaned up. In our fractional-reserve lending example, Steal Second Bank embezzled reserves, issued loans, and created lie-abilities—created additional deposits which were unbacked by reserves. Being totally trustworthy, Totally Trustworthy Bank won't create lie-abilities, so it also has no excess reserves and is loaned up.

$100 of reserves were initially deposited at Infinite Integrity Bank as a demand deposit, and after a $90 loan was issued there are still only $100 of demand deposits, $10 at Infinite Integrity Bank and $90 at Totally Trustworthy Bank. Time deposits are not money which depositors can spend, only demand deposits are money which depositors can spend. The demand deposit supply which is the money supply has not increased, and is still $100. All demand deposits are 100% backed by reserves.

Jane R. Debtor wants an $81 car loan. Totally Trustworthy Bank's depositors agree to convert $81 of their demand deposits into 1-year time deposits, but want half of the prevailing 6% interest rate, or 3%. Totally Trustworthy Bank agrees to this interest rate demand. Depositors surrender $81 of demand deposits, and Totally Trustworthy Bank begins paying them 3% interest. The updated ledgers:

Infinite Integrity Bank

Assets	Liabilities
$10 (Reserves)	$10 (Demand Deposits)
$90 (1 Year Loan)	$90 (1 Year Time Deposits)
$100	$100

Totally Trustworthy Bank

Assets	Liabilities
$90 (Reserves)	**$9 (Demand Deposits)**
	$81 (1 Year Time Deposits)
$90	$90

100% Reserve Ratio

The $81 time deposit can't be demanded for a year, so for that time it is not a liability and doesn't have to be backed by reserves. Only the demand deposit has to be backed by reserves. After Totally Trustworthy Bank sets $9 of reserves aside to honor its $9 of demand deposits, it has $81 of excess reserves:

Infinite Integrity Bank

Assets	Liabilities
$10 (Reserves)	$10 (Demand Deposits)
$90 (1 Year Loan)	$90 (1 Year Time Deposits)
$100	$100

Totally Trustworthy Bank

Assets	Liabilities
$9 (Reserves)	$9 (Demand Deposits)
$81 ("Excess" Reserves)	$81 (1 Year Time Deposits)
$90	$90

100% Reserve Ratio

Totally Trustworthy Bank has $81 of excess reserves which were obtained honestly. It has $81 of reserves which it can use to honor a loan check if that check is deposited at another bank and that bank demands payment. Totally Trustworthy Bank therefore issues the $81 loan to Jane R. Debtor:

Infinite Integrity Bank

Assets	Liabilities
$10 (Reserves)	$10 (Demand Deposits)
$90 (1 Year Loan)	$90 (1 Year Time Deposits)
$100	$100

Totally Trustworthy Bank

Assets	Liabilities
$9 (Reserves)	$9 (Demand Deposits)
$81 ("Excess" Reserves)	$81 (1 Year Time Deposits)
$81 (1 Year Loan)	
$171	$90

100% Reserve Ratio

Jane R. Debtor signs the loan contract, agreeing to make payments to Totally Trustworthy Bank for 1 year. Only after Debtor signs the loan contract does Totally Trustworthy Bank issue Debtor a loan check. Totally Trustworthy Bank's updated ledger:

Infinite Integrity Bank

Assets	Liabilities
$10 (Reserves)	$10 (Demand Deposits)
$90 (1 Year Loan)	$90 (1 Year Time Deposits)
$100	$100

Totally Trustworthy Bank

Assets	Liabilities
$9 (Reserves)	$9 (Demand Deposits)
$81 (1 Year Loan)	$81 (1 Year Time Deposits)
$81 ("Excess" Reserves)	**$81 (Loan Check)**
$171	**$171**

100% Reserve Ratio

The excess reserves will be used to honor the loan check. They back the loan check. They were therefore moved to the same ledger row as the loan check to simplify visualization.

Jane R. Debtor deposits her check at Vast Virtue Bank, which is also an honest 100% reserve bank:

Infinite Integrity Bank

Assets	Liabilities
$10 (Reserves)	$10 (Demand Deposits)
$90 (1 Year Loan)	$90 (1 Year Time Deposits)

$100	$100

Totally Trustworthy Bank

Assets	Liabilities
$9 (Reserves)	$9 (Demand Deposits)
$81 (1 Year Loan)	$81 (1 Year Time Deposits)
$81 ("Excess" Reserves)	$81 (Loan Check) ⟶ ≫ ≫

$171	$171

Vast Virtue Bank

Assets	Liabilities
	$81 (Demand Deposits) ⟵ ≪ ≪

$0	$81

100% Reserve Ratio

After the loan check is deposited at Vast Virtue Bank, it is no longer on Totally Trustworthy Bank's ledger:

Infinite Integrity Bank

Assets	Liabilities
$10 (Reserves)	$10 (Demand Deposits)
$90 (1 Year Loan)	$90 (1 Year Time Deposits)
$100	$100

Totally Trustworthy Bank

Assets	Liabilities
$9 (Reserves)	$9 (Demand Deposits)
$81 (1 Year Loan)	$81 (1 Year Time Deposits)
$81 ("Excess" Reserves)	
$171	**$90**

Vast Virtue Bank

Assets	Liabilities
	$81(Demand Deposits)
$0	$81

100% Reserve Ratio

$81 of deposit liabilities were transferred from Totally Trustworthy Bank to Vast Virtue Bank. The transfer of money was not permanent, as with a purchase, but was a loan. Thus the depositor lending the money maintains an IOU (a UOI actually) which is a promise of repayment. This IOU is the $81 time deposit entry.

Vast Virtue Bank contacts Totally Trustworthy Bank and requests payment for the loan check. It demands $81 of assets to offset the $90 liability it has incurred. Totally Trustworthy Bank transfers its $81 of excess reserves to Vast Virtue Bank to honor the loan check it issued:

Infinite Integrity Bank

Assets	Liabilities
$10 (Reserves)	$10 (Demand Deposits)
$90 (1 Year Loan)	$90 (1 Year Time Deposits)
$100	$100

Totally Trustworthy Bank

Assets	Liabilities
$9 (Reserves)	$9 (Demand Deposits)
$81 (1 Year Loan)	$81 (1 Year Time Deposits)
$81 ("Excess" Reserves)	
$171	$90

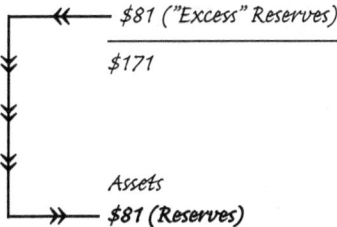

Vast Virtue Bank

Assets	Liabilities
$81 (Reserves)	$81 (Demand Deposits)
$81	$81

100% Reserve Ratio

On Vast Virtue Bank's ledger, the excess reserves are entered as reserves. This is because Vast Virtue Bank's $81 deposit is a demand deposit which must be 100% backed by reserves. Vast Virtue Bank can only obtain excess reserves by converting demand deposits into time deposits.

The excess reserves are removed from Totally Trustworthy Bank's ledger because they were transferred to Vast Virtue Bank:

Infinite Integrity Bank

Assets	Liabilities
$10 (Reserves)	$10 (Demand Deposits)
$90 (1 Year Loan)	$90 (1 Year Time Deposits)
$100	$100

Totally Trustworthy Bank

Assets	Liabilities
$9 (Reserves)	$9 (Demand Deposits)
$81 (1 Year Loan)	$81 (1 Year Time Deposits)
$90	$90

Vast Virtue Bank

Assets	Liabilities
$81 (Reserves)	$81 (Demand Deposits)
$81	$81

100% Reserve Ratio

None of the banks have excess reserves, nor will they be able to obtain excess reserves unless depositors convert demand deposits into time deposits. All banks are loaned up.

In this honest 100% reserve banking system, depositors control loan issuance because they must convert demand deposits into time deposits before loans can be issued. Depositors can easily limit excessive bank profits by demanding higher interest rates for time deposits, and refusing to convert demand deposits into time deposits unless banks pay higher interest rates. An honest 100% reserve banking system like this in which depositors have recourse against bankers and control loan issuance is totally unacceptable to Speculatos, which is why such a banking system doesn't exist. Speculatos prefer a fraudulent fractional-reserve banking system in which they conjure all the loan money they please without having to obtain permission from depositors, or having their actions otherwise impeded or regulated by depositors.

$100 was initially deposited at Infinite Integrity Bank as a demand deposit, and after $90 and $81 loans were issued there are still only $100 of demand deposits, $10 at Infinite Integrity Bank, $9 at Totally Trustworthy Bank, and $81 at Vast Virtue Bank. Time deposits are not money which depositors can spend, only demand deposits are money which depositors can spend. The demand deposit supply which is the money supply has not increased, and is still $100. All demand deposits are 100% backed by reserves.

Though the money supply is only $100, there is $171 of loans. This is not a paradox, nor it is dishonest. In an honest money system, commercial banks can create and uncreate debts, but they can't create and uncreate money. This concept of more debt than money seems paradoxical, and leads many ranting kooks to claim that anytime there is more debt than money, there is not enough money to pay off all debt, and the money system is therefore tyrannical. If I owe you $1 and pay you a $1 bill, and you owe John $1 and pay him with the same $1 bill, and John owes Mary $1 and pays Mary with the same $1 bill, then $3 of debts have been paid with a single $1 bill. This absurd "there isn't enough money to pay all loans" fallacy, and a similar "there isn't enough money to pay interest on all loans" fallacy, will be addressed in more detail in the *Recycling Money* chapter in *Bubblenomics 3*.

For this money system to remain honest, time deposits which are promises to repay money can't be circulated as money. If time deposits are allowed to circulate as money, then each loan is effectively money creation. There would not be multiple claims on reserves if time deposits were circulated as money. No matter who possesses a time deposit, it can't be used to claim reserves until a period of time has passed. Circulating time deposits as money would therefore not decrease reserve ratios of banks or create lie-abilities or bank-ruptcies. However, yo-yo-ing the money supply creates the business cycle and Depressions. Circulating time deposits as money would increase the money supply and manufacture a business cycle.

One form of time deposit is the certificate of deposit which anyone can obtain at a real bank. You hand a bank reserves, and it hands you a certificate promising you to repay those reserves plus interest at some future time. To get your reserves back at the end of the specified time period, you bring the certificate back to the bank, it takes the certificate, and gives your loan principal back plus interest. One oversimplified way to envision an honest 100% reserve banking system is to picture no savings accounts, only checking accounts and certificates of deposit.

In some cases, certificates of deposit resemble cashier's checks. However, you can't take a certificate of deposit—or any other time deposit—to a grocery store or gas station or bar and spend it like money. Thus the assumption that time deposits don't circulate as money is reasonable.

A time deposit is credit. A demand deposit is money. Credit is not money. Credit is a promise to pay (or be paid) money at a future time. Heinous misconceptions and boundless confusion arise when people confuse credit and money.

To avoid these misconceptions and confusion, deposit credit and deposit money will be defined one more time. Time deposits are a promise made by a bank to pay reserves to a depositor at a future time. Time deposits are credit. A bank creating additional time deposits is issuing additional credit. Demand deposits are a promise made by a bank to pay reserves to a depositor at any time, including the present time. Demand deposits are money. A bank creating additional demand deposits is issuing additional money.

Confusing money and credit is an easy mistake to make when trying to understand a money & banking system which exists primarily on computer ledgers, and which purposely muddles the difference between money and credit. The fundamental difference between an honest 100% reserve banking system and a fraudulent fractional-reserve banking system is that one issues loans by creating credit (time deposits) and the other issues loans by creating money (demand deposits).

There is no theoretical limit to the amount of loans that could be created in an honest 100% reserve banking system. Each new depositor could choose to convert their demand deposit into a time deposit, which would be lent, deposited somewhere else, converted into a time deposit, and relent... The amount of loans and time deposits would increase with each iteration, but the total amount of demand deposits would not exceed $100 or whatever the initial amount of deposited reserves is.

In a fractional-reserve banking system, the maximum amount of loans that can be created is some multiple of the initial deposit of reserves. At a 10% reserve ratio, that multiple is 9, and the maximum number of loans that can be issued is 9 times the initial deposit of reserves.

A fractional reverse lending system has a cap on loan creation because each additional loan is an additional deposit, and eventually so many deposits have been created that reserves are a miniscule fraction of those deposits. When the reserve ratio of a bank decreases so much that the statutory reserve ratio requirement has been reached, no more deposits can be created, and as a commercial bank loan can only be issued by creating a deposit, no more loans can be issued. An honest 100% reserve banking system always has a 100% reserve ratio; additional loans don't require the creation of additional deposits which decrease the reserve ratio, so infinite loan creation is theoretically possible.

In theory, an honest 100% reserve banking system allows more credit to be issued than a fraudulent fractional-reserve banking system, but in practice the opposite is true. Depositors in the honest 100% reserve banking system could have chosen to convert any amount of their demand deposits into time deposits. The loan amounts chosen in this example were the exact same as those in the fraudulent fractional-reserve lending example so that the two lending methods could be easily contrasted. In real life, the amounts of demand deposits which depositors chose to convert into time deposits would have been much, much smaller.

People converting demand deposits into time deposits are setting aside their money and saving it. Most people need most of their money to pay bills and survive. When most people have extra money, they choose to buy frivolous luxuries rather than save it. Very few sheeple save even 10% of their money. China's 40% savings rate is the highest of any nation in the world, and America's 4% savings rate is the lowest. In an honest 100% reserve banking system the savings rate would be different than under our fraudulent fractional-reserve banking system. One could debate that rate, but it would almost certainly be less than 40%.

A fraudulent fractional-reserve banking system with a 10% reserve ratio allows 90% of reserves to be recategorized as "excess" reserves and used to issue loans. For 90% of reserves to be recategorized as excess reserves in an honest 100% reserve banking system, 90% of demand deposits would have to be converted into time deposits. This is a 90% savings rate. Thus, very roughly, the 10% reserve ratio in a fraudulent fractional-reserve banking system (i.e., the 90% embezzle-and-lend ratio) is analogous to a 90% savings rate which has not and never will exist in the real world. Fractional-reserve lending mimics an artificially high savings rate which can never exist in the free market, allowing much higher debt levels than would otherwise be possible. This generates massive profit for banks and Speculatos.

This difference in savings and lending rates for honest 100% reserve banking and fraudulent fractional-reserve banking is especially pronounced when the recursive nature of lending is factored in. In fraudulent fractional-reserve lending, 90% of each new deposit is "saved" (i.e., embezzled) and lent, resulting in recursive loan issuance and deposit creation. For this 90% "savings" (i.e., embezzlement) rate and the exorbitant lending it facilitates to be mimicked by an honest 100% reserve banking system in which loan money must actually be saved, each new depositor must choose to save 90% of their deposit, which is absurdly improbable.

Suppose John Q. Frugal saves 90% of his deposit, converts it to a time deposit, and allows it to be lent. Jane R. Thrift is selling the car, house, or whatever the loan was issued to pay for, is paid a loan check which is Frugal's surrendered money, and must save 90% of the money she is paid and convert it into a time deposit for loan creation to proceed in a manner analogous to fractional-reserve lending. This would then result in another loan being issued, and the person paid this loan check would have to convert 90% of it into a time deposit for loan creation to continue in a manner analogous to fractional-reserve lending. . .

If any party in the recursive process decides to spend money rather than save it, or refuses to convert their demand deposit into a time deposit, the recursive loan issuing process is truncated and all additional loan creation that might have occurred down the line is eliminated. Again, there is no such truncation mechanism in fraudulent fractional-reserve lending, especially not one which puts depositors in the driver's seat and lets them control loan issuance, creating a more democratic banking, lending, and money system.

Hundreds of millions of individuals in an economy, especially Americans, will never attain or sustain a 90% savings rate or anything close, much less a 98.54% savings rate. A 98.54% savings rate would have been necessary for an honest 100% reserve banking system to approximate the 1.46% reserve ratio which prevailed under fraudulent fractional-reserve lending in September 2008 just before the economy collapsed and The Bailout passed. Again, while it would have been theoretically possible for an honest 100% reserve banking system to produce as much lending as a fraudulent fractional-reserve banking system, this would have required millions of depositors to recursively save 98.54% of what they were paid when selling homes, cars, etc.

A 98.54% recursive savings rate would also have required businesses taking out loans to save 98.54% of what they borrowed. However, businesses don't take out loans to save money, they take out loans to spend money in an attempt to grow and prosper, and they usually use loan money to pay other businesses who spend most money in an attempt to grow and prosper.

At any iteration, someone spending money rather than converting it to a time deposit may pay another person who saves 98.54% of it, but it is extremely improbable for this process to occur repeatedly in a virtually endless manner as in fraudulent fractional-reserve lending. While some people who sell homes, cars, etc. save a percentage of what they are paid, it is exceptionally rare for them to save even 50%, much less 98.54%, and it is simply impossible for millions of people economy wide to repeatedly save 98.54% of what they are paid. Thus it is impossible for an honest 100% reserve banking system to mimic the recursive loan issuance of a fraudulent fractional-reserve banking system, and this is a good thing.

The recursive examples in the paragraphs above also don't factor in the creditworthiness of borrowers. Even if every person paid a loan check saves 98.54% of it, and there are funds available for an endless succession of loans, borrowers with good enough credit to obtain those loans are required, and the pool of such qualified borrowers is limited. As noted, an honest 100% reserve banking system can't rely on Bailouts, nor the ability to conjure money for many additional loans to provide income streams which can honor defaulted loans. An honest 100% reserve banking system is thus much more judicious about issuing loans than a fraudulent fractional-reserve banking system. This is yet another reason an honest 100% reserve banking system would not issue as many loans as a fraudulent fractional-reserve banking system.

Pardon some of the redundancy in the last several paragraphs, but this is another one of those topics that confuses many people. Additional explanation was therefore provided, as it is extremely beneficial to some readers.

In honest 100% reserve banking, all demand deposits are backed by reserves, but all loans must also back time deposits of equal or lesser duration. On Infinite Integrity Bank's ledger, a 1-year time deposit was backed by a 1-year loan:

Assets	Liabilities
$10 (Demand Reserves)	$10 (Demand Deposits)
$90 (1 Year Loan)	$90 (1 Year Time Deposits)
$100	$100

100% Reserve Ratio

When the time deposit expired in 1 year, the depositor would once again have a demand deposit which they can withdraw, obtaining reserves. By that time, the 1-year loan would also be repaid, so Infinite Integrity would have reserves to honor the deposit.

Half Honest Bank has loans and time deposits of different duration:

Assets	Liabilities
$10 (Demand Reserves)	$10 (Demand Deposits)
$90 (5 Year Loan)	$90 (1 Year Time Deposits)
$100	$100
	100% Reserve Ratio

This seems like honest 100% reserve banking, but is not. The time deposit will expire in 1 year and be converted back into a demand deposit. At that time, the depositor may demand reserves, but Half Honest bank doesn't have reserves, it only has a loan. This is just a clever variation of the fractional-reserve fraud, as can be seen by viewing Half Honest Bank's ledger at the end of the 1-year time deposit:

Assets	Liabilities
$10 (Demand Reserves)	$100 (Demand Deposits)
$90 (4 Year Loan)	
$100	$100
	10% Reserve Ratio

Half Honest Bank's ledger is now the ledger of a fractional-reserve bank. Half Honest Bank can only make its books legit by convincing the depositor to convert a demand deposit into a time deposit again. If it can't do so, it has lie-abilities which are not allowed in honest 100% reserve banking. Thus no honest bank issues a loan which exceeds the duration of the time deposit surrendered to make the loan. As the time deposit is issued before the loan, this is not problematic procedurally.

The formal term for synchronizing the duration of loan assets with the duration of time-deposit liabilities is "maturity matching." Maturity is the duration of a loan. When a loan ends, it has reached maturity and no longer exists. Loan assets and time-deposit liabilities are both loans, and for banking to be honest, the maturities of both loans must be the same. The maturity of the loan by one depositor to the bank must be the same as the maturity of the loan by the bank to another depositor. The maturities must match. Most modern banking textbooks portray maturity matching as an anachronistic absurdity which constrains banks unduly. It is not.

No honest bank issues a loan without a time deposit and then tries to find demand depositors willing to convert deposits into time deposits later, as it has then embezzled reserves and lent them without the permission of depositors, and has engaged in fraudulent fractional-reserve lending. Speculatos utilize this method to subvert an honest 100% reserve banking system and convert it into a fraudulent fractional-reserve banking system.

It is acceptable to issue a loan which is of shorter duration than the time deposit. Infinite Integrity Bank's ledger:

Assets	Liabilities
$10 (Demand Reserves)	$10 (Demand Deposits)
$90 (1 Year Loan)	$90 (5 Year Time Deposits)
$100	$100

100% Reserve Ratio

The depositor is not expecting their money for 5 years, but the loan will be repaid in 1 year. At that time, Infinite Integrity Bank can relend the money for as long as 4 more years.

One other loophole is variable rate loans with interest rates that change with market conditions. In all our examples, interest rates were fixed at a certain percentage rate and did not change. For an honest financial intermediary to turn a profit, it must charge higher interest rates on a loan than it pays a time depositor. With fixed interest rates this is simple, but what if a bank pays a time depositor 3% interest and then issues a variable rate mortgage? Suppose the mortgage pays 4% interest initially. The bank is making a 1% profit which is the difference between the 4% interest the mortgage pays and the 3% interest the time depositor is paid. Interest rates plummet, and the interest rate on the mortgage decreases to 2%. Now the bank is paying the time depositor 3% interest, but only earning 2% interest on the mortgage, meaning it is incurring a 1% loss. The bank has to pay the time depositor an interest rate 1% higher than it is earning on its mortgages. On a large scale with many loans, this could easily rupt a bank. A similar principle applies if the bank pays variable interest rates on time deposits rather than variable interest rates on loans.

Though the ledgers and some of the nuances can seem tricky, honest lending isn't rocket science. To issue a loan, you must actually have preexisting money. You can't lend demand deposits, or the reserves backing demand deposits, or create additional deposit money to lend. If all depositors demand all their reserves, Infinity Integrity Bank, Totally Trustworthy Bank, and Vast Virtue Bank always have enough reserves to honor these demands. These honest banks are never insolvent because they never fraudulently create lie-abilities. This is honest lending as it existed for most of human history before the goldsmiths.

In these simple examples, a loan was requested and then a time depositor surrendered money for the loan. In an actual honest 100% reserve banking system, interest rates for time deposits would be established, and some depositors would surrender money and convert demand deposits into time deposits. Banks would have unlent time deposits, and they would be able to make loans immediately. The pool of money available for loans would be much smaller than under a corrupt fractional-reserve system, as it would have to be saved and relinquished, rather than merely conjured.

Under honest 100% reserve banking, Speculatos can't fleece sheeple, but such integrity comes at a price. Infinite Integrity Bank has $100 in demand deposits. John Q. Debtor wants a $90 30-year mortgage. Infinite Integrity Bank asks Jane R. Depositor to surrender her deposit money for 30 years. She hesitates. 30 years is a long time. She might be willing to lend $60 for 15 years, as her 3 year old will need the money for college at that time. Even then, she might need the money sooner, but if she tightens her belt, she could manage and be able to send her child to a better college when she got the money back plus interest. Giving up the money is a risk and a sacrifice, so Jane won't do so cheaply, and wants 8% interest. Infinite Integrity Bank adds 1% to earn a profit and the interest rate on the mortgage is 9%. Infinite Integrity Bank's balance sheet:

Assets	Liabilities
$40 (Reserves)	$40 (Demand Deposits)
$60 (15 Year Loan)	$60 (15 Year Time Deposits)
$100	$100
	100% Reserve Ratio

With a 30-year, 6%, $90 mortgage John Q. Debtor would have purchased a McMansion, but a 15-year, 9%, $60 mortgage means a modest home. John Q. Debtor nonetheless feels lucky to have the $60 loan. Many want mortgages, few obtain them. When banks embezzle reserves and create money out of thin air, there are more funds than borrowers and unsound loans are made. When each loan is a voluntarily-forsaken asset, there are far more borrowers than funds. Only those with good credit receive loans, and they pay them. A tidal wave of foreclosures never ravages the economy.

To the ignorant, the difference between fraudulent fractional-reserve lending and honest 100% reserve lending seems insignificant. In one type of lending the loan amount is subtracted from the deposit, in another type of lending the loan amount isn't subtracted from the deposit. What's the big deal?

To appreciate the big deal, the scam needs to be viewed with big numbers. Real big numbers. Here is the ledger for the U.S. banking system in September 2008 just before The Bailout:

```
Assets                                      Liabilities
  #102,736,000,000 (Reserves)                 #7,052,700,000,000 (Deposits)
#6,949,964,000,000 (Loans)


#7,052,700,000,000                          #7,052,700,000,000
                                                    1.46% Reserve Ratio
```

Initially, $102 billion of reserves were deposited into the U.S. banking system, and these reserves backed $102 billion of deposits. After numerous iterations of fraudulent fractional-reserve lending, banks had created $6.95 trillion out of thin air and lent it, increasing the deposit supply to $7.05 trillion.

Had honest 100% reserve banking prevailed, the ledger for the U.S. banking system would have been:

Assets   *Liabilities*

$102,736,000,000 (Reserves)   *$102,736,000,000 (Demand Deposits)*

$102,736,000,000   *$102,736,000,000*

                                          100% Reserve Ratio

$6.95 trillion of deposits could not have been created out of thin air and lent under an honest 100% reserve banking system. If you were the banking lobby, how much would you spend to prevent reform which denies you interest payments on $6.95 trillion? At a 3% interest rate, which is far less than most banks charge, $6.95 trillion of loans pay $202 billion of interest per year. Assume banks use 95% of this interest income to pay expenses, and keep 5% as profit. That's $10 billion in profit, which is a very, very, very conservative reckoning, as total bank profits often exceed $100 billion per year. Suppose banks keep $9 billion of their $10 billion, and spend $1 billion influencing politicians, judges, funding pro-fractional-reserve think tanks, etc. If banks give $1 million to all 535 members of the U.S. Congress, that still leaves $465 million. $1 million to every state governor, $415 million left. $50,000 to each of the 3,500 federal judges, $240 million left. $50,000 honorariums to 1,000 prominent intellectuals who will champion corrupt banking via position papers, journal articles, dissertations, newspaper and magazine editorials, textbooks, college classes, and news appearances. $190 million left. . .

These examples are simplistic and heavy handed, but they are not inaccurate. If the American sheeple were shown a list of all the dishonest yet legal ways in which money is channeled to politicians and judges, they would probably stop voting and stop watching the news. With so much profit at stake, Speculatos don't hesitate to bribe, smear, or even murder rabble-rousing JFK-types who get in their way. No one can match banks' political donations—or their political influence—because no one else can create money out of thin air.

Loans would have been issued in an honest 100% reserve banking system with $102 billion of reserves, but not nearly as many as in a fraudulent fractional-reserve banking system. The exact amount of loans which would have been issued is debatable, and can't be known with certainty, as there is not a single honest 100% reserve bank anywhere on Earth, much less an entire country utilizing an honest 100% reserve banking system. There is no empirical evidence of what the savings rate in an honest 100% reserve banking system would be because an honest 100% reserve banking system has not existed for centuries.

Assume that an honest 100% reserve banking system creates 25% as many loans as a fraudulent fractional-reserve lending system, which is a very, very generous assumption as we'll see later. In September 2008 just before The Bailout passed, the fraudulent fractional-reserve banking system had issued $6,949,964,000,000 of loans. Total loans issued by an honest 100% reserve banking system would have been $1,737,491,000,000 or $1.73 trillion ($6,949,964,000,000 x 0.25 = $1,737,491,000,000) and the ledger for the U.S. banking system would have been:

Assets	Liabilities
$102,736,000,000 (Reserves)	$102,736,000,000 (Demand Deposits)
$1,737,491,000,000 (Loans)	$1,737,491,000,000 (Time Deposits)
$1,840,227,000,000	$1,840,227,000,000
	100% Reserve Ratio

No additional money would have been created when the $1.7 trillion of loans were issued. The money supply would have stayed constant at $102 billion. As yo-yo-ing the money supply is what creates the business cycle, no Depression could have arisen under this system. Which means no housing bubble. A few loans might have been defaulted upon, causing a recession, but there would have been no tsunami of defaults which caused a Depression. Banks would have issued $5.2 trillion less loans than under the fraudulent fractional-reserve lending system. At 6% interest rates, this would have meant $312 billion less interest paid by sheeple to bankers each year—$1,000 per American. The interest that was paid would have been less profitable to bankers because much of it would have been paid to time depositors. Most importantly, banks could have honored every deposit, wouldn't have been rupted by withdrawals, and wouldn't have wanted Bailouts.

Most Americans today haven't seen a bank run, but people alive in 1946 had survived The Great Depression, in which 9,000 banks went rupt. The movie *It's a Wonderful Life* made shrewd use of a scene all Americans were familiar with. Most everyone has watched this movie and seen Jimmy Stewart calm depositors during a bank run, but few stop and ask how everyone can think their money is "back in a safe," when it isn't there? 1940s sheeple who'd seen bank runs first-hand didn't note this paradox, much less sheeple today, which doesn't bode well for the prospects for monetary reform.

If your bank is not forcing you to surrender your money for a period of time, but is paying you interest, then it is practicing fraudulent fractional-reserve lending. The same is true of "free" checking accounts. If reserves are not embezzled, and the depositor doesn't give permission for their reserves to be lent, then the bank not only couldn't pay interest, it would have to charge a warehousing fee for storing reserves and additional fees for services. Honest, 100% reserve banks that warehouse money and don't lend it without permission would have fee structures much higher than fraudulent fractional-reserve banks. To sheeple accustomed to fractional-reserve banks, paying a bank to hold money seems ludicrous, perhaps even fraudulent, which is the perversest of ironies. Warehousing fees and additional or higher fees are a trivial price to pay to eliminate inflation taxes and the business cycle and establish honest 100% reserve banking.

There are no "warehouse" banks—no 100% reserve banks—because fraudulent fractional-reserve lending is so profitable. Why open an honest bank when embezzlement and money creation are legalized and a banking cartel with a monopoly on these practices is protected by the Federal Reserve?

If people in Bedford Falls understood banking, one might've confronted George Bailey with a gun. "You told me my deposit is a demand deposit, not a time deposit. Before converting my demand deposit to a time deposit, you should have asked me." Blam, blam. "Have a not-so-wonderful death, you shyster."

You now understand the scam, and are hopefully beginning to see solutions. No, not shooting bankers, but rather honest 100% reserve banking in which there are no lie-abilities and demand deposits must be converted into time deposits before the reserves backing deposits can be lent.

Honest Banking Picture Pages

To skip the picture pages after this chapter, please turn to page 132

DIVORCE MONEY CREATION & UNCREATION FROM BANKING!

Many economists consider Irving Fisher the greatest American economist. Fisher was horrified by the inflation and hyperdeflation which caused the Great Depression, as well as the public's inability to understand its true cause and thus support a true solution. Fisher wrote *The Debt Deflation Theory of Great Depressions* and *100% Money* during the Great Depression to educate people. *100% Money* advocated the correct solution, an honest 100% reserve banking system. This solution was snubbed by John Maynard Keynes and other "Keynesian" economists who held politicians' ears, including President Franklin D. Roosevelt's. Keynesian economists champion fraudulent fractional-reserve banking, and government "stimulus" programs as "solutions" to Depressions. Fisher's explanation of the causes of and solutions to Great Depressions were ignored, but have become esteemed since. Excerpts from *100% Money* are provided below:

"There is little practical difference between permitting banks to issue book credits which perform monetary service, and permitting them to issue paper currency. It is essentially the same unsound practice. ... The revival now of the ancient 100% [reserve] system, with the readjustments demanded by modern conditions, would effectually restrain the monetary inflation and deflation incident to our present system; that is, would actually stop the irresponsible creation and destruction of circulating medium by our thousands of commercial banks which now act like so many private mints. ... The 100% proposal is the opposite of radical. It is a return from the present extraordinary and ruinous system of lending the same money 8 or 10 [or 50 or more] times over, to the conservative safety-deposit system of the old goldsmiths, before they began lending out improperly what was entrusted to them for safekeeping. It was this abuse of trust which, after being accepted as standard practice, evolved into modern deposit banking. ... The essence of the 100% plan is to make money independent of loans, to divorce the process of creating and destroying money from the business of banking. ... Great inflations and deflations would be eliminated because banks would be deprived of their present power virtually to mint check-book money and to destroy it; making loans would not inflate our circulating medium and calling [unmaking] loans would not deflate it. ... Even if depositors withdraw all deposits at once, or pay all their loans at once, or default on all of them at once, the nation's volume of money would not be affected. ... The most important result would be the prevention of great booms and depressions by ending the chronic inflations and deflations which have ever been the curse of mankind and which have sprung largely from banking."

FRAUDULENT FRACTIONAL-RESERVE LENDING GENERATES EXORBITANT BANK PROFITS

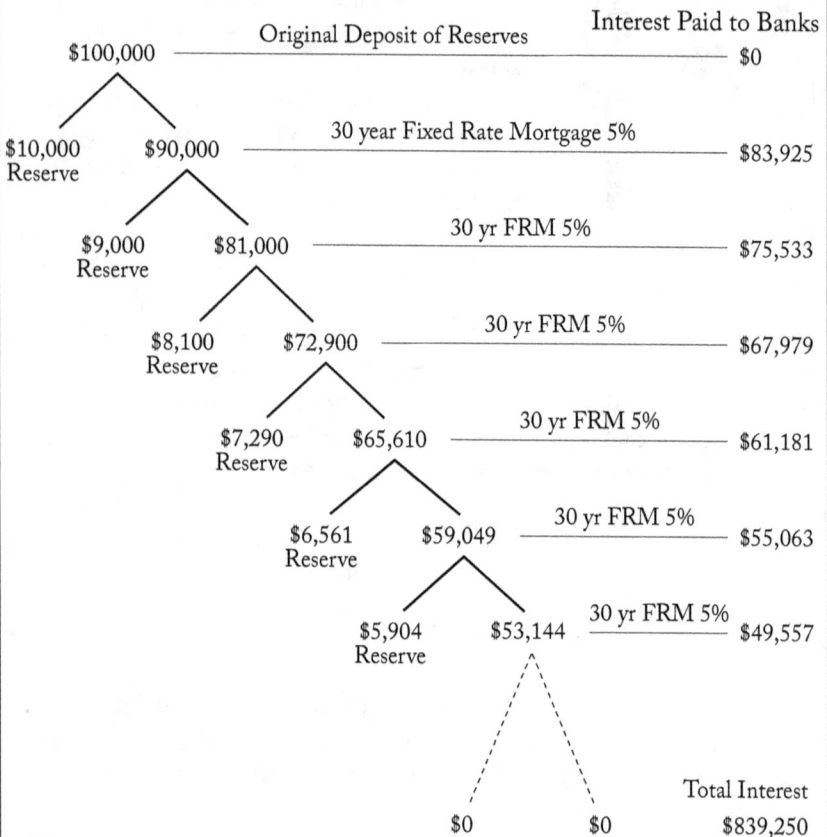

	Original Deposit of Reserves	Interest Paid to Banks
$100,000		$0
$10,000 Reserve $90,000	30 year Fixed Rate Mortgage 5%	$83,925
$9,000 Reserve $81,000	30 yr FRM 5%	$75,533
$8,100 Reserve $72,900	30 yr FRM 5%	$67,979
$7,290 Reserve $65,610	30 yr FRM 5%	$61,181
$6,561 Reserve $59,049	30 yr FRM 5%	$55,063
$5,904 Reserve $53,144	30 yr FRM 5%	$49,557

		Total Interest
$0	$0	$839,250

This is the diagram from *Bubblenomics* showing the exorbitant interest profits which fraudulent fractional-reserve lending generates for banks. An initial $100,000 deposit of reserves is made into the banking system, and additional loans equal to 9 times this original deposit are created via fraudulent fractional-reserve lending. Banks charge interest on each loan, earning much more interest than they would under an honest system. Contrast this fraudulent fractional-reserve banking system with the honest 100% reserve banking system shown on the next two diagrams.

HONEST 100% RESERVE LENDING
PREVENTS EXORBITANT BANK PROFITS

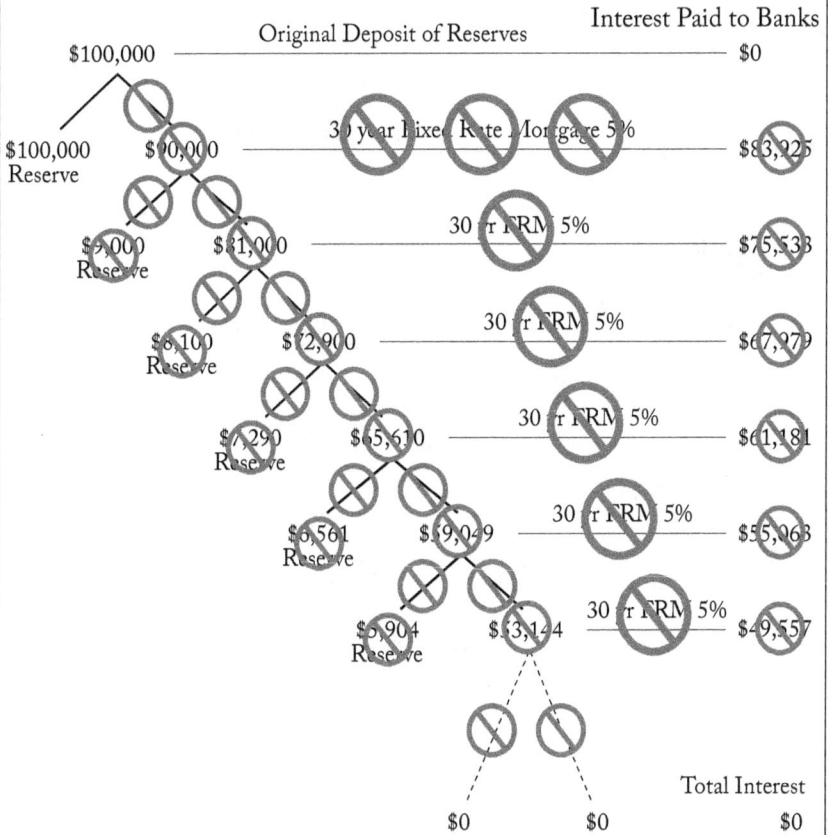

Original Deposit of Reserves

Interest Paid to Banks

$100,000 ——————————————————————— $0

$100,000
Reserve

$90,000

30 year Fixed Rate Mortgage 5% ——— $83,925

$9,000
Reserve

$81,000

30 yr FRM 5% ——— $75,533

$8,100
Reserve

$72,900

30 yr FRM 5% ——— $67,979

$7,290
Reserve

$65,610

30 yr FRM 5% ——— $61,181

$6,561
Reserve

$59,049

30 yr FRM 5% ——— $55,063

$5,904
Reserve

$53,144

30 yr FRM 5% ——— $49,557

Total Interest

$0 $0 $0

Under an honest 100% reserve system, no fractional-reserve lending is allowed. Demand deposits must be 100% backed by reserves. A banking system like this makes Speculatos angry. They give up $839,250 of interest profit.

To Speculatos, this system has another disadvantage: sheeple understand it. Money only exists once, in a single place. To issue loans, banks can't create additional money out of thin air. Rather, banks must obtain permission from depositors to lend deposited money. The way people intuitively sense a money system and lending should work.

HONEST 100% RESERVE LENDING
ALLOWS REASONABLE BANK PROFITS

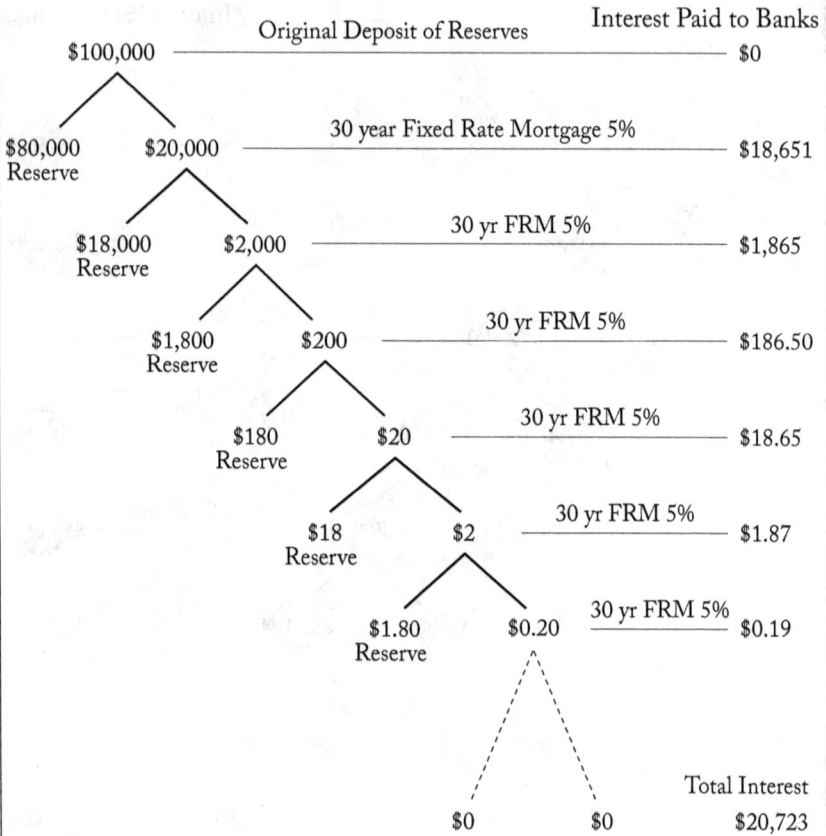

		Interest Paid to Banks
$100,000 — Original Deposit of Reserves —		$0
$80,000 Reserve / $20,000 — 30 year Fixed Rate Mortgage 5% —		$18,651
$18,000 Reserve / $2,000 — 30 yr FRM 5% —		$1,865
$1,800 Reserve / $200 — 30 yr FRM 5% —		$186.50
$180 Reserve / $20 — 30 yr FRM 5% —		$18.65
$18 Reserve / $2 — 30 yr FRM 5% —		$1.87
$1.80 Reserve / $0.20 — 30 yr FRM 5% —		$0.19

		Total Interest
$0	$0	$20,723

No loans were shown on the previous page, but honest 100% reserve banking systems issue loans which are shown here. This diagram presumes a 20% savings rate, meaning every depositor converts 20% of demand deposits into time deposits. A 20% savings rate is at least five times America's savings rate, a generous assumption. With fraudulent fractional-reserve lending, a $100,000 deposit led to $900,000 of loans which earned bankers $839,250. With honest 100% reserve lending and a 20% savings rate, a $100,000 deposit leads to $22,222 of loans which earn bankers $20,723. Banks earn $818,527 less under honest 100% reserve banking, 97% less. This is before banks pay higher interest rates to time depositors who must explicitly surrender money. There are many assumptions, with this example a rough approximation, but it still gives a sense of the massive profit Speculatos would be denied under an honest 100% reserve banking system.

LOANS: TIME RESERVES

In honest 100% reserve banking, the duration of a liability and the asset which backs it are the same. A time deposit is a promise made by the bank to repay a deposit to a depositor at a future time. A loan is a promise made by a borrower to repay reserves to the bank at a future time. A loan is essentially time reserves, reserves which will be repaid to the bank at a future time. Reserves themselves are essentially demand reserves, reserves which the bank possesses and which can be demanded at any time. Thus Infinite Integrity Bank's ledger could be rewritten as:

Assets	*Liabilities*
$10 (Demand Reserves)	*$10 (Demand Deposits)*
$90 (1 Year Time Reserves)	*$90 (1 Year Time Deposits)*
$100	*$100*

100% Reserve Ratio

As the time reserves and time deposits are mere promises to provide reserves and deposits at a future time, and are not reserves or deposits which are actually possessed, they are greyed out to reflect this fact. First Fraud Bank's ledger could be rewritten as:

Assets	Liabilities
$10 (Demand Reserves)	$10 (Demand Deposits)
$90 (Time Reserves)	$90 ("Demand" Deposits)
$100	$100

10% Reserve Ratio

On First Fraud Bank's ledger there is a lack of synchronicity between deposit liabilities and reserve assets. Every demand deposit should be backed by demand reserves, and only time deposits should be backed by time reserves. Demand deposits should not be backed by time reserves. If $90 of First Fraud Bank's "demand" deposits are demanded, it has no demand reserves to honor them, just time reserves (loans), which are promises to pay reserves in the future. First Fraud Bank doesn't refer to its deposits as demand deposits, but nonetheless promises to redeem all deposits upon demand. It represents all its deposits as demand deposits, even though it can't honor them all. First Fraud Bank misrepresents time deposits, deposits which can only be redeemed at a future time when a loan is repaid and embezzled reserves are replenished, as demand deposits. This is the essence of fractional-reserve lending: misrepresenting time deposits as demand deposits.

30-YEAR MORTGAGES DO NOT EXIST IN A FREE MARKET

Fannie Mae and Freddie Mac were created during the Great Depression as part of the President Franklin D. Roosevelt's New "Deal," along with Social Security and the Federal Deposit Insurance Corporation (FDIC). The Roaring 1920s or Roaring '20s was the boom period that preceded the bust which was the Great Depression. During the Roaring '20s, most of the money that the Fed and commercial banks created went into the stock market rather than the real estate market, which is why there was a stock bubble rather than a housing bubble. This also meant that free-market mortgage lending prevailed prior to the Great Depression. People had to put 50% down to buy a house, only a few individuals with exceptional credit could obtain mortgages longer than 10 years, and 5-year mortgages were common. Many borrowers couldn't afford to pay off their house in 5 years, so had lump sum "balloon" payments due at the end of 5-year mortgage terms, which they then obtained additional 5-year mortgages to finance. Without these balloon payments, mortgage payments would have been too high for most borrowers to afford.

Moderners consider such high down payments and short mortgage terms absurd, even tyrannical, but they are a natural consequence of free market lending. In an honest 100% reserve banking system, someone must surrender the reserves used for loans. Would you surrender money for 30 years? For 20 years? That is a long time. Few people will surrender demand deposits and allow them to be converted to time deposits for a decade or longer, and if they did, they would want to earn much more than the 3% - 7% rate charged on most modern mortgages. An investor looking to surrender money 10 to 30 years would probably invest it in a factory or other large-scale industrial venture with potential for stupendous returns, rather than a mortgage. Thus in an honest 100% reserve banking system there are no 20-year or 30-year mortgages, except perhaps a few funded by extremely conservative investors; they would be rare, highly sought after, and only granted to individuals with pristine credit.

If Thomas Jefferson were transported to the present, and only shown widespread 30-year mortgages, he would instantly realize that America's money & banking system are corrupt. For all of human history prior to the New "Deal," 20-year and 30-year mortgages never existed. And they never can and never will exist in a free market with honest 100% reserve banking where loans utilize time deposits and surrendered reserves.

Sheeple view 30-year mortgages as a progressive development rather than a corruption. That is why they are sheeple. The subversion of the free market which allows 30-year mortgages is the same subversion which allows the Speculato looting and Bailouts that sheeple oppose. Like stupid children, sheeple want to end Speculato looting, but still be able to obtain 30-year mortgages. One can't be eliminated without eliminating the other. Tragically, if given a choice, most sheeple would choose a world with 30-year mortgages, Depressions, Bailouts, and Speculato plunder, rather than a world without all of them.

When the Great Depression descended, many Americans were able to make mortgage payments, but could not find refinancing for the balloon portion of their loans, and therefore lost their homes. In betting that they could find refinancing in 5 years, they had taken a risk and been burned. These individuals could have bought more modest homes or saved longer, and purchased homes that could have been paid off in full in 5 years, but they wanted homes sooner rather than later, larger homes rather than smaller homes, or luxurious homes instead of modest homes. Today sheeple consider being forced to save for a home or only being allowed a 5-year mortgage or 10-year mortgage injustices, but such requirements are characteristic of an honest money system.

The fundamental cause of the Great Depression was a Fed-initiated Great Inflation that crashed the economy, and the only real solution was reform that prevented future Great Inflations. Franklin D. Roosevelt never seemed to understand the true cause of the Great Depression. To FDR, the solution to Americans losing homes wasn't more savings or people buying more modest homes or eliminating Great Inflations, it was longer duration mortgages that didn't have balloons due at the end of their terms. Then home buyers wouldn't have to find financing every 5 years and risk losing their home. No free market lenders would offer longer duration mortgages, so guv'ment would have to intervene in the free market, insuring mortgages, issuing mortgages, and selling mortgages. FDR created the Federal Housing Administration to guarantee (insure) preexisting mortgages, the Federal National Mortgage Association to issue new mortgages, and the Federal Home Loan Mortgage Corporation to sell mortgages. This guv'ment intervention gradually transformed mortgages from 5-year critters into the 30-year (and longer) monstrosities of today.

It is instructive to stop a moment and ponder what the Founding Fathers at the Constitutional Convention would have said if someone had stood up and suggested that the U.S. government insure and/or issue a huge percentage of the nation's mortgages. The Founding Fathers probably would have been petrified by the potential for corruption and economic devastation inherent in such a centralized power, and would have viewed it as the provenance of individuals and private business, not the U.S. government. A person suggesting such an absurd policy at the Constitutional Convention probably would have been derided mercilessly by the Founding Fathers. Stated more indelicately, the Founding

Fathers probably would have considered FDR a tyrant or rube, and would have been horrified by his New Deal policies.

The Federal National Mortgage Association is nicknamed "Fannie Mae." The Federal Home Loan Mortgage Corporation is nicknamed "Freddie Mac." The names for these agencies contain ludicrous incongruencies which suggest their inherent conflicts of interest. A "Federal National" Mortgage Association? A "federal" government is a compact of states in which most powers are reserved to states. A "national" government is one in which the nation as a whole is dominant and states and localities are subordinate. The media never uses the term "national government." Propagandists generally call things what they are not. As states' rights have been neutered and our government is undoubtedly national, the media calls our government what it isn't and uses the term "federal government." The media never uses the term "federal national government" because it is nonsensical gibberish, except in the Fantasia of government, where it is beneficial to try to please everyone, be everything to everyone, promise everything to everyone.

A "Federal Corporation" for Home Loan Mortgages is equally absurd. Corporations are private. Federal is governmental. Is a "federal corporation" governmental or private? Almost a century after "federal corporations" were first created, we can answer this question. A "federal corporation" is private when turning a profit, federal when in need of a Bailout. Speculatos keep profits, taxpayers pay losses, the usual formula.

The very existence of a U.S. government corporation with the power to issue mortgages (try and find a clause explicitly enumerating that power in the U.S. Constitution) suggests a national government rather than a federal. It would be much more honest to call the Federal Home Loan Mortgage Corporation the National Home Loan Mortgage Corporation, which is of course why it is called the Federal Home Loan Mortgage Corporation. If national were swapped for federal, the nickname would be Neddie Mac rather than Freddie Mac. With national swapped for federal in Fannie Mae, it would be Nannie Mae, a fitting name for a nanny state government agency that subverts the free market.

The term "federal" income tax is also misleading. As a federal government is a compact of states, a federal income tax is levied against states rather than individual citizens. The original U.S. Constitution imposed truly federal direct taxes which had to be apportioned among the states and could not be levied directly against individuals. An income tax levied directly against each individual citizen in America is a national income tax, not a federal income tax.

The Federal Reserve Bank should be called the National Reserve Bank. There are 12 regional Federal Reserve Bank branches each responsible for a region of the country, which gives the "Federal" Reserve "System" a superficial appearance of regionality and federalism. However, the real power is wielded by the 7-member Board of Governors of the Federal Reserve System, which is headed by the Inflator General (Chairman of the Board of Governors of the Federal Reserve System). The Inflator General and Fed Governors decree the supply of reserves, and set the statutory reserve requirements that bind all banks. Regional Federal Reserve Bank branches simply obey these decrees and are mere underlings. When first proposed to sheeple, the "Federal" Reserve "System" was misrepresented as a federal apparatus with distributed power, but today it is inarguably a National Reserve Bank with a monopoly on the ability to create and uncreate reserves.

To sheeple, emphasizing the difference between national and federal seems anal. To sheeple, this is hair splitting with an electron microscope. If America still had a truly federal government instead of a national government, most corruptions which sheeple rail against would not exist, but sheeple can never be made to accept this fact.

Propagandized Mary Poppins nicknames like Fannie Mae and Freddie Mac keep people from questioning incongruencies. There is also a "Government National Mortgage Association" which is called "Ginnie Mae." It at least has national in its name. Fannie Mae, Freddie Mac and Ginnie Mae are the Ronald McDonald of mortgages. They are also called "Government Sponsored Enterprises" (GSEs). Enterprise would seem to imply free market entrepreneurship. More Mary Poppins propaganda. Government enterprise is a supreme oxymoron. When you hear government and enterprise in the same sentence, hide your wallet.

Fannie Mae can issue mortgages without concern for market forces because it knows guv'ment will use tax revenues to cover any mortgage defaults. Freddie Mac sells Fannie Mae mortgages to Wall Street as Mortgage-Backed Securities (MBSs). Money from Freddie MBS sales gives Fannie more money to lend for more mortgages. In theory, Fannie and Freddie are private corporations, but they are nonetheless referred to as Government Sponsored Enterprises. Everyone understands that guv'ment will bail Fannie and Freddie out if they go rupt— which it did during Depression v9.2006-201x when Fannie and Freddie went rupt. Guv'ment is committed to intervening in the free market and creating Frankenstein 30-year mortgages. Government's guarantee to honor all Fannie & Freddie mortgages if they default causes investors to lend to Fannie & Freddie at lower rates than they would normally charge, distorting the capital allocation and ultimately the resource allocation of the entire economy.

As an aside, note how the frequent use of Freddie and Fannie in discussion makes these agencies seem more personal, less Orwellian. This is why they are given such soothing names in the first place. Having the agencies repeatedly referred to in such personalized, humanistic terms profoundly alters sheeple's psychological perception of them. The nicknames give faceless agencies a face. The nicknames truly perform the same function for GSEs which Ronald McDonald does for McDonald's. Sheeple recognize this ploy when seeing a McDonald's commercial. They understand that the clown is a marketing gimmick intended to make McDonald's seem appealing to simple minded children. Sheeple don't connect the dots and realize that Fannie Mae, Freddie Mac(Donald's), and Ginnie Mae are a marketing gimmick intended to make GSEs seem appealing to simple minded adults, namely them. A huge portion of the wording and imagery used by the guv'ment, media, and advertising industry for everything that it presents to sheeple is crafted in a similar way. A GSE by any other name is not just as sweet sounding.

The Federal Housing Administration (FHA) guarantees (insures) mortgages issued to people who would be unable to obtain a mortgage otherwise. The FHA website chirps:

> Unlike conventional loans that adhere to strict underwriting guidelines, FHA-insured loans require very little cash investment to close a loan. There is more flexibility in calculating household income and payment ratios.

"Strict underwriting guidelines" means not lending to irresponsible individuals with shoddy credit and demanding large down payments on mortgages. In a free market, there is little "flexibility" in calculating household income and payment ratios—limits on the maximum percentage of household income that is acceptable to allocate to a mortgage payment to prevent inevitable defaults. In a free market, people who don't pay bills or can't save money don't get mortgages, period. The FHA circumvents all this sinister free market, capitalist accountability by agreeing to pay any defaulted mortgage it guarantees (insures). How wonderful. Responsible people get to subsidize the irresponsible, by paying defaulted mortgages with tax dollars or via the inflation tax.

To sheeple, eliminating boondoggles like the FHA is cruel. Sheeple gripe about Bailouts necessary to support boondoggles, and erroneously consider them a failure of the "free" market and capitalism. One far-from-absurd explanation of the housing bubble is that banks simply applied FHA lending guidelines to all borrowers. In 2003, Rep. Ron Paul offered an excellent summary of the Fannie-Freddie-Ginnie-FHA hydra:

One of the major government privileges granted to GSEs is a line of credit with the United States Treasury. According to some estimates, the line of credit may be worth over $2 billion. [This was before The Bailout. The line of credit actually ended up being trillions of dollars.] This explicit promise by the Treasury to bail out GSEs in times of economic difficulty helps the GSEs attract investors who are willing to settle for lower yields than they would demand in the absence of the subsidy [because investors know GSE loans won't be allowed to default]. Thus, the line of credit distorts the allocation of capital [decisions about what goods & services the economy should produce]. More importantly, the line of credit is a promise on behalf of the government to engage in a huge unconstitutional and immoral income transfer from working Americans to holders of GSE debt.

At the end of 2012, mortgage debt outstanding in America was $13.4 trillion. $10.2 trillion of this $13.4 trillion was one-to-four family homes (homes for 1-4 families that most people think of when using the word home). Fannie, Freddie, FHA, and Ginnie guaranteed (insured) or originated (created) at least 75% of family mortgages, or about $7.63 trillion worth. At the end of 2012, GSEs held 49% of family mortgages, $5.03 trillion worth. Financial institutions and private investors held the remaining 51% or $5.17 trillion, both directly and as M-BSs, but GSEs had guaranteed roughly $2.1 trillion of these.

There are many terms we could use to describe this system of massive government intervention in mortgage issuance, but a free market isn't one of them. Maybe you like this system of government intervention in mortgage markets. Maybe you don't. Fine either way. But it is totally inaccurate to call such a system a free market, or to blame failures caused by this system a failure of the free market.

30-year mortgages might still exist to some degree without GSEs because of fraudulent fractional-reserve banking, but if guv'ment let GSEs go bank-rupt, 30-year mortgages would be much less common. At least 75% less common. Most mortgages guaranteed by GSEs would not have been created without their backing. If created without GSE backing in a true free market, these mortgages would have been issued at higher interest rates for shorter terms (time periods), and would have required larger down payments, higher income levels, etc. Fewer people would have borrowed under these terms, and defaults would have been rare. Yet still sheeple regurgitate the fallacy that Depression v9.2006-201x was caused by too much free market capitalism.

Free markets rewards savings and frugality. Enslaved markets reward consumption and extravagance. Fannie, Freddie, Ginnie, and the FHA allow borrowers to obtain larger mortgages than the free market would allow, for lower interest rates and longer durations than the free market would allow. Guv'ment is guaranteeing everything and will pay mortgages in the event of default—just make the damn loan! Everyone with a Fannie, Freddie, or Ginnie mortgage is subsidized by taxpayers. Guv'ment essentially confiscated money from one person and used it to honor the mortgage of another.

The thieves running Fannie and Freddie knew that guv'ment would not let them be rupted. This is why they committed so much fraud. The Bailout was part of their business plan. Again, this the usual formula, GSEs are private as long as they are making money, public when they lose it. Profits go to Speculatos, losses are paid by taxpayers. By 2012, The Bailout of these two "GSEs" had cost sheeple more than $1 trillion—more than $3,300 per American. Much of this was loans rather than overt handouts, but even so, this is a staggering financial commitment. Conventional summaries of GSE Bailout costs cite much lower numbers which are lies. Moreover, GSEs helped cause the collapse of the U.S. economy, and that is tough to put a price on. Prolonged economic stagnation is a priceless gift that just keeps on giving. Thanks, FDR!

While we're thanking FDR, let's not forget Social Security and the FDIC. Along with Fannie, Freddie, and FHA, they are the backbone of FDR's New "Deal." In the 1920s and 1930s, Speculatos abused corrupt banking to destroy the economy, causing sheeple to lose houses, bank deposits, and retirement money invested in the stock market. Don't eliminate corrupt banking and prevent all future Depressions, instead give guv'ment control of mortgages, have it insure all bank deposits, and make it the trustee of the nation's retirement savings. Have guv'ment guarantee everyone a retirement income, mortgage financing, and a safe bank deposit. Sheeple who'd lost everything in the Stock Market Crash, Bank Runs, and Great Depression were so petrified and despondent they would have agreed to anything. FDR promised to replace the retirement they had squandered in stocks, guaranteed them a mortgage which would allow them to replace the home many had lost, and was willing to insure bank deposits so no one would ever have to worry about bank runs again. What a guy! A true working man's hero!

Politicians in control of sheeple's bank deposits, mortgages, and retirement savings. What could possibly go wrong?

Only imbeciles are surprised by the truck wreck we face almost a century later. Exhibit QQQ, Social Security. Politicians embezzled almost $3 trillion from the Social Security "Trust" Fund, used it to fund the national guv'ment, and still ran gargantuan deficits even after this embezzlement. Few young Americans believe Social Security will provide for their retirement, but all must pay 6.2% of their income into it, plus 1.45% of their income for Medicare, and all employers must match this contribution. This 6.2% payroll deduction will increase to at least 8% once baby boomers retire, Social Security goes broke, and it too requires a Bail-out. The longer guv'ment waits to face the music, admit the insolvency to the public, and raise the Social Security tax rate, the higher the eventual increase will be. An increase to 9%, 10%, or even 11% or 12% is hardly unthinkable. What if you would rather keep 8% (or 9% or 10% or 11% or 12%) of what you earn, exercise personal responsibility and accountability, and handle your own retire-ment? Tough. Do what you're told, serf. Cough up approximately 1/10th of your pay and return to the herd.

Our Founding Fathers would be astounded and saddened. They paid 6% - 9% for *all* taxes, and revolted when Britain tried to increase taxes just a few percent. Sheeple today cough up that much just for FICA with no resistance whatso-ever. FICA is the Federal "Insurance" Contribution Act, the federal law which instituted "FICA" payroll deductions which fund Social Security and Medicare.

President Woodrow Wilson put our Founding Fathers' republic on life support by creating the Federal Reserve and National Income Tax. FDR pulled the plug and performed the final euthanasia with the New "Deal." Most every New "Deal" program that still exists has required or will require a massive Bailout, yet Spec-ulato scholars and textbooks teach sheeple that FDR was one of the greatest Presidents. Collectivism that bails out and enriches Speculatos must be glorified.

The core American principle is now looting one group of people and handing their wealth to some other group. We do this externally to other nations with our military and world reserve currency, and we do it internally via income, FICA, and inflation taxes. The Bailout was and is the inevitable progression of what Woodrow Wilson and FDR began.

Sheeple pay homage to our Founding Fathers, unaware that modern America bears little resemblance to the peaceful, free republic our Founders intended. Sheeple worship America's Founding Fathers with religious ignorance.

We've veered off yellow brick road a bit, but before we return, let's ponder a free market America with honest 100% reserve banking in which there are only 10-year mortgages. And less car loans. And fewer credit cards. An America whose citizens live in smaller, modest homes, but are not drowning in debt. An Ameri-ca in which people pay off a new car, drive it 8 more years, and save up enough money to pay for most new cars with cash. An America in which most citizens have saved 6 months of income, so that if laid off they can they travel, fish, or chill for months before looking for a new job, and only accept a job they love. An America where the focus isn't possessions, but each other. An America that saves, lives within its means, whose future is secure. A nation where people don't ponder their country's financial future, and think, "Thank God I'll be dead by then."

Imagine it. I wonder if you can. A nation where Speculatos didn't use inflation to impoverish the common man. A nation where people save for a house until age 25, pay it off by 35, and then spend the rest of their lives freed from debt servitude. A nation where this house is given to children who are content with its modesty, never pay a mortgage, but own a home. A nation where inflation has not been used to siphon the wealth produced by technology and transfer it to Speculatos. Colonial Americans produced most everything by hand; modern Americans produce most everything via automation but work almost as long as colonial Americans. If sheeple were not transferring so much wealth to Speculatos, there could be a 4-day, 32-hour work week! Imagine you had no mortgage, and a 3-day weekend every week! How different would your life be?

There is something chillingly dysfunctional about Americans' neurotic obsession with ever larger homes, and possessions in general. As homes grow larger, and sheeple amass more possessions, the American soul seems to grow emptier. If you could remove half the clothes from your closet, swap your car for one half as nice, live in a house half as big, and be debt free, would you? For most Americans, the answer is a resounding yes—but they don't think of such things until it is too late and they are locked and loaded with debt for life.

40-year mortgages are becoming common. As Speculatos gain power, even a 50-year mortgage may become commonplace. People will buy monstrous mansions and smorgasbords of other possessions, and slave paying them off until the day they die. Speculatos will earn even more interest profits, increasing their clandestine tithe.

THE DEPOSIT "INSURANCE" FUND FARCE

The Federal Deposit "Insurance" Corporation (FDIC) was created in 1933 by President Franklin D. Roosevelt. After more than 9,000 bank runs, bank failures that defrauded depositors, FDR's gold confiscation and outlawing of gold, and bank "holidays" that denied depositors the ability to demand reserves, no one trusted the banking system. The FDIC was cooked up to restore confidence in a banking system that had defrauded the entire U.S. population. The FDIC was and is a con to convince a gullible public that a fraudulent fractional-reserve banking system is honest.

Commercial banks create deposits which drastically exceed reserves, and have no ability to honor any widespread demand for reserves. No matter how careful bankers are, a few banks will always be rupted by this lie-ability exposure. If sheeple are to trust a banking system that exploits them, they can't lose their deposits when banks are rupted. All banks therefore pay an "assessment"—a tax—into the FDIC Deposit "Insurance" Fund (DIF). When banks are rupted by lie-ability exposure, depositors that would normally lose their deposit money are paid out of the Deposit "Insurance" Fund.

Bank assessments are computed using a complex methodology that forces banks with a greater risk of bank-ruptcy to pay higher assessments. Each year, banks pay an assessment equal to 0.05% - 0.35% of total deposits, depending on their risk of bank-ruptcy. The total assessment is divided up into 4 quarterly payments. A bank with $100 of deposits would pay an assessment of 5¢ - 35¢. If the bank issued conservative loans, had a track record of profitability and few historical loan defaults, and kept ample capital and reserves, it would be considered low risk and its assessment would be 5¢. If the bank issued risky loans, had not always been profitable, had a history of loan defaults, and did not always keep ample capital or reserves, it would be considered high risk and its assessment would be 35¢. Assessments greater than 5¢ and less than 35¢ might also be levied if the bank was neither low risk or high risk, but rather medium risk. If the bank owed an assessment of 5¢, it makes 4 payments of 1.25¢, one every 90 days throughout the year. If the bank owed an assessment of 35¢, it makes 4 payments of 8.75¢.

Every bank that practices fraudulent fractional-reserve lending should be considered high risk, as no bank that practices fraudulent fractional-reserve lending can honor even a small fraction of its deposits. The FDIC is oblivious to this fundamental fraud which lies at the core of the banking system, as it is designed to perpetuate fraudulent fractional-reserve lending and prop up a banking system predicated upon it. Most banks are considered low risk by the FDIC, and pay low assessment fees. A low risk bank with $1 million of deposits would pay an annual assessment of $500, and the FDIC would commit to honoring all the bank's deposits if it is bank-rupted. This "insurance" has no deductible, and represents a staggering bargain. An individual with a $1 million home would pay at least $2,000 per year for insurance, and a deductible would have to be paid if the home owner attempted to collect on the policy. Banks pay far below typical market value for their "insurance."

Assessments paid by banks accumulate in the Deposit "Insurance" Fund year to year. The FDIC attempts to maintain a balance in the Deposit "Insurance" Fund that is equal to 2% of total "insured" deposits. That is, the Deposit "Insurance" Fund attempts to maintain a 2% reserve ratio. FDIC deposit "insurance" is simply another nested layer of the fractional-reserve fraud.

An honest 100% reserve banking system which applies a 100% statutory reserve ratio requirement to demand deposits doesn't require "insurance" on those demand deposits. In an honest 100% reserve banking system, the FDIC and deposit "insurance" would be superfluous.

As banks don't pay 2% of deposits per year into the Deposit "Insurance" Fund, but rather $1/40^{th}$ (0.05% of deposits) to $1/6^{th}$ (0.35% of deposits) this amount, it can take years or decades to build up a balance in the Deposit "Insurance" Fund equal to 2% of all guaranteed deposits. This is especially true because most banks pay annual assessments equal to $1/40^{th}$ of 2% (0.05%), rather than annual assessments equal to $1/6^{th}$ of 2% (0.35%).

Under normal, healthy economic conditions in which there are no widespread runs on banks, few banks fail, and a Deposit balance equal to 2% of deposits is sufficient to honor the deposits of any banks that are rupted. Under abnormal, unhealthy economic conditions in which there are widespread runs on banks, many banks fail, the Deposit "Insurance" Fund is rapidly exhausted, and is insufficient to honor all defaulted deposits.

The FDIC Deposit "Insurance" Fund was rapidly exhausted during Depression v9.2006-201x. The table on the following page shows the balance in the Deposit "Insurance" Fund from 2006 - 2013. All amounts are millions of dollars. Negative amounts are red. The Deposit "Insurance" Fund had a balance that was billions of dollars, and this balance guaranteed or "insured" trillions of dollars of deposits. The reserve ratio of the FDIC is the Deposit "Insurance" Fund balance divided by total insured deposits, and is shown.

Prior to Depression v9.2006-201x, the FDIC was required by law to target a 1.25% reserve ratio. This would be an amount of money in the Deposit "Insurance"

FDIC Deposit "Insurance" Fund
During Depression v9.2006-201x
All Amounts Millions of Dollars

Date	Deposit "Insurance" Fund Balance	Deposits Insured	Reserve Ratio
June 2006	$49,564	$4,040,353	1.23%
September 2006	$49,992	$4,100,013	1.22%
December 2006	$50,165	$4,153,786	1.21%
March 2007	$50,745	$4,245,266	1.20%
June 2007	$51,227	$4,235,044	1.21%
September 2007	$51,754	$4,242,607	1.22%
December 2007	$52,413	$4,292,221	1.22%
March 2008	$52,843	$4,437,870	1.19%
June 2008	$45,217	$4,467,570	1.01%
September 2008	$34,588	$4,545,098	0.76%
December 2008	$17,276	$4,750,608	0.36%
March 2009	$13,007	$4,831,090	0.27%
June 2009	$10,368	$4,817,577	0.22%
September 2009	-$8,243	$5,296,533	-0.16%
December 2009	-$20,850	$5,391,876	-0.39%
March 2010	-$20,717	$5,472,395	-0.38%
June 2010	-$15,247	$5,437,411	-0.28%
September 2010	-$8,009	$5,421,425	-0.15%
December 2010	-$7,352	$6,302,329	-0.12%
March 2011	-$1,023	$6,380,407	-0.02%
June 2011	$3,916	$6,524,750	0.06%
September 2011	$7,813	$6,756,302	0.12%
December 2011	$11,827	$6,974,690	0.17%
March 2012	$15,292	$7,032,875	0.22%
June 2012	$22,693	$7,083,433	0.32%
September 2012	$25,224	$7,250,062	0.35%
December 2012	$32,958	$7,406,652	0.44%
March 2013	$35,742	$6,010,216	0.59%
June 2013	$37,871	$5,963,323	0.64%
September 2013	$40,758	$5,969,177	0.68%

Fund equal to 1.25% of all deposits insured by the FDIC. As some banks are always failing and their defrauded depositors are being reimbursed by the FDIC, banks are regularly paying assessments to the FDIC, and the total amount of insured deposits increases as the money supply is inflated, the reserve ratio of the FDIC will fluctuate and can't always be maintained at the exact value decreed by statute. However, under healthy economic conditions the FDIC reserve ratio is usually kept very close to the legally mandated level.

In early 2006, runs on banks commenced as Inflator General Alan Greenspan popped the housing bubble. As the economic collapse snowballed, bank failures increased, and the Deposit "Insurance" Fund was rapidly depleted. The balance in the fund decreased, as did the FDIC reserve ratio. By December 2009, the Deposit "Insurance" Fund had a negative $20 billion balance. The FDIC owed $20 billion to defrauded depositors that it did not possess. The fractional-reserve fraud all over again.

The FDIC can borrow up to $500 billion from the U.S. Treasury, and the U.S. Treasury can have Fed monetize massive quantities of T-debts, so the FDIC is simply another iteration of the same old story. Speculatos keep profits, sheeple pay losses.

When the balance in the Deposit "Insurance" Fund became negative in 2009, the FDIC drew upon its U.S. Treasury credit line to stay solvent over the short term. It then asked banks to prepay three years of assessments in advance to replenish the Deposit "Insurance" Fund. Banks' willingness to pay these assessments was portrayed as an altruistic act, but the opposite is true. Propping up the FDIC props up the entire corrupt edifice of fractional-reserve lending. If banks had refused to prepay three years of FDIC assessments, and the Deposit "Insurance" Fund had maintained a negative balance for years while assessments trickled in, then depositors at failed banks would have waited years to be reimbursed and might have begun complaining and demanding bank reform.

During Depression v9.2006-201x, several legislative "reform" packages were passed, to purportedly prevent future Depressions. The FDIC reserve ratio requirement was increased from 1.25% to 2%, and the FDIC insurance limit was increased from $100,000 per depositor per institution to $250,000 per depositor per institution. An honest 100% reserve banking system that would truly prevent future Depressions was never contemplated by "reformers." Instead, the Deposit "Insurance" Fund was forced to accumulate a slightly greater amount of reserves, and depositor panic was prevented by increasing the amount of deposits that the FDIC guaranteed. Here are the FDIC deposit insurance limits since the FDIC was created in 1933:

Date	FDIC Deposit "Insurance" Limit
1934 - 1949	$5,000
1950 - 1965	$10,000
1966 - 1968	$15,000
1969 - 1973	$20,000
1974 - 1979	$40,000
1980 - 2007	$100,000
2008 - 2014	$250,000

The 2% FDIC reserve ratio was implemented in 2010. FDIC estimates that the balance in the Deposit "Insurance" Fund will be equal to 2% of insured deposits in 2018. It will take almost a decade to replenish the Deposit "Insurance" Fund and attain the 2% reserve ratio.

The FDIC's 2% reserve ratio is a major reason, but not the only major reason, for the doctrine of "Too Big To Fail." Some behemoth banks hold 5% - 10% of total deposits. If one of these behemoth banks went rupt and the FDIC had to honor its lie-abilities, the Deposit "Insurance" Fund would be immediately depleted and incur a negative balance that was tens of billions of dollars. Too Big To Fail actually means Too Big To Bail—out that is. In an honest 100% reserve banking system, there is no bogus "insurance" fund to be bank-rupted, and behemoth banks can be allowed to fail.

Banks accept a $100 deposit of reserves, create $6,700 of additional deposits that can't be honored, and have $6,800 of total deposits. Banks then pay an annual FDIC assessment equal to 0.05% - 0.35% of total deposits, which for $6,800 of deposits is an assessment of $3.40 - $23.80. As always, these are real world ratios which prevailed in September 2008 when The Bailout passed. Banks create additional deposits to lend them out, and banks that create $6,700 of deposits and lend them at 6% interest earn $402 per year of interest payments. So banks earn $402 a year in income by practicing fraudulent fractional-reserve lending, and pay $3.40 - $23.80 to "insure" deposits, thereby protecting the fractional-reserve scam. Most banks pay low FDIC assessments, meaning most banks would earn $402 in income and pay $3.40, which is a mere 0.8% of income. The FDIC "insurance" assessment only requires banks to surrender a tiny percentage of their income on conjured deposits, yet grants banks total immunity from prosecution (and persecution) by defrauded depositors because the FDIC must honor all the conjured deposits. True reform would prevent the creation of the $6,700 of additional deposits. The FDIC deposit "insurance fund" is not real protection for depositors, but rather a ruse to give the appearance of protection, and prevent true banking reform.

BANK RUNS THROUGHOUT HISTORY

1 George Bailey faces a bank run in the 1946 movie *It's a Wonderful Life.*
2 "Run on the Seaman's Savings' Bank During the Panic." That is, the Banking Panic during Depression v3.1857-1861.

Our banking system is built upon a lie. Bankers promise to pay interest on deposits by lending reserves, but simultaneously tell all depositors that they can withdraw their reserves at any time. Bank runs have occurred throughout history when depositors demand reserves that banks don't possess and expose this lie. It is depressing that sheeple can't deduce such a simple fraud, and that bank runs continue to occur generation after generation after generation...

3 Run on the 4th National Bank in New York City. This occurred during Depression v4.1873-1879. The black blotch is a hole in the original image.
4 "The run on the Montreal City and District Savings Bank. The Mayor addressing the crowd." In 1872, just before Depression v4.1873-1879.

5 An 1873 bank run in Vienna, Austria. American sheeple are not the only herd with amnesia about bank runs. Sheeple worldwide are ravaged repeatedly.
6 The 1873 Banking Panic on Wall Street.

7 The failure of Grant & Wood Bank caused runs on Wall Street in 1884.

8 A run during the Banking Panic of 1907. Widespread Panics such as this one precipitated Depression v6.1907-1908.
9 A run at American Union Bank of New York in 1931, during The Great Depression.

After the 9,000 bank runs during the Great Depression, Speculatos took steps to prevent their scam from being exposed in the future. They created the Federal Deposit Insurance Corporation (FDIC). As explained in the previous section, the FDIC is a guv'ment created—and guv'ment backed—corporation. Banks pay an FDIC assessment equal to a tiny percentage of deposits. These assessments are deposited in the FDIC Deposit "Insurance" Fund. The Deposit "Insurance" Fund rescues banks on the verge of ruptcy, or honors the lie-abilities (defaulted deposits) of rupted banks that are liquidated. A few large bank failures quickly exhausts the Deposit "Insurance" Fund; guv'ment then funds the FDIC with tax revenues, Fed creates money and funds it via the inflation tax, or banks increase assessment payments. The FDIC is quintessential collectivism that taxes competent, solvent banks to aid incompetent, insolvent banks. In the case of widespread bank failures, the FDIC transfers costs of Speculato reserve embezzlement to sheeple. Calling this Bailout process "insurance" is shrewd propaganda.

Sheeple don't think it through on this level. They know nothing about the FDIC, except that the guv'ment backs it and their bank deposits. Americans have seen few bank runs since Franklin D. Roosevelt created the FDIC in 1934. Sheeple usually don't withdraw currency from bank accounts during a banking crisis because they believe that the FDIC will protect them. This confidence has prevented most physical bank runs. There have been silent computer bank runs that don't involve herds of sheeple physically congregating at banks. Silent computer bank runs can be (and have been) hidden, but physical bank runs can't be hidden and create panic that leads to additional bank runs. The real purpose of the FDIC is to prevent a chain reaction of bank runs which would expose lie-abilities of all banks and implode the fraudulent fractional-reserve banking system.

10 (PREVIOUS PAGE) Countrywide Financial Corporation was crooked even by shady "subprime" standards. It created IndyMac Bank to "collateralize" loans. IndyMac promised depositors reserves upon demand yet lent those reserves out for subprime mortgages. When mortgages were defaulted, IndyMac couldn't honor deposits. Runs occurred in 2008. The FDIC placed IndyMac into "conservatorship" and replenished embezzled deposits. This let IndyMac executives pocket millions in origination fees and walk away scot-free, and kept depositors at other banks from questioning the safety of their deposits and creating additional runs.

11 Northern Rock was England's 5th largest bank. In 2007, it experienced runs at locations nationwide. Sheeple expecting Northern Rock to become insolvent camped outside branches the night before. The Bank of England computered massive sums of British-pound reserves and provided British-pound currency which Northern Rock used to honor deposits, but runs continued. Imagine 67 of every 68 people in this mob being told that they could never redeem their deposit for reserves. Word of the lie-ability fraud would have spread with super-liminal speed. Northern Rock was nationalized, meaning losses were transferred to taxpayers. If this had not been done, all banks might have soon faced similar demands for reserves they did not possess, vaporizing England's economy.

The global banking system is a cartel whose protector is the FDIC and Federal Reserve System, or their counterparts in foreign nations. All claims that this system avoids moral hazard are propaganda for rubes. The system is designed to protect Speculatos from financial losses caused by their own greed, by granting them gargantuan Bailouts. Bailouts are the fundamental reason Central Banks and the FDIC are created—they are the core principle at the heart of the banking system.

There is a massive difference between individual bank failures and a systemic failures of many banks. Individual bank failures can be weathered. System-wide failures can't. In bailing out bank-rupt banks, the FDIC is essentially handing out hush money. If it did not, defrauded depositors would tell other depositors about lie-abilities, creating doubts about the integrity of a banking system that is borrowed short and lent long, and which therefore can't honor its commitments.

Runs in 2008 at Hong Kong's Bank of East Asia. An employee made derivative bets, lost, and hid the data. When the fraud was discovered, previous year's profits were decreased by 12%, creating panic. London's *Evening Standard* reported:

> Hong Kong faced its first bank run in a decade today as hundreds of depositors queued to withdraw money from the Bank of East Asia (BEA). The bank blamed "malicious rumours" for the crisis and chairman David Li rushed back to Hong Kong from the U.S. to reassure depositors. Hong Kong's Central Bank jumped to BEA's defence and police are investigating phone messages questioning its health. "The rumours were groundless," Li said. "The bank has no problem." BEA's woes underline fragile public sentiment towards lenders and financial firms and echo scenes last week in Singapore as customers rushed to AIG's local offices to terminate insurance policies. Joseph Yam, chief executive of Hong Kong's Central Bank, urged depositors to "stay calm." Under Hong Kong's deposit insurance programme, depositors are protected by just HK$100,000 (£7,000) in case of a bank failure. The Hong Kong Monetary Authority [Hong Kong's Central Bank] injected HK$3.88 billion [of reserves] into the banking system, after the interbank lending rate surged. Hundreds of depositors lined up outside BEA branches to withdraw money. ... Other banks moved to reassure the public about their finances. Fears were growing over a run on DBS Group, South-east Asia's biggest lender, but its Hong Kong unit was "in a strong financial and capital position," the bank said.

In all times and nations, the Speculato formula is the same. When depositors try to demand their "demand" deposits, a Central Bank creates reserves to help the besieged bank survive, and sheeple are Fed lies which convince them not to demand reserves. Other banks project confidence to prevent widespread runs. One wonders about the "criminals" investigated by the police. Police investigate those warning about fractional-reserve lending rather than the crooks practicing it!

In a banking system in which only time deposits are lent and demand deposits are warehoused, none of the depositors pictured on these pages would have had to worry that banks didn't have their reserves. In such a system, banks would be audited regularly to make sure that all demand deposits are warehoused, not lent. Banks would charge fees for warehousing demand deposits rather than paying interest on them and lending them without permission. The only solvency problem an honest bank would encounter is distribution of reserves among different branches, which could result in delays for widespread currency withdrawals while funds are transferred between banks. But every customer at an honest bank could withdraw the reserves backing their demand deposit. In an honest 100% reserve banking system, every demand depositor at every bank could withdraw their reserves—an impossibility in the present system.

Time depositors could lose their reserves if banks made bad loans, but they accepted this risk when voluntarily surrendering reserves for a loan. A time depositor could not suddenly demand their reserves from their bank, but they could sell their time deposit in a secondary market for less than face value. You might have a receipt entitling you to your $100 time deposit in 1 year. I would buy it for $90 right now, earning $10 profit in 1 year.

The real solution to bank runs isn't Central Banks or deposit "insurance," it is honest banks which don't fraudulently create an amount of deposits that exceeds reserves. Depositors should lose money when banks fail, so that they learn to use banks that don't embezzle reserves or issue bad loans. Sheeple conditioned to believe in cradle to grave guv'ment protection can never be made to accept this premise. They gripe about Bailouts, but refuse to accept the risk and personal accountability which are necessary to eliminate Bailout mechanisms. Banking Panics will continue for all of history—unless honest 100% reserve banking is instituted.

"That men do not learn very much from the lessons of history is the most important of all the lessons that history has to teach."—Aldous Huxley

THE ROAD TO 0% RESERVES

"Reserve requirements are applied only to transaction deposits ... A depository institution's reserve requirement expands or contracts with the level of its transaction deposits."
—*The Federal Reserve System Purposes & Functions*, Federal Reserve Publication

"The [savings] depositor is permitted or authorized to make no more than six transfers and withdrawals, or a combination of such transfers and withdrawals, per calendar month or statement cycle (or similar period) of at least four weeks ... a depository institution must prevent withdrawals or transfers of funds from account that are in excess of the [six withdrawal] limit ... [when the six withdrawal limit is exceeded] the depository institution must either close the account and place the funds in another account that the depositor is eligible to maintain, or take away the transfer and draft capacities of the account. An account that authorizes withdrawals or transfers in excess of the permitted number [six] is a transaction account regardless of whether the authorized number of transactions is actually made. ... A deposit may continue to be classified as a savings deposit even if the depository institution exercises its right to require notice of withdrawal. . ."
—Section 204.2(d) of the Federal Reserve Act
"Regulation D"

We're done with honest 100% reserve banking for now. Back to the credit cornucopia that is our fraudulent fractional-reserve banking system. The next several chapters will summarize frauds which banks utilize to further decrease reserve ratios which are already ridiculously low.

In 2008 just before The Bailout passed, U.S. banks had $102.7 billion of reserves to honor $7.053 trillion of deposits, which is a 1.46% reserve ratio. If the Federal Reserve decrees a statutory reserve ratio requirement of 10%, how can a 1.46% reserve ratio be legal? The demand deposits and time deposits which honest banks use are abandoned for TRANSACTION DEPOSITS and NON-TRANSACTION DEPOSITS. The 10% statutory reserve ratio requirement is applied only to transaction deposits, not non-transaction deposits, which decreases the overall statutory reserve ratio requirement for all deposits taken as a whole.

Transaction deposits are those which the depositor has unrestricted access to for use in day to day economic transactions. Transaction deposits have no limitations on withdrawal or access to funds—assuming the bank can honor lie-abilities.

Non-transaction deposits can't be accessed without limitation. Non-transaction deposits place restrictions upon depositors' ability to withdraw funds. Non-transaction deposits are therefore not suitable for use in day to day economic transactions. Checking accounts are transaction accounts. Savings accounts are non-transaction accounts. The statutory reserve ratio requirement is 10% on transaction deposits and 0% on non-transaction deposits. No reserves have to be set aside to honor non-transaction deposits.

Most savings accounts pay interest, and most checking accounts don't. Some special hybridized checking accounts with withdrawal limitations pay interest, but it is less than the interest rate on savings accounts. Most people attempt to maximize interest payments, and therefore keep a small percentage of their bank deposits in checking accounts and a large percentage of their bank deposits in savings accounts. This means that non-transaction deposits with a 0% statutory reserve ratio requirement are a significant portion of deposits at most banks, and that banks don't have to keep any reserves to back a significant portion of deposits.

Suppose you have $100 deposited at a Tenth Transaction Bank, $20 in a checking account, $80 in a savings account. If the 10% statutory reserve ratio requirement was applied to both accounts, Tenth Transaction Bank would have to keep $10 in reserve (10% of $100). The $80 savings account is a non-transaction deposit with a 0% statutory reserve ratio requirement. The 10% statutory reserve ratio requirement for transaction accounts is only applied to the $20 checking account. Tenth Transaction Bank only has to keep reserves to back the $20 checking account, not the $80 savings account. Tenth Transaction Bank's statutory reserve requirement is $2 (10% of $20). $2 is 2% of $100, so the statutory reserve ratio requirement for all deposits taken as a whole is 2%. Implementing the non-transaction ruse decreased the statutory reserve requirement from $10 to $2, an 80% reduction.

Here is the process on ledgers. Tenth Transaction Bank accepts a $100 deposit of reserves. Depositors choose to open $20 of checking accounts and $80 of savings accounts:

Assets	Liabilities
$20 (Reserves)	$20 (Checking Deposits)
$80 (Reserves)	$80 (Savings Deposits)
$100	$100

100% Reserve Ratio

The reserves backing each deposit type will be shown separately to aid visualization.

The 10% statutory reserve ratio requirement is applied to checking deposits and savings deposits. 90% of reserves are recategorized as "excess" reserves, embezzled, and lent:

```
Assets                          Liabilities
  $2 (Reserves)                   $20 (Checking Deposits)
 $18 (Loans)
  $8 (Reserves)                   $80 (Savings Deposits)
 $72 (Loans)


$100                            $100
                                     10% Reserve Ratio
```

Tenth Transaction Bank's ledger after combining reserves and loans:

```
Assets                          Liabilities
 $10 (Reserves)                   $20 (Checking Deposits)
 $90 (Loans)                      $80 (Savings Deposits)


$100                            $100
                                     10% Reserve Ratio
```

Tenth Transaction Bank has $100 of deposits, $10 of reserves and $90 of loans. This is the same ledger we have seen many times, except that on this ledger deposits are not all lumped together. On this ledger, transaction deposits and non-transaction deposits are differentiated.

The $80 savings deposit is a non-transaction deposit with a 0% statutory reserve ratio requirement. Tenth Transaction Bank only has to apply the 10% statutory reserve ratio requirement to the $20 checking deposit which is a transaction deposit. Tenth Transaction Bank only has to hold reserves to back the $20 checking deposit:

```
Assets                          Liabilities
  $2 (Reserves)                   $20 (Checking Deposits)
 $18 (Loans)
  $0 (Reserves)                   $80 (Savings Deposits)
 $80 (Loans)


$100                            $100
                                      2% Reserve Ratio
```

Tenth Transaction Bank's ledger after combining reserves and loans:

Assets	Liabilities
$2 (Reserves)	$20 (Checking Deposits)
$98 (Loans)	$80 (Savings Deposits)
$100	$100
	2% Reserve Ratio

Tenth Transaction Bank has $2 of reserves backing $100 of deposits, a 2% reserve ratio. Implementing the non-transaction ruse has decreased its statutory reserve requirement from $10 to $2, by 80%. Tenth Transaction Bank could issue a $90 loan before the non-transaction ruse, a $98 loan after the non-transaction ruse.

In the real world, banks don't apply a 10% statutory reserve ratio requirement to checking deposits and savings deposits, and then decrease reserves once a 0% statutory reserve ratio requirement is applied to savings deposits. This step was shown to aid learning. In the real world, banks immediately apply a 0% statutory reserve ratio requirement to non-transaction deposits and never apply a higher statutory reserve ratio requirement to them. When you deposit $100 of reserves into a savings account, those $100 of reserves are promised to you upon demand, and then immediately embezzled and lent out.

Checking account and saving account are terms sheeple use. Speculatos and bankers use the terms transaction deposits and non-transaction deposits. We'll insert these terms into Tenth Transaction Bank's ledger:

Assets	Liabilities
$2 (Reserves)	$20 (Transaction Deposits)
$98 (Loans)	$80 (Non-Transaction Deposits)
$100	$100
	2% Reserve Ratio

In September 2008 just before The Bailout passed, Bank of America had $672 billion of deposits, $89 billion of transaction deposits and $583 billion of non-transaction deposits. For every $1 of transaction deposits, Bank of America had $6.55 of non-transaction deposits. If Bank of America had applied a 10% statutory reserve ratio requirement to non-transaction deposits and transaction deposits, its statutory reserve requirement would have been $67.2 billion (10% of $672 billion). Instead Bank of America applied a 0% statutory reserve ratio requirement to its $583 billion of non-transaction deposits, and only had to apply the 10% statutory reserve ratio requirement to its $89 billion of transaction deposits, which resulted in an overall statutory reserve requirement of $8.9 billion. $8.9 billion of reserves is 1.3% of the $672 billion of deposits—a 1.3% statutory reserve ratio requirement. By applying a 0% statutory reserve requirement to non-transaction deposits, Bank of America decreased its overall statutory reserve requirement by $58.3 billion or 87%. This allowed Bank of America to create and lend an additional $58.3 billion.

Here is the process on ledgers. Bank of America held $672.1 billion of deposits. Depositors chose to open $88.7 billion of checking accounts and $583.4 billion of savings accounts. There are other types of non-transaction accounts besides savings accounts, but we haven't discussed them yet. Bank of America didn't actually have $583.4 billion of savings accounts, it had $583.4 billion of non-transaction accounts. Again, it is more accurate to use the transaction account and non-transaction account terminology that Speculatos and bankers prefer, rather than the checking account and savings account terminology that sheeple prefer. Bank of America's ledger:

Assets	Liabilities
∦88,656,723,000 (Reserves)	∦88,656,723,000 (Transaction Deposits)
∦583,410,654,000 (Reserves)	∦583,410,654,000 (Non-Transaction Deposits)
∦672,067,377,000	∦672,067,377,000
	100% Reserve Ratio

The 10% statutory reserve ratio requirement is applied to both transaction and non-transaction deposits. 90% of reserves are recategorized as "excess" reserves, embezzled, and lent:

Assets	Liabilities
$8,865,672,300 (Reserves)	∦88,656,723,000 (Transaction Deposits)
$79,791,050,700 (Loans)	
$58,341,065,400 (Reserves)	∦583,410,654,000 (Non-Transaction Deposits)
$525,069,588,600 (Loans)	
∦672,067,377,000	∦672,067,377,000
	10% Reserve Ratio

Bank of America's ledger after combining reserves and loans:

```
Assets                              Liabilities
  $67,206,737,700 (Reserves)         $88,656,723,000 (Transaction
$604,860,639,300 (Loans)                            Deposits)
                                    $583,410,654,000 (Non-Transaction
                                                     Deposits)
──────────────────────────────────────────────────────────────────────
$672,067,377,000                    $672,067,377,000
                                              10% Reserve Ratio
```

Bank of America has $672.1 billion of deposits, $67.2 billion of reserves, and $604.9 billion of loans. This is the same ledger we have seen many times, except that on this ledger deposits are not all lumped together. On this ledger, transaction deposits and non-transaction deposits are differentiated.

Non-transaction accounts have a 0% statutory reserve ratio requirement. Bank of America only has to apply the 10% statutory reserve ratio requirement to the $88.7 billion of transaction deposits. It only has to hold reserves to back the $88.7 billion of transaction deposits:

```
Assets                              Liabilities
  $8,865,672,300 (Reserves)          $88,656,723,000 (Transaction
 $79,791,050,700 (Loans)                            Deposits)
              $0 (Reserves)         $583,410,654,000 (Non-Transaction
$583,410,654,000 (Loans)                             Deposits)
──────────────────────────────────────────────────────────────────────
$672,067,377,000                    $672,067,377,000
                                            1.32% Reserve Ratio
```

Bank of America's ledger after combining reserves and loans:

```
Assets                              Liabilities
  $8,865,672,300 (Reserves)          $88,656,723,000 (Transaction
$663,201,704,700 (Loans)                            Deposits)
                                    $583,410,654,000 (Non-Transaction
                                                     Deposits)
──────────────────────────────────────────────────────────────────────
$672,067,377,000                    $672,067,377,000
                                            1.32% Reserve Ratio
```

Bank of America has $8.9 billion of reserves backing $672 billion of deposits, a 1.32% reserve ratio. Implementing the non-transaction ruse decreased Bank of America's statutory reserve requirement from $67.2 billion to $8.9 billion, by $58.3 billion or 87%. Bank of America could issue $604.8 billion of loans before the non-transaction ruse, but $663.2 billion of loans after the non-transaction ruse. If lent at 5% interest, the additional $58.3 billion of loans generates almost $3 billion of interest payments per year.

$583 billion of transaction deposits which can be demanded at anytime, and Bank of America kept no reserves to back them? $0 of reserves back $583 billion of deposits?

No. Reserves backing transaction deposits are used to honor non-transaction deposits. Banks don't segregate reserves, meaning all reserves can be used to honor any type of deposit. Also, some of Bank of America's non-transaction deposits are certificates of deposit (time deposits) which can't be demanded, rather than savings deposits (demand deposits) which can be demanded, as will be shown later. This description is a bit inaccurate as of now—but not by much.

Still. Bank of America had $672 billion of deposits and only set aside $8.9 billion of reserves to honor them?

No. Bank of America actually held $7.6 billion of reserves to honor $672 billion of deposits, as previously shown. $7.6 billion is less than $8.9 billion. $8.9 billion is Bank of America's overall statutory reserve requirement after applying the 0% statutory reserve ratio requirement to non-transaction deposits. Another scam called sweeps decreased Bank of America's overall statutory reserve requirement and statutory reserve ratio requirement even more, but sweeps haven't been described yet.

Pardon the perplexing maze of frauds. The author didn't concoct them, he is simply trying to explain them.

So Bank of America had $672 billion of deposits. Under honest 100% reserve banking, Bank of America would have had a 100% statutory reserve ratio requirement and a statutory reserve requirement of $672 billion. Fraudulent fractional-reserve banking set a 10% statutory reserve ratio requirement, decreasing the statutory reserve requirement to $67.2 billion. The non-transaction deposit ruse allowed Bank of America to apply a 0% statutory reserve ratio requirement to $583 billion of non-transaction deposits, decreasing its overall statutory reserve requirement to $8.9 billion and its overall statutory reserve ratio requirement to 1.3%.

A 1.3% statutory reserve ratio requirement?
A 1.3% statutory reserve ratio requirement!
1.3%?

Promise depositors access to all their money upon demand, but only keep enough reserves to back 1.3% of deposits?

Yep. Sickening, but true. Bank of America isn't the only perpetrator of this fraud. Every bank in America applies a 0% statutory reserve ratio requirement to non-transaction deposits, and has statutory reserve ratio requirements which are as absurdly low as Bank of America's. A 10% statutory reserve ratio requirement is paltry to depositors who may demand their reserves, as 90% of promised reserves literally are not reserved, but to banks a 10% statutory reserve ratio requirement is excessive.

In September 2008 just before The Bailout passed, the U.S. banking system had $7.053 trillion of deposits, $631 billion of transaction deposits and $6,422 billion ($6.422 trillion) of non-transaction deposits. For every $1 of transaction deposits, U.S. banks had $10.18 of non-transaction deposits. If U.S. banks applied a 10% statutory reserve ratio requirement to non-transaction deposits and transaction deposits, their statutory reserve requirement would have been $705.3 billion (10% of $7.053 trillion). Instead U.S. banks applied a 0% statutory reserve ratio requirement to their $6.422 trillion of non-transaction deposits, and a 10% statutory reserve requirement to their $631 billion of transaction deposits, which resulted in an overall statutory reserve requirement of $63.1 billion. $63.1 billion of reserves is 0.89% of the $7.053 trillion of deposits—a 0.89% statutory reserve ratio requirement. By applying a 0% statutory reserve ratio requirement to non-transaction deposits, the U.S. banking system decreased its overall statutory reserve requirement by $642.2 billion or 91%. This allowed U.S. banks to create and lend an additional $642.2 billion.

Here is the process on ledgers. Banks in America held $7.053 trillion of deposits. Depositors chose to open $631 billion of transaction accounts and $6,422 billion ($6.422 trillion) of non-transaction accounts:

Assets	Liabilities
₦631,100,000,000 (Reserves)	₦631,100,000,000 (Transaction Deposits)
₦6,421,600,000,000 (Reserves)	₦6,421,600,000,000 (Non-Transaction Deposits)
₦7,052,700,000,000	₦7,052,700,000,000
	100% Reserve Ratio

If the 10% statutory reserve ratio requirement had been applied to both transaction and non-transaction deposits, the ledger would have been:

Assets	Liabilities
$63,110,000,000 (Reserves)	₦631,100,000,000 (Transaction Deposits)
$567,990,000,000 (Loans)	
$642,160,000,000 (Reserves)	₦6,421,600,000,000 (Non-Transaction Deposits)
$5,779,440,000,000 (Loans)	
₦7,052,700,000,000	₦7,052,700,000,000
	10% Reserve Ratio

90% of the reserves backing deposits have been recategorized as "excess" reserves, embezzled, and lent.

Don't let the large numbers confuse you. This is the same ledger we have seen many times. The fact that the numbers may be too large for you to add in your head or easily visualize doesn't change this fact.

If the 10% statutory reserve ratio requirement had been applied to both transaction and non-transaction deposits, the U.S. banking system's ledger after combining reserves and loans would have been:

```
Assets                                 Liabilities

  $705,270,000,000 (Reserves)            $631,100,000,000 (Transaction
$6,347,430,000,000 (Loans)                                 Deposits)
                                       $6,421,600,000,000 (Non-Transaction
                                                           Deposits)
_____          _____
$7,052,700,000,000                     $7,052,700,000,000

                                                   10% Reserve Ratio
```

The U.S. banking system would have had $7.053 trillion of deposits, $705.3 billion of reserves, and $6.347 trillion of loans. This is the same ledger we have seen many times, except that on this ledger deposits are not all lumped together. On this ledger, transaction deposits and non-transaction deposits are differentiated.

Total reserves in the U.S. banking system at this time were only $102.7 billion. It would have been impossible for the banking system to have $705.3 billion of reserves, as this many reserves did not exist (prior to The Bailout anyway). This ledger shows the amount of reserves which would have been required if less fraudulent banking prevailed, to provide a baseline for comparison.

In reality, if $7.053 trillion of deposits had to be backed by $705.3 billion of reserves, and there were only $102.7 billion of reserves, then U.S. banks could not have created $7.053 trillion of deposits, but rather "only" $1.027 trillion of deposits. If a 10% statutory reserve ratio requirement is applied, $102.7 billion of reserves can "only" back $1.027 trillion of deposits. That is, a U.S. banking system with a 10% statutory reserve ratio requirement which accepted initial reserve deposits of $102.7 billion could "only" create $924.3 billion of additional deposits and lend those deposits out at interest:

```
Assets                                 Liabilities

  $102,700,000,000 (Reserves)          $1,027,000,000,000 (Deposits)
  $924,300,000,000 (Loans)
_____          _____
$1,027,000,000,000                     $1,027,000,000,000

                                                   10% Reserve Ratio
```

If forced to apply a mere 10% statutory reserve ratio requirement to non-transaction deposits, which is a 10% statutory reserve ratio requirement on all deposits, bankers would have had their deposit creation decreased by $6.026 trillion!

Fortunately for bankers, and unfortunately for sheeple, non-transaction deposits have a 0% statutory reserve ratio requirement. The U.S. banking system only has to apply the 10% statutory reserve ratio requirement to the $631.1 billion of transaction deposits. The U.S. banking system only has to hold reserves to back the $631.1 billion of transaction deposits:

Assets	Liabilities
$63,110,000,000 (Reserves)	$631,100,000,000 (Transaction Deposits)
$567,990,000,000 (Loans)	
$0 (Reserves)	$6,421,600,000,000 (Non-Transaction Deposits)
$6,421,600,000,000 (Loans)	
$7,052,700,000,000	$7,052,700,000,000
	0.89% Reserve Ratio

The U.S. banking system's ledger after combining reserves and loans:

Assets	Liabilities
$63,110,000,000 (Reserves)	$631,100,000,000 (Transaction Deposits)
$6,989,590,000,000 (Loans)	$6,421,600,000,000 (Non-Transaction Deposits)
$7,052,700,000,000	$7,052,700,000,000
	0.89% Reserve Ratio

The U.S. banking system has $63.1 billion of reserves backing $7,053 billion of deposits, a 0.89% reserve ratio. Implementing the non-transaction ruse decreased the U.S. banking system's statutory reserve requirement from $705.3 billion to $63.1 billion, by $642.2 billion or 91%. The U.S. banking system could "only" have issued $924.3 billion of loans before the non-transaction ruse, but issued $6.990 trillion of loans after the non-transaction ruse. If lent at 5% interest, the additional $6.065 trillion of loans generates almost $303 billion of interest payments annually—approximately $1,000 per American.

Banks obtain hundreds of billions of dollars of additional revenue each year from this one simple change in the way that statutory reserve requirements are computed. This revenue comes at a price: decreased reserve levels which mean increased lie-ability exposure. If even modest numbers of depositors attempt to withdraw reserves, banks don't have them and are rupted.

In September 2008 just before The Bailout passed, the U.S. banking system held $7.053 trillion of deposits and had a statutory reserve requirement of $63.1 billion, but actually kept $102.7 billion of reserves. $102.7 billion of reserves backing $7.053 trillion of deposits is a 1.46% reserve ratio. Even with a paltry 1.46% reserve ratio, the U.S. banking system was not loaned up and had $39.6 billion more reserves than regulations required. That is, the U.S. banking system had $39.6 billion of "excess" reserves.

An honest banker would consider a 1.46% reserve ratio obscenely low and feel that they had a catastrophic reserve shortage, but in our corrupt banking system a 1.46% reserve ratio was 164% greater than the statutory reserve ratio requirement. This was just before the U.S. banking system imploded and required trillions of dollars of Bailouts. Fraud this masterful is breathtaking to behold, isn't it?

Just to beat it to death: the law allows $7.053 trillion of deposits to be backed by $102.7 billion of reserves. When $102.7 billion of reserves are deposited into the banking system, the law allows commercial banks to create an additional $6.950 trillion of deposits out of thin air and lend them. As long as such blatant fraud is legalized and considered acceptable banking practice, there will always be Depressions and Bailouts.

In the simple example in which $100 of reserves are deposited into the banking system, it is easy to imagine one person making a single $100 deposit. With $672 billion of deposits, as in the Bank of America example, there are many depositors. It is important to remember that people didn't deposit $672 billion of reserves at Bank of America all at once, nor did they deposit $7.053 trillion of reserves at U.S. banks all at once. This would be impossible because total reserves of the U.S. banking system were "only" $102 billion. Rather, a small amount of reserves are initially deposited into the banking system, and commercial banks create deposits far in excess of those reserves by issuing loans. The ledgers for Bank of America and all banks in America show the money supply after numerous iterations of this deposit creation and loan issuing process.

The difference between the statutory reserve requirement and actual reserve levels confuses some people. In the ledgers in this chapter, the statutory reserve ratio requirement and statutory reserve requirement were computed. The statutory reserve ratio requirement is a percentage. The statutory reserve requirement is an amount of reserves. The statutory reserve ratio requirement is 10% on transaction deposits, 0% on non-transaction deposits. The overall statutory reserve ratio requirement for transaction deposits and non-transaction deposits taken as a whole will be less than 10%, but greater than 0%. The greater the percentage of non-transaction deposits a bank or banking system holds, the closer to 0% the overall statutory reserve ratio requirement will be (which is why banks sweep accounts, as we will see). Banks can't have a lower reserve ratio than the statutory reserve ratio requirement. Banks can hold more reserves than required by the statutory reserve requirement, but not less.

It is also important not to get lulled by the gargantuan sums of money involved. It is easy to begin talking about billions of dollars and small percentages of total deposits as if they were trivial, and to lose sight of their true real world meaning. A bank can honor a huge number of deposits with a "few" billion dollars of additional reserves, and in decreasing reserves by "just" a few billion dollars, a bank is creating an inability to honor a huge number of deposits.

The Monetary Control Act of 1980 created a 0% statutory reserve ratio requirement for non-transaction deposits. Realizing the obscene lie-ability risk this would subject banks to, the Monetary Control Act limited depositors' ability to withdraw funds from non-transaction accounts. Two of the more important limits are "reservation of rights" and "convenient withdrawals."

The fine print of savings account contracts contains a "reservation of rights" clause which requires the depositor to give the bank 7 days notice for any withdrawal. The bank rarely exercises this clause, but it could at any time. Doing so would erode confidence in the banking system and precipitate bank runs, but if a bank faced massive, instantaneous runs the 7-day delay for withdrawals could be used as a stalling tactic while Fed conjured ledger reserves, printed and shipped out physical-currency reserves, and tried to restore confidence. Banks have the legal right to declare a 7-day FDR-style bank holiday anytime they want, at least on savings accounts and other non-transaction accounts which constitute the bulk of their lie-abilities.

Bank Holidays can also be applied to checking accounts called Negotiated Order of Withdrawal (NOW) accounts. NOWs are just a ploy banks came up with to circumvent laws which prevent transaction accounts from paying interest (a restriction which was eliminated during Depression v9.2006-201x). A depositor can demand money from a standard checking transaction account anytime, and the bank must comply immediately. Checks written on NOW accounts are not standard checks that have to be paid immediately, they are actually "negotiated orders of withdrawal" with the negotiated condition that the bank can demand 7 days notice before processing a check. This notice is not usually invoked, but it can be. Having to potentially wait 7 days to withdraw reserves anytime the bank chooses scares many depositors, so few depositors opt for NOWs. By statute, NOWs are considered transaction accounts—checking accounts—and have a 10% statutory reserve ratio requirement.

Again, note the slick Mary Poppins propaganda name: an account from which you may not obtain funds immediately is called a NOW. In Bankerville, everything is called the exact opposite of what it is.

When panic strikes, banks face runs, and financial markets freeze, hours can be an eternity. The ability to not honor deposit contracts for 7 days is a huge ace in the hole for banks.

By law, only 6 withdrawals per month are allowed from non-transaction accounts. This limit on withdrawals keeps sheeple from using non-transaction accounts for day-to-day transactions, which would expose bank lie-abilities. Banks want savings deposits sitting dormant and unused by depositors, so that they don't have to worry about withdrawals that expose lie-abilities. There are of course no limits on deposits into non-transaction accounts, as this provides additional reserves that banks can embezzle and lend, increasing their profit.

Bankers refer to limits on deposit withdrawals as Regulation D, or Reg. D, because they are enumerated in Section D of the portion of the Code of Federal Regulations (CFR) containing the Federal Reserve Act and Monetary Control Act. The Code of Federal Regulations is basically a huge list of every administrative law in America. It makes a set of encyclopedias look like a pamphlet.

Bankers love to use Reg D to blame guv'ment and make it the scapegoat for withdrawal limitations. Hey, we'd love to give you unlimited access to your savings deposits, but we're just following the law. Never mind that banks own Congress and essentially write the laws.

Most commercial banks also set a limit on "convenient withdrawals" from non-transaction accounts. Convenient withdrawals are any withdrawal that is not physical-currency reserves (cash) from an ATM or bank branch. Payments via check, debit card, automatic payment withdrawal, etc., are all "convenient." Banks don't want depositors habitually using non-transaction accounts to make large payments such as mortgages, car loans, etc., so often limit depositors to 3 convenient withdrawals per month, and charge fees for withdrawals in excess of this amount. Few depositors pay large bills such as mortgages using physical-currency reserves, and most depositors want the ability to make withdrawals from savings accounts a few times per month in case of emergency without incurring fees, so limits on convenient withdrawals cause most depositors to avoid using their savings accounts for large regular transactions that cause severe lie-ability exposure.

The Regulation D limit on withdrawals from non-transaction accounts is a ruse which allows banks to promise depositors perpetual access to reserves while simultaneously limiting access to those reserves. With withdrawal demands minimized, reserves can be embezzled and lent out with minimal risk. Deposits which drastically exceed reserves can be created with minimal risk.

Banks have other types of accounts besides just checking and savings accounts, but any deposit with restriction on reserve access is a non-transaction deposit with a 0% reserve requirement, which is most accounts at most banks. NOW checking accounts are the only major exceptions.

Defenders of 0% statutory reserve ratio requirements argue that savings deposits pay interest, which is impossible if the reserves backing savings deposits are not invested. True. It is also true that banks promise to redeem non-transaction deposits upon demand while keeping 0% of those deposits in reserve. Banks should not promise all depositors access to their reserves if that promise can't be honored *simultaneously for all depositors*. For the reserves backing a demandable deposit to be lent, it should be converted to a time deposit. Always. The reserves backing demandable deposits—whether "transaction" deposits or "non-transaction" deposits—should always be warehoused, never lent or invested, as this is the only way a bank can maintain the ability to redeem all deposits for reserves.

At a more fundamental level, claiming that the reserves backing savings deposits are invested is fraudulent. It is preposterous to create an amount of deposits equal to 9 - 100 times reserves, yet claim that some sort of honest reserve investment process is utilized to pay interest on deposits. While any single bank may make this fallacious claim, for the banking system as a whole such a claim is preposterous. Fractional-reserve lending is not a process of accepting a deposit of reserves, investing those reserves to earn interest, paying some of that interest to depositors, and keeping some of that interest as profit. Fractional-reserve lending is a process of fraudulently creating deposits which drastically exceed reserves. Low statutory reserve ratio requirements are not instituted to facilitate the investment of reserves that back deposits, they are instituted to facilitate the creation of deposits that drastically exceed reserves. Any statutory reserve ratio requirement less than 100% is a fraudulent absurdity, and a 0% statutory reserve ratio requirement is a grotesquely fraudulent absurdity.

THE ROAD TO 0% RESERVES PICTURE PAGES

TO SKIP THE PICTURE PAGES AFTER THIS CHAPTER, PLEASE TURN TO PAGE 155

BANK OF AMERICA'S SEPTEMBER 2008 FDIC CALL REPORT

BANK OF AMERICA, NATIONAL ASSOCIATION   FFIEC 031
RSSD-ID 480228   Quarter End Date 9/30/2008
Last Updated on 3/16/2009   23

Dollar amounts in thousands	(Column A) Transaction Accounts Total Transaction accounts (including total demand deposits)	(Column B) Transaction Accounts Memo: Total demand deposits (included in column A)	(Column C) Nontransaction Accounts Total nontransaction accounts (including MMDAs)	
	RCONB551		RCONB552	
4. Commercial banks and other depository institutions in the U.S.......	8,591,442		9,846,109	4.
	RCON2213		RCON2236	
5. Banks in foreign countries.................................	261,364		105,883	5.
6. Foreign governments and official institutions (including foreign central banks)..................................	RCON2216 185,749		RCON2377 163,606	6.
	RCON2215	RCON2210	RCON2385	
7. Total.................................	88,656,723	78,480,834	583,410,654	7.

Schedule RC-E Part I - Deposits in Domestic Offices
Dollar amounts in thousands

1. Selected components of total deposits:			M.1.
a. Total Individual Retirement Accounts (IRAs) and Keogh Plan accounts......................	RCON6835	16,074,727	M.1.a.
b. Total brokered deposits..	RCON2365	32,417	M.1.b.
c. Fully insured brokered deposits (included in Memorandum item 1.b above):			M.1.c.
1. Brokered deposits issued in denominations of less than $100,000......................	RCON2343	32,317	M.1.c.1.
2. Brokered deposits issued in denominations of $100,000 and certain brokered retirement deposit accounts........................	RCON2344	100	M.1.c.2.
d. Maturity data for brokered deposits:			M.1.d.
1. Brokered deposits issued in denominations of less than $100,000 with a remaining maturity of one year or less (included in Memorandum item 1.c.(1) above).............	RCONA243	31,148	M.1.d.1.
2. Brokered deposits issued in denominations of $100,000 or more with a remaining maturity of one year or less (included in Memorandum item 1.b above)................	RCONA244	0	M.1.d.2.
e. Preferred deposits (uninsured deposits of states and political subdivisions in the U.S. reported in item 3 above which are secured or collateralized as required under state law)..	RCON5590	NR	M.1.e.
2. Components of total nontransaction accounts:			M.2.
a. Savings deposits:			M.2.a.
1. Money market deposit accounts (MMDAs)..	RCON6810	238,940,207	M.2.a.1.
2. Other savings deposits (excludes MMDAs).......................................	RCON0352	133,166,338	M.2.a.2.
b. Total time deposits of less than $100,000..	RCON6648	101,278,178	M.2.b.
c. Total time deposits of $100,000 or more..	RCON2604	110,025,931	M.2.c.
1. Individual Retirement Accounts (IRAs) and Keogh Plan accounts included in Memorandum item 2.c, "Total time deposits of $100,000 or more," above................	RCONF233	1,795,434	M.2.c.1.
3. Maturity and repricing data for time deposits of less than $100,000:			M.3.
a. Time deposits of less than $100,000 with a remaining maturity or next repricing date of:			M.3.a.
1. Three months or less..	RCONA579	23,529,878	M.3.a.1.
2. Over three months through 12 months........................	RCONA580	70,411,674	M.3.a.2.
3. Over one year through three years.........................	RCONA581	5,340,043	M.3.a.3.
4. Over three years..	RCONA582	1,996,583	M.3.a.4.
b. Time deposits of less than $100,000 with a REMAINING MATURITY of one year or less (included in Memorandum items 3.a.(1) and 3.a.(2) above)........................	RCONA241	93,941,552	M.3.b.

This is page 23 of the Call Report that Bank of America submitted to the FDIC in September 2008 just before The Bailout passed. In the section "Schedule RC-E Part I - Deposits in Domestic Offices," line items M2a1, M2a2, M2b, and M2c are the individual components of non-transaction deposits. When summed, these 4 items give the total amount of domestic non-transaction deposits, which is $583,410,654,000 or $583 billion. Bank of America held $672 billion of total deposits, $583 billion of which were non-transaction deposits. The remaining $89 billion of deposits were transaction deposits.

10% RESERVE RATIO ON ALL DEPOSITS VS. 10% RESERVE RATIO ON TRANSACTION DEPOSITS FOR A SINGLE BANK

Assets	Liabilities
$10 (Reserves)	$100 (Deposits)
$90 (Loans)	
$100	$100

Total Reserves: $10
Reserve Ratio: 10%
Total Loans: $90

Assets	Liabilities
$2 (Reserves)	$20 (Transaction Deposits)
$18 (Loans)	
$0 (Reserves)	$80 (Non-Transaction Deposits)
$80 (Loans)	
$100	$100

Total Reserves: $2
Reserve Ratio: 2%
Total Loans: $98

The ledger on the left shows a fractional-reserve bank which applies a 10% statutory reserve ratio requirement to all deposits. The ledger on the right shows a fractional-reserve bank which applies a 10% statutory reserve ratio requirement to transaction deposits and a 0% statutory reserve ratio requirement to non-transaction deposits. This 0% statutory reserve ratio requirement drastically decreases overall statutory reserve ratio requirements and increases the amount of loans which banks can issue.

10% RESERVE RATIO ON ALL DEPOSITS VS. 10% RESERVE RATIO ON TRANSACTION DEPOSITS FOR THE U.S. BANKING SYSTEM

```
Assets                          Liabilities
$705,270,000,000  (Reserves)    $7,052,700,000,000  (Deposits)
$6,347,430,000,000 (Loans)

$7,052,700,000,000              $7,052,700,000,000

Total Reserves: $705,270,000,000
Reserve Ratio: 10%
Total Loans: $6,347,430,000,000
```

```
Assets                          Liabilities
$63,110,000,000  (Reserves)     $631,100,000,000  (Transaction Deposits)
$567,990,000,000 (Loans)
$0  (Reserves)                  $6,421,600,000,000 (Non-Transaction Deposits)
$6,421,600,000,000 (Loans)

$7,052,700,000,000              $7,052,700,000,000

Total Reserves: $63,110,000,000
Reserve Ratio: 0.89%
Total Loans: $6,989,590,000,000
```

The upper ledger shows a 10% statutory reserve ratio requirement applied to all deposits. This was not and is not done. The lower ledger shows a 10% statutory reserve ratio requirement applied to transaction deposits and a 0% statutory reserve ratio requirement applied to non-transaction deposits. This decreased the statutory reserve requirement by $642 billion and decreased the statutory reserve ratio requirement from 10% to 0.89%, by 9.11%. The statutory reserve requirement was $63.1 billion, but banks actually kept $102.7 billion of reserves—$39.6 billion more than the statutory reserve requirement, a 1.46% reserve ratio. Banks were not being careful. Rather, the statutory reserve requirement was so absurdly low that it was useless, and allowed banks to set whatever reserve level they wanted.

BANK OF AMERICA WITHDRAWAL LIMITS ON 0% RESERVE SAVINGS ACCOUNTS

Bank of America® Clarity Statement®   **Bank of America** 🇺🇸

Overview of Regular Savings key policies and fees
Your Regular Savings Account

Monthly Maintenance Fee	$5.00 each month	You can avoid the **Monthly Maintenance Fee** when you meet **one** of the following requirements during each statement period:

- Maintain a minimum daily balance of $300 or more, **OR**
- Link your account to your Bank of America Interest Checking® or Bank of America Advantage® account (waiver applies to first 4 savings accounts), **OR**
- Are enrolled in the Preferred Rewards¹ program (waiver applies to first 4 savings accounts)

You can also avoid the Monthly Maintenance Fee if you make combined monthly automatic transfers of $25 or more from your Bank of America checking account to your savings account during the immediately preceding statement cycle.

Withdrawal Limit Fee and Transaction Limitations

	It Applies To	How It Works
Withdrawal Limit Fee	**All** types of withdrawals and transfers from a savings account, including: • ATM withdrawals and transfers • Financial center teller withdrawals • Online and Mobile Banking transfers or payments • Automatic or pre-authorized transfers (includes an automatic payment to a merchant or bank) • Telephone transfers • Checks, drafts or debit card transactions	*Each monthly statement cycle:* • You can make a total of 6 withdrawals and transfers with no Withdrawal Limit Fee • After your first 6, the Withdrawal Limit Fee is **$10.00** for each additional withdrawal or transfer • No more than 6 Withdrawal Limit Fees will be charged • You can avoid the Withdrawal Limit Fee by maintaining a minimum daily balance of $2,500 or more in your savings account If you receive a quarterly statement, please note that we calculate and apply these fees to each monthly period in the quarter. This means that the first 6 transactions in each month of the quarter can be made with no Withdrawal Limit Fee.
Transaction Limitations	**Certain** types of withdrawals and transfers from a savings account, including: • Online and Mobile Banking transfers or payments • Automatic or pre-authorized transfers (includes an automatic payment to a merchant or bank) • Telephone transfers • Checks, drafts or debit card transactions	Certain types of withdrawals and transfers from savings accounts are limited to a total of 6 per monthly cycle. This limit is governed by federal Regulation D and our deposit agreement. However, this limit doesn't apply to transactions made at financial centers, by mail or at an ATM. (Please note that Withdrawal Limit Fees still apply to these types of transactions.) **If you exceed the transaction limitations on more than an occasional basis, we'll convert your account to a checking account that will no longer earn interest.**

The image above is a Bank of America "Clarity Statement" that explains the fee structures for a standard savings account. This was the fee structure in May 2016. The author is not trying to demonize Bank of America, it is simply the largest bank in America and therefore the logical bank to use as an example. All major banks operate in a similar manner.

Bank of America applies a 0% statutory reserve ratio requirement to savings deposits, keeps no reserves to back savings deposits, embezzles the reserves that should back savings deposits, lends these reserves by creating additional savings deposits, "backs" savings deposits with mortgages and other loans that pay a 2% - 10% annual interest rate, and then charges savings depositors a monthly fee! With robust interest rates being earned on the loans backing all savings deposits, interest is effectively being earned on every savings deposit, and there should therefore be no monthly fees, but this doesn't stop Bank of America from gouging customers and charging monthly fees.

The monthly fee is waived if a minimum daily balance of $300 is maintained, which decreases Bank of America's lie-ability exposure because most depositors strive not to dip below the $300 minimum balance. Bank of America has about 57 million American depositors, including small businesses. Assume 50 million depositors. If 50 million sheeple have $500 in a savings account, that is $25 billion in non-transaction deposits. Few sheeple will dip below the $300 minimum balance because they don't want to incur fees, meaning $15 billion (50,000,000 x $300) of the $25 billion won't be withdrawn. This greatly decreases Bank of America's lie-ability risk. It also allows Bank of America to create more deposits than it might otherwise, because it knows that a significant portion of deposits will be savings deposits, and a significant portion of savings deposits will never be demanded.

The monthly fee is also waived if the depositor agrees to an automatic monthly transfer of $25 from a checking account to the savings account. Checking deposits have a 10% statutory reserve ratio requirement and savings deposits have a 0% statutory reserve ratio requirement, so every nickel transferred from checking accounts to savings accounts has its statutory reserve ratio requirement decreased from 10% to 0%. This allows Bank of America to decrease reserve levels. If Bank of America doesn't decrease reserve levels but decreases its statutory reserve ratio requirement, it can create additional deposits and lend them (which will usually decrease reserve levels when reserves are paid out to honor the loan). More on this concept in the Infinite Money Creation chapter. $25 transferred from a checking account to a savings account might not seem like much—until you sum it over tens millions of customers. If 50 million depositors transfer $25 per month from a checking account to a savings account, that is $1.25 billion per month, and $15 billion over a 12-month year. $15 billion lent at 5% interest earns $750 million a year. Almost a billion dollars a year! From this one simple, seemingly innocuous policy! Many depositors choose larger amounts than $25 for their monthly transfer from checking to savings. Also, seeing money transferred from checking accounts to savings accounts on banking statements causes customers to transfer additional money to savings accounts, thereby decreasing Bank of America's reserve requirements further.

The monthly fee is also waived if savings accounts are linked to "Advantage" checking accounts. Linking means that the accounts can be accessed with one debit card, and funds can be transferred between accounts easily. Most banks offer premium checking accounts to depositors with large balances, which include perks like interest payments and waiving service fees that regular customers pay. At Bank of America this premium account is the "Advantage" checking account, and to avoid its $25 monthly service fee depositors must maintain a $5,000 minimum balance. Bank of America would love to have these huge checking account deposits transferred to savings accounts, so that they are subject to a 0% statutory reserve ratio requirement rather than a 10% statutory reserve ratio requirement, and it no longer has to back them with any reserves. Thus four savings accounts can be obtained for free if linked to a large-balance Advantage checking account, because this facilitates the transfer of funds from the checking account to the savings accounts. A few large depositors at a bank may have more money than thousands of normal customers, and encouraging these whales to transfer as much money as possible to savings accounts is critical. The minimum balance requirements for premium checking accounts usually include the balances in linked savings accounts, to further encourage transfer of funds to savings accounts.

Banks summarize withdrawal limitations, fee structures, and account features without explaining their true purpose: to maximize non-transaction deposits subject to a 0% statutory reserve ratio requirement, minimize transaction deposits subject to a 10% statutory reserve ratio requirement, and prevent reserve withdrawals that expose lie-abilities. You could visit the websites of thousands of banks, and each would have info similar to Bank of America's. You will never find a candid summary of the 0% statutory reserve ratio requirement for non-transaction deposits on any bank website, brochure, contract, nor any other communication designed for sheeple.

The Bank of America "Clarity Statement" also explains the "Withdrawal Limit Fee" and "Transaction Limits" for savings accounts. As Bank of America applies a 0% statutory reserve ratio requirement to savings accounts, it could be rupted very easily if depositors were given freedom to use savings accounts for day-to-day transactions. Depositors are therefore only allowed 6 free withdrawals per month on their savings account—"convenient" or otherwise. Each additional withdrawal costs $10! This limits demands for reserves, and gouges depositors with unnecessary fees if they attempt to demand reserves.

A defender of fraudulent fractional-reserve lending would argue that savings by definition is not intended to be accessed frequently or used for day-to-day transactions. That is why you *save* money. Of course savings deposits have a 0% statutory reserve ratio requirement, they have to be invested to pay interest! True, yet again. Though it must yet again be emphasized that no matter what a deposit is called, if the reserves backing it are promised upon demand and simultaneously lent out, or if multiple deposits which exceed reserves are simply created, the bank doing so is insolvent and committing fraud. To invest the reserves backing demand deposits in an ethical manner, the demand deposits should be converted to time deposits. Also, it must yet again be emphasized that fractional-reserve lending creates deposits that exceed reserves and fraudulently attempts to back multiple deposits with reserves that should only back a single deposit. This is far different than honestly lending the reserves backing a single deposit.

You may be willing to pay "Withdrawal Limit Fees" to access reserves that should be freely available, but even then you are only allowed 12 withdrawals per month. Bank of America's "Clarity Statement" notes that "No more than 6 Withdrawal Limit Fees will be charged." What this means in real-world terms is that a depositor can make 6 free withdrawals and 6 more which are charged a $10 "Withdrawal Limit Fee." By the time the 13th withdrawal is reached, Bank of America will have warned the depositor to limit withdrawals in the future or convert the savings account to a checking account. They can't let depositors use savings accounts for day-to-day transactions, as this would bank-rupt them. Bank of America generally won't issue the warning until the 13th withdrawal is reached though, so that they can make the easy $60 off "Withdrawal Limit Fees."

The 12-withdrawal scenario assumes that all 12 withdrawals are currency withdrawals from an ATM or a brick & mortar bank branch. Such withdrawals are necessarily small, as ATMs have withdrawal limits, banks demand notice for large currency withdrawals, and few people make large payments in cash regardless. If any of the withdrawals are not physical cash, then Regulation D limitations come into play. Regulation D covers the non-currency, non-physical-cash transactions that are the bulk of all economic activity. If your savings account withdrawals are online bill payments or transfers, automatic or pre-authorized payments or transfers, transfers by telephone, or any checks, drafts, or debit card transactions, then only 6 per month are allowed by Regulation D. If you conduct these sorts of transactions using your "non-transaction" account more than 6 times a month, it must be converted to a transaction account. Federal law forces banks to do this. Banks can't use the term transaction account and non-transaction account without making sheeple suspicious, so the language is massaged.

The Regulation D withdrawal limit was imposed to prevent irresponsible banks from creating huge amounts of non-transaction deposits, applying a 0% statutory reserve ratio requirement, keeping no reserves to back the huge amount of non-transaction deposits, and being rupted when depositors made frequent, erratic withdrawals that exposed reserve shortages. Anytime depositors use non-transaction accounts more than 6 times a month, the accounts are converted into transaction accounts which are subject to a 10% statutory reserve ratio requirement. The statutory reserve ratio requirement on converted accounts instantaneously increases from 0% to 10%. When this happens, Bank of America must obtain reserves to back the converted deposit. Bank of America may have "excess" reserves, but if it doesn't, it must obtain additional reserves. Bank of America therefore tries to discourage such conversions by warning that converted accounts may no longer earn interest. Not for the depositor anyway. 90% of the reserves that should back a converted transaction deposit can still be embezzled and lent by Bank of America, and earn interest for it.

BANKS ENCOURAGE TRANSFERS TO SAVINGS ACCOUNTS TO REDUCE RESERVES

Bank of America

Keep the Change® Savings Program

Spend with your debit card. Add to your savings. Only at Bank of America.

Every time you buy something with a Bank of America Visa® debit card[1], we'll round up your purchase to the nearest dollar amount and transfer the difference from your checking to your savings account[2] free of charge. Because every bag of groceries, every coffee and every tank of gas adds up to more savings for you.

So you get to keep the change and grow your savings. What could be easier?

We'll even match your savings.

For the first three months, we'll match your Keep the Change™ savings at 100%. That means for every Keep the Change transfer, we'll contribute the same amount to your Bank of America savings account. And when the three months are over, to make it even easier to save, we'll continue matching 5% a year, every year[3].

Many seemingly altruistic bank policies have hidden purposes that only become apparent once you understand the fractional-reserve scam. One example is Bank of America's "Keep the Change" program. An image of a portion of the Keep the Change webpage is shown above. Technological limitations prevent website images of exceptional clarity, but this website image and others throughout the book have been made as clear and readable as possible.

The "Keep the Change" program rounds every debit card transaction up to the nearest dollar and this "change" amount is transferred from a customer's checking account to their savings account. If you purchase a Coke for $1.27, the transaction would be rounded up to $2.00, and the 73¢ difference—the change—is transferred from your checking account to your savings account.

Bank of America wants to help you save and really cares about you. Right?

Wrong.

Ever see someone put all their change into a bottle or bowl? It fills up fast. Now imagine doing the same thing virtually on computers with billions of dollars of economic transactions by millions of customers. All this "change" is transferred from transaction accounts with a 10% statutory reserve ratio requirement into non-transaction accounts with a 0% statutory reserve ratio requirement. This allows Bank of America to increase the amount of deposits it can create and lend, without attracting more depositors of reserves or increasing its total amount of reserves.

This additional deposit creation is so lucrative to Bank of America that when depositors sign-up for "Keep the Change," it will match their savings for three months. For ninety days, Bank of America will give depositors an amount of money equal to the amount that they transfer from checking to savings using Keep the Change. After the three-month period of 100% matching ends, Bank of America will give depositors an amount of money equal to 5% of the amount that they transfer from checking to savings using Keep the Change. This 5% matching will continue indefinitely.

No honest bank could afford such largesse. When a bank is willing to simply give hundreds of dollars to tens of millions of customers—billions of dollars total—this should make sheeple suspicious. It of course doesn't. Bank of America was willing to give depositors more than a billion dollars to "Keep the Change" because it would make far more than this off the loan money conjured as a result of the decreased statutory reserve requirement which the program creates.

"Keep the Change" exploits most people's unwillingness to change. Once most people enroll in the program, they will keep using it indefinitely. This means that every time people use their debit cards for day-to-day transactions, they transfer money out of their checking accounts into savings accounts and increase the amount of loan money Bank of America can conjure and loan.

Bank of America may "Keep the Change," but it certainly doesn't keep the reserves. Each policy at banks is carefully crafted to abet fractional-reserve lending, in ways which sheeple are not told and are unaware of.

THE RESERVE REQUIREMENT EXEMPTION & LOW-RESERVE TRANCHE

"The burden of reserve requirements is structured to bear generally less heavily on smaller institutions. At every depository institution, a certain amount of reservable liabilities [liabilities such as deposits which must be backed by reserves] is exempt from reserve requirements, and a relatively low required reserve ratio is applied to reservable liabilities up to a specific level. The amounts of reservable liabilities exempt from reserve requirements and subject to the low required reserve ratio are adjusted annually to reflect growth in the banking system."
—*The Federal Reserve System Purposes & Functions*, Federal Reserve Publication

"Requiring depositories to hold idle, non-interest-bearing balances [reserves] is essentially like taxing these institutions in an amount equal to the interest they could have earned on these balances in the absence of reserve requirements."
—1993 *Federal Reserve Bulletin*

Banks constantly scheme ways to decrease reserve requirements so they can create and lend more deposits. The Federal Reserve is happy to help them, as the *Bulletin* quote above indicates. In the Fed's view, forcing "depositories" (banks) to hold reserves to honor deposits is like taxing them! This despite the fact that banks create exorbitant amounts of deposits which dwarf reserves, and essentially earn interest on a single deposit of reserves multiple times. To analyze such a system of rampant deposit creation and exorbitant profit, and demonize the paltry amount of reserves that banks hold by characterizing them as "a tax" is not just astounding, but absolutely diabolical. To let commercial banks create $6.95 trillion out of thin air and loan that money at interest, and then complain that the $102 billion of reserves backing the deposits are a "tax" is despicable. Fed lets each individual bank embezzle and lend more than 98% of the reserves backing deposits, and then argues that the remaining 2% of reserves that were not embezzled are a tax because they could also earn money if embezzled and lent. Fed isn't just in bed with banks, it puts the condom on for them to make sure the rape of the citizenry will be safe sex. Taxpayers spent trillions of dollars bailing out banks, and Fed's rationale for the meager reserve requirements that created the need for The Bailout is a desire not to "tax" banks! Any claim that Fed is a regulator of banks or a protector of the American people is farcical.

As shown, a 0% statutory reserve ratio requirement is applied to non-transaction deposits, and a 10% statutory reserve ratio requirement is applied to transaction deposits. Sort of. In 2012, a bank's first $11.5 million in transaction deposits were subject to a 0% statutory reserve ratio requirement. Transaction deposits over $11.5 million and up to and including $71.0 million—$59.5 million worth—were subject to a 3% statutory reserve ratio requirement. Transaction deposits above $71.0 million were subject to the 10% statutory reserve ratio requirement. As the 10% statutory reserve ratio requirement applies to most bank deposits, it is usually cited.

Here are the 2012 statutory reserve ratio requirements for different deposits, presented in table form:

Deposit Type	Cutoff	Statutory Reserve Ratio Requirement	Name
Transaction	$0 to $11.5 million	0%	Reserve Requirement Exemption
Transaction	$11.5 million to $71.0 million	3%	Low-Reserve Tranche
Transaction	Above $71.0 million	10%	Standard Reserve Requirement
Non-Transaction	All non-transaction deposits	0%	No Reserve Requirement

The cutoff at $11.5 million is called the "Reserve Requirement Exemption." For a bank's first $11.5 million of deposits, there is no statutory reserve requirement, banks are exempt from the reserve requirement, it is a Reserve Requirement Exemption.

A tranche is a slice or portion of something. For example, M-BSs (Mortgage-Backed Securities) combined "tranches" of low quality mortgages with "tranches" of high quality mortgages. The Low-Reserve Tranche is that portion of transaction deposits which have a low-reserve requirement, that is, a reserve requirement less than the normal or "high" reserve requirement of 10%. A tranche of transaction deposits over $11.5 million and up to and including $71.0 million had a low-reserve ratio of 3%. This is the Low-Reserve Tranche.

Bankers would say that the Reserve Requirement Exemption in 2012 was $11.5 million and the Low-Reserve Tranche in 2012 was $71.0 million. Other bankers would know exactly what they are talking about. Bankers would understand that the first $11.5 million of deposits were subject to a 0% statutory reserve ratio requirement, and the next $59.5 of deposits ($71 million - $11.5 million = $59.5 million) were subject to a 3% statutory reserve ratio requirement

The Federal Reserve indexes the Reserve Requirement Exemption and Low-Reserve Tranche just like Social Security, increasing them each year to account for the ever increasing money supply. Bankers understand the inflation scam, and are not dumb enough to agree to any fixed-number cutoff for the Reserve Requirement Exemption and Low-Reserve Tranche that is not increased and which is therefore subject to bracket creep. If the total deposit supply increases, but the Reserve Requirement Exemption and Low-Reserve Tranche don't increase, then a smaller percentage of total deposits qualify for the Reserve Requirement Exemption and Low-Reserve Tranche. Bankers won't let themselves get shafted the way sheeple do with income tax bracket creep, in which an increasing money supply increases annual pay, bumping sheeple who are earning less real wealth into higher tax brackets, forcing them to surrender more wealth to guv'ment. More information about bracket creep is available on pages 30 and 171 of *Bubblenomics*. The Reserve Requirement Exemption was $10.7 million in 2010, $11.5 million in 2011, a 7.5% increase. The Low-Reserve Tranche was $58.8 million in 2010, $71.0 million in 2011, a 20.7% increase. These increases are indexed according to the increase in bank deposits that are literally the money supply. When adjusting for inflation for bankers, the Fed doesn't use the bogus 3% inflation rate it feeds sheeple.

For large banks with billions of dollars of deposits, the Reserve Requirement Exemption and Low-Reserve Tranche only apply to a miniscule portion of deposits, and have a negligible effect on overall statutory reserve ratio requirements. For small and medium-sized banks with millions of dollars of deposits, the Reserve Requirement Exemption and Low-Reserve Tranche apply to a significant portion of deposits, and greatly decrease overall statutory reserve ratio requirements.

In September 2008 just before The Bailout passed, Bank of America had about $6 in non-transaction deposits for every $1 in transaction deposits, and the U.S. banking system as a whole had about $10 in non-transaction deposits for every $1 in non-transaction deposits. The exact distribution of non-transaction and transaction deposits varies bank to bank with customer preferences (and with the aggressiveness of sweeping, as we'll see), but as a rough approximation, assume Bank of America's 6-to-1 ratio is the nationwide average. We chose Bank of America's 6-to-1 ratio rather than the 10-to-1 ratio for the banking system as a whole because sweeping converts transaction deposits to non-transaction deposits, increasing the amount of non-transaction deposits and decreasing the amount of transaction deposits, thereby increasing the ratio of non-transaction deposits to transaction deposits unnaturally. You won't understand that totally until you read the SweepsTakes chapter, for now just accept that the 6-to-1 ratio of non-transaction deposits to transaction deposits is more realistic.

Twelfth Tranche Bank has $497 million in total deposits and $6 of non-transaction deposits for every $1 of transaction deposits, which is $426 million in non-transaction deposits and $71 million in transaction deposits. Twelfth Tranche Bank's statutory reserve ratio requirement on the $426 million in non-transaction deposits would be 0%, its statutory reserve ratio requirement on the first $11.5 million of transaction deposits would be 0% (Reserve Requirement Exemption), and its statutory reserve ratio requirement on the remaining $59.5 million of transaction deposits would be 3% or $1.785 million (Low-Reserve Tranche). Twelfth Tranche Bank has $497 million of deposits but could legally hold a mere $1.785 million of reserves to back those deposits—a 0.3% reserve ratio, about 1/3 of 1%. $1 of reserves for every $278 deposits.

In September 2008 just before The Bailout passed, more than 6,000 banks in America each had less than $497 million of deposits. That is, more than 6,000 banks in America each had less than half a billion dollars of deposits. These calculations are rough, but there are thousands of banks which can legally attain an overall statutory reserve ratio requirement of less than 1%, and probably less than 0.5%. It is not absurd to say that there are probably more than 5,000 U.S. banks with an overall statutory reserve requirement of less than 1%. That is without resorting to sweeps.

A bank with $11.5 million in transaction deposits applies a 0% statutory reserve ratio requirement to its non-transaction deposits and a 0% statutory reserve ratio requirement to its transaction deposits (Reserve Requirement Exemption), and has an overall statutory reserve ratio requirement of 0%. Such a bank is legally allowed to hold no reserves. Applying Bank of America's 6-to-1 non-transaction deposit to transaction deposit ratio, a bank with $80.1 million in total deposits would have $69 million in non-transaction deposits, and $11.5 million in transaction deposits. Roughly 2,500 U.S. commercial banks hold $80.1 million of deposits or less, are subject to a statutory reserve ratio requirement of 0%, and could legally hold no reserves. A bank can't hold no reserves, as it needs reserves to honor day-to-day depositor withdrawals and transactions, but this doesn't change the fact that banking regulations are absurdly lax.

Let's follow the process on ledgers. Eighth Exemption Bank has $80.1 million of deposits and $6 of non-transaction deposits for every $1 of transaction deposits, which is $68.6 million of non-transaction deposits and $11.5 million of transaction deposits. Eighth Exemption Bank's initial ledger with a 10% statutory reserve ratio requirement for all transaction deposits and a 0% statutory reserve ratio requirement for all non-transaction deposits:

Assets	Liabilities
$1,150,000 (Reserves)	$11,500,000 (Transaction Deposits)
$10,350,000 (Loans)	
$0 (Reserves)	$68,600,000 (Non-Transaction Deposits)
$68,600,000 (Loans)	
$80,100,000	$80,100,000

1.44% Reserve Ratio

Eighth Exemption Bank's ledger after combining reserves and loans:

Assets	Liabilities
$1,150,000 (Reserves)	$11,500,000 (Transaction Deposits)
$78,950,000 (Loans)	$68,600,000 (Non-Transaction Deposits)
$80,100,000	$80,100,000

1.44% Reserve Ratio

Eighth Exemption Bank has $1.15 million of reserves backing $80.1 million of deposits, a 1.44% reserve ratio.

Eighth Exemption Bank applies the Reserve Requirement Exemption. Eighth Exemption Bank's first $11.5 million of transaction deposits are exempt from reserve requirements and therefore subject to a 0% statutory reserve ratio requirement:

```
Assets                              Liabilities
        $0 (Reserves)               $11,500,000 (Transaction Deposits)
$11,500,000 (Loans)
        $0 (Reserves)               $68,600,000 (Non-Transaction Deposits)
$68,600,000 (Loans)
_____
$80,100,000                         $80,100,000
                                              0% Reserve Ratio
```

Eight Exemption Bank's ledger after combining reserves and loans:

```
Assets                              Liabilities
        $0 (Reserves)               $11,500,000 (Transaction Deposits)
$80,100,000 (Loans)                 $68,600,000 (Non-Transaction Deposits)
_____
$80,100,000                         $80,100,000
                                              0% Reserve Ratio
```

Eighth Exemption Bank has $0 of reserves backing $80.1 million of deposits, a 0% reserve ratio. Applying the Reserve Requirement Exemption decreased Eighth Exemption Bank's statutory reserve requirement from $1.15 million to $0.

Twelfth Tranche Bank has $497 million of deposits and $6 of non-transaction deposits for every $1 of transaction deposits, which is $426 million of non-transaction deposits and $71 million of transaction deposits. Twelfth Tranche Bank's initial ledger with a 10% statutory reserve ratio requirement for all transaction deposits and a 0% statutory reserve ratio requirement for all non-transaction deposits:

```
Assets                              Liabilities
  $7,100,000 (Reserves)             $71,000,000 (Transaction Deposits)
 $63,900,000 (Loans)
         $0 (Reserves)              $426,000,000 (Non-Transaction Deposits)
$426,000,000 (Loans)
_____
$497,000,000                        $497,000,000
                                              1.43% Reserve Ratio
```

Twelfth Tranche Bank's ledger after combining reserves and loans:

```
Assets                               Liabilities
  #7,100,000 (Reserves)                #71,000,000 (Transaction Deposits)
$489,900,000 (Loans)                  #426,000,000 (Non-Transaction Deposits)

#497,000,000                          #497,000,000
                                              1.43% Reserve Ratio
```

Twelfth Tranche Bank has $7.1 million of reserves backing $497 million of deposits, a 1.43% reserve ratio.

Twelfth Tranche Bank applies the Reserve Requirement Exemption and Low-Reserve Tranche. Twelfth Tranche Bank's first $11.5 million of transaction deposits are subject to a 0% statutory reserve ratio requirement (Reserve Requirement Exemption), and its next $59.5 million of transaction deposits are subject to a 3% statutory reserve ratio requirement (Low-Reserve Tranche):

```
Assets                               Liabilities
         $0 (Reserves)                $11,500,000 (Transaction Deposits)
$11,500,000 (Loans)
 $1,785,000 (Reserves)                $59,500,000 (Transaction Deposits)
$57,715,000 (Loans)
         $0 (Reserves)               #426,000,000 (Non-Transaction Deposits)
$426,000,000 (Loans)

#497,000,000                          #497,000,000
                                              0.36% Reserve Ratio
```

Twelfth Tranche Bank's ledger after combining reserves and loans:

```
Assets                               Liabilities
 $1,785,000 (Reserves)                $71,000,000 (Transaction Deposits)
$495,215,000 (Loans)                  #426,000,000 (Non-Transaction Deposits)

#497,000,000                          #497,000,000
                                              0.36% Reserve Ratio
```

Twelfth Tranche Bank has $1.785 million of reserves backing $497 million of deposits, a 0.36% reserve ratio. Applying the Reserve Requirement Exemption and Low-Reserve Tranche decreased Twelfth Tranche Bank's reserve requirement from $7.1 million to $1.785 million, by $5.315 million or 75%.

First Fraud Bank has $11 billion of deposits and $6 of non-transaction deposits for every $1 of transaction deposits, which is $9.4 billion of non-transaction deposits and $1.6 billion of transaction deposits. First Fraud Bank's initial ledger with a 10% statutory reserve ratio requirement for all transaction deposits and a 0% statutory reserve ratio requirement for all non-transaction deposits:

Assets		Liabilities	
$160,000,000	(Reserves)	$1,600,000,000	(Transaction Deposits)
$1,440,000,000	(Loans)		
$0	(Reserves)	$9,400,000,000	(Non-Transaction Deposits)
$9,400,000,000	(Loans)		
$11,000,000,000		$11,000,000,000	
		1.45% Reserve Ratio	

First Fraud Bank's ledger after combining reserves and loans:

Assets		Liabilities	
$160,000,000	(Reserves)	$1,600,000,000	(Transaction Deposits)
$10,840,000,000	(Loans)	$9,400,000,000	(Non-Transaction Deposits)
$11,000,000,000		$11,000,000,000	
		1.45% Reserve Ratio	

First Fraud Bank has $160 million of reserves backing $11 billion of deposits, a 1.45% reserve ratio.

First Fraud Bank applies the Reserve Requirement Exemption and Low-Reserve Tranche. First Fraud Bank's first $11.5 million of transaction deposits are subject to a 0% statutory reserve ratio requirement (Reserve Requirement Exemption), its next $59.5 million of transaction deposits are subject to a 3% statutory reserve ratio requirement (Low-Reserve Tranche), and its remaining $1,529 million ($1.529 billion) of transaction deposits are subject to the standard 10% statutory reserve ratio requirement:

Assets	Liabilities
$0 (Reserves)	$11,500,000 (Transaction Deposits)
$11,500,000 (Loans)	
$1,785,000 (Reserves)	$59,500,000 (Transaction Deposits)
$57,715,000 (Loans)	
$152,900,000 (Reserves)	$1,529,000,000 (Transaction Deposits)
$1,447,100,000 (Loans)	
$0 (Reserves)	$9,400,000,000 (Non-Transaction Deposits)
$9,400,000,000 (Loans)	
$11,000,000,000	$11,000,000,000
	1.41% Reserve Ratio

First Fraud Bank's ledger after combining reserves and loans:

Assets	Liabilities
$154,685,000 (Reserves)	$1,600,000,000 (Transaction Deposits)
$10,845,315,000 (Loans)	$9,400,000,000 (Non-Transaction Deposits)
$11,000,000,000	$11,000,000,000
	1.41% Reserve Ratio

First Fraud Bank has $154.7 million of reserves backing $11 billion of deposits, a 1.41% reserve ratio. Applying the Reserve Requirement Exemption and Low-Reserve Tranche decreased First Fraud Bank's reserve requirement from $160 million to $154.7 million, by $5.3 million or 3.3%.

Applying the Reserve Requirement Exemption and Low-Reserve Tranche "only" decreased First Fraud Bank's reserve requirement by $5.3 million. As the $71 million of transaction deposits which qualify for the Reserve Requirement Exemption and Low-Reserve Tranche were but a small fraction of First Fraud Bank's total transaction deposits, they did not decrease First Fraud Bank's overall statutory reserve ratio requirement significantly. Contrast this with Eighth Exemption Bank and Twelfth Tranche Bank, which were able to drastically decrease their overall statutory reserve ratio requirements.

In general, as a bank's total amount of deposits increases, the percentage of its deposits which qualify for the Reserve Requirement Exemption and Low-Reserve Tranche decreases, and the Reserve Requirement Exemption and Low-Reserve Tranche decrease its overall statutory reserve ratio requirement to an ever-diminishing degree. Conversely, as a bank's total amount of deposits decreases, the percentage of its deposits which qualify for the Reserve Requirement Exemption and Low-Reserve Tranche increases, and the Reserve Requirement Exemption and

Low-Reserve Tranche decrease its overall statutory reserve ratio requirement to an increasing degree.

The Reserve Requirement Exemption and Low-Reserve Tranche primarily benefit smaller banks, but most banks are smaller banks. The Fed argues that smaller banks are highly localized, know their communities, and can therefore lend smartly and manage their loan portfolios aggressively. This is but one of the many fallacious justifications for such low reserve levels.

There is no justification for such low reserve levels. All banks keeping such low reserve levels eventually have their lie-abilities exposed, are rupted, and require Bailouts.

No commercial bank could hold no reserves. A commercial bank must keep some reserves to operate, including physical-currency reserves that customers withdraw, and ledger reserves deposited in bank accounts at the Federal Reserve which are used to make digital reserve payments to other banks. Though no commercial bank could hold no reserves, it is comforting to know that draconian banking "regulations" allow so much flexibility.

From a profitability standpoint, lower reserve requirements are better for a bank, as they allow the bank to issue more loans. Through trial and error, banks have determined the lowest reserve ratio which they can maintain. 1% - 2% is usually the absolute lowest reserve ratio possible, and is the ratio which the most greedy and irresponsible banks strive for. This is most banks. Keeping such paltry reserve levels is incredibly risky, but banks don't care about the risk because they bank on Bailouts in which reserves are lent by government or conjured by the Fed, alleviating lie-ability exposure. To banks, keeping any more reserves than the bare minimum needed to honor depositor withdrawals and process payments in their Fed accounts is uneconomical. Banks care only about creating and lending as much deposit money as possible to maximize profit.

Banks want, and easily obtain, statutory reserve requirements that are well below the reserve levels they must maintain to honor depositor withdrawals and process payments in their Fed accounts. This allows them to set whatever reserve levels they choose and to be essentially unregulated.

THE RESERVE REQUIREMENT EXEMPTION & LOW-RESERVE TRANCHE PICTURE PAGES

TO SKIP THE PICTURE PAGES AFTER THIS CHAPTER, PLEASE TURN TO PAGE 172

RESERVE RATIO ON INCREASING AMOUNTS OF TRANSACTION DEPOSITS
USING 2012 RESERVE REQUIREMENT EXEMPTION & LOW-RESERVE TRANCHE

	Total Transaction Deposits	Low Reserve Tranche	Standard Reserve Requirement	Total Reserves	Reserve Ratio
1	$0	$0	$0	$0	0.0%
2	$1,000,000	$0	$0	$0	0.0%
3	$2,000,000	$0	$0	$0	0.0%
4	$3,000,000	$0	$0	$0	0.0%
5	$4,000,000	$0	$0	$0	0.0%
6	$5,000,000	$0	$0	$0	0.0%
7	$6,000,000	$0	$0	$0	0.0%
8	$7,000,000	$0	$0	$0	0.0%
9	$8,000,000	$0	$0	$0	0.0%
10	$9,000,000	$0	$0	$0	0.0%
11	$10,000,000	$0	$0	$0	0.0%
12	$11,000,000	$0	$0	$0	0.0%
13	$11,500,000	$0	$0	$0	0.0%
14	$11,500,001	$0.03	$0	$0.03	0.0%
15	$12,000,000	$15,000	$0	$15,000	0.1%
16	$13,000,000	$45,000	$0	$45,000	0.3%
17	$14,000,000	$75,000	$0	$75,000	0.5%
18	$15,000,000	$105,000	$0	$105,000	0.7%
19	$16,000,000	$135,000	$0	$135,000	0.8%
20	$17,000,000	$165,000	$0	$165,000	1.0%
21	$18,000,000	$195,000	$0	$195,000	1.1%
22	$19,000,000	$225,000	$0	$225,000	1.2%
23	$20,000,000	$255,000	$0	$255,000	1.3%
24	$21,000,000	$285,000	$0	$285,000	1.4%
25	$31,000,000	$585,000	$0	$585,000	1.9%
26	$41,000,000	$885,000	$0	$885,000	2.2%
27	$51,000,000	$1,185,000	$0	$1,185,000	2.3%
28	$61,000,000	$1,485,000	$0	$1,485,000	2.4%
29	$71,000,000	$1,785,000	$0	$1,785,000	2.5%
30	$71,000,001	$1,785,000	$0.10	$1,785,000.10	2.5%
31	$81,000,000	$1,785,000	$1,000,000	$2,785,000	3.4%
32	$91,000,000	$1,785,000	$2,000,000	$3,785,000	4.2%
33	$100,000,000	$1,785,000	$2,900,000	$4,685,000	4.7%
34	$200,000,000	$1,785,000	$12,900,000	$14,685,000	7.3%
35	$300,000,000	$1,785,000	$22,900,000	$24,685,000	8.2%
36	$400,000,000	$1,785,000	$32,900,000	$34,685,000	8.7%
37	$500,000,000	$1,785,000	$42,900,000	$44,685,000	8.9%
38	$600,000,000	$1,785,000	$52,900,000	$54,685,000	9.1%
39	$700,000,000	$1,785,000	$62,900,000	$64,685,000	9.2%
40	$800,000,000	$1,785,000	$72,900,000	$74,685,000	9.3%
41	$900,000,000	$1,785,000	$82,900,000	$84,685,000	9.4%
42	$1,000,000,000	$1,785,000	$92,900,000	$94,685,000	9.5%
43	$2,000,000,000	$1,785,000	$192,900,000	$194,685,000	9.7%
44	$3,000,000,000	$1,785,000	$292,900,000	$294,685,000	9.8%
45	$4,000,000,000	$1,785,000	$392,900,000	$394,685,000	9.9%
46	$5,000,000,000	$1,785,000	$492,900,000	$494,685,000	9.9%
47	$6,000,000,000	$1,785,000	$592,900,000	$594,685,000	9.9%
48	$7,000,000,000	$1,785,000	$692,900,000	$694,685,000	9.9%
49	$8,000,000,000	$1,785,000	$792,900,000	$794,685,000	9.9%
50	$9,000,000,000	$1,785,000	$892,900,000	$894,685,000	9.9%
51	$10,000,000,000	$1,785,000	$992,900,000	$994,685,000	9.9%
52	$11,000,000,000	$1,785,000	$1,092,900,000	$1,094,685,000	10.0%

The table on the previous page shows the overall reserve ratio on increasing amounts of transaction deposits. The first $11.5 million of transaction deposits qualify for the Reserve Requirement Exemption and are subject to a 0% statutory reserve ratio requirement. In row 14 the deposit amount jumps from $11,500,000 to $11,500,001, and the 3% statutory reserve ratio requirement for the Low-Reserve Tranche is applied for the first time. The 3% statutory reserve ratio requirement for the Low-Reserve Tranche is applied to the next $59.5 million of deposits, until there are $71,000,000 of deposits. In row 30, the deposit amount jumps from $71,000,000 to $71,000,001, and the 10% statutory reserve ratio requirement for the Standard Reserve Requirement is applied for the first time. The 10% Standard Reserve Requirement is applied to all additional transaction deposits. In the table, "Total Reserves" are reserves for the Low-Reserve Tranche plus reserves for the Standard Reserve Requirement. The ratio of total reserves to total transaction deposits is the reserve ratio for transaction deposits, which is "Reserve Ratio" in the table.

Without the Reserve Requirement Exemption and Low-Reserve Tranche, all banks would apply a 10% statutory reserve ratio requirement to all transaction deposits. With the Reserve Requirement Exemption and Low-Reserve Tranche decreasing the overall statutory reserve ratio requirement, only banks with at least $11 billion of transaction deposits apply a 10% statutory reserve ratio requirement to transaction deposits, as shown on line 52 of the table. Banks with an amount of transaction deposits less than $11 billion are able to decrease their overall statutory reserve ratio requirement below 10%. At a 6-to-1 non-transaction to transaction deposit ratio, a bank with $11 billion of transaction deposits would have $66 billion of non-transaction deposits and $77 billion total deposits. There are roughly 7,000 banks in America, but less than 24 have more than $77 billion of deposits. All banks except for these huge banks benefit from the Reserve Requirement Exemption and Low-Reserve Tranche.

The reserve ratio shown in the previous table is not the reserve ratio for all deposits, it is just the reserve ratio for transaction deposits. As no reserves are set aside to back non-transaction deposits, reserves for transaction deposits also back non-transaction deposits. The overall reserve ratio for all deposits (transaction deposits and non-transaction deposits) will therefore be much lower than the reserve ratio shown on this table. For example, a bank with $11 billion of transaction deposits and $66 billion of non-transaction deposits applies a 10% overall statutory reserve ratio requirement to its $11 billion of transaction deposits and a 0% statutory reserve ratio requirement to its non-transaction deposits, and its overall statutory reserve ratio requirement is 1.4%, which is $1.1 billion. $1.1 billion of reserves backs $77 billion of deposits, meaning each $1 of reserves backs $70 of deposits.

RESERVE REQUIREMENT EXEMPTION AND LOW-RESERVE TRANCHE SINCE 1982
ALL AMOUNTS MILLIONS OF DOLLARS

Date Implemented	Reserve Requirement Exemption	% Change from Previous Year	Low-Reserve Tranche	% Change from Previous Year
January 14, 1982	26.0	N/A	2.1	N/A
December 23, 1982	26.0	0%	2.1	0%
January 13, 1983	26.3	1%	2.1	0%
January 12, 1984	28.9	10%	2.2	5%
January 3, 1985	29.8	3%	2.4	9%
January 2, 1986	31.7	6%	2.6	8%
January 1, 1987	36.7	16%	2.9	12%
December 31, 1987	40.5	10%	3.2	10%
December 29, 1988	41.5	2%	3.4	6%
December 28, 1989	40.4	-3%	3.4	0%
December 27, 1990	41.1	2%	3.4	0%
December 26, 1991	42.2	3%	3.6	6%
December 24, 1992	46.8	11%	3.8	6%
December 23, 1993	51.9	11%	4.0	5%
December 22, 1994	54.0	4%	4.2	5%
December 21, 1995	52.0	-4%	4.3	2%
December 31, 1996	49.3	-5%	4.4	2%
January 1, 1998	47.8	-3%	4.7	7%
December 31, 1998	46.5	-3%	4.9	4%
December 30, 1999	44.3	-5%	5.0	2%
December 28, 2000	42.8	-3%	5.5	10%
December 27, 2001	41.3	-4%	5.7	4%
December 26, 2002	42.1	2%	6.0	5%
December 25, 2003	45.4	8%	6.6	10%
December 23, 2004	47.6	5%	7.0	6%
December 22, 2005	48.3	1%	7.8	11%
December 21, 2006	45.8	-5%	8.5	9%
December 20, 2007	43.9	-4%	9.3	9%
January 1, 2009	44.4	1%	10.3	11%
December 31, 2009	55.2	24%	10.7	4%
December 30, 2010	58.8	7%	10.7	0%
December 29, 2011	71.0	21%	11.5	7%
December 27, 2012	79.5	12%	12.4	8%
January 23, 2014	89.0	12%	13.3	7%
January 22, 2015	103.6	16%	14.5	9%
January 21, 2016	110.2	7%	15.2	5%

The total amount of transaction deposits in the U.S. banking system usually increases each year, so the Reserve Requirement Exemption and Low-Reserve Tranche are also usually increased to index them for inflation, as shown in the table above. A stark exception is the years 1995 - 2001, when the Reserve Requirement Exemption decreased. During this time, the money supply increased steadily, but the total amount of transaction deposits plummeted because of sweeps. Sweeps were first instituted in 1994 and became widespread early in 1995. The Reserve Requirement Exemption and Low-Reserve Tranche were not increased in 2013. The omission of 2013 from the table is not an error.

FEDERAL RESERVE WEBSITE SHOWING
RESERVE REQUIREMENT EXEMPTION & LOW-RESERVE TRANCHE

Board of Governors of the Federal Reserve System

About the Fed	News & Events	Monetary Policy	Banking Information & Regulation	Payment Systems	Economic Research & Data	Consumer Information	Community Development

Reserve Requirements

About Reserve Maintenance Manual

Reserve requirements are the amount of funds that a depository institution must hold in reserve against specified deposit liabilities. Within limits specified by law, the Board of Governors has sole authority over changes in reserve requirements. Depository institutions must hold reserves in the form of vault cash or deposits with Federal Reserve Banks.

More Information

- Regulation D
- Interest on Required Balances and Excess Balances

The dollar amount of a depository institution's reserve requirement is determined by applying the reserve ratios specified in the Federal Reserve Board's Regulation D to an institution's reservable liabilities (see table of reserve requirements). Reservable liabilities consist of net transaction accounts, nonpersonal time deposits, and Eurocurrency liabilities. Since December 27, 1990, nonpersonal time deposits and Eurocurrency liabilities have had a reserve ratio of zero.

The reserve ratio on net transactions accounts depends on the amount of net transactions accounts at the depository institution. The Garn-St Germain Act of 1982 exempted the first $2 million of reservable liabilities from reserve requirements. This "exemption amount" is adjusted each year according to a formula specified by the act. The amount of net transaction accounts subject to a reserve requirement ratio of 3 percent was set under the Monetary Control Act of 1980 at $25 million. This "low-reserve tranche" is also adjusted each year (see table of low-reserve tranche amounts and exemption amounts since 1982). Net transaction accounts in excess of the low-reserve tranche are currently reservable at 10 percent.

For more history on the changes in reserve requirement ratios and the indexation of the exemption and low-reserve tranche, see the annual review table. Additional details on reserve requirements can be found in the *Reserve Maintenance Manual* and in the article (119 KB PDF) in the Federal Reserve Bulletin, the appendix of which has tables of historical reserve ratios.

This page and the next 5 pages show the Reserve Requirements webpage on the website of the Board of Governors of the Federal Reserve System in May 2016. The Reserve Requirements webpage summarizes statutory reserve ratio requirements, including the Reserve Requirement Exemption, the Low-Reserve Tranche, and the Standard Reserve Requirement.

Board of Governors of the Federal Reserve System

| About the Fed | News & Events | Monetary Policy | Banking Information & Regulation | Payment Systems | Economic Research & Data | Consumer Information | Community Development |

Reserve Requirements

Liability Type	Requirement	
	% of liabilities	Effective date
Net transaction accounts[1]		
$0 to $15.2 million[2]	0	1-21-16
More than $15.2 million to $110.2 milllion[3]	3	1-21-16
More than $110.2 million	10	1-21-16

Note. Required reserves must be held in the form of vault cash and, if vault cash is insufficient, also in the form of a deposit maintained with a Federal Reserve Bank. An institution can maintain that deposit directly with a Reserve Bank or with another institution in a pass-through relationship. Reserve requirements are imposed on commercial banks, savings banks, savings and loan associations, credit unions, U.S. branches and agencies of foreign banks, Edge corporations, and agreement corporations.

1. Total transaction accounts consists of demand deposits, automatic transfer service (ATS) accounts, NOW accounts, share draft accounts, telephone or preauthorized transfer accounts, ineligible bankers acceptances, and obligations issued by affiliates maturing in seven days or less. Net transaction accounts are total transaction accounts less amounts due from other depository institutions and less cash items in the process of collection. For a more detailed description of these deposit types, see Form FR 2900 at http://www.federalreserve.gov/apps/reportforms/default.aspx Return to table

2. The amount of net transaction accounts subject to a reserve requirement ratio of zero percent (the "exemption amount") is adjusted each year by statute. The exemption amount is adjusted upward by 80 percent of the previous year's (June 30 to June 30) rate of increase in total reservable liabilities at all depository institutions. No adjustment is made in the event of a decrease in such liabilities. Return to table

3. The amount of net transaction accounts subject to a reserve requirement ratio of 3 percent is the "low-reserve tranche." By statute, the upper limit of the low-reserve tranche is adjusted each year by 80 percent of the previous year's (June 30 to June 30) rate of increase or decrease in net transaction accounts held by all depository institutions. Return to table

The table above shows the Reserve Requirement Exemption, Low-Reserve Tranche, and Standard Reserve Requirement on commercial bank transaction accounts for 2016. This is a continuation of the webpage shown on the previous page. It is not scintillating reading. However, it does provide factual confirmation of reserve requirements from the Federal Reserve's own website. As noted, this is important because many individuals exhibit a dogmatic unwillingness to believe criticisms of the banking system, characterizing them as inaccurate or conspiratorial, or simply flat-out denying their existence.

The webpage on the previous page notes that, "Reserve requirements are imposed on commercial banks, savings banks, savings and loan associations, credit unions, U.S. branches and agencies of foreign banks, Edge corporations, and agreement corporations." In aggregate, these institutions are referred to as "depository institutions." They are institutions that accept deposits of reserves. All depository institutions can engage in fraudulent fractional-reserve lending. When this book speaks of commercial banks, it is referring to all depository institutions. Most people are more familiar with the term bank, which is why it was used, even though the term depository institution is more inclusive and technically more accurate.

Board of Governors of the Federal Reserve System

| About the Fed | News & Events | Monetary Policy | Banking Information & Regulation | Payment Systems | Economic Research & Data | Consumer Information | Community Development |

Low-Reserve Tranche Amounts and Exemption Amounts since 1982

Effective date (beginning of maintenance period)	Low-reserve tranche amount (millions of U.S. dollars)	Exemption amount (millions of U.S. dollars)
January 14, 1982	26.0	n.a.
December 23, 1982	n.a.	2.1
January 13, 1983	26.3	***
January 12, 1984	28.9	2.2
January 3, 1985	29.8	2.4
January 2, 1986	31.7	2.6
January 1, 1987	36.7	2.9
December 31, 1987	40.5	3.2
December 29, 1988	41.5	3.4
December 28, 1989	40.4	3.4
December 27, 1990	41.1	3.4
December 26, 1991	42.2	3.6
December 24, 1992	46.8	3.8
December 23, 1993	51.9	4.0
December 22, 1994	54.0	4.2
December 21, 1995	52.0	4.3
December 31, 1996	49.3	4.4
January 1, 1998	47.8	4.7
December 31, 1998	46.5	4.9
December 30, 1999	44.3	5.0
December 28, 2000	42.8	5.5

Low-Reserve Tranche Amounts and Exemption Amounts since 1982

Effective date (beginning of maintenance period)	Low-reserve tranche amount (millions of U.S. dollars)	Exemption amount (millions of U.S. dollars)
December 27, 2001	41.3	5.7
December 26, 2002	42.1	6.0
December 25, 2003	45.4	6.6
December 23, 2004	47.6	7.0
December 22, 2005	48.3	7.8
December 21, 2006	45.8	8.5
December 20, 2007	43.9	9.3
January 1, 2009	44.4	10.3
December 31, 2009	55.2	10.7
December 30, 2010	58.8	10.7
December 29, 2011	71.0	11.5
December 27, 2012	79.5	12.4
January 23, 2014	89.0	13.3
January 22, 2015	103.6	14.5
January 21, 2016	110.2	15.2

This page and the previous page show a table of the historical increases in the Reserve Requirement Exemption and Low-Reserve Tranche on the Federal Reserve website. This is the same table shown a few pages earlier, on page 166, though it doesn't contain the percentage increases.

Board of Governors of the Federal Reserve System

About the Fed	News & Events	Monetary Policy	Banking Information & Regulation	Payment Systems	Economic Research & Data	Consumer Information	Community Development

Regulatory Changes in Reserve Requirements and Indexation of the Low Reserve Tranche and the Reserve Requirement Exemption

The following list covers regulatory changes in reserve requirements and indexation of the low reserve tranche and the reserve requirement exemption beginning December 1, 1959, and their effects on required reserves.

105. Effective for the reserve maintenance period beginning December 27, 2012, the low reserve tranche for net transaction accounts will rise from $71.0 million to $79.5 million. The reserve requirement exemption will rise from $11.5 million to $12.4 million. These actions will lower total required reserves by an estimated $971 million.

104. Effective for the reserve maintenance period beginning December 29, 2011, the low reserve tranche for net transaction accounts will rise from $58.8 million to $71.0 million. The reserve requirement exemption will rise from $10.7 million to $11.5 million. These actions will lower total required reserves by an estimated $1.33 billion.

103. Effective for the reserve maintenance period beginning December 30, 2010, the low reserve tranche for net transaction accounts was raised from $55.2 million to $58.8 million. The reserve requirement exemption remained at $10.7 million. These actions lowered total required reserves by an estimated $353 million.

102. Effective for the reserve maintenance period beginning December 31, 2009, the low reserve tranche for net transaction accounts was raised from $44.4 million to $55.2 million. The reserve requirement exemption was raised from $10.3 million to $10.7 million. These actions lowered total required reserves by an estimated $1.24 billion.

101. Effective for the reserve maintenance period beginning January 1, 2009, the low reserve tranche for net transaction accounts was raised from $43.9 million to $44.4 million. The reserve requirement exemption was raised from $9.3 million to $10.3 million. The actions lowered total required reserves by an estimated $270 million.

This is the appendix which appears after the table shown on the previous two pages. It lists the decrease in statutory reserve requirements which resulted from each increase in the Reserve Requirement Exemption and Low-Reserve Tranche. For example, the increase in the Reserve Requirement Exemption and Low-Reserve Tranche implemented in 2012 lowered the statutory reserve requirement for the entire banking system by $971 million. The increase in the Reserve Requirement Exemption and Low-Reserve Tranche implemented in 2011 lowered the statutory reserve requirement for the entire banking system by $1.33 billion. And so forth. There are 105 changes listed as of May 2016, but only the 5 most recent are shown.

Lowering the statutory reserve requirement allows commercial banks to embezzle and lend more reserves, beginning the recursive process of fractional-reserve deposit creation. Commercial banks ultimately end up creating an amount of additional deposits which drastically exceed the amount of the statutory reserve requirement reduction. Thus increases in the Reserve Requirement Exemption and Low-Reserve Tranche allow commercial banks to create large amounts of additional deposits.

SweepsTakes

"Although reserve requirement ratios have not been changed since the early 1990s, the level of reserve requirements and required reserve balances has fallen considerably since then because of the widespread implementation of retail sweep programs ... a depository institution sweeps amounts above a predetermined level from a depositor's checking account into a special-purpose money market [savings] deposit account created for the depositor. In this way, the depository institution shifts funds from an account that is subject to reserve requirements to one that is not and therefore reduces its reserve requirement."

—*The Federal Reserve System Purposes & Functions*, Federal Reserve Publication

"The willingness of bank regulators to permit use of deposit-sweeping software has made statutory reserve requirements a 'voluntary constraint' for most banks. That is, with adequately intelligent software, many banks seem easily to be able to reduce their transaction deposits by a large enough amount that the level of their required reserves is less than the amount of reserves that they require for day-to-day operation of the bank. For these banks at least, the economic burden of statutory reserve requirements is zero."

—Richard G. Anderson, Federal Reserve Economist

Large banks want the same super-low statutory reserve ratio requirements that small banks obtain via the Reserve Requirement Exemption and Low-Reserve Tranche, but most of their transaction deposits are subject to a 10% statutory reserve ratio requirement. Also, small banks hope to become large banks, and when they do, most of their transaction deposits will be subject to that pesky 10% statutory reserve ratio requirement. Banks need another scam to lower the 10% statutory reserve ratio requirement, and it is called SWEEPING or SWEEPS.

Most sheeple keep a cushion in their checking account which is their personal reserves. That is, sheeple don't spend every nickel in their checking account each day or week or month, but rather keep extra money which they rarely or never spend. In many cases, a lot of extra money. This is especially true because bank fees for bounced checks or bounced debits are so high and interest rates on savings accounts are often so low. This extra money in checking accounts sits dormant and is not really used by the depositor, but the bank must still apply a 10% statutory reserve ratio requirement to it and hold reserves to back it. Banks hate this. In banks' view, the "unused" reserves backing the undemanded portion of checking deposits should be embezzled and lent, not held in reserve. Banks therefore "sweep" (transfer) this unused checking account money into a savings account without telling depositors. That is, banks secretly convert the "unused" portions of checking deposits into savings deposits, which are then subject to a 0% statutory reserve ratio requirement and don't have to be backed by reserves.

Most money doesn't exist physically. Rather, most money is credit on computer bank ledgers. Sweeping "extra" checking account funds into savings accounts is a completely computerized process. Bank computers carefully monitor each transaction account, track the payment history and withdrawal tendencies of the depositor, and predict how much money the depositor uses. The unused portion of every checking account is swept into a savings account. The software algorithms which determine how much to sweep out of each transaction account are sophisticated, and can predict checking account withdrawals with amazing accuracy.

Most sheeple lead predictable lives. They are paid at regular intervals, deposit money at regular intervals, and spend most of their money at regular intervals on basic living expenses such as mortgages, car payments, credit cards, loans, food, utilities, and gas for vehicles. For most sheeple, these expenses vary minimally. Viewed month to month, even seemingly erratic spending like eating out and recreation modulates into a pattern. Sheeple may spend their disposable income on different goods & services, and some sheeple may keep more checking-account cushions than others, but by the time they settle into their chosen profession, their spending stabilizes and forms a predictable pattern which banks exploit via sweeps.

Banks secretly "recategorize" or "reclassify" each transaction account. They recategorize a transaction account by converting it into a transaction sub-account and a non-transaction sub-account. Once transaction accounts are recategorized as two sub-accounts, they are swept. Initially, all money that was in the original transaction account is placed in the transaction sub-account. Unused funds are swept—that is, transferred—from the transaction sub-account into the non-transaction sub-account. Unswept funds—funds not transferred into the non-transaction sub-account—remain in the transaction sub-account. The sub-accounts are invisible to depositors, who simply see a checking account. Sweeping is a slang term for this process used by many economists and bankers, but the formal name is DEPOSIT RECLASSIFICATION. Deposit reclassification is the process of secretly reclassifying a portion of every transaction deposit as a non-transaction deposit.

Sweeping is very rudimentary in a technological sense. The software is simply an addition to a bank's preexisting computer infrastructure, and is installed in much the same way home users install programs such as Microsoft Office, Adobe Photoshop, or Quickbooks. Once installed, the sweep software runs for several hours and analyzes all transaction histories, determines sweep thresholds, and then sweeps all accounts. A bank manager uses a simple, user-friendly interface to set the aggressiveness of the sweep thresholds, set the time when accounts will be swept, and is shown statistical summaries of the total amounts swept, total reserves freed up, etc. Instituting such a massive fraud is remarkably simple.

Sweeping software is also extremely cheap. Small banks can purchase and implement sweep software for less than $10,000 and use it to drastically decrease their statutory reserve ratio requirement and statutory reserve requirement. A bank spending thousands of dollars on sweep software can free up millions of dollars of reserves. These millions of dollars of reserves can then be embezzled and lent, generating interest income which far exceeds the cost of sweep software.

You deposit $100 at Sixth Sweep Bank, $30 in a checking account, $70 in a savings account. A 0% statutory reserve ratio requirement is applied to the $70 transaction deposit, a 10% statutory reserve ratio requirement is applied to the $30 non-transaction deposit, and the overall statutory reserve requirement is $3. $3 of reserves back $100 of deposits, a 3% reserve ratio. This is before your checking account is swept.

Banks are able to sweep 60% - 90% of checking account deposits into savings sub-accounts. More sophisticated (and expensive) sweep software can sustain 90% sweep rates or higher. An 80% sweep rate is fairly typical, can be implemented by inexpensive sweep software, and is assumed. In the previous example, you deposited $100 at Sixth Sweep Bank and placed $30 in a checking account. 80% of $30 is $24. $24 of your checking account is swept into a savings account. Sixth Sweep Bank now has $94 in savings deposits, $6 in checking deposits. A 0% statutory reserve ratio requirement is applied to the $94 of transaction deposits, a 10% statutory reserve ratio requirement is applied to the $6 of non-transaction deposits, and the overall statutory reserve requirement is 60¢. 60¢ of reserves back $100 of deposits, a 0.6% reserve ratio. Sweeping decreased the statutory reserve requirement from $3 to 60¢ and the statutory reserve ratio requirement from 3% to 0.6%, which is an 80% reduction.

Let's examine the deposit reclassification process on ledgers. $100 of reserves are deposited at Sixth Sweep Bank, $70 as savings deposits, $30 as checking deposits. Sixth Sweep Bank applies a 10% statutory reserve ratio requirement to all transaction deposits and a 0% statutory reserve ratio requirement to all non-transaction deposits. Sixth Sweep Bank's ledger before transaction deposits are swept:

```
Assets                          Liabilities

 $3 (Reserves)                   $30 (Transaction Deposits)
$27 ("Excess" Reserves)
 $0 (Reserves)                   $70 (Non-Transaction Deposits)
$70 ("Excess" Reserves)
```

```
$100                            $100

                                    100% Reserve Ratio
```

Sixth Sweep Bank's ledger after combining reserves and "excess" reserves:

Assets	Liabilities
$3 (Reserves)	$30 (Transaction Deposits)
$97 ("Excess" Reserves)	$70 (Non-Transaction Deposits)

$100	$100

100% Reserve Ratio

Sixth Sweep Bank has $3 of reserves backing $100 of deposits, a 3% reserve ratio.

Transaction deposits are reclassified. Each transaction account is broken up into a transaction sub-account and a non-transaction sub-account:

Assets	Liabilities
$3 (Reserves)	$30 (Transaction Deposits)
$27 ("Excess" Reserves)	$30 (Transaction Deposits)
	$0 (Non-transaction Deposits)
$0 (Reserves)	$70 (Non-Transaction Deposits)
$70 ("Excess" Reserves)	

$100	$100

100% Reserve Ratio

The depositor only sees the original transaction account, which has been greyed out. This nomenclature indicates that there are $30 of total transaction deposits at Sixth Sweep Bank, $30 which are in the transaction sub-account, and $0 which are in the non-transaction sub-account. Counting the original transaction account and the sub-accounts would result in $60 of liabilities for $30 of transaction deposits, which is double the actual amount and therefore incorrect. The original transaction account is nonetheless shown to avoid confusion, but only the sub-accounts will be used when totalling the ledger. In previous examples, when loans or time deposits were greyed out, they were still counted in ledger totals, but that won't be done in this case. Limited horizontal space requires the sweeping to be shown in this somewhat cumbersome way.

No money has been swept yet, the sub-accounts have simply been created. All the money in the original transaction account has been moved into the transaction sub-account. The total amount of transaction deposits has not changed and Sixth Sweep Bank's statutory reserve requirement has not changed.

Sixth Sweep Bank sweeps 80% or $24 of transaction deposits, transferring them from the transaction sub-account to the non-transaction sub-account:

```
Assets                              Liabilities
  $0.60 (Reserves)                    $30 (Transaction Deposits)
  $29.40 ("Excess" Reserves)           $6 (Transaction Deposits)
                                      $24 (Non-transaction Deposits)
  $0.00 (Reserves)                    $70 (Non-Transaction Deposits)
  $70.00 ("Excess" Reserves)
```

```
$100.00                             $100
```

                                              0.6% Reserve Ratio

The $24 in the non-transaction sub-account is treated as a standard non-transaction deposit, and a 0% statutory reserve ratio requirement is applied. Sixth Sweep Bank only has to apply the 10% statutory reserve ratio requirement to the $6 in the transaction sub-account. Its statutory reserve requirement has decreased from $3 to 60¢. This change is easier to visualize if we combine reserves, "excess" reserves, and non-transaction deposits:

```
Assets                              Liabilities
  $0.60 (Reserves)                     $6 (Transaction Deposits)
  $99.40 ("Excess" Reserves)          $94 (Non-Transaction Deposits)
```

```
$100.00                             $100
```

                                              0.6% Reserve Ratio

Sixth Sweep Bank has 60¢ of reserves backing $100 of deposits, a 0.6% reserve ratio.

Criminals often keep two sets of books, one seemingly honest set which shows lies, and one fraudulent set which shows the true criminal activity. U.S. banks that sweep do the same thing with every checking (transaction) account. Depositors are not shown the sub-accounts. Depositors see $30 of transaction accounts which are a lie. The true criminal activity is shown on the actual ledger with the sub-accounts. This true, fraudulent sub-account ledger is the one that the bank uses on "Call Reports" and "FR2900" forms when reporting its deposits and reserves to the Federal Deposit Insurance Corporation (FDIC) and Federal Reserve. This true, fraudulent sub-account ledger is the ledger from which statutory reserve ratio requirements and statutory reserve requirements are computed.

In the real world, banks that sweep can decrease statutory reserve requirements well below 1%. Banks must usually keep 1% - 2% reserves in vault cash to honor physical currency withdrawals. Sweeping sets the statutory reserve ratio requirement well below the real-world reserve ratio which banks must maintain to honor customer transactions. This means banks are free to set whatever reserve ratio they want without concern for laws and regulations. The 10% statutory reserve ratio requirement becomes as meaningless as campaign contribution laws.

Most reductions in statutory reserve requirements obtained by sweeping are used to decrease reserves held in Federal Reserve accounts. Commercial banks hold two types of reserves: physical-currency reserves and Fed-account reserves. Most commercial banks have already decreased physical-currency reserves to the lowest level that is possible. Physical-currency reserves are also called vault-cash reserves because they are currency or cash kept in bank vaults in case depositors demand them. Commercial banks keep only enough physical-currency reserves to honor day-to-day withdrawal demands by depositors, and can't decrease physical-currency reserves further, or they would not have physical currency to give to depositors who show up at banks and demand it. The remaining reserves a commercial bank holds are non-physical, Fed-account reserves, and when commercial banks sweep and lower statutory reserve requirements, they decrease reserve levels by decreasing the non-physical reserves held in their Federal Reserve account.

Commercial banks that sweep will often decrease their Fed-account balance to $0 or very close to it. They do so because they once again rely on the Federal Reserve to assist with their fraud, in this case via the Discount Window and Daylight Overdrafts. No honest business or individual would ever think of keeping no money in its checking account and then processing hordes of transactions, but this is exactly what commercial banks do with their Fed accounts.

Shortages of physical vault-cash reserves are a catastrophe for commercial banks, but shortages of non-physical Fed-account reserves are more manageable. Commercial banks that are short non-physical, Fed-account reserves can have Fed conjure virtually limitless quantities of these reserves at the Discount Window. Commercial banks are allowed to run massive "Daylight Overdrafts" in their Fed accounts. That is, they are allowed to have negative balances in their bank accounts at the Federal Reserve which are literally negative reserve positions or reserve shortages. However, these overdrafts are only allowed during the business day, thus the term Daylight Overdrafts. Commercial banks are punished severely by Fed if they are irresponsible and incur "Overnight Overdrafts," and Fed will close the accounts of banks that do so regularly, which is basically closing the bank. Commercial banks eliminate Daylight Overdrafts which persist at the end of a business day by scaring up reserves. This is not hard during healthy economic conditions, as commercial banks can simply borrow preexisting reserves from other banks that have "excess" reserves in the "Fed Funds" market, pawn loans for preexisting reserves in Repurchase Agreement or "repo" markets, or pawn loans for newly conjured reserves at the Discount Window.

The previous three paragraphs were long and may have confused you. Don't worry. You don't need to understand them fully now, as every concept mentioned will be described in detail later, especially the corrupt processes of Daylight Overdrafts and Discount Window loans. The main thing to understand is that reserve reductions obtained by sweeping are not usually reductions in physical, vault-cash reserves, but rather reductions in non-physical, Fed-account reserves.

Back to the sweep process. Suppose 1,000 depositors all have checking accounts containing $100. Advanced sweep software would monitor and analyze the account activity of each individual depositor, and sweep different amounts of money out of each account. Perhaps $90 out of the account of a thrifty person who spends little, $50 out of the account of a person who spends modestly, maybe nothing out of the account out of a person who lives paycheck to paycheck and sometimes only has a few dollars in their account. As a rough rule, when these differing sweep amounts are averaged out, 80% of a bank's total checking account deposits can be swept. If 1,000 depositors each have $100 in their checking account, there is $100,000 of total transaction deposits, and $80,000 of transaction account deposits would be swept into non-transaction sub-accounts.

The fine print of the contract signed when opening a checking account gives banks permission to sweep it. When a bank first implements sweeps, it sends out notices which disclose the practice to all depositors who already have accounts. The language in such disclosures is carefully crafted to obscure what is happening so that sheeple are not alarmed. Most sheeple are unaware that their checking account deposits are secretly swept into savings accounts. If given a candid explanation of the decreased reserve levels and increased lie-ability risk which sweeping creates, most sheeple would oppose sweeping vehemently.

Sweeping is fraud. If the Federal Reserve were actually a regulator of banks rather than their partner in crime, it would have banned the practice of sweeping the moment it was first proposed in 1994 by First Union Bank of North Carolina. First Union Bank was the very first bank to think up the scam. First Union Bank was acquired by Wachovia, which was bank-rupted by low-reserve levels during Depression v9.2006-201x, and acquired by Wells Fargo. A fitting parable of the fractional-reserve fraud.

Sweeping was approved in 1994 by Alan Greenspan, who was Inflator General (Chairman of the Board of Governors of the Federal Reserve System) at that time. Greenspan was also the single person most responsible for the housing bubble, as we will see. His legacy is a veritable truckwreck of fraud and economic devastation, which is why a media that calls everything what it isn't refers to him as "The Maestro."

The Federal Reserve must give explicit approval to a commercial bank before it is allowed to implement sweeping. Bankers call this Fed approval a "no objection." The Fed is complicit in the sweeping scheme, and could completely eliminate sweeping by simply refusing to issue "no objections" and telling banks that they are not allowed to sweep accounts. Fed actually provides guidance to banks which are implementing deposit reclassification, and helps banks use soothing language to describe the process so that depositors are not alarmed. The last thing Fed wants is runs on commercial banks which result when depositors become alarmed, as it then has to Bailout banks by monetizing their loans and creating reserves.

If the Fed wants lower statutory reserve ratio requirements, why not just ban sweeps and decree a lower statutory reserve ratio requirement? By law, the Fed can only lower the statutory reserve ratio requirement on transaction deposits to 8% (except for the Reserve Requirement Exemption and Low-Reserve Tranche). Changing this law would erode confidence in the banking system. Any public admission of how paltry reserve levels are erodes confidence in a banking system that requires confidence to continue its con.

Bankers are ballsy, huh? They are asked to apply a mere 10% statutory reserve ratio requirement only to that small portion of deposits which are transaction deposits, are granted a Reserve Requirement Exemption and Low-Reserve Tranche which exempts many transaction deposits from this 10% statutory reserve ratio requirement, and yet scheme to evade even these paltry safeguards.

It is absolutely insane for banks to hold such miniscule amounts of reserves. Banks that hold such miniscule amounts of reserves always have their lie-abilities exposed eventually, but know they will be bailed out by a Federal Reserve that can conjure infinite reserves, so could care less about risk. Banks are only interested in lowering statutory reserve requirements as much as possible so they can conjure as many deposits as possible, lend those deposits out, and earn as much profit on interest payments as possible.

What if a bank sweeps a transaction sub-account into a non-transaction sub-account, and then the depositor with the original checking account demands a greater percentage of their deposit than is in the transaction sub-account? Money is then "unswept"—transferred out of the non-transaction sub-account and into the transaction sub-account. When this is done, the transferred funds are suddenly subject to a 10% statutory reserve ratio requirement rather than a 0% statutory reserve ratio requirement, and the bank experiences a sudden increase in its statutory reserve requirement. If the bank doesn't have "excess" reserves which can be used to meet the sudden increase in its statutory reserve requirement, it must rapidly obtain additional reserves. A depositor withdrawal is a demand for reserves, so the bank may also require enough additional reserves to honor the full amount withdrawn by the depositor, rather than just 10% of it.

If there were a run on a bank in which large numbers of depositors suddenly spent or withdrew checking deposits, then millions or billions of dollars of deposits might be suddenly transferred from non-transaction sub-accounts with a 0% statutory reserve ratio requirement to transaction sub-accounts with a 10% statutory reserve ratio requirement. This massive "unsweeping" would increase banks' statutory reserve requirements and exacerbate their reserve shortages. Massive unsweeping occurred during Depression v9.2006-201x, worsening banks' plight.

Sweeps could theoretically be used by banks to help alleviate minor reserve shortages. If transaction accounts are swept more aggressively, the amount of deposits in transaction sub-accounts subject to a 10% statutory reserve ratio requirement decreases, the amount of deposits in non-transaction sub-accounts subject to a 0% statutory reserve ratio requirement increases, and the overall statutory reserve ratio requirement decreases.

Shrewder customers are aware of sweeps and want in on the action, so some banks tout sweeping as a service, especially for businesses or extremely rich depositors. Funds swept into savings sub-accounts are invested and earn interest. Usually this interest isn't paid to depositors, but some banks pay a portion of their sweeping profits back to depositors. The majority of sweeping profit accrues to banks, not depositors, but sweeping was first implemented to circumvent laws which prevent interest from being paid on checking accounts. Though sweeps were initially a scheme to allow interest to be paid on checking accounts, they are now primarily used to evade statutory reserve requirements. A fraud designed to circumvent one fairly-important regulation is now primarily used to circumvent a critically-important regulation.

The Regulation D savings account withdrawal rule applies to savings sub-accounts. By law, if more than 6 withdrawals are made from a non-transaction account in a month, that non-transaction account must be converted into a transaction account. If a customer occasionally made more than 6 withdrawals from a transaction account which involved trifling sums of money, the bank might simply issue them a warning and might not convert the non-transaction account into a transaction account, but sweeps are designed to systematically exploit the 6-withdrawal rule, so there is no leeway.

There is no Regulation D limit on deposits into a savings account, so funds can be swept out of the checking sub-account into the savings sub-account as much as the sweep software wants. However, the sweep software must predict depositor usage patterns very accurately to avoid having to make 6 transfers from the savings sub-account back into the checking sub-account in a month. If a 6th transfer is made, Regulation D requires the entire savings sub-account to be emptied into the checking sub-account and the checking sub-account can't be swept again that month. The 6-withdrawal rule is per monthly billing cycle, so the sweeping can begin again in the next monthly billing cycle.

Suppose you have $100 in a checking account with Sixth Sweep Bank, which sweeps $80 of it into a savings sub-account, leaving $20 in the checking sub-account. You still only see a checking account with $100, and write a check for $30. $10 is transferred out of the savings sub-account and into the checking sub-account, so the checking sub-account contains the $30 needed to honor your $30 check.

A smart sweep program would actually transfer $24 out of the savings sub-account and into the checking sub-account, rather than $10, so that there is $14 in the checking sub-account after the depositor withdrawal is processed. After the withdrawal, there would be $14 in the checking sub-account, and $56 in the savings sub-account. The depositor has $70 of deposits remaining after the $30 withdrawal. If this $70 deposit was swept at an 80% rate, $56 would be transferred into the savings sub-account and $14 would remain in the checking sub-account. By transferring $24 into the checking sub-account rather than $10, the 80% sweep threshold is maintained. The $24 transfer is 1 of the 6 monthly withdrawals from the savings sub-account which Regulation D allows.

Anytime a depositor withdraws more money than is in the checking sub-account, money must be transferred from the savings sub-account to the checking sub-account to cover the shortage. Depositors can't withdraw money directly from the savings sub-account, they can only withdraw money from the checking sub-account. In the example above, if the $30 withdrawal is processed and $10 is taken from the savings sub-account to honor it, that is 1 of the 6 withdrawals allowed by Regulation D for the month. After the depositor withdrawal is honored, there is no money in the checking sub-account, so another $14 transfer is made from the savings sub-account to checking sub-account. The same end result of $14 in the checking sub-account was accomplished, but in a much less efficient manner which frittered 2 of the 6 Regulation D withdrawals rather than 1.

Here is the process on ledgers. $100 is deposited in a checking account with a 10% reserve requirement:

Assets	Liabilities
$10 (Reserves)	$100 (Transaction Deposits)
$90 ("Excess" Reserves)	
$100	$100
	100% Reserve Ratio

The checking account is reclassified as a checking sub-account and savings sub-account, and all funds are initially placed in the checking sub-account:

Assets	Liabilities
$10 (Reserves)	$100 (Transaction Deposits)
$90 ("Excess" Reserves)	$100 (Transaction Deposits)
	$0 (Non-transaction Deposits)
$100	$100
	100% Reserve Ratio

80% of the funds in the transaction sub-account are swept into the non-transaction sub-account:

```
Assets                          Liabilities
  $2 (Reserves)                 $100 (Transaction Deposits)
  $98 ("Excess" Reserves)          $20 (Transaction Deposits)
                                   $80 (Non-transaction Deposits)
_____
$100                            $100
                                        100% Reserve Ratio
```

Reserves decreased. "Excess" reserves increased. This is because transaction deposits subject to a 10% statutory reserve ratio requirement decreased, and non-transaction deposits subject to a 0% statutory reserve ratio requirement increased.

"Excess" reserves can be loaned. On all ledgers in this section, "excess" reserves could be replaced with loans. "Excess" reserves are increased to increase loans. To banks, more loans equal more interest profits.

The depositor withdraws $30. To honor this withdrawal, the sweep software transfers $24 from the non-transaction sub-account into the transaction sub-account. The withdrawal has not been processed yet, the sub-accounts are merely being changed to facilitate honoring the withdrawal:

```
Assets                          Liabilities
  $4.40 (Reserves)              $100 (Transaction Deposits)
  $95.60 ("Excess" Reserves)       $44 (Transaction Deposits)
                                   $56 (Non-transaction Deposits)
_____
$100.00                         $100
                                        100% Reserve Ratio
```

Reserves increased. "Excess" reserves decreased. This is because transaction deposits subject to a 10% statutory reserve ratio requirement increased, and non-transaction deposits subject to a 0% statutory reserve ratio requirement decreased.

There is now enough money in the transaction sub-account to honor the $30 depositor withdrawal. It is therefore processed:

```
Assets                          Liabilities
  $1.40 (Reserves)              $70 (Transaction Deposits)
  $68.60 ("Excess" Reserves)       $14 (Transaction Deposits)
                                   $56 (Non-transaction Deposits)
_____
$70.00                          $70
                                        100% Reserve Ratio
```

The $30 withdrawal was subtracted from the transaction sub-account. The original transaction deposit was also decreased by $30. $30 of reserves are paid to the depositor to honor the deposit withdrawal, so $30 is subtracted from reserves.

There is now a $70 transaction deposit. 80% or $56 of this $70 deposit is in the non-transaction sub-account. The 80% sweep threshold has been maintained.

It would be smart to play it extremely safe and only sweep modest amounts of money out of checking accounts so that there is always enough money for transactions and the 6-transfer limit out of the savings sub-account is never reached. Except that we're talking about bankers. Safety doesn't concern bankers as much as maximizing profit because they know they'll always be bailed out. Banks know they can obtain additional reserves in the repo market, or from Fed. The Federal Reserve will monetize loans for banks and instantly conjure all the reserves they require, and does so daily at the Discount Window. More information on the Fed conjuring reserves, the Discount Window, and the repo market will be provided later.

Average sweep software will ensure that less than 10% of swept accounts reach the Reg-D 6 transfer limit per month. Good software will get the rate well below 5%. Thus a competent bank can ensure that more than 95% of transaction accounts remain perpetually swept.

Sweeping a small amount of extra money out of a transaction account might not seem like a big difference—until it is summed over millions of transaction accounts. The difference can be billions of dollars. Banks work relentlessly to hone their sweeping software settings and make them more aggressive.

The Federal Reserve doesn't report pre-sweep deposit data. Fed used to publish a list of the total amount of money swept each month by all U.S. banks, but stopped doing so in May 2012. As with M3 money supply data that is no longer published, Fed hopes to hide distortions and frauds by simply refusing to quantify them.

Prior to May 2012, an individual who wanted accurate pre-sweep transaction deposit and non-transaction deposit data for the U.S. banking system had to back-correct deposit data using Fed sweep estimates. No individual bank was required to publicly report its sweeping levels, nor would Fed disclose this information. The only statistic on sweeps that Fed reported was the lone monthly estimate of total sweeping by the entire U.S. banking system.

Fed used to defend its non-reporting of pre-sweep data by saying that it simply reports the deposit data that banks submit on FR2900 forms ("Report of Transaction Accounts, Other Deposits, and Vault Cash") which are used to determine statutory reserve requirements. At a deeper and more absolute ethical level, it is ridiculous to distort fundamental economic statistics to abet bank fraud.

Bank deposits are money. The deposit supply is literally the money supply. The money supply is a critical piece of data which economists and investors use to gauge the health of the economy. In particular, economists trying to forecast the economy's future health, or determine when an unhealthy economy will recover, rely on money supply data.

Economists differentiate transaction and non-transaction deposits, viewing transaction deposits as the money being used to buy goods & services, and non-transaction deposits as the level of savings. Sweeping causes artificial decreases in transaction deposits, and artificial increases in non-transaction deposits. An artificial and illusory increase in non-transaction deposits makes savings rates appear higher than they actually are, making it seem like the economy is investing more in its future than it actually is. An artificial and illusory decrease in transaction deposits makes the amount of money chasing goods & services and setting the general price levels in the economy seem smaller than it actually is, which causes predictions of price inflation and forecasts of general demand for goods & services to be understated.

Stated another way, the amount of money which depositors have in checking accounts is the money they have available for spending in day to day commerce (assuming they only draw on savings deposits in an emergency or for some future purchase which they are saving for, which is true of most people). After sweeping, the amount of transaction deposits reported is smaller than the amount of transaction deposits that actually exist, which drastically understates the amount of money used for economic transactions. After sweeping, the amount of non-transaction deposits reported is larger than the amount of non-transaction deposits that actually exist, which drastically overstates the amount of money saved. An economist performing calculations using the fraudulent transaction-money and savings data will have a distorted sense of price pressures, demand for goods & services, and investment, and draw conclusions about the economy which deviate sharply from reality.

Some shoddy researchers claim that sweeping decreases the M2 money supply, which in oversimplified terms is physical currency in circulation plus checking deposits and savings deposits. Sweeping does not decrease the M2 money supply, it decreases the M1 money supply. The M1 money supply is currency in circulation plus checking deposits, and is meant to approximate total money available for day-to-day economic transactions. In oversimplified terms, M2 is M1 plus savings deposits. Sweeping decreases checking deposits and increases savings deposits, which decreases M1 but has no effect on M2. As M1 includes checking deposits but not savings deposits, sweeping that decreases checking deposits decreases M1. As M2 includes checking deposits and savings deposits, transferring money from checking accounts to savings accounts has no effect on M2. In formal economic terms, M1 (cash + checking deposits) is transaction money, and sweeping decreases M1, distorting the fundamental measure of the amount of money which is available for commerce and which sets prices, causing it to be drastically understated.

Until Fed stopped reporting sweeps data, economists could correct for sweeps, but precise data provided by banks would have eliminated this unnecessary guesswork. As Fed will no longer report even a single aggregate sweeps statistic, hoping it will provide more exhaustive data about the sweeping activity of individual banks is pitifully naive.

The Fed can't publish two sets of money supply data, just as a mobster can't show an IRS auditor both sets of books. Fed can't publish just the pre-sweep books which depositors see because statutory reserve requirements computed from the pre-sweep books would be much higher than the reserve levels which banks actually maintain, meaning every bank would have illegally low-reserve levels. Banks compute their statutory reserve requirements from the crooked swept books, not the honest un-swept books. If Fed published two sets of money supply data, one with sweeps and one without sweeps, it would draw attention to the fraudulent nature of sweeps.

Fed used to disseminate a single statistic about sweeps because it understood that economists denied accurate money supply data would be incapable of analyzing the economy. Fed published the post-sweep books as money supply data on the "releases" section of its Board of Governors website which sheeple visit, and then discreetly made sweep data available via less publicized portions of the website of its St. Louis branch. The website of the St. Louis branch of the Federal Reserve is primarily accessed by professional bankers and economists rather than sheeple.

Most people looking at money supply data have no idea that sweeping even occurs, and Fed doesn't mention sweeps unless someone asks. Fed won't lie about sweeps if specifically asked, but this only-tell-if-asked policy can hardly be considered honest disclosure. Again, it is obscene and absurd to propagate fallacious economic data to facilitate bank fraud, but this is the unfortunate reality.

Sweeping decreases the statutory reserve requirements of the U.S. banking system dramatically. Here is the ledger for the U.S. banking system in September 2008 just before The Bailout passed:

```
Assets                                    Liabilities
   $63,110,000,000 (Reserves)                $631,100,000,000 (Transaction
  $567,990,000,000 (Loans)                                    Deposits)
              $0 (Reserves)               $6,421,600,000,000 (Non-Transaction
$6,421,600,000,000 (Loans)                                    Deposits)

$7,052,700,000,000                        $7,052,700,000,000
                                                   0.89% Reserve Ratio
```

This ledger uses the statutory reserve requirement, not the actual reserves that banks kept, as the way that sweeps lower statutory reserve requirements is being shown.

This ledger is easier to visualize if we combine reserves and loans:

```
Assets                                    Liabilities
   $63,110,000,000 (Reserves)                $631,100,000,000 (Transaction
$6,989,590,000,000 (Loans)                                    Deposits)
                                          $6,421,600,000,000 (Non-Transaction
                                                              Deposits)
```

```
$7,052,700,000,000                        $7,052,700,000,000
                                                0.89% Reserve Ratio
```

The ledger contains the transaction and non-transaction data that the Fed released. This is post-sweep data, even though sweeps were not shown or acknowledged by the Fed. Sweeps are not even mentioned on the exhaustive footnotes at the bottom of the Fed release which contained this transaction deposit and non-transaction deposit data. This data gives the false impression that depositors with $7.052 trillion of total deposits chose to place $631.1 billion of their money in transaction accounts and $6.421 trillion in non-transaction accounts.

In reality, $779.7 billion of transaction deposits were swept into non-transaction accounts. This is an estimate produced by Fed economists which may be inaccurate, but again, it is the only public statistic which quantifies total sweep activity for the U.S. banking system. It would be a fairly simple matter for Fed to demand that all banks report both the amount of transaction and non-transaction deposits which depositors see and the amount of transaction and non-transaction deposits which exist after sweeping. Subtracting the two amounts would give an exact total for deposit reclassification, but Fed is unwilling to require this reporting. We therefore have no choice but to use the estimate Fed provides, which may drastically understate total sweep activity. It is abominable that an honest accounting of the actual amount of transaction deposits prior to sweeping is not reported, so that the exact amount of sweeping performed could be determined. The Fed purports to be a regulator of banks and protector of the public, but it is not. Any true regulator of banks and protector of the public would demand honest reporting of sweeping activity—and of course outlaw sweeping.

Prior to sweeping, transaction deposits would have been $779.7 billion larger, and non-transaction deposits would have been $779.7 billion smaller. Making these adjustments, we obtain the true ledger for the U.S. banking system prior to the sweep fraud:

Assets		Liabilities	
$141,080,000,000 (Reserves)		$1,410,800,000,000 (Transaction	
$1,269,720,000,000 (Loans)		Deposits)	
$0 (Reserves)		$5,641,900,000,000 (Non-Transaction	
$5,779,440,000,000 (Loans)		Deposits)	

‡7,052,700,000,000   ‡7,052,700,000,000

2% Reserve Ratio

If sweeping had not been allowed, this would have been the ledger for the U.S. banking system. This is the data Fed should have published, and would have published if it were a regulator of banks rather than their partner in crime. Without sweeping, the statutory reserve requirement for the entire U.S. banking system was $141.08 billion. After sweeping, the statutory reserve requirement for the entire U.S. banking system was $63.11 billion. Sweeping decreased the statutory reserve requirement of the entire U.S. banking system by $77.97 billion—the amount of reserves which backed the $779.7 billion of swept funds when they were still un-swept transaction deposits and subject to a 10% statutory reserve ratio requirement.

This oversimplified example neglects the Reserve Requirement Exemption and Low-Reserve Tranche. Fed doesn't report the total amount of deposits in the U.S. banking system that qualified for the Reserve Requirement Exemption and Low-Reserve Tranche. This makes it difficult to include the Reserve Requirement Exemption and Low-Reserve Tranche in aggregate deposit information for the entire U.S. banking system.

In 2008 just before The Bailout passed, 55% of the transaction deposits in the U.S. banking system were swept and converted into non-transaction deposits. There were $4 of non-transaction deposits for every $1 of transaction deposits prior to sweeping, and $10 of non-transaction deposits for every $1 of transaction deposits after sweeping. The non-transaction to transaction deposit ratio increased from 4-to-1 to 10-to-1, a significant distortion.

Total reserves in the banking system at this time were $102.7 billion, yet this ledger shows a statutory reserve requirement of $141.8 billion, which is $39.1 billion greater than $102.7 billion. If banks had not used sweeps, the statutory reserve requirement would have exceeded the amount of reserves which existed by $39.1 billion, which the Fed would never allow. Banks would have created fewer deposits to avoid decreasing reserve levels below statutory reserve requirements, and the total amount of deposits would have therefore been smaller. Without sweeping, bank deposit creation would have been drastically curtailed, which is why banks sweep—to decrease statutory reserve ratio requirements and thereby increase deposit creation.

Sophisticated sweeping software can sweep 90% of transaction deposits and maintain that sweep threshold. Forrest Gump could write software that sweeps 60%

of transaction deposits. Why were "only" 55% of transaction deposits in the U.S. banking system swept? Not all banks use sweep software. Smaller banks for whom the Reserve Requirement Exemption and Low-Reserve Tranche provide significant reductions in statutory reserve requirements often choose not to implement sweeping. Fed won't reveal how many banks sweep, so we also don't know how many banks don't sweep. Banks which use simpler sweep software or choose conservative sweep settings may only sweep 60%, 70%, or 80% of deposits. So some banks sweep at an aggressive 90% level, some at levels as low as 60%, and some don't sweep at all which is a 0% level. When all these levels are combined the average estimated sweep level for the U.S. banking system is 55%—assuming Fed sweep estimates were correct. This may be a very dubious assumption. Again, it is preposterousness to guess such fundamental economic data when it could easily be tabulated.

Here are the sweep ledgers for the U.S. banking system. Transaction accounts are broken up into transaction sub-accounts and non-transaction sub-accounts:

Assets	Liabilities	
$141,080,000,000 (Reserves)	$1,410,800,000,000 (Transaction	
$1,269,720,000,000 (Loans)		Deposits)
	$1,410,800,000,000	(Transaction
		Deposits)
	$0	(Non-Transaction
		Deposits)
$0 (Reserves)	$5,641,900,000,000 (Non-Transaction	
$5,641,900,000,000 (Loans)		Deposits)
$7,052,700,000,000	$7,052,700,000,000	
		2% Reserve Ratio

Depositors only see the original transaction accounts, which have been greyed out. No money has been swept yet, the sub-accounts have simply been created. All the money in the original transaction accounts has been moved to the transaction sub-accounts. The total amount of transaction deposits has not changed and the U.S. banking system's statutory reserve requirement has not changed.

Thousands of banks sweep $779.7 billion of transaction deposits, transferring them from millions of transaction sub-accounts into millions of non-transaction sub-accounts:

Assets	Liabilities
$63,110,000,000 (Reserves)	$1,410,800,000,000 (Transaction Deposits)
$1,347,690,000,000 (Loans)	
	$631,100,000,000 (Transaction Deposits)
	$779,700,000,000 (Non-Transaction Deposits)
$0 (Reserves)	$5,641,900,000,000 (Non-Transaction Deposits)
$5,641,900,000,000 (Loans)	
$7,052,700,000,000	$7,052,700,000,000
	0.89% Reserve Ratio

$1.4 trillion of transaction deposits is an average of $4,700 per American. Businesses have transaction accounts, and the transaction accounts of rich individuals like Bill Gates also distort the average, so $4,700 is a rough, brute-force statistic, but it nonetheless gives an individualized sense of the magnitude of the sweeping fraud. $631 billion of transaction deposits is an average of $2,100 per American. Very, very, very roughly, banks converted $2,600 of transaction deposits per American into non-transaction deposits.

The $779.7 billion in the non-transaction sub-accounts are treated as standard non-transaction deposits, and have a 0% statutory reserve ratio requirement. U.S. banks only have to apply the 10% statutory reserve ratio requirement to the $631.1 billion in the transaction sub-accounts. U.S. banks' statutory reserve requirement has decreased from $141.08 billion to $63.11 billion. This change is easier to visualize if we combine reserves, loans, and non-transaction deposits:

Assets	Liabilities
$63,110,000,000 (Reserves)	$631,100,000,000 (Transaction Deposits)
$6,989,590,000,000 (Loans)	
	$6,421,600,000,000 (Non-Transaction Deposits)
$7,052,700,000,000	$7,052,700,000,000
	0.89% Reserve Ratio

This is the ledger initially shown, which is the post-sweep data Fed published without ever mentioning sweeps. U.S. banks had $7.052 trillion of deposits, but the statutory reserve requirement was only $63.1 billion, a 0.89% reserve ratio. Banks could never back $7.052 trillion of deposits with only $63.1 billion of reserves. Banks must hold reserves equal to 1% - 2% of deposits to honor day-to-day withdrawals and transactions. U.S. banks actually kept $102.7 billion of reserves.

U.S. banks did not hold reserves which exceeded the statutory reserve requirement because they were being careful. The statutory reserve requirement was so much lower than the reserve level needed to honor day-to-day transactions and withdrawals that banks were free to set whatever reserve level they wanted without concern for statutory reserve requirements.

There is still and is always a deposit creation aspect. This is the master ledger for all U.S. banks after thousands of banks have repeatedly embezzled reserves, issued loans equal to their "excess" reserves, and created new deposits equal to the loan amounts. The final ledger for the entire banking system and economy showing deposits which greatly exceed reserves is always the result of this recursive deposit-creation, reserve-leveraging process.

The $63.1 billion statutory reserve requirement in this example was higher than the actual statutory reserve requirement because all transaction deposits were assumed to have a 10% statutory reserve ratio requirement. Many transaction deposits qualified for the Reserve Requirement Exemption and Low-Reserve Tranche and were subject to 0% or 3% statutory reserve ratio requirements. This decreased the statutory reserve requirement from $63.1 billion to $42.7 billion. $42.7 billion of reserves could legally back $7.05 trillion of deposits—a 0.6% reserve ratio. At a 0.6% reserve ratio, there are $165 of deposits for every $1 of reserves. Commercial banks were legally allowed to accept a $1 deposit of reserves and create $164 of additional deposits. They were allowed to create $164 of lie-abilities for every $1 of reserves they held!

Banks sweep to "reduce their transaction deposits by a large enough amount that the level of their required reserves is less than the amount of reserves that they require for day-to-day operation of the bank. For these banks at least, the economic burden of statutory reserve requirements is zero." For U.S. commercial banks as a whole, statutory reserve requirements are very close to zero. The important thing to commercial banks is that they determine their reserve levels, not regulators. Sweeps are a scam which give commercial banks this ability.

Sweepstakes Picture Pages

To skip the picture pages after this chapter, please turn to page 234

UNSWEPT TRANSACTION DEPOSITS VS. SWEPT TRANSACTION DEPOSITS

```
Assets                              Liabilities
$3  (Reserves)                      $30 (Transaction Deposits)
$27 (Loans)
$0  (Reserves)
$70 (Loans)                         $70 (Non-Transaction Deposits)

$100                                $100

Total Reserves: $3
Reserve Ratio: 3%
Total Loans: $97
```

```
Assets                              Liabilities
$0.60  (Reserves)                   $30 (Transaction Deposits)
$29.40 (Loans)                      $6  (Transaction Deposits)
$0.00  (Reserves)                   $24 (Non-transaction Deposits)
$70.00 (Loans)                      $70 (Non-Transaction Deposits)

$100.00                             $100

Total Reserves: $0.60 (60¢)
Reserve Ratio: 0.6%
Total Loans: $99.40
```

The upper ledger shows unswept transaction deposits. The lower ledger shows swept transaction deposits. Each transaction account is reclassified as a transaction sub-account and non-transaction sub-account. 80% of money in transaction sub-accounts (10% reserve ratio) is "swept" into non-transaction sub-accounts (0% reserve ratio). This decreases the overall statutory reserve ratio requirement.

UNSWEPT TRANSACTION DEPOSITS VS. SWEPT TRANSACTION DEPOSITS FOR THE U.S. BANKING SYSTEM IN 2008 JUST BEFORE THE BAILOUT

Assets

$141,080,000,000 (Reserves)
$1,269,720,000,000 (Loans)
$0 (Reserves)
$5,641,900,000,000 (Loans)

$7,052,700,000,000

Liabilities

$1,410,800,000,000 (Transaction Deposits)

$5,641,900,000,000 (Non-Transaction Deposits)

$7,052,700,000,000

Total Reserves: $141,080,000,000
Reserve Ratio: 2%
Total Loans: $6,911,620,000,000

Assets

$63,110,000,000 (Reserves)
$1,347,690,000,000 (Loans)
$0 (Reserves)
$5,641,900,000,000 (Loans)

$7,052,700,000,000

Liabilities

$631,100,000,000 (Transaction Deposits)
$779,700,000,000 (Non-transaction Deposits)
$5,641,900,000,000 (Non-Transaction Deposits)

$7,052,700,000,000

Total Reserves: $63,110,000,000
Reserve Ratio: 0.89%
Total Loans: $ 6,989,590,000,000

The upper ledger shows unswept transaction deposits. The lower ledger shows swept transaction deposits. Reserves shown are the statutory reserve requirements. After sweeping, banks were only required to hold $63.1 billion of reserves to honor $7.05 trillion of deposits.

AN APPALLINGLY CANDID SUMMARY OF SWEEPS BY A COMPANY MARKETING ITS SWEEP SOFTWARE TO BANKS

Most banks massage their description of sweeps so as not to anger depositors, but a company marketing sweep software to banks has no such limitation. It has to highlight the corrupt benefits of sweeping to sell its product. The website of such a company is therefore illuminating. And chilling.

FINANCIAL INSTITUTION
SOLUTIONS

Financial Institution Services
Solutions for Community Banks and Credit Unions

Deposit Reclassification: Benefits and Strategies
By Joe Moss

Deposit reclassification offers financial institutions a way to dramatically lower their reserve requirements. This opportunity was approved by the Federal Reserve Board (Fed) in 1994 and has been implemented by most large banks. Now, as transactional deposits are increasing in small and medium-sized financial institutions, community banks are also able to reap the benefits of deposit reclassification. We examine the benefits and the way reclassification works in this article.

What Is Deposit Reclassification

Deposit reclassification represents a significant change in the method by which transaction accounts (both interest and non-interest) are reported for reserve requirement calculations under the Fed's Regulation D. As a result of deposit reclassification, interest and non-interest checking accounts are segmented into separate subaccounts unique to each account. The savings subaccount of the combined account balance is not subject to the 10 percent reserve requirement. The net impact is that your bank's reserve requirements fall to insignificant levels. Other than an initial, non-adverse notice to the customer, this process of transferring funds to the savings subaccount is invisible to your customer.

The checking and savings sub-accounts are evaluated daily. Funds are automatically transferred from the savings sub-account to the checking subaccount if required to cover activity in the account. Concurrent with the sixth such transfer during a calendar month, the entire balance is transferred to the checking subaccount to remain in compliance with restrictions on savings accounts imposed by Regulation D.

"Deposit reclassification offers financial institutions a way to dramatically lower their reserve requirements. ... The net impact is that your bank's reserve requirements fall to insignificant levels." These are not exaggerated marketing claims, but rather facts. "This process of transferring funds to the savings sub-account is invisible to your customer." Wonderful. The reserves backing your deposits have been decreased to virtually nil, and your bank doesn't even have to tell you. "This opportunity was approved by the Federal Reserve Board (Fed) in 1994." To banks, sweeps are not a risk or fraud, but an opportunity.

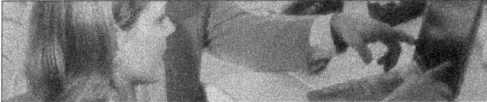

FINANCIAL INSTITUTION
SOLUTIONS

Sample Account Example

Deposit reclassification maximizes the balance of the savings subaccount each day. This process is best described by showing the impact on a sample checking account. The chart in Exhibit 1 tracks a checking account with a starting balance of $10,000 through each day of the month. Initially, the savings subaccount would be $8,000, leaving $2,000 in the checking subaccount.

On a daily basis, deposit reclassification compares the ending balance of the customer's checking account to the balance of the savings subaccount from yesterday and the status of the transfer counter. If the account balance is lower than the savings subaccount, a transfer is made from the savings subaccount to the checking subaccount. In that event, the transfer counter is incremented by one. In the event that the account balance multiplied by the threshold percentage exceeds the savings subaccount, a transfer is made from the checking subaccount to the savings subaccount. Since only debit transfers are counted, no increment is made to the transfer counter.

This process continues until the transfer counter reaches six. In the event of a sixth transfer, the entire account balance resides in the checking subaccount until the end of the month when the savings subaccount and transfer counters are reset.

Establishing Thresholds

Threshold percentages are established by checking product type and by balance range to identify relative volatility of checking accounts. A high balance and low volatility account (e.g., a high balance senior NOW account) would use a high threshold percentage. A low balance, high volatility account (e.g., a small business account) would use a low threshold percentage. On a macro level, the threshold percentage matrix should allow no more than 5 percent of total checking accounts to achieve the maximum of six transfers

The impact on reserve requirements is dramatic. Before deposit reclassification, the entire checking account balance would be reserved at 10 percent. After deposit reclassification, only the checking subaccount is subject to reserve requirements.

On a macro level, 80 percent of the transaction accounts of a financial institution can be reported as savings deposits, and all the calculations and transfers are invisible to the customer!

"On a macro level, 80 percent of the transaction [checking] accounts of a financial institution can be reported as savings deposits [even though they are not], and all the calculations and transfers are invisible to the customer!" To banks, invisibility to the customer is a plus. Customers would be unamused if sweeps were explained candidly. What if sweeps couldn't remain invisible? Imagine that swept funds were subtracted from the checking account balance depositors observe, and moved into a newly created savings account the depositor could also see but had never opened. If depositors could view these hidden sweeps and the decreased statutory reserve requirement which is the impetus for them was explained, would they consider the sweeping honest? Of course not, but even if depositors tolerated sweeps they would at least demand interest payments on the savings sub-account.

FINANCIAL INSTITUTION
SOLUTIONS

Customer Disclosure

The Fed allows the use of deposit reclassification only if it is properly disclosed to the customer, which means proper disclosure is critical to the process. In the Fed's opinion, the savings subaccount must be interpreted as a legally separate savings account to qualify as a savings account for purposes of Reg D. Since this process is invisible to the customer, the disclosure is the process by which the savings subaccount becomes legally separate.

There has been considerable debate about this issue among the Reg D purists. Since the customer is unaffected and no adverse change is being made to the customer's account, the need for disclosure has been questioned. However, the Fed has been quite adamant on this issue. This process is a contractual change in the way the customer's account is processed. To effect this change to the contract, the customer must be notified. Continued use of the account after disclosure constitutes acceptance.

We know of financial institutions that have chosen not to disclose deposit reclassification to their customers. But after their regulatory compliance examination, some have had to suspend deposit reclassification and restate reserve requirements with penalties as a result of not disclosing.

Financial institutions have also tried to disclose to the customer without truly informing the customer of the entire process. Disclosures referring to deposit reclassification as "an internal bookkeeping process only" or "an internal reclassification of deposit accounts" have also been denied by the Fed. The customer must be told that checking and savings subaccounts will be created and maintained and that transfers may occur between these subaccounts. However, the customer may be told that it will not negatively affect their account.

Many financial institutions have been concerned that the disclosure may create substantial dissension among their customers. The empirical evidence from actual disclosures suggests that negative customer reaction has been minimal, probably because they can be assured that the change is a non-adverse change to their account.

"Since the customer is unaffected and no adverse change is being made to the customer's account, the need for disclosure has been questioned." Questioned by who? What depositor wouldn't want to know that most of their checking account with a 10% statutory reserve ratio requirement is secretly converted into a savings account with a 0% statutory reserve ratio requirement? What depositor wouldn't want to know that their bank earns interest on the money swept into savings sub-accounts but doesn't pay any portion of that interest to them? The need for disclosure has been questioned by banks, of course. They want to decrease reserves to "insignificant" levels without telling depositors. The customer is not "unaffected" if large numbers of depositors attempt to withdraw reserves which are only sufficient to honor 1% or 2% of deposits. The change is "adverse" because it increases the risk of a bank defaulting on its contractual obligation to redeem all deposits upon demand. Banks consider this risk negligible because they rely on Bailouts.

"The [sweep] process is a contractual change in the way the customer's account is processed. To effect this change to the contract, the customer must be notified. Continued use of the account after disclosure constitutes acceptance." For most agreements involving money a contract is signed. It would be unrealistic to force all customers to resign deposit agreements every time trivial changes in bank policies were made, but sweeping is a major change which should be authorized only by having depositors sign a revised deposit agreement. This would require banks to explain the process candidly, and few depositors given a candid description of this fraudulent practice would agree to it. Thus there is a mere notification. Anyone continuing to use an account after the notice is sent—usually as a "statement stuffer"—is presumed to have agreed to it. Thus sweeps are instituted and "accepted" without most depositors having any idea that the practice was instituted.

"We know of financial institutions that have chosen not to disclose deposit reclassification to their customers. But after their regulatory compliance examination, some have had to suspend deposit reclassification and restate reserve requirements with penalties as a result of not disclosing." Some banks that swept accounts without telling depositors had to suspend it. But not all banks. How many banks sweep accounts without notifying depositors and were not punished or forced to come clean? Fed never releases such information.

"Financial institutions have also tried to disclose to the customer without truly informing the customer of the entire process." All banks in America that sweep meet legal disclosure requirements without truly informing customers. 99.99% of sheeple have no idea that their checking account is swept. In a broader sense, sheeple are uninformed about the most basic operational principles of our banking system. Fraudulent fractional-reserve lending could not be perpetrated or perpetuated without widespread ignorance. A smart, educated citizenry would never allow fraudulent fractional-reserve banking. Ever. Most sheeple are not even aware that fractional-reserve lending exists, and the few sheeple that know about fractional-reserve lending consider criticisms of the practice a ludicrous conspiracy theory. Someone who doesn't understand fraudulent fractional-reserve lending can't understand the significance of paltry reserve levels, and the obscene risk that fraudulent fractional-reserve lending and sweeping expose sheeple to. All bank depositors are harmed by the Depressions that result from the rampant money creation which low statutory reserve ratio requirements allow. Everyone is harmed when multi-trillion dollar bank Bailouts cause prolonged economic stagnation—everyone except Speculatos who profit from fraudulent fractional-reserve lending and sweeping.

"… the customer may be told that it [sweeping] won't negatively affect their account." A carefully worded misrepresentation masquerading as truth. Sweeping doesn't negatively affect any individual account, which from the depositor's viewpoint functions in the same manner as an unswept account. Sweeping negatively affects banks' ability to honor withdrawals by numerous depositors, reducing this ability precariously. The essence of fractional-reserve lending is that banks can honor deposit withdrawals by a few depositors, but can't honor deposit withdrawals by many depositors, even though all depositors think their deposit can be honored. The number of deposits which banks can honor is precariously low before sweeping. After sweeping, the number of deposits which banks can honor is decreased to absurdly low levels.

"Many financial institutions have been concerned that the disclosure [of sweeps] may create substantial dissension among their customers." Of course it would. If disclosed in a way customers understood, which sweeps are not. "... negative customer reaction has been minimal, probably because they can be assured that the change is a non-adverse change to their account." No, negative customer reaction has been minimal because customers don't know their accounts are swept. Even if customers know their accounts are swept, they don't understand the true reasons for sweeping and the true consequences of the practice because they don't understand fraudulent fractional-reserve lending. Again, no bank disclosure mentions the decreased statutory reserve requirement which is the impetus for sweeps. A thousand sheeple could call banks and ask about sweeping, and the decreased statutory reserve requirement for savings accounts would never be mentioned, unless the caller broached the topic and specifically asked about it. An honest disclosure of sweeps would explain fractional-reserve banking, the 0% statutory reserve ratio requirement for non-transaction deposits, and the increased risk this creates for depositors Any "disclosure" of sweeps which doesn't explain these facts to depositors is not honest, and is not real disclosure.

FINANCIAL INSTITUTION
SOLUTIONS

Implementation Action Steps

Implementation of deposit reclassification is much more than a data processing change because it involves a contractual change in the way a customer's account is processed, using a unique interpretation of Reg D. It also represents a dramatic change in the way transaction accounts are reported to the Fed. As a result, the steps required for implementation go beyond the installation of a new piece of software. Use of this action plan ensures the proper implementation of deposit reclassification, consistent with Fed directives.

1. *Obtain Federal Reserve Bank "No Objection."* We recommend highly that a letter be delivered to your Federal Reserve bank outlining in detail how the program will work in your institution. You will receive a verbal confirmation if your program is consistent with programs previously approved. Included in this letter should be the actual customer disclosure developed in the next work step.

2. *Develop disclosure strategy and complete the disclosure.* Disclosure language must be developed and included in your letter to the Fed. It is critical that your disclosure be consistent with Federal Reserve bank directives. A statement stuffer can be used as the disclosure for existing accounts. You need to modify your Terms and Conditions sheet for new accounts.

3. *Develop algorithm to maximize the balance of the savings subaccount.* The algorithm used to maximize the savings subaccount should contain threshold percentages allowing only 5 percent to 10 percent of accounts to reach six transfers by the end of month. These threshold percentages should be established by balance range and account type to carefully match the volatility of specific account types. This provides a smooth reserve reduction across the entire month. A three-month sampling of actual account activity is required to develop the threshold percentage matrix.

4. *Develop systems solution and implement the process.* The database approach using existing download extract language from DDA systems allows the most efficient implementation. Implementation can typically begin immediately upon completion of the disclosure, since it is a nonadverse change.

Deposit reclassification represents a major opportunity for your bank to improve its net interest margins. You would be remiss not to consider it.

To insiders who profit off our corrupt banking system, sweeping isn't fraud, but rather a "unique interpretation of Regulation D." This "unique interpretation" results in a "dramatic change in the way transaction accounts are reported to the Fed." The "dramatic change" is that swept transaction accounts aren't reported.

"Deposit reclassification represents a major opportunity for your bank to improve its net interest margins. You would be remiss not to consider it." As the Fed and guv'ment Bailout banks anytime their lie-abilities are exposed, this statement is the sad truth. When do bankers stop their relentless drive for lower reserves? When statutory reserve ratio requirements are 0% for every bank deposit everywhere, and not a moment before. When do fractional-reserve bankers stop concocting ways to defraud sheeple? Never.

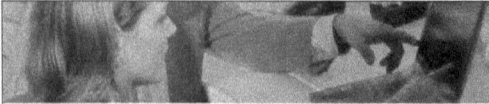

FINANCIAL INSTITUTION
SOLUTIONS

Exhibit 1. Account Example

Day	Ledger Balance	Threshold %	Checking Sub-account	Savings Sub-account	Transfer Counter
Start	$10,000	80%	$2,000	$8,000	0
1	$8,000	80%	$0	$8,000	0
2	$5,000	80%	$1,000	$4,000	1
3	$6,000	80%	$1,200	$4,800	1
4	$5,500	80%	$700	$4,800	1
5	$5,400	80%	$600	$4,800	1
6	$10,000	80%	$2,000	$8,000	1
7	$9,000	80%	$1,000	$8,000	1
8	$500	80%	$100	$400	2
9	$5,000	80%	$1,000	$4,000	2
10	$2,000	80%	$400	$1,600	3
11	$1,500	80%	$300	$1,200	4
12	$1,000	80%	$200	$800	5
13	$2,500	80%	$500	$2,000	5
14	$1,000	80%	$200	$800	6
15 to 30	$5,000	80%	$5,000	$0	6
Month 2	$5,000	80%	$1,000	$4,000	0

The sweep-company website included an example of deposit reclassification, which is shown above. "Ledger Balance" is the balance a depositor sees in their checking account. "Threshold %" is the percentage of the deposit swept out of the account. Advanced sweep software would set a different threshold percentage—a different sweep rate—for each depositor depending upon the depositor's spending habits. In this example, an 80% sweep rate is applied to all deposits. No matter how much money the depositor has in their checking account, 80% is swept into the savings sub-account.

The depositor in this example begins with an initial balance of $10,000 in their checking account. The checking account is swept at an 80% rate. 80% of the $10,000 deposit is $8,000, which is swept into a savings sub-account. $2,000 is kept in the checking sub-account.

Day 1 the depositor withdraws $2,000, decreasing the balance in their checking account from $10,000 to $8,000. $2,000 is withdrawn from the checking sub-account to honor the transaction. With an $8,000 deposit and an 80% sweep rate, there should be $800 in the checking sub-account and $7,200 in the savings sub-account. After the $2,000 withdrawal by the depositor, there is $0 in the checking sub-account and $8,000 in the savings sub-account. The sweep software doesn't withdraw $800 from the savings sub-account and transfer it to the checking sub-account, as this would squander one of the 6 monthly withdrawals that are allowed from the savings sub-account.

Day 2 the depositor withdraws $3,000, decreasing the balance in their checking account from $8,000 to $5,000. There is no money in the checking sub-account to honor the withdrawal, and money can't be taken directly from the savings sub-account to honor the withdrawal. Money can only be taken from the checking sub-account to honor the withdrawal. $4,000 is transferred from the savings sub-account to the checking sub-account. This is more than is needed to honor the $3,000 withdrawal, but after the $3,000 withdrawal there is $1,000 in the checking sub-account and $4,000 in the savings sub-account. The $4,000 in the savings sub-account is 80% of the $5,000 balance in the original checking account, so that the 80% sweep level is preserved. This withdrawal from the savings sub-account is one of the 6 permitted by Regulation D, and is added to the "Transfer Counter" which tracks such withdrawals. This process of withdrawing funds from the savings sub-account and transferring them to the checking sub-account is repeated whenever a withdrawal from the original checking account exceeds the amount of money in the checking sub-account. This occurred on Days 2, 8, 10, 11, 12, and 14. The software always withdraws an amount of money from the savings sub-account which will restore an 80% sweep rate after the withdrawal from the original checking account is completed.

There is no limit on deposits into the savings sub-account, which don't trigger the transfer counter. On Days 3,6,9, and 13, deposits are made into the original checking account and money is swept into the savings sub-account, but the transfer counter doesn't increase.

When additional deposits are made into the original checking account, the software automatically sweeps an amount of money into the savings sub-account which will restore an 80% sweep rate. For example, on Day 5 there is $5,400 in the original checking account, $600 in the checking sub-account and $4,800 in the savings sub-account. $4,800 (savings sub-account) is 89% of $5,400 (original checking account), which is an 89% sweep rate. The software prefers an 80% sweep rate, but withdrawals on previous days have decreased the balance in the checking sub-account, and the software won't withdraw funds from the savings sub-account and transfer them into the sub-account unless it absolutely has to, as this squanders one of the 6 withdrawals from the savings sub-account allowed by Regulation D. When $4,600 is deposited into the original checking account on Day 6, the software transfers $1,400 of the $4,600 into the checking sub-account, and the remaining $3,200 into the savings sub-account. The software only sweeps 70% of the $4,600 into the savings sub-account. After sweeping the additional $4,600 deposit at a 70% rate, there is $10,000 in the original checking account, $2,000 in the checking sub-account and $8,000 in the savings sub-account. The 80% sweep rate has been restored. This process of sweeping additional deposits at whatever rate will restore on overall 80% sweep rate is repeated whenever an additional deposit is made into the original checking account.

The sweep software self-adjusts each night in response to depositor activity, as is shown day by day in the table. On Day 14, the 6th withdrawal is made and the Regulation D limit on withdrawals is exceeded, so the account must be converted to a checking account for the rest of the month. Even advanced sweep software will occasionally lose its sweep "bet" (exceed the 6 withdrawal limit), and have to unsweep the account until the next billing cycle, forsaking extra income derived from lower statutory reserve ratio requirements.

Sweeping a checking account into a savings sub-account doesn't free up reserves equal to 100% of the swept amount because 90% of the reserves backing the swept amount have already been embezzled and lent. Sweeping frees up an amount of reserves equal to 10% of the swept amount, which can then be embezzled and lent. These reserves were backing transaction deposits subject to a 10% statutory reserve ratio requirement, and are no longer needed when the transaction deposit becomes a non-transaction deposit subject to a 0% statutory reserve ratio requirement. Banks make overnight reserve loans in the federal funds and repo markets, which will be described later, so freeing up millions of dollars of reserves for even a few days is profitable.

The sweep software in this example is rather primitive, but is cost effective for small banks that can't afford in-house sweep specialists. Larger banks have much more sophisticated sweep software which varies the sweep percentages as the month progresses. For example, software might set a more conservative sweep threshold after the 5th withdrawal from the savings sub-account, so that a 6th withdrawal is not made and the account is not completely converted to a checking account and can still be swept. Advanced software might have halved the threshold to 40% after the 5th withdrawal on Day 12, leaving $1,500 in the checking sub-account. This was enough to honor the next depositor withdrawal of $1,000 and avoid the 6th savings sub-account withdrawal, preventing the account from being completely unswept for the rest of the month. Advanced software would perform trending on accounts, note the amounts of withdrawals that cause accounts to be completely unswept, and utilize this historical information to calculate optimal sweep percentages for each account.

When advanced sweep software is first run, it analyzes historical account data, trends deposit and withdrawal tendencies, and determines optimal sweep rates for each depositor. There is no initial learning period in which the software guesses wrong frequently and many accounts have to be completely unswept. The software functions optimally immediately when implemented.

Advanced software would sweep more aggressively near the end of the month if few savings sub-account withdrawals had occurred. If there are 5 days left in the month, and only 1 of the 6 allowed transfers has occurred, the entire checking account could be swept into a savings sub-account, and only the amount withdrawn by the depositor would be transferred back into the checking sub-account each night. The 6th withdrawal would occur on the last night of the month, but the next day a new month would begin and 6 more withdrawals would be allowed. When making the withdrawal on the last night of the month, the software would decrease the sweep rate to a more modest beginning-of-month level.

Advanced software would account for large, regular payments such as loans and bills. If you deposit $5,000 a month into your checking account and pay a $2,000 mortgage on the 15th of each month, the sweep software knows the $2,000 probably won't be withdrawn before the 15th, and can sweep aggressively prior to the 15th. Systematic trending of such tendencies maximizes effectiveness of sweep software.

At a large bank like Citibank or Bank of America with hundreds of billions of dollars of deposits, sophisticated sweep algorithms free up billions of dollars of reserves. These reserves are embezzled and lent. As always, loan creation is deposit creation, which simultaneously increases both the money supply and interest profit "earned" by banks.

Bank Account Rules Facilitate Sweeps

citi

Banking   Credit Cards   Lending   Investing   Business   Rewards & Offers   Services   Citigold

Basic Banking Package: Summary of Common Fees and Features

Minimum Deposit Needed to Open Account

Monthly Service Fee

Waived When Requirements Are Met

Waived if you satisfy ONE of the following:

1. 1 Qualifying Direct Deposit credited to a Regular Checking, Day-to-Day Savings Account or money market account in a Basic Banking Package and 1 Qualifying Bill Payment posted to a Regular Checking account per statement cycle

OR

2. Maintain $1,500 or more in combined average monthly balances in a Regular Checking account and linked Day-to-Day Savings Account or money market accounts in a Basic Banking Package.

You've seen sweeps from banks' point of view. How are they disclosed to customers? In these examples we'll use information from Citibank, the second largest bank in America after Bank of America. The webpage above shows Citibank's basic checking account in May 2016. Citi calls this basic checking account its "Basic Banking Package."

Bank of America has the same minimum balance requirement of $1,500 and a $12 monthly "service" fee. Are banks colluding and fixing fees? As with Bank of America, the linked savings account is important to Citibank (and all banks) because the depositor can then be encouraged to transfer funds from a checking account with a 10% statutory reserve ratio requirement into a savings account with a 0% statutory reserve ratio requirement. Ideally, these transfers would be automatic via inducements like Bank of America's "Keep the Change."

Direct deposit and direct bill paying are also encouraged because they are periodic and predictable, and greatly improve the efficiency of sweep programs. If you are handed a physical check, you may wait days to deposit it if you are busy and not broke, but direct deposit will add funds to your account at the same time each month, with only minor variation. The same is true of direct bill pay. If you mail a mortgage check to your bank each month, it may arrive at the bank at different times each month, and be deposited at different times each month, depending on how long it takes mail services to transport and deliver it and bank employees to process it. Your mortgage payment is thus deducted from your account at different times each month. Not so with direct withdrawals which are entirely computerized and take mere nanoseconds. With direct withdrawals, the funds are withdrawn at the exact same time each month.

Citibank waves account "service" fees if 1 direct deposit and 1 direct withdrawal are made per month. Many individuals who don't keep $1,500 in their checking account all month long but who want to avoid fees setup direct deposits and direct withdrawals. They often find that they like the convenience of these direct withdrawals, have all paychecks direct deposited, and pay all major bills via direct withdrawals including their mortgage, car loan, student loans, insurance, cell phone bill, etc. Any bill whose amount doesn't vary month to month, and even some bills that do, can be paid in this manner.

Direct deposit and direct withdrawal decrease bank labor and overhead and improve customer service because they don't require tellers or physical checks which must be processed, but they also make sweeping aggressively a breeze for banks. The sweep software knows exactly when funds will be direct deposited, and exactly when the major direct withdrawals which are the bulk of most sheeple's expenditures will be made. The remaining expenditures are trivial by comparison.

If you have a $5,000 check direct deposited on the 1st of each month, and have a $2,000 mortgage payment direct withdrawn on the 15th of each month, then sweep software can transfer $2,000 to the savings sub-account on the 1st, and it knows it won't be withdrawn until the 15th. Spending need only be analyzed on the remaining $3,000, most of which can also be swept. Yet again, when summed over millions of accounts containing billions of dollars' worth of deposits, these large numbers of direct deposits and direct withdrawals greatly increase the total amounts of funds that can be swept. Banks advertise direct deposit and direct withdrawal as conveniences for customers, which they are, but their primary purpose is to make sweeping easier and limit lie-ability exposure.

"NON-INTRUSIVE" DISCLOSURE: TELLING WITHOUT REVEALING

Ceto and Associates
Consultants To Bank Management

services

Deposit Reclassification

Notify Federal Reserve Bank

Prior to implementation, you must notify the Federal Reserve Bank outlining the details of the Deposit Reclassification program. To do this, Ceto and Associates will write a customized letter for submission to your local Federal Reserve Bank. Included in this initial assistance is the development of a customer disclosure language that will be both acceptable to the Federal Reserve Bank as well as non-intrusive to the customer.

Ceto and Associates
Consultants To Bank Management

services

Deposit Reclassification

Develop and Deploy Disclosure

Upon receiving a No Objection from the Federal Reserve Bank, the customer disclosure process begins. We recommend utilizing a two sided statement stuffer for disclosing to existing accounts. This allows the disclosure to be complemented by a friendly marketing message. At the same time, the Terms and Conditions for new account holders must be modified by the insertion of a separate paragraph outlining this process.

Ceto and Associates is a leading sweep software company which has implemented sweeps at over 1,500 U.S. banks. Ceto was surprisingly candid in marketing sweeps. The two webpages shown above have been removed from the Ceto website, probably because it was deemed inadvisable to portray sweeps so honestly on a site that the public can view.

Translated from deceptive banker-speak into English, these two webpages say that Ceto and Associates will draft disclosure language which meets the legal disclosure requirements the Federal Reserve demands, without alarming depositors by telling them the truth about their bank's absurdly-low reserve levels and its inability to honor the majority of its deposits. The "disclosure" will therefore be "non-intrusive to the customer," meaning customers won't truly understand what is being done to their account and therefore won't object.

Ceto and Associates recommends using a "two sided statement stuffer" for "disclosing to existing accounts." This doesn't just allow the "disclosure" to "be accompanied by a friendly marketing message," it ensures that it will be mistaken for a marketing message. The "disclosure" on the back of the "friendly marketing message" will be presumed to be fine print about the message and ignored by the customer. In this way, banks meet the technical requirements of "disclosure," but implement it in a deceptive way which ensures that the disclosure will be not be read by most customers. Those few customers that actually read the "disclosure" are fooled by the deceptive language, don't understand what it means, and consider it "non-intrusive."

Two examples of actual bank "disclosures" of deposit reclassification follow. The deceptions in these "disclosures" will be meticulously documented.

Boiling Springs Savings Bank

Come Home to *Better Banking*

About us   Deposits   Loans   Products and Services   Rate Information   Resources   Community Alliance Program

RESOURCES

Deposit Reclassification

Under federal law, we are required to report our deposits in a certain way for regulatory reporting purposes. We are simply changing the way we report checking accounts and we are notifying you of this change. It does not affect you in any way.

Effective immediately, the Bank may make a change in your Checking Account that will not affect your available balance, interest earnings, FDIC Insurance, or bank statement. This account will consist of a checking sub-account and a savings sub-account. The Bank may periodically transfer funds between these two sub-accounts. On a sixth transfer during a calendar month, any funds in the savings sub-account will be transferred back to the checking sub-account. If an account is a Plan on which interest is paid, your interest calculation will remain the same. Otherwise, the savings sub-account will be non-interest bearing. The savings sub-account will be governed by the rules governing our other savings accounts.

Frequently Asked Questions Regarding Deposit Reclassification

What are you doing to my account? Why are you doing this?
Under federal law, we are required to classify our deposits in a certain way for regulatory reporting purposes. We are simply changing the way we report checking accounts and we are notifying you of this change. It does not affect you in any way.

Has my availability of funds been changed?
No, our funds availability will not be affected in any way.

Is my account still insured by the FDIC?
The FDIC insurance on your account will remain as it is today.

How is Boiling Springs Savings Bank benefiting from this?
This change will lower the amount of funds that we are required to keep on deposit at the Federal Reserve Bank, providing more funds for lending and investment purposes.

Will you increase your rate on my interest bearing accounts?
No, but this change will allow us to continue to pay competitive rates on all of our deposit products.

Will my fees go up?
No, this change will not affect your account in any way.

Boiling Springs Savings Bank is a New Jersey bank. Its September 2008 "Call Report" filed with the FDIC lists $961.2 million of deposits, $39.5 million of transaction deposits and $921.7 million of non-transaction deposits. This is after sweeping. The 23 to 1 non-transaction deposit to transaction deposit ratio suggests extremely aggressive sweeping, though Boiling Springs Bank does bill itself as a "savings" bank and might have a significant amount of non-transaction or savings accounts. Boiling Springs Savings Bank's statutory reserve ratio requirement was 0% on its $921.7 million of non-transaction deposits, 0% on its first $9.3 million of transaction deposits (Reserve Requirement Exemption in 2008) and 3% on its remaining $30.2 million of transactions deposits (the Low-Reserve Tranche in 2008 was $43.9 million). None of its transaction deposits were subject to the 10% standard reserve ratio requirement. Boiling Springs Savings Bank's statutory reserve requirement was 3% of $30.2 million, or $0.906 million ($906,000). Boiling Springs Savings Bank could legally keep a mere $906,000 of reserves to back $961.2 million of deposits—a 0.098% reserve ratio which would require each $1 of reserves to back $1,107 of deposits. Boiling Springs Savings Bank actually kept $2.1 million of reserves to back $961.2 million of deposits—a 0.22% reserve ratio which required each $1 of reserves to back $457 of deposits. No bank is required to disclose sweeping data, so Boiling Springs Savings Bank doesn't have to reveal how aggressive its sweeping is. We therefore have no idea what Boiling Springs Savings Bank's statutory reserve requirement would have been if it hadn't swept transaction accounts.

The website "disclosure" on the previous page shows how Boiling Springs Savings Bank justifies sweeping to its depositors. The term Faustian doesn't do this "disclosure" justice. Several lies jump out:

"Under federal law, we are required to report our deposits in a certain way for regulatory reporting purposes." True, but that reporting "way" doesn't require deposit reclassification. Sweeping is not necessary to meet regulatory reporting purposes. A bank can choose not to reclassify deposits and meet all regulatory reporting guidelines.

"We are simply changing the way we report checking accounts and we are notifying you of this change. It doesn't affect you in any way." This makes sweeping sound like an inert accounting change, which it is not. Sweeping is a reclassification of transaction accounts into non-transaction accounts for the purpose of drastically decreasing statutory reserve requirements. This drastic decrease in statutory reserve requirements affects depositors if the bank doesn't hold enough reserves to honor simultaneous withdrawal demands by all depositors.

"Effective immediately, the Bank may make a change in your Checking Account that won't affect your available balance, interest earnings, FDIC Insurance, or bank statement." All true—especially the claim that the "change … won't affect your … interest earnings." Interest earnings paid to the depositor should increase when their account is swept and their money is transferred from a checking account to a savings account. Interest earnings not changing actually means that the depositor is getting screwed, but the bank claims this is an advantage or benefit. Banks obviously have little respect for the intelligence of their depositors, and rightly so. A smart depositor who is told that their no-interest checking account is being converted to an interest-bearing savings account would immediately ask why they are not being paid any of the interest that the savings account earns.

"This account will consist of a checking sub-account and a savings sub-account. The Bank may periodically transfer funds between these two sub-accounts. On a sixth transfer during a calendar month, any funds in the savings sub-account will be transferred back to the checking sub-account." No mention of the 0% statutory reserve ratio requirement on savings accounts which is the reason why there is a limit on transfers out of savings accounts. Also no mention of the decreased statutory reserve requirement which is the impetus for the transfer.

"If an account is a Plan on which interest is paid, your interest calculation will remain the same. Otherwise, the savings sub-account will be non-interest bearing." Again, this means that none of the profit generated by sweeping will be shared with the depositor. The bank keeps all the profit generated by sweeping.

"The savings sub-account will be governed by the rules governing our other savings accounts." Especially the unmentioned 0% reserve ratio rule. The only rule that might benefit the depositor, the paying interest rule, is the only rule ignored.

"Has my availability of funds been changed? No, our funds availability won't be affected in any way." This is the most egregious lie. Availability of "funds" means availability of reserves. Reserves are used to honor deposits. Reducing the amount of "funds" or reserves can of course decrease their availability if many depositors demand "funds" or reserves which the bank has promised them but doesn't possess.

"How is Boiling Springs Savings Bank benefiting from this? This change will lower the amount of funds [reserves] that we are required to keep on deposit at the Federal Reserve Bank, providing more funds for lending and investment purposes." Banks that sweep don't decrease vault-cash reserves, as they have already decreased vault-cash reserves as much as possible. Sweeping generally lowers the Fed-account reserves that commercial banks must hold, and these are the funds "on deposit at the Federal Reserve Bank" that Boiling Springs Savings Bank is referring to. Note that Boiling Springs Savings Bank's description of how it is benefitting from sweeping isn't something honest and direct like, "This change will lower the amount of reserves that we are required to keep on hand to honor deposits, allowing Boiling Springs Savings Bank to create additional deposits, lend those deposits, and earn more profit in the form of interest income. The lower reserve level will also make Boiling Springs Savings Bank more susceptible to depositor runs, and increase the chance that it might not be able to honor demands for reserves made by depositors." Imagine some incompetent bank executive who actually sent a message like this out or posted it on their website. Depositors would flip out, mob the bank, withdraw all their money and close accounts, and the bank would be rapidly rupted. Which is of course why "disclosures" full of lies are utilized instead.

There is scarcely a sentence in the whole "disclosure" that is not a lie or misrepresentation. The Fed approved the exact wording of this "disclosure," and similar "disclosures" utilized by every bank which implemented sweeps. The Fed is a co-conspirator of commercial banks, not a regulator of commercial banks, and any claim otherwise is simply another lie.

The website "disclosure" on the following page shows how Capital Bank justifies sweeping to its depositors. The tiresome reserve calculations performed for Boiling Springs Savings Bank won't be repeated with Capital Bank. Capital Bank is a fairly new bank created in 2009, so the September 2008 data that has been used as a common reference point throughout most of this book doesn't exist regardless. Note that Capital Bank's "disclosure" sounds almost exactly like Boiling Springs Savings Bank's disclosure. In some cases, the wording is exactly the same. Either both banks used the same sweep software company, or they both used the same Fed sweep guidelines. It is a bit chilling to have thousands of banks regurgitating the exact same lies using the exact same wording, but it is not surprising.

None of the extremely large banks are foolish enough to put deposit reclassification "disclosure" pages on their websites. As most large banks implemented sweeping at least a decade ago, no disclosures are available from them except in the fine print of agreements signed when opening new accounts. Small banks were also shown because the author did not want to single out the same few large banks repeatedly.

⊕ CAPITAL BANK

Deposit Reclassification

Effective immediately, the Bank will make a change in your Checking Account that will not affect your available balance, interest earnings, FDIC insurance, or bank statement. This Account will consist of a checking sub-account and a savings sub-account. The bank may periodically transfer funds between these two sub-accounts. On a sixth transfer during a calendar month, any funds in the savings sub-account will be transferred back to the checking sub-account. If your Account is a Plan on which interest is paid, your interest calculation will remain the same. Otherwise, the savings sub-account will be non-interest bearing. The savings sub-account will be governed by the rules governing our other savings accounts.

Questions and Answers

What are you doing to my account? Why are you doing this?
Under federal law, we are required to classify our deposits a certain way for regulatory reporting purposes. We are simply changing the way we report deposit accounts to the government and the government requires that we notify you of this change. **It does not affect you in any way.**

Has my availability of funds been changed?
No. Funds are still immediately available from Non Interest Checking Accounts.

Is my account still insured by FDIC?
Yes. The FDIC insurance on your account will remain as it is today.

Is Capital Bank benefiting?
This change will lower the amount of funds that we have to keep on deposit at the Federal Reserve Bank, providing more funds for lending and investment purposes.

Will you adjust my analysis credit rate or change my marginal reserve requirement on analyzed business account?
No. Our already competitive analysis prices will be unchanged. This change is allowing these prices to remain competitive. The marginal reserve requirement will remain because our marginal reserve requirement is unchanged.

Will you increase the rate on my Interest Checking Account?
No. Not immediately. But the change will allow us to continue to pay competitive rates on all of our deposit products.

Will my fees go up?
No. This change will not affect your account or fees in any way.

BANKERS RAVE ABOUT RESERVE REDUCTIONS SWEEPING CREATES

IMPACT your bottom line

Deposit Reclassification™

CetoLogic's solution, Deposit Reclassification has assisted thousands of depository institutions increase their profitability by reducing their Federal Reserve Bank Required Reserves. The following are testimonials from our Deposit Reclassification clients discussing their success using our solution.

"Prior to Deposit Reclassification, we were holding a reserve balance close to $1.2 million which was non-interest bearing. We were able to lower our reserve to the minimum as soon as we started using Deposit Reclassification and our reserve has stayed there ever since. The implementation of Deposit Reclassification directly impacted our bottom line by $70,000 within the first year!
Ceto's Deposit Reclassification conversion was very easy. During the Fed required customer disclosure process, Ceto and Associates' expertise and guidance on the compliance steps was especially beneficial and contributed to the limited number of questions we received from our customers. The implementation was seamless and a non-event for our institution."

Neil Burke
Vice President – Senior Financial Officer
Benchmark Community Bank
Kenbridge, VA

"We are very pleased with the Deposit Reclassification program Ceto and Associates presented to us. Utilizing their program, we were able to completely eliminate the need to maintain a non-interest bearing balance of almost $8 million with the Federal Reserve. The elimination of this non-earning asset provided us the opportunity to lessen our wholesale funding balances, thereby providing a meaningful positive impact on our earnings. We are most appreciative of the Ceto and Associates' consultants and their insight and guidance throughout the process."

Mr. Charles Christmas
Senior Vice President & Chief Financial Officer
Mercantile Bank of Michigan
Grand Rapids, MI

"Deposit Reclassification was a great solution for us. Prior to Deposit Reclassification, our non-interest earning reserve balance at our Federal Reserve Bank was close to $3,000,000. We reclaimed this entire amount within 2 weeks! Our implementation of Ceto and Associates' Deposit Reclassification system was seamless and required minimal staff time. We highly recommend it to anyone seeking a permanent increase in earning assets."

Mr. Charles Burnett
Chief Financial Officer
Jeff Bank
Jeffersonville, NY

"Over the years, our holding company has built up an excellent business relationship with Ceto and Associates. Our banks are very familiar with the Ceto Deposit Reclassification program which has been implemented in eight of our banks. Implementation is very easy and requires minimal efforts from bank staff. Their consultants are great to work with and they ensure client satisfaction every step of the way. We are pleased to refer other banks to them."

Mr. Don McCarthy
Chief Financial Officer
Glacier Bancorp
Kalispell, MT

CetoLogic

Ceto and Associates revamped its website. The old Ceto website shown previously no longer exists, but testimonials from bankers that have implemented sweep software were added to a new CetoLogic website. Bankers brazenly laud the way deposit reclassification decreases the amount of Fed-account reserves they must hold to virtually nil, usually within weeks. They also consider the "limited number of questions … received from our customers" a plus, which is a discrete way of warning other bankers that Ceto "expertise and guidance on the compliance steps" keeps customers from understanding what is happening and complaining.

This is the second page of the CetoLogic deposit reclassification testimonials. Bankers utilizing sweep software note that "our FRB [Federal Reserve Bank] reserve balance is now zero" and that sweeping "significantly reduced our reserve requirement." Duping customers remains critical, and bankers are again careful to note that "the disclosure process went smoothly and we received very few questions from our customers." Yay! Especially disturbing is the claim that decreasing reserves "by more than $4 million on a permanent basis" is "good for the communities we serve as well as the bank." Reducing Fed-account reserves allows any bank to embezzle more reserves, create additional deposits, and lend them. While this additional credit could be a benefit to the community, decreasing reserve levels "excess"-ively is what eventually implodes the economy. The most heartwarming portion of the testimonial page is the admonition to fax "two of your most recent FR2900s" to CetoLogic for a free analysis of reserve reductions that can be obtained via deposit reclassification. As we'll see, the Fed could easily require disclosure of sweeps using the FR2900 form, but refuses to do so.

Though the author made the webpage snapshots as clear as technologically possible, their clarity is not optimal. Ceto banker testimonials on the previous two pages are reproduced here so that they are easier to read:

"Prior to Deposit Reclassification, we were holding a reserve balance close to $1.2 million which was non-interest bearing. We were able to lower our reserve to the minimum as soon as we started using Deposit Reclassification and our reserve has stayed there ever since. The implementation of Deposit Reclassification directly impacted our bottom line by $70,000 within the first year! Ceto's Deposit Reclassification conversion was very easy. During the Fed required customer disclosure process, Ceto and Associates' expertise and guidance on the compliance steps was especially beneficial and contributed to the limited number of questions we received from our customers. The implementation was seamless and a non-event for our institution."

—Neil Burke
Vice President – Senior Financial Officer
Benchmark Community Bank
Kenbridge, VA

"Deposit Reclassification was a great solution for us. Prior to Deposit Reclassification, our non-interest earning reserve balance at our Federal Reserve Bank was close to $3,000,000. We reclaimed this entire amount within 2 weeks! Our implementation of Ceto and Associates' Deposit Reclassification system was seamless and required minimal staff time. We highly recommend it to anyone seeking a permanent increase in earning assets."

—Mr. Charles Burnett
Chief Financial Officer
Jeff Bank
Jeffersonville, NY

"We are very pleased with the Deposit Reclassification program Ceto and Associates presented to us. Utilizing their program, we were able to completely eliminate the need to maintain a non-interest bearing balance of almost $8 million with the Federal Reserve. The elimination of this non-earning asset provided us the opportunity to lessen our wholesale funding balances, thereby providing a meaningful positive impact on our earnings. We are most appreciative of the Ceto and Associates' consultants and their insight and guidance throughout the process."

—Mr. Charles Christmas
Senior Vice President & Chief Financial Officer
Mercantile Bank of Michigan
Grand Rapids, MI

"Over the years, our holding company has built up an excellent business relationship with Ceto and Associates. Our banks are very familiar with the Ceto Deposit Reclassification program which has been implemented in eight of our banks. Implementation is very easy and requires minimal efforts from bank staff. Their consultants are great to work with and they ensure client satisfaction every step of the way. We are pleased to refer other banks to them."

—Mr. Don McCarthy
Chief Financial Officer
Glacier Bancorp
Kalispell, MT

"We are very pleased to be a client of Ceto's Deposit Reclassification software. It has enabled us to increase revenue with minimal time and effort. Our FRB reserve balance is now zero. We have placed these new funds into our loan portfolio and other earning assets. We implemented the Ceto Solution in less than 45 days."

—Roseanne DeLucia
Accounting Officer
Suffolk County National Bank
Riverhead, NY

"We have been very pleased with the results of Ceto and Associates' Deposit Reclassification solution. The Deposit Reclassification product has worked exactly as described. Shortly after implementation, we significantly reduced our reserve requirement. This reduction allowed us to reclaim our bank's assets from our reserve balance at the FRB. These recouped assets are now working for our bank's bottom line. We would highly recommend Ceto's Deposit Reclassification."

—Greg Dunlap
Chief Operations Officer
Farmers & Merchants Bank
Milford, NE

"Ceto and Associates and their Deposit Reclassification solution exceeded our expectations. Our merger partner brought attention to the benefits of Deposit Reclassification, including their favorable results from the solution and outstanding experience with Ceto. Ceto and Associates consultants were extremely helpful and their solution was simple to implement. We have continuously received excellent customer service and support. Deposit Reclassification provides the credit union with a competitive advantage by helping us to minimize our non-earning assets. Ceto made a promise to us and delivered on that promise."

—Greg Hughes
Assistant Vice President, Finance
California Coast Credit Union
San Diego, CA

"Deposit Reclassification is as easy to implement and use as Ceto and Associates described. We have recommended and, even bragged, to other institutions on how simple it was to implement. The disclosure process went smoothly and we received very few questions from our customers. The change was seamless and our benefits of $3,600,000 were quickly reclaimed. I firmly believe that Deposit Reclassification is a great benefit to the banking industry and Ceto and Associates is the Firm to use."

—Mr. Ken Junker
Vice President
Central Bank
Stillwater, MN

"Ceto's Deposit Reclassification solution enabled us to increase our earning assets by more than $4 million on a permanent basis, which is good for the communities we serve as well as the bank. Implementation was very smooth and required very little time of our people, and the daily process takes only about five minutes per day. Their system has been virtually trouble-free for us, but it's good to know our one-time fee includes unlimited support. Overall, we've found Ceto to be a pleasure to work with—their expertise and customer focus is refreshing."

—Richard Jackson
Executive Vice President
Northwestern Bank
Traverse City, MI

FEDERALRESERVE.GOV DATA RELEASES: NO SWEEPS DATA AVAILABLE

Board of Governors of the Federal Reserve System

About the Fed	News & Events	Monetary Policy	Banking Information & Regulation	Payment Systems	Economic Research & Data	Consumer Information	Community Development	Reporting Forms	Publications

Home > Economic Research & Data

Bank Assets and Liabilities

Aggregate Reserves of Depository Institutions and the Monetary Base - H.3

Agricultural Finance Databook - E.15

Assets and Liabilities of Commercial Banks in the U.S. - H.8

Assets and Liabilities of U.S. Branches and Agencies of Foreign Banks

Charge-Off and Delinquency Rates on Loans and Leases at Commercial Banks

Country Exposure Lending Survey - E.16
(on the website of the FFIEC)

Home Mortgage Disclosure Act Data
(on the website of the FFIEC)

Insured Commercial Bank Assets and Liabilities, Domestic and Foreign Offices

Senior Financial Officer Survey

Senior Loan Officer Opinion Survey on Bank Lending Practices

Survey of Terms of Business Lending - E.2

Bank Structure Data

Large Commercial Banks

Minority-Owned Depository Institutions

Structure and Share Data for the U.S. Offices of Foreign Banks

Business Finance

Commercial Paper

Corporate Medium-Term Notes

Finance Companies - G.20

New Security Issues, State and Local Governments

New Security Issues, U.S. Corporations

Survey of Small Business Finances

Dealer Financing Terms

Senior Credit Officer Opinion Survey on Dealer Financing Terms

Exchange Rates and International Data

Country Exposure Lending Survey - E.16
(on the website of the FFIEC)

Foreign Exchange Rates (H.10/G.5)

International Summary Statistics

Securities Holdings and Transactions

Statistics Reported by Banks and Other Financial Firms in the United States

Statistics Reported by Nonbanking Enterprises in the United States

Structure and Share Data for U.S. Offices of Foreign Banks

Financial Accounts

Financial Accounts of the United States - Z.1

Household Finance

Principal Economic Indicator

Consumer Credit - G.19

Finance Companies - G.20

Home Mortgage Disclosure Act
(on the website of the FFIEC)

Household Debt Service and Financial Obligations Ratios

Mortgage Debt Outstanding

Survey of Consumer Finances

Industrial Activity

Principal Economic Indicator

Industrial Production and Capacity Utilization - G.17, Annual Revision

Interest Rates

Selected Interest Rates - H.15 Daily | Weekly

Money Stock and Reserve Balances

Aggregate Reserves of Depositor Institutions and the Monetary Base - H.3

Factors Affecting Reserve Balances - H.4.1

Money Stock Measures - H.6

This is the Federal Reserve Data Releases webpage where economic data is published. This webpage is maintained by the Board of Governors of the Federal Reserve System and is where most people look for economic data. There is no sweeps data.

SWEEPS DATA WAS POSTED AT OBSCURE WEBSITE BUT IS DISCONTINUED

ECONOMIC RESEARCH
FEDERAL RESERVE BANK OF ST. LOUIS

MY ACCOUNT | REGISTER | SIGN IN

Search

FRED® Economic Data   Information Services   Publications   Working Papers   Economists   About

Home > Monetary Aggregates

Federal Reserve Board Data on OCD Sweep Account Programs

On Wednesday, May 2, 2012, the Board of Governors of the Federal Reserve System discontinued the publication of their retail deposit sweeps data. The existing data will continue to be hosted on this website, however no new observations will be reported.

Monthly Sweeps Data
ascii format | excel format

Since January 1994, hundreds of banks and other depository financial institutions have implemented automated computer programs that reduce their required reserves by analyzing customers' use of checkable deposits (demand deposits, ATS, NOW, and other checkable deposits) and "sweeping" such deposits into savings deposits (specifically, MMDA, or money market deposit accounts). Under the Federal Reserve's Regulation D, MMDA accounts are personal saving deposits and, hence, have a zero statutory reserve requirement. For a fuller description of sweep programs, see Richard Anderson and Robert Rasche, "Retail Sweep Programs and Bank Reserves, 1994-1999," Federal Reserve Bank of St. Louis Review, January/February 2001.

Some early sweep software operated over weekends. These programs reclassified transaction deposits as savings deposits (MMDA) just prior to the close of business on Friday and moved the funds back to the transactions account just prior to the opening of business on Monday. Because reserve requirements are computed on the daily close of business level of deposits, including Saturday and Sunday, doing so avoided (on average) more than 3/7 of the reserve requirement on these deposits (Friday, Saturday and Sunday, plus an occasional Monday holiday). Later software chooses an optimal strategy based on customer's payment patterns. A constraint is that the number of "transfers" (reclassifications) from MMDA to a checkable deposit must be six or less each month. (More than six and the MMDA is subject to reserve requirements as a transaction deposit.) Hence, all of a customer's funds must be reclassified as checkable deposits on the sixth transfer.

These 1990s "retail" sweep programs are not to be confused with the sweep programs initiated by banks during the 1960s and 1970s. In those programs, business demand deposits were swept overnight (typically) into non-deposit interest-earning assets such as repurchase agreements and money market mutual funds. Although these programs also reduced banks' required reserves, their primary intent was to allow firms to earn interest overnight on demand deposits because, under the Banking Acts of 1933 and 1935, banks are prohibited from paying explicit interest on such deposits.

Anything posted on the world wide web and indexed by search engines is hardly being hidden, but there is a monumental difference between publishing sweeps data on the main FederalReserve.gov site which most economists and investors on Earth visit, and posting sweeps data on the site of a regional Federal Reserve branch. The FederalReserve.gov site is the site for the Board of Governors of the Federal Reserve System, which is the executive council in charge of the Federal Reserve System. This is the site most of the world associates with the Federal Reserve, and visits. There are 12 Federal Reserve branches, each which regulates banks in a different geographical region of the country and maintains its own website. Each Fed branch employs its own staff of economists, and these economists have different specialties. Economists which studied sweeps were employed by the St. Louis Fed branch, and the sweep data was therefore published on its website.

This webpage includes a summary of sweeps in the Fed's own words. As noted, sheeple often refuse to accept the factuality of fraudulent banking practices and dogmatically claim that factual summaries of the operation of the banking system are outlandish. Reasonably-well-informed people who understand fraudulent fractional reserve lending have often never heard of sweeping. The author has dealt with many über skeptics who argue that it is impossible for banks to secretly reclassify tens of millions of checking accounts as savings accounts. As with other fraudulent banking practices, conclusive, irrefutable documentation of sweeping is therefore being provided.

The Fed webpage notes that, "these 1990s 'retail' sweep programs [the types of sweeps being summarized] are not to be confused with the sweep programs initiated by banks during the 1960s and 1970s. … Although these programs [non-retail sweep programs] also reduced banks' required reserves, their primary intent was to allow firms to earn interest overnight on demand deposits." Though stated delicately, this is an admission that "retail" sweeps are a ruse solely intended to decrease the amount of reserves banks must hold. Non-retail sweeps had the effect of reducing required reserves, but this was not their primary intention, as is the case with retail sweeps.

Non-retail sweeps only occur overnight, or over the weekend. Retail sweeps can be permanent, so long as Regulation D withdrawal limitations are not violated. This is a key distinction.

The terms retail and non-retail can be confusing. Non-retail sweeps were primarily offered as a perk to business customers, which are non-retail or non-consumer customers. "Non-retail" business customers are a relatively small percentage of total accounts at most commercial banks. Retail customers, the millions of individual consumers holding checking and savings accounts, are the bulk of accounts at most commercial banks. Retail sweeps were thus a massive expansion of the practice of sweeping. Rather than stating this distinction and its implication honestly and directly, Fed resorts to the deceptive "non-retail" and "retail" descriptions.

The Fed webpage explains that, "Their [non-retail sweeps] primary intent was to allow firms to earn interest overnight on demand deposits because, under the Banking Acts of 1933 and 1935, banks are prohibited from paying explicit interest on such deposits." The Banking Acts of 1933 and 1935 were passed during Depression v8.1929-1942 (The "Great" Depression), and were an attempt to limit the money creation that causes Depressions. Depression v8.1929-1942 will be explained in detail in *Bubblenomics 3*, but the basic gist is that banks created exorbitant amounts of money for stock loans, thereby creating the stock market bubble. If banks are paying interest on checking accounts, then they must be loaning out the reserves backing checking accounts to obtain the income to pay the interest, which means they are not holding sufficient reserves to honor checking accounts. At this time, reserves were still gold. Gold reserves could not simply be conjured like ledger reserves. As noted, there were 9,000 bank failures during Depression v8.1929-1942. 9,000 bank failures! Nine-freaking-thousand! Legislators were serious about forcing banks to hold adequate reserves, so as to prevent thousands of bank failures at some future date. Thus they outlawed paying interest on demand deposits, including checking deposits, which was intended to force banks to hold reserves to honor demand deposits.

One might think that the Fed, the supposed regulator of banks and the protector of the public, would have immediately disallowed non-retail sweeps in the 1960s when banks first began implementing them, as they are a clear violation of both the spirit and the letter of the Banking Act laws. One might think that the Fed would respect the authority of Congress and only change its checking account policies if Congress amended or rescinded the Banking Act. By now it should be clear that such hopes are naive, as is the expectation of any real oversight from the Fed. The Fed will approve most any fraud which increases the profit earned by commercial banks, with total disregard for negative effects on We the People. In allowing non-retail sweeps, the Fed emboldened commercial banks to attempt even more brazen frauds, which they eventually did with retail sweeps.

Commercial banks should not be allowed to lend the reserves backing demand deposits, not even overnight as is done in non-retail sweeps. Commercial banks should not be allowed to secretly reclassify tens of millions of demand deposits as time deposits to evade statutory reserve requirements. Fed's regulatory laxness in this regard is inexcusable, but typical.

Retail sweep programs have substantially distorted the growth of M1, total reserves and the monetary base, as Chairman Greenspan noted in his July 1995 Humphrey-Hawkins Act testimony to the Congress. (See "Monetary Policy Report to the Congress," Federal Reserve Bulletin, August 1995, pp. 772-3.) In the fall of 1995, the Board staff began releasing monthly data on the amount of newly initiated sweep programs to the public. On October 12, 1995, the Board of Governors' staff released the following statement:

"To avoid misinterpretation of monetary and reserves data on the part of the public, the Federal Reserve Board intends to release to the public information regarding sweeps from NOW accounts to MMDAs. On an historical basis, monthly estimates of the nationwide change in NOW accounts attributable to the implementation of sweeps during the month would be provided on request to any member of the public. No names of individual institutions, no specific dates and no disaggregation of the data by District or any other category will be provided. Rather, only a single national monthly average will be provided."

The data in this file are these estimates.

These data are the estimated cumulative daily-average effect of new sweep programs on the month-average level of the aggregate checkable deposits included in M1. For example, a sweep program that reclassifies $30 million of OCD as MMDA would reduce the average level of OCD for a 30-day month by $30 million if implemented on the first day of the month, $15 million if implemented on the 15th day, $10 million if implemented on the 20th day, etc. These calculations correspond to those used in published monetary and reserve aggregates based on averages of daily deposit data. (For general discussion of the reporting of deposit data and construction of monetary aggregates, see Richard Anderson and Kenneth Kavajecz, "A Historical Perspective on the Federal Reserve's Monetary Aggregates," and Kenneth Kavajecz, "The Evolution of the Federal Reserve's Monetary Aggregates: A Timeline," both in Federal Reserve Bank of St. Louis Review, March/April 1994.

The Fed webpage admits that "Retail sweep programs have substantially distorted the growth of M1, total reserves, and the monetary base." These are key economic indicators that the public uses to gauge the health of the economy and assess the rate inflation. "To avoid misinterpretation of monetary and reserves data on the part of the public, the Federal Reserve Board intends to release to the public information regarding sweeps." This is a clear admission that distorted money-supply data results in critical misinterpretations unless sweep data is published. However, "no names of individual institutions, no specific dates, and no disaggregation of the data by District or any other category will be provided. Rather, only a single monthly aggregate will be provided." So the public will never learn about the sweeping activity of any specific bank or banking sector, not even the sweeping of their own accounts. The public is only given a single monthly statistic representing the total amount of money swept by all banks. Thus the Fed shields commercial banks against all demands for disclosure of sweeping activity.

ECONOMIC RESEARCH
FEDERAL RESERVE BANK OF ST. LOUIS

MY ACCOUNT | REGISTER | SIGN IN

Search

FRED® Economic Data   Information Services   Publications   Working Papers   Economists   About

Home > Monetary Aggregates

Inferences regarding distortions to narrow monetary and reserve aggregates from these data should be made with caution. In particular, these are not the current amounts being swept, and no data are available regarding the aggregate volume of deposits currently affected by sweep programs. Depositories do not report to the Federal Reserve the size of their sweep programs. The MMDA used in the sweep are included with all other savings deposits in deposit reports filed the Federal Reserve. MMDA have been included with reported savings deposits since September 1991.

Estimates suggest that retail deposit sweep programs have reduced aggregate required reserves by about 10 percent of aggregate amount of deposits reclassified from transaction deposits to MMDA. Although sweep programs have been implemented in some smaller institutions subject to only a 3 percent marginal reserve requirement ratio, most programs have been implemented in larger depository institutions subject to a 10 percent marginal reserve requirement.

In the July 1995 Humphrey-Hawkins report on monetary policy, Federal Reserve Board staff noted that sweep programs "...this year..." had reduced OCD by about $12 billion and required reserves by about $1.2 billion. Based on a panel of 1231 larger banks likely sensitive to changes in reserve requirements, Anderson and Rasche (2001) estimated that sweep programs had reduced required reserves as of December 1999 by $34.1 billion. Because some banks could not, subsequent to implementing a sweep program, reduce their balances at Federal Reserve Banks by as much as the programs had reduced their required reserves, Anderson and Rasche estimated that banks' actual reserves had decreased only $25.8 billion. Note that sweep programs do not directly affect M2, since MMDA are included in M2. Sweep programs might indirectly affect M2 growth if they affect deposit offering rates paid on MMDA, OCD or other deposits.

The data reported here on the reduction in M1 due to the initiation of sweep programs are produced by staff of the Money and Reserves Projections Section, Division of Monetary Affairs, Board of Governors of the Federal Reserve System, Washington, D.C. They are reported here as a convenience. New data for each month will be available during the last week of the following month. Data for September, for example, are expected to be available during the last week of October. These data may understate initial amounts being swept. Depositories are not required to notify the Federal Reserve prior to beginning a sweep program and some may have started programs that have not been detected by Federal Reserve staff. The amount of any such undetected sweep activity, however, is likely small: The initiation of a sweep program of any importance sharply decreases a depository's reported checkable deposits and increases its reported savings deposits.

Here we have the key admission by the Fed that "no data are available regarding the aggregate volume of deposits currently being affected by sweep programs. Depositories do not report to the Federal Reserve the size of their sweep programs." Again, it is incredible that the Fed would allow such a monumental fraud and not even make banks report the scope of their activity. This is doubtless because the scope is much larger than estimated. Also, gathering sweep data would draw attention to it, inviting massive undesired scrutiny.

So if the Fed didn't force banks to report sweep data, where did it obtain the sweep data it reported? Fed economists had to estimate sweep activity from the historical deposit data commercial banks report. This is absurd and abominable. Regional Fed economists had to labor at taxpayer expense estimating sweep data that the Board of Governors of the Federal Reserve should be forcing commercial banks to report.

Finally, we have the galling statement that the sweep data are "reported here as a convenience." Fed is doing you a favor by releasing even this paltry information, and is under no obligation to continue doing so—which it didn't. On the top of the first webpage shown in this section, the Fed decreed: "On Wednesday, May 2, 2012, the Board of Governors of the Federal Reserve System discontinued the publication of their retail sweeps data. The existing data will continue to be hosted on this website, however no new observations will be reported." That's it. No reason for the termination of reporting was given. The omnipotent Fed does not have to explain itself. Only rubes need to ask such questions anyway, and they almost deserve the deceptive answers they would be given.

Commercial bank sweeping data should have been—and still should be—incorporated into the money stock measures and commercial bank asset & liability information published on the FederalReserve.gov website. Unfortunately, it never was, and never will be.

Fed's sweeping webpage is a disturbing exercise in Orwellian doublethink. It admits that sweeps distort fundamental economic statistics and that sweep data is important to avoid misinterpretation of monetary data. Which is true. This admission was on the website for years, but it is now juxtaposed with the terse explanation that sweeps data will no longer reported. So sweeps data is critical to avoid distortion of fundamental economic statistics, but Fed will no longer report it, meaning interpretations of fundamental economic statistics will be distorted and only insiders will have accurate information. Banks will be able to fraudulently reclassify deposits in absolute secrecy without any fear of oversight or public outrage.

THE FED'S **FR2900 FORM DOES NOT REQUIRE COMMERCIAL BANKS TO DOCUMENT SWEEPING**

FR 2900
OMB Number 7100–0087
Approval expires July 31, 2018
Page 1 of 2

Board of Governors of the Federal Reserve System

Report of Transaction Accounts, Other Deposits, and Vault Cash—FR 2900

PLEASE READ INSTRUCTIONS PRIOR TO COMPLETION OF THIS REPORT.

For the week ended Monday, _____ Month / Day / Year (9909)

This report is required by law (12 U.S.C. §§ 248(a), 461, 603, and 615). The Federal Reserve System regards the information provided by each respondent as confidential. If it should be determined subsequently that any information collected on this form must be released, respondents will be notified. The Federal Reserve may not conduct or sponsor, and an organization (or a person) is not required to respond to, a collection of information unless it displays a currently valid OMB control number.

Report all balances as of the close of business each day to the nearest thousand dollars.

Items	For FRB Use Only	Tuesday Column 1			Wednesday Column 2			Thursday Column 3			Friday Column 4			Saturday Column 5			Sunday Column 6			Monday Column 7			Total Column 8			
Dollar Amounts in Thousands		Bil	Mil	Thou	Bil	Mil	Thou	Bil	Mil	Thou	Bil	Mil	Thou	Bil	Mil	Thou	Bil	Mil	Thou	Bil	Mil	Thou	Bil	Mil	Thou	
A. Transaction Accounts																										
1. Demand deposits:																										
a. Due to depository institutions	2698																										A.1.a.
b. Of U.S. Government	2280																										A.1.b.
c. Other demand	2340																										A.1.c.
2. ATS accounts and NOW accounts/share drafts, and telephone and preauthorized transfers	6917																										A.2.
3. Total transaction accounts (must equal sum of Items A.1 through A.2 above)	2215																										A.3.
B. Deductions from Transaction Accounts																										
1. Demand balances due from depository institutions in the U.S.	0063																										B.1.
2. Cash items in process of collection	0020																										B.2.

Name and Address of Reporting Institution: I certify that the information shown on this report is correct.

Name (9017) _____   Authorized Signature (H321) _____   Person to be contacted concerning this report (please print) (8901) _____

Address (9028) _____   Title (C491) _____   Area Code / Phone Number (9902) _____

City (9130) _____   State (9200) _____   Zip Code (9220) _____   E-mail Address (4086) _____

Public reporting burden for this information collection is estimated to average 3 hours per response for quarterly filers and 1.25 hours per response for weekly filers, including time to gather and maintain data in the required form and to review instructions and complete the information collection. Comments regarding this burden estimate or any other aspect of this information collection, including suggestions for reducing the burden, may be sent to Secretary, Board of Governors of the Federal Reserve System, 20th and C Streets, NW, Washington, DC 20551, and to the Office of Management and Budget, Paperwork Reduction Project (7100-0087), Washington, DC 20503.

07/2015

FR 2900, Page 2 of 2

Report all balances as of the close of business each day to the nearest thousand dollars.

Dollar Amounts in Thousands	For FRB Use Only	Tuesday Column 1			Wednesday Column 2			Thursday Column 3			Friday Column 4			Saturday Column 5			Sunday Column 6			Monday Column 7			Total Column 8		
		Bil	Mil	Thou	Bil	Mil	Thou	Bil	Mil	Thou	Bil	Mil	Thou	Bil	Mil	Thou	Bil	Mil	Thou	Bil	Mil	Thou	Bil	Mil	Thou

Items—Continued

C. 1. **Total Savings Deposits (including MMDAs)** ... 2389 ... C. 1.

D. 1. **Total Time Deposits** ... 2514 ... D. 1.

E. 1. **Vault Cash** ... 0080 ... E. 1.

F. **Memorandum Item**

1. All time deposits with balances of $100,000 or more (included in Item D.1 above) ... 2604 ... F. 1.

☐ If your institution has no funds obtained through use of ineligible acceptances or through issuance of obligations by affiliates, please check this box and do not complete Schedule AA. (H017)

Schedule AA:

1. Ineligible acceptances and obligations issued by affiliates *maturing in less than 7 days* ... 2245 ... AA. 1.

The following items should be reported in June only.

Weekly reporters: Report balance as of close of business on June 30 each year.
Quarterly reporters: Report balance as of close of business on Monday of June report week each year.

Schedule BB: Nonpersonal Items

	For FRB Use Only	June Report Day Bil	Mil	Thou	

1. Total nonpersonal savings and time deposits (included in Items C. 1 and D. 1 above) ...
   Dollar Amounts in Thousands ... 6918 ... BB. 1.

☐ If your institution had no funds obtained through use of ineligible acceptances or through issuance of obligations by affiliates, please check this box and do not complete Item BB.2. (H029)

2. Ineligible acceptances and obligations issued by affiliates *maturing in 7 days or more (Nonpersonal Only)* ...
   Dollar Amounts in Thousands ... 6919 ... BB. 2.

☐ If your institution had no foreign borrowings, please check this box and do not complete Schedule CC. (H030)

Schedule CC:

1. Net Eurocurrency liabilities ...
   Dollar Amounts in Thousands ... C434 ... CC. 1.

☐ If your institution had no foreign (non-U.S.) currency denominated deposits at any of your U.S. offices, please check this box. If you did not check this box, your institution is responsible for filing the quarterly FR 2915 Report of Foreign (non-U.S.) Currency Deposits. (H020)

07/2015

The Federal Reserve FR2900 form, "Report of Transaction Deposits, Other Deposits, and Vault Cash," is shown on the previous two pages. All commercial banks must fill this form out each week and submit it to the Fed. Banks must list their daily transaction deposits, non-transaction deposits, and vault cash. This allows the Fed to track the amount of deposit money commercial banks are creating, and to ensure that they are complying with statutory reserve requirements.

Post-sweep transaction deposit and post-sweep non-transaction deposit levels are currently reported on the FR2900 form. The Fed could easily add a few lines to the FR2900 which would require banks to list pre-sweep transaction deposit and pre-sweep non-transaction deposit levels. The aggressiveness of all commercial bank sweeping could then be precisely calculated, and the amount of sweeping would be conclusively known. Most banks fill out electronic FR2900 forms and submit them digitally. The FR2900 data from thousands of banks is automatically plucked from digital forms and tabulated by the Fed's computers, so the amount of work involved in compiling comprehensive sweeps data would be trifling. The Fed nonetheless refuses to make commercial banks reveal their sweeping activity.

Earlier we saw companies selling sweep software ask commercial banks for recent FR2900 forms, so that the gains realized from sweeping could be estimated. The FR2900 form supposedly exists to obtain information from commercial banks which is used to ensure their compliance with regulations. What perverse irony! The FR2900 can be used to assist with the implementation of fraudulent sweeping, but not for its intended purpose of providing an accurate summary of a bank's deposits. Par for the course in our corrupt banking system.

CITIBANK LIES ABOUT SWEEPING CHECKING ACCOUNTS

Banks are honest about sweeps, right? Even if you oppose the practice, banks will at least admit to it, right? Wrong. They can't attract new customers if they are candid about such fraud. The following is a transcript of a conversation between the author and a Citibank online chat representative in December 2011:

Welcome
A Citi representative will help you in approximately 0 minutes 12 seconds. For your protection, we'll never ask you for passwords, PINs, User IDs, security words or any part of your social security number during a chat. Other information may be required to help us verify your identity.

You are now chatting with 'VERA' from Citibank, N.A.

VERA: Welcome to Citibank's Online Chat. My name is VERA. How may I help you?

LAWRENCE: Thinking of opening a checking account. Do you sweep your checking accounts? If so, could I have a copy of the disclosure that outlines the process?

VERA: I am sorry what do you mean by sweep the checking accounts?

LAWRENCE: Convert them into a checking sub-account and savings sub-account, and sweep unused checking funds into a savings sub-account to lower reserve requirements. As a depositor, I am concerned by this lower reserve requirement. Can I open an account and refuse to allow Citi to sweep it?

VERA: No we don't sweep accounts.

LAWRENCE: You're positive on that?

VERA: Yes I am positive on this.

LAWRENCE: At first you didn't know what sweeps were, so I just want to be sure. Did you ask someone?

VERA: When you explained it that made it clear. We don't sweep accounts.

LAWRENCE: I was told that Citi sweeps checking accounts when I called a branch. I just want to be sure. I want a bank that holds sufficient reserves.

VERA: Yes, I completely understand.

LAWRENCE: I am not trying to be difficult. Why would a local Citibank tell me they sweep accounts then?

VERA: No I understand your concern.

LAWRENCE: Is there an online copy of the checking account form used for opening a checking account?

VERA: Do you mean a customer manual. Now we don't sweep accounts on personal account we may with our business.

[Business checking accounts are those which actually pay some of the profits from sweeps to the depositor. The bank acknowledges these sweeps to business customers because they are smarter and know about sweeps. In this case, the interest revenue generated by sweeping and the portion paid to the depositor is a selling point.]

LAWRENCE: The agreement you sign which opens the account and includes all fine print.

[A lengthy exchange followed in which VERA guided the author to the portion of the website containing the "Client Manual" which the author downloaded.]

LAWRENCE: [Referring to the Client Manual.] This is the form they'll hand me to sign when I open a checking account?

VERA: The form that only sign is the "Signature Card" at our branch.

LAWRENCE: But this manual is everything I'm agreeing to legally when I sign that card, yes?

VERA: Yes that is correct.

LAWRENCE: The legal contract outlining account terms, is what this is?

VERA: The Signature Card is to verify you when a deposit and write checks to make sure that is your signature.

LAWRENCE: I know that. But when I open an account I agree to contractual terms for management of that account by Citibank. This "Client Manual" is that contract?

VERA: Okay sorry can you clarify the question. What type of account are you looking to open?

LAWRENCE: Basic checking.

VERA: Yes the client manual is that contract.

LAWRENCE: Thanks. Happy Holidays.

The "Client Manual" contains 64 small pages of fine print. 8 point font size. 31,000 words—about one-third the length of a typical mass market novel. When was the last time you or anyone you know stopped before opening a bank account and read all the fine print? Or read the fine print "statement stuffers" which disclose sweeping to those with preexisting accounts? Maybe it is sheeple's own stupid fault, but few read the fine print or any of the print in deposit agreements or statement stuffers.

Banks could encourage depositors to read the "fine" print by making it un-fine. That is, normal size. The paper cost would be trivial. Few sheeple question why the fine print on deposit contracts is even fine. Contracts truly designed to be read are printed in standard-size print. A contract printed with text so small it would make a Lilliputian squint should make sheeple suspicious and determined to read every word in the contract, but of course doesn't.

The author is trained in speed reading, but still required more than an hour to read the Client Manual. Contrary to what the Citibank employee said, sweeps are authorized in the Client Manual. The table of contents of the Client Manual lists, "Checking Account Sub-Accounts" on page 11. On page 11, the Client Manual says:

Checking Account Sub-accounts
For regulatory reporting and accounting purposes, all Citibank consumer checking accounts consist of two sub-accounts: a transaction sub-account to which all financial transactions are posted; and a savings sub-account into which available balances above a pre-set level are transferred daily.

Funds will be transferred to your transaction sub-account to meet your transactional needs. For Regular Checking (all non-interest bearing checking accounts), both sub-accounts are non-interest bearing. For all types of Interest Checking, the savings sub-accounts pay the same interest rate as their corresponding transaction sub-accounts. Transfers can occur on any Business Day. Transfers to the savings sub-account will be made whenever available balances in the transaction sub-account exceed a preset level. Transfers from the savings sub-account to the transaction sub-account will be made whenever the transaction sub-account balances fall below a predetermined level. Because banking regulations limit the number of transfers between these types of sub-accounts, all balances in the savings sub-account will be transferred to the transaction sub-account with the sixth transfer in any statement period. Both sub-accounts are treated as a single account for purposes of the customer's deposits and withdrawals, access and information, tax reporting, fees, etc.

So the Citibank employee denied that personal checking accounts are swept, yet the fine print of the Citibank account contract clearly says that all checking accounts swept. Maybe the employee was merely incompetent, but the fact remains that a Citibank employee misrepresented a practice which goes to the very heart of its ability to honor (or inability to honor) deposits.

Let's translate the massaged corporate-speak into English. "For regulatory reporting and accounting purposes, all Citibank consumer checking accounts consist of two sub-accounts." Why on Earth would "regulatory reporting and accounting purposes" necessitate the creation of sub-accounts? Superficially, this would seem absurd and illogical. If accounting were done honestly, there would be no such need. This slick wording is technically true, but literally a lie. "Regulatory reporting" means statutory reserve requirements. If savings sub-accounts were not used to artificially and fraudulently lower statutory reserve requirements, bank reserve levels would be insufficient to meet the statutory reserve requirement on checking accounts. Note that there is no mention of the 0% statutory reserve ratio requirement for savings accounts, which is the real reason for sweeping.

"For Regular Checking (all non-interest bearing checking accounts), both sub-accounts are non-interest bearing." Citibank can earn interest on your checking account deposit when it is swept into a savings account, but won't pay any of that interest to you. The savings sub-account doesn't pay interest to depositors. Why even classify it as a savings account then? To lower reserve requirements. The lack of interest payments by the savings sub-account is a sign that something shady is happening, and should arouse suspicion.

"For all types of Interest Checking, the savings sub-accounts pay the same interest rate as their corresponding transaction sub-accounts." One might think that a savings sub-account would pay savings account interest rates, which are generally higher than checking account rates, but this is not the case. If Citibank earns higher interest rates by covertly converting your interest-bearing checking deposit into a savings deposit, you don't share in that profit. If "savings accounts" used for sweeps don't pay savings account interest rates, they should not be called savings accounts, but rather something which more accurately reflects their true purpose. Reserve Requirement Avoidance Accounts?

"Both sub-accounts are treated as a single account for purposes of the customer's deposits and withdrawals, access and information, tax reporting, fees, etc." This process will remain invisible to you the depositor, so that you don't get angry or worried, and demand the termination of this practice, or a fair share of the profits it generates.

The author went into a Citibank branch and tried to open a checking account which could not be swept. He crossed out the sweeping portion of the Client Manual, and informed the employee that he would only open an account if sweeping were explicitly prohibited. The author also provided a typed addendum which explicitly disallowed sweeping. The employee called the manager, who smiled wryly and said that such ad-hoc revisions of the deposit agreement were not allowed. The author asked if any bank offered non-swept checking accounts. The bank manager said he didn't know of any but couldn't be sure that there weren't any (many small banks don't sweep accounts, as explained). The author asked the manager if Citibank offered any accounts which were 100% backed by reserves. The manager said he was sure no bank offered such accounts, as they would "completely eliminate" bank profits.

No bank executive would try to deny sweeps. They are a fundamental part of modern banking which all insiders know about, and which all executives factor into their strategic planning. Keeping sweeps hidden from sheeple is the name of the game. Banks meet the technical legal requirement of disclosure, without truly informing most sheeple about sweeps. Not one depositor in 10,000 is aware that their checking account is swept. Those rare times that average customers ask banks about sweeping, banks simply lie, as Citibank did to the author.

Infinite Money Creation

"Laws requiring banks and other depository institutions to hold a certain fraction of their deposits in reserve have been a part of our nation's banking history for many years. ... Before the establishment of the Federal Reserve System, reserve requirements were thought to help ensure the liquidity of bank notes and deposits, particularly during times of financial strains. ... Since the creation of the Federal Reserve System as a lender of last resort, capable of meeting the liquidity needs of the entire banking system, the notion of and need for reserve requirements as a source of liquidity has all but vanished."

—Joshua N. Feinman, Federal Reserve Economist

There are no more reserve-reducing machinations to document. In September 2008 just before The Bailout passed, the U.S. banking system had $7.05 trillion of deposits and a statutory reserve requirement of $42.7 billion. $7.05 trillion of deposits only had to be backed by $42.7 billion of reserves—a 0.6% reserve ratio. "Regulations" only required commercial banks to hold $1 of reserves to honor every $165 of deposits.

Fed justifies this blatant insolvency by portraying reserves as decadent. Miniscule amounts of reserves are not a risk. In some bygone era, "reserve requirements were thought to help ensure the liquidity of bank notes and deposits, particularly during times of financial crisis." Thought to help ensure? How could reserves not help ensure "liquidity" of bank deposits? Liquidity is the ability to redeem deposits for reserves. Without reserves, deposits can't be redeemed, "particularly during times of financial strains." That is, particularly during times when many depositors demand the reserves supposedly backing their deposits. Banks then have a "liquidity" problem because there are not enough reserves to honor all deposits. Luckily for us, "Since the creation of the Federal Reserve System as a lender of last resort, capable of meeting the liquidity needs of the entire banking system, the notion of and need for reserve requirements as a source of liquidity has all but vanished." So no commercial bank needs reserves. They have the Fed. The Fed ends up "meeting the liquidity needs of the entire banking system" by conjuring limitless reserves out of thin air. It is difficult for a non-economist to appreciate the true meaning of Fed "meeting the liquidity needs of the entire banking system." Please remember that harmless-sounding phrase when reading about the trillions of dollars of reserves that the Fed conjured during Depression v9.2006-201x to effect The Bailout.

The perversion of statutory reserve ratio requirements was gradual. In 1913 when Fed was created, it set the statutory reserve ratio requirement for demand deposits at 18%. When banks failed during the Great Depression, Fed increased the statutory reserve ratio requirement to 26% and did not decrease it below 20% until the 1950s. After the 1950s, Fed steadily decreased the statutory reserve ratio requirement to as low as 12.75% on most demand deposits. The Monetary Control Act of 1980 created the transaction deposit and non-transaction deposit categorizations and the 3% Low-Reserve Tranche. After the Monetary Control Act took effect, the Fed set a 12% statutory reserve ratio requirement on transaction deposits. The Garn–St. Germain Depository Institutions Act of 1982 created the Reserve Requirement Exemption. In 1992, the Fed decreased the statutory reserve ratio requirement on transaction deposits from 12% to 10% and has not changed it since, excepting annual indexing of the Reserve Requirement Exemption and Low-Reserve Tranche.

In 1913 when Fed was created, it set the statutory reserve ratio requirement on time deposits at 5%. Fed changed the statutory reserve ratio requirement on time deposits many times prior to the 1970s; the lowest statutory reserve ratio requirement on time deposits was 1% during the stagflation (high unemployment and high inflation) of the 1970s, the highest was 7.5% in the late 1940s just after World War II. After the Monetary Control Act created the "non-transaction" deposit categorization in 1980, Fed set a 3% statutory reserve ratio requirement on non-transaction deposits. Fed decreased this statutory reserve ratio requirement to 0% in 1990, and began strictly enforcing the Regulation D limit of 6 withdrawals per month from non-transaction accounts.

In 1994, banks began sweeping transaction accounts, circumventing Fed's statutory reserve requirements, and reducing overall statutory reserve ratio requirements to less than 1%. The only banks not using sweeping to lower statutory reserve ratio requirements are small banks which have miniscule statutory reserve requirements because most of their transaction deposits qualify for the Reserve Requirement Exemption and Low-Reserve Tranche.

Surprisingly, these "regulations" are not explained in the pamphlets and signs that litter bank lobbies. Guess what, dunce, this bank only has to keep 0.6% of your deposit in reserve, even though it has promised you the whole deposit upon demand. Or imagine the following giant signs above banks:

Bank of America
Less Than 2% Reserves Since 1994

Wells Fargo
Conjuring Loan Money Since 1852

Banks could hire a famous magician to do bank advertisements and pull money out of a hat rather than a rabbit. Or maybe an Ethiopian to emphasize how slim reserve margins really are. A ballsy bank might have a McDonald's-like sign that increases each time a new loan is monetized:

Citibank
$1,491,373,852,416 of Loan Money Created

These quips are far from funny. They are the brutal truth. Low statutory reserve ratio requirements are a simple thing, but they are applied by banks worldwide on a colossal scale, resulting in money creation on a colossal scale.

While we're dreaming of absurd theoreticals in which banks represent themselves honestly, imagine going to FederalReserve.gov, and seeing a banner that said: there are currently $102.7 billion of reserves backing $7,052 billion of commercial-bank deposits, which is a 1.46% reserve ratio. $6.95 trillion of deposits can't be honored. Such honesty would precipitate runs on banks that would collapse the entire financial system and economy.

When fractional-reserve banks decrease reserve ratios, they can lend more money, but they always lend more money by creating more money. Previous examples showed the total deposit creation with a 10% statutory reserve ratio requirement, but at the much lower statutory reserve ratio requirements which actually prevail, much more money is created. How much more?

At a 10% reserve ratio, an initial $100 deposit has 10% reserve backing. $10 is reserved, $90 is lent by creating new deposits. The 10% reserve ratio is applied to the $90 of new deposits. $9 is reserved, $81 is lent by creating new deposits. . . If this process of recursive money creation proceeds to its theoretical maximum, $900 in new money is created, 9 times the original deposit.

At a 5% reserve ratio, an initial $100 deposit has 5% reserve backing. $5 is reserved, $95 is lent by creating new deposits. The 10% reserve ratio is applied to the $95 of new deposits. $4.75 is reserved, $90.25 is lent by creating new deposits. . . If this process of recursive money creation proceeds to its theoretical maximum, $1,900 of new deposits are created, 19 times the original deposit.

At a 2.5% reserve ratio, an initial $100 deposit has 2.5% reserve backing. $2.50 is reserved, $97.50 is lent by creating new deposits. The 10% reserve ratio is applied to the $97.50 of new deposits. $2.44 is reserved, $95.06 is lent by creating new deposits. . . If this process of recursive money creation proceeds to its theoretical maximum, $3,900 of new deposits are created, 39 times the original deposit.

At a 1.25% reserve ratio, an initial $100 deposit has 1.25% reserve backing. $1.25 is reserved, $98.75 is lent by creating new deposits. The 10% reserve ratio is applied to the $98.75 of new deposits. $1.23 is reserved, $97.52 is lent by creating new deposits. . . If this process of recursive money creation proceeds to its theoretical maximum, $7,900 of new deposits are created, 79 times the original deposit.

At a 0.625% reserve ratio, an initial $100 deposit has 0.625% reserve backing. $0.63 is reserved, $99.37 is lent by creating new deposits. The 10% reserve ratio is applied to the $99.37 of new deposits. $0.62 is reserved, $98.75 is lent by creating new deposits... If this process of recursive money creation proceeds to its theoretical maximum, $15,900 of new deposits are created, 159 times the original deposit.

Decreasing the reserve ratio 16-fold from 10% to 0.625% allows banks to increase their money creation 150-fold. Stated another way, decreasing the reserve ratio 94% increased money creation 1,667%.

At a 10% reserve ratio the first-iteration loan is $90, at a 2.5% reserve ratio the first-iteration loan is $97.50, and at a 0.625% reserve ratio the first-iteration loan is $99.37. At a 10% reserve ratio the second-iteration loan is $81, at a 2.5% reserve ratio the second-iteration loan is $95.06, and at a 0.625% reserve ratio the second-iteration loan is $98.75. At the end of the second iteration, money creation totals $171 for a 10% reserve ratio, $192.56 for a 2.5% reserve ratio, and $198.12 for 0.625% reserve ratio. As the reserve ratio decreases, the amount of money created and lent with each iteration increases, which drastically increases total money creation when summed over many iterations. Reserve ratios are the throttle of the deposit creation process. Decreasing reserve ratios drastically is like slamming one's foot on the gas pedal of a car. Rapid and voluminous money creation results.

Here is the money creation in table form:

Reserve Ratio	Money Multiplier	Additional Deposit Money Created From Initial $100 Deposit of Reserves
100%	0 times initial deposit of reserves	$0
50%	1 times initial deposit of reserves	$100
25%	3 times initial deposit of reserves	$300
10%	9 times initial deposit of reserves	$900
5%	19 times initial deposit of reserves	$1,900
2.5%	39 times initial deposit of reserves	$3,900
1.25%	79 times initial deposit of reserves	$7,900
0.625%	159 times initial deposit of reserves	$15,900

In honest 100% reserve banking, the reserve ratio is 100%, and an initial deposit of reserves only results in a single deposit being created which is equal to the amount of reserves. In honest 100% reserve banking, if $100 of reserves are deposited into the banking system initially, a single $100 deposit is all that is created. Any additional deposit creation results in deposit lie-abilities not fully backed by reserves, and is fraudulent. The creation of a single deposit when reserves are deposited is not fraudulent, and this first deposit which is 100% backed by reserves is not counted in the deposit creation in the table above. In the table above, $0 of additional deposit money is created at a 100% reserve ratio, but this doesn't mean there are no deposits, as there is still the initial $100 deposit fully backed by reserves. $100 of additional deposit money is created at a 50% reserve ratio, but there is $200 of total deposits when the initial $100 deposit is counted. $100 of additional deposit money is created at a 50% reserve ratio, but there is $200 of total deposits when the initial $100 deposit is counted. $7,900 of additional deposit money is created at a 1.25% reserve ratio, but there is $8,000 of total deposits when the initial $100 deposit is counted...

Under a system of fraudulent fractional-reserve banking, the maximum amount of additional deposit lie-abilities that can be created is always some multiple of the initial amount of reserves deposited into the banking system. That multiple is the MULTIPLIER. Deposits are money, in creating additional deposits the money supply is being increased or multiplied. The multiplier is therefore called the MONEY MULTIPLIER. The money multiplier is the fundamental parameter that reveals the aggressiveness of fractional-reserve deposit creation—besides deposit and reserve statistics, of course.

In honest 100% reserve banking, the money multiplier is 0 and no new deposits are created. Anytime the money multiplier is greater than 0, fraudulent fractional-reserve lending is taking place. The larger the money multiplier, the greater the deposit creation, and the greater the fraud.

In our simple examples, $100 of reserves are initially deposited at the first bank. In the real economy, the Fed made a $102 billion deposit of reserves. At a 10% reserve ratio, commercial banks could create an additional $918 billion of deposits (9 x $102 billion = $918 billion). At a 2.5% reserve ratio, commercial banks could create an additional $3.978 trillion of deposits (39 x $102 billion = $3,978 billion = $3.978 trillion). At a 0.625% reserve ratio, commercial banks could create an additional $16.218 trillion of deposits (159 x $102 billion = $16,218 billion = $16.218 trillion).

Did commercial banks actually create $16.22 trillion? No. Total deposits in the U.S. banking system were "only" $7.05 trillion. The statutory reserve requirement for the U.S. banking system was $42.7 billion, 0.6% of the $7.05 trillion of deposits, a 0.6% reserve ratio.

At a 0.6% statutory reserve ratio requirement, the money multiplier is 164 (which doesn't include the initial deposit of reserves or the first deposit created which is a promise to redeem the deposited reserves). For every $1 of reserves initially deposited into the banking system, commercial banks can create $164 of additional deposits, and when deposit creation concludes there are deposits equal to 165 times reserves. For $42.7 billion of reserves, banks exercised this deposit-creation prerogative and created $7.05 trillion of deposits (165 x $42.7 billion = $7,050 billion = $7.05 trillion).

Banks kept reserves in excess of the statutory reserve requirement. $60 billion excess. Banks held $102.7 of total reserves, $42.7 billion were required, so there was a $60 billion "excess." Banks did not exercise their deposit-creation prerogative for these $60 billion of "excess" reserves. Assuming a 0.6% statutory reserve ratio requirement, banks could have created an additional amount of deposits equal to

165 times "excess" reserves, which is $9.9 trillion (165 x $60 billion = $9,900 billion = $9.9 trillion).

A banking system which is loaned up has no "excess" reserves. If a banking system with $102.7 billion of reserves is loaned up at a 0.6% statutory reserve ratio requirement, total deposits would be 165 times reserves, or $16.9 trillion (165 x $102.7 billion = $16,900 billion = $16.9 trillion). $16.90 trillion is $9.85 trillion more than the $7.05 trillion of deposits which banks actually created.

Here is the information in visual form:

```
    $42.7 billion     +     $60 billion     =     $102.7 billion
      Required               "Excess"              Total
      Reserves               Reserves              Reserves


  Deposit Creation         No Deposit
  165 Times Reserves        Creation


    $7.05 trillion    +         $0         =      $7.05 trillion
      Deposits               Deposits              Deposits
```

The $42.7 billion of reserves back the $7.05 trillion of deposits. $42.7 billion is the minimum amount of reserves that can back $7.05 trillion of deposits at the prevailing statutory reserve ratio requirement. Additional deposits can be created because "excess" reserves can back them. If $165 of deposits are created for each dollar of the $60 billion of "excess" reserves, the result is:

```
    $42.7 billion     +     $60 billion     =     $102.7 billion
      Required               "Excess"              Total
      Reserves               Reserves              Reserves


  Deposit Creation       Deposit Creation
  165 Times Reserves     165 Times Reserves


    $7.05 trillion    +    $9.85 trillion  =      $16.9 trillion
      Deposits               Deposits              Deposits
```

The $60 billion of "excess" reserves now back deposits, so are required reserves rather than "excess" reserves:

$102.7 billion	+	$0 billion	=	$102.7 billion
Required Reserves		"Excess" Reserves		Total Reserves
Deposit Creation 165 Times Reserves		No Deposit Creation		
$16.9 trillion	+	$0	=	$16.9 trillion
Deposits		Deposits		Deposits

There are no "excess" reserves. The banking system is loaned up and no more deposits can be created—unless deposits are uncreated or additional reserves are injected into the banking system.

Speculatos' greed is boundless. If Speculatos were legally allowed to create an additional $9.9 trillion of deposits and lend them at interest, why didn't they? The 0.6% reserve ratio is the absurdly-low statutory reserve ratio requirement created by sweeping deposits. Banks have no intention of decreasing reserves to this absurdly-low level. Banks decreased the statutory reserve requirement so that it is far less than the reserves they need for day to day operations, which allows them to ignore statutory reserve requirements and set whatever reserve level they prefer.

Banks thought that $102.7 billion of reserves would be sufficient to honor normal withdrawal demands on $7.05 trillion of deposits. Banks actually needed trillions of dollars more reserves than this when runs manifested, as evidenced by The Bailout, but ignore that inconsistency for now. When runs manifest, banks always need Fed Bailouts, but runs are not a normal occurrence. Banks hold enough reserves to honor day-to-day depositor withdrawals under normal, healthy economic conditions in which runs have not manifested. $102.7 billion of reserves backing $7.05 trillion of deposits is a 1.46% reserve ratio. $102.7 billion of reserves backing $16.9 trillion of deposits would have been a 0.6% reserve ratio, which is not enough reserves to honor normal, day-to-day depositor withdrawal demands. 1.46% is already a razor-thin reserve ratio, anything lower is lunacy and then some. If the U.S. banking system had only backed 0.6% of all deposits with reserves, depositors would have come to banks to withdraw reserves, and banks would have said, "sorry, we're all out." This would have precipitated widespread bank runs which would have rupted every bank and vaporized the economy—unless a Bailout were implemented to prevent such an econolypse.

To maintain a 1.46% reserve ratio with $16.9 trillion of deposits, $246.7 billion of reserves would have been required. The banking system only had $102.7 billion of reserves. Commercial banks can't create reserves, they can only create deposits. Even though the statutory reserve ratio requirement allowed additional deposit creation, banks need to hold sufficient reserves to honor depositor withdrawals prevented them from creating additional deposits.

It is nonetheless staggering that our banking system's "regulations" are so corrupt and lax that private commercial banks had the prerogative of creating almost $17 trillion out of thin air. Banks "only" exercised $7 trillion of their $17 trillion money-creation prerogative. Yet again, it is sickening and tyrannical for a privileged class of bankers to create almost $7 trillion out of thin air while sheeple must work to obtain money.

In our corrupt banking system, "excess" reserves can be viewed as latent deposits, deposits that have not been created but can be. This critical insight helps avoid confusion later, when the Federal Reserve creates and uncreates reserves, and the amount of reserves is changing. More on latent deposits later.

The 0.6% statutory reserve ratio requirement for the entire banking system is not a single decreed statutory reserve ratio requirement. Each individual bank may have different amounts of transaction deposits subject to the Reserve Requirement Exemption, Low-Reserve Tranche, or Standard Reserve Requirement. Depositors at different banks may choose different ratios of transaction and non-transaction deposits. Different banks may sweep or not sweep, and those that sweep often set different sweep thresholds. Individual banks thus have different statutory reserve ratio requirements. When the deposits and reserves of more than 7,000 banks are summed and a single statutory reserve ratio requirement is computed for that summation by dividing total reserves by total deposits, the 0.6% statutory reserve ratio requirement results.

A Central Bank concerned about protecting depositors increases statutory reserve ratio requirements—ideally to 100%. A Central Bank concerned about increasing commercial bank profits decreases statutory reserve ratio requirements, which is what the Fed has done continually since it was created in 1913.

Paltry statutory reserve ratio requirements are important enough to Speculatos that they leave nothing to chance. Though Speculatos spend significant resources to make sure that each Inflator General (Chairman of the Board of Governors of the Federal Reserve System) is a proponent of fraudulent fractional-reserve banking, it is theoretically possible that some JFK-esque Inflator General might try to subvert the natural order and institute a 100% statutory reserve ratio requirement. Speculatos ensured the passage of laws which make this impossible. By statute, the Federal Reserve can only set a statutory reserve ratio requirement of 8% - 14% on transaction deposits, and 0% - 9% on non-transaction deposits. No Inflator General in history has ever uttered a single syllable supporting honest 100% reserve banking while in power, but even if an Inflator General wanted to institute honest 100% reserve banking, doing so would be illegal.

Speculatos are ruthless geniuses. They think of *every* eventuality, and have contingencies for every eventuality. There is *nothing* Speculatos overlook.

The Federal Reserve and Congress are supposed to regulate banks, but instead act as getaway drivers for banks, allowing the creation of classes of accounts with 0% statutory reserve ratio requirements, and then allowing the fraudulent transfer of money from accounts with statutory reserve ratio requirements to accounts with 0% statutory reserve ratio requirements. This lowers overall statutory reserve requirements to negligible levels.

Low statutory reserve requirements make Depressions inevitable. When significant amounts of additional reserves are injected into the banking system, huge amounts of deposit money are created, bad loans are made with this money, and when these bad loans are defaulted upon depositors grow worried about bank solvency, withdraw money, and banks face runs that are demands for reserves that they don't possess.

Even with the need to hold enough reserves to honor depositor withdrawals limiting deposit creation, banks were still able to create so much money that they lent to every single responsible borrower seeking credit, and then still lent trillions of dollars more to Crayola chimps who shouldn't have been allowed to finance a pack of chewing gum much less a home. After all this money creation, banks were nowhere near the maximum money creation that "regulations" allowed. Statutory reserve requirements no longer limit deposit creation—which they are supposed to do. Absurdly low statutory reserve ratio requirements allow commercial banks that practice fraudulent fractional-reserve lending to create as much money as they want virtually without limitation.

Infinite Money Creation Picture Pages

To skip the picture pages after this chapter, please turn to page 259

DECREASING THE RESERVE RATIO INCREASES DEPOSIT CREATION

20% RESERVE RATIO

	Deposit	Reserves	Loans
1	$100.00	$20.00	$80.00
2	$80.00	$16.00	$64.00
3	$64.00	$12.80	$51.20
4	$51.20	$10.24	$40.96
5	$40.96	$8.19	$32.77
6	$32.77	$6.55	$26.21
7	$26.21	$5.24	$20.97
8	$20.97	$4.19	$16.78
9	$16.78	$3.36	$13.42
	$432.89	$86.57	$346.31

"Excess" Reserves $13.43
Latent Deposits $67

10% RESERVE RATIO

	Deposit	Reserves	Loans
1	$100.00	$10.00	$90.00
2	$90.00	$9.00	$81.00
3	$81.00	$8.10	$72.90
4	$72.90	$7.29	$65.61
5	$65.61	$6.56	$59.05
6	$59.05	$5.90	$53.14
7	$53.14	$5.31	$47.83
8	$47.83	$4.78	$43.05
9	$43.05	$4.30	$38.74
	$612.58	$61.24	$551.32

"Excess" Reserves $38.76
Latent Deposits $388

5% RESERVE RATIO

	Deposit	Reserves	Loans
1	$100.00	$5.00	$95.00
2	$95.00	$4.75	$90.25
3	$90.25	$4.51	$85.74
4	$85.74	$4.29	$81.45
5	$81.45	$4.07	$77.38
6	$77.38	$3.87	$73.51
7	$73.51	$3.68	$69.83
8	$69.83	$3.49	$66.34
9	$66.34	$3.32	$63.02
	$739.50	$36.98	$702.52

"Excess" Reserves $63.02
Latent Deposits $1,260

2.5% RESERVE RATIO

	Deposit	Reserves	Loans
1	$100.00	$2.50	$97.50
2	$97.50	$2.44	$95.06
3	$95.06	$2.38	$92.69
4	$92.69	$2.32	$90.37
5	$90.37	$2.26	$88.11
6	$88.11	$2.20	$85.91
7	$85.91	$2.15	$83.76
8	$83.76	$2.09	$81.67
9	$81.67	$2.04	$79.62
	$815.07	$20.38	$794.69

"Excess" Reserves $79.62
Latent Deposits $3,185

1.25% RESERVE RATIO

	Deposit	Reserves	Loans
1	$100.00	$1.25	$98.75
2	$98.75	$1.23	$97.52
3	$97.52	$1.22	$96.30
4	$96.30	$1.20	$95.09
5	$95.09	$1.19	$93.90
6	$93.90	$1.17	$92.73
7	$92.73	$1.16	$91.57
8	$91.57	$1.14	$90.43
9	$90.43	$1.13	$89.30
	$856.29	$10.69	$845.59

"Excess" Reserves $89.31
Latent Deposits $7,144

0.625% RESERVE RATIO

	Deposit	Reserves	Loans
1	$100.00	$0.63	$99.38
2	$99.38	$0.62	$98.75
3	$98.75	$0.62	$98.14
4	$98.14	$0.61	$97.52
5	$97.52	$0.61	$96.91
6	$96.91	$0.61	$96.31
7	$96.31	$0.60	$95.71
8	$95.71	$0.60	$95.11
9	$95.11	$0.59	$94.51
	$877.83	$5.49	$872.34

"Excess" Reserves $94.51
Latent Deposits $15,122

In the tables on the previous page, $100 of reserves are initially deposited into the banking system and total reserves for the banking system are $100. Banks then practice fractional-reserve lending, at different statutory reserve ratio requirements which are shown just above each of the 6 separate tables. Each row numbered 1-9 on a table corresponds to a newly created deposit. On all tables, the initial deposit is $100. In any given row, the statutory reserve ratio requirement is applied to a deposit shown in the "Deposit" column, an amount of reserves necessary to meet this statutory reserve ratio requirement is set aside in the "Reserves" column, and the remaining reserves are used to issue a loan whose amount is indicated in the "Loans" column. All loans are issued by creating deposits, and when the loan in one column is deposited at another bank, the new deposit created is shown in the next column in the table in the "Deposit" column. The process of fractional-reserve backing, loan issuance, and deposit creation is then repeated multiple times, with new deposits being created on successive rows of the table...

For example, in the first table with a 20% reserve ratio, $100 of reserves are deposited initially in row 1. A 20% statutory reserve ratio requirement is applied to the $100 deposit, meaning it must be backed by $20 of reserves (0.20 x $100 = $20). $80 of reserves remain and are lent out, resulting in an $80 deposit being created in row 2. The deposit supply that is the money supply has increased from $100 to $180. The $100 deposit is backed by $20 of reserves. The $80 deposit is backed by $80 of reserves—until fraudulent fractional-reserve lending proceeds. A 20% statutory reserve ratio requirement is applied to the $80 deposit, meaning it must be backed by $16 of reserves (0.20 x $80 = $16). $64 of reserves remain and are lent out, resulting in a $64 deposit being created in row 3...

Total deposit creation through 9 iterations of fractional-reserve lending is shown at the bottom of each table, as are total reserves backing deposits and total loans issued. "Excess" reserves that can still be lent in the 10th iteration of fractional lending and beyond are also shown. The maximum amount of deposits that can be created using these "excess" reserves are the "Latent Deposits" table entries. Latent deposits are deposits that have not been created but can be created. In the tables, "Latent Deposits" are the maximum amount of newly created deposits that the "excess" reserves can back at the prevailing reserve ratio.

After the 9th iteration of deposit creation at a 10% reserve ratio, $61.24 of reserves back $612.58 of deposits. As there $100 of total reserves, and $61.24 of reserves back deposits, there are $38.76 ($100 - $61.24) of "excess" reserves that can be used to back additional deposits which banks can create. After the 9th iteration of deposit creation at a 1.25% reserve ratio, $10.69 of reserves back $856.29 of deposits. As there $100 of total reserves, and $10.69 of reserves back deposits, there are $89.31 ($100 - $10.69) of "excess" reserves that can be used to back additional deposits which banks can create. At the 1.25% reserve ratio, 33% more deposits have been created than at the 10% reserve ratio, but they are backed by 82% less reserves. Moreover, at a 1.25% reserve ratio, each $1 of "excess" reserves can back $80 of additional deposits, while at a 10% reserve ratio, each $1 of "excess" reserves can "only" back $10 of additional deposits. Thus the bank with the 1.25% reserve ratio can create an additional $7,144 of deposits, while the bank with the 10% reserve ratio can "only" create $388 of additional deposits.

At lower statutory reserve ratio requirements, banks create more deposits and keep less reserves to honor those deposits, leaving larger amounts of "excess" reserves available for additional deposit creation. At lower statutory reserve ratio requirements, each $1 of "excess" reserves can back increasing amounts of deposits. All else being equal, banks with lower statutory reserve ratio requirements have more "excess" reserves and can create more deposits from each $1 of those "excess" reserves.

Sheeple view the banking system as having a fixed amount of deposits, but it is more accurate to view it as having a fixed amount of reserves. Decreased statutory reserve ratio requirements don't usually cause banks to decrease reserve holdings, but rather allow banks to increase deposit creation. Sheeple viewing reserve ratios from a perspective in which there is a fixed amount of deposits focus on the amount of reserves needed to back those deposits. Most sheeple don't know that banks conjure deposits to issue loans, and erroneously assume that reducing banks' statutory reserve ratio requirement will cause banks to hold less reserves. In this erroneous view, if banks have $100 of deposits and the statutory reserve ratio requirement is decreased from 10% to 2%, banks decrease reserves from $10 to $2. In reality, banks as a whole hold a fixed amount of reserves, and create additional deposits. The amount of additional deposits that can be created is limited by the statutory reserve ratio requirement. If banks hold $10 of reserves and the statutory reserve ratio requirement is decreased from 10% to 2%, the amount of deposits banks can create increases from $100 to $500. Banks create $400 of additional deposits, decreasing the reserve ratio from 10% to 2% by increasing the deposit supply rather than by decreasing the reserve supply.

Lower statutory reserve ratio requirements don't usually cause decreases in reserve holdings, but rather increases in deposit creation. In reality, the amount of reserves and deposits that banks hold are always fluctuating, so the situation is never this simple, but the basic principle holds.

GRAPHS OF DEPOSIT CREATION AT DIFFERENT RESERVE RATIOS

THE EXPANSION OF $100 THROUGH FRACTIONAL-RESERVE BANKING WITH VARYING RESERVE REQUIREMENTS (ACCUMULATION OF DEPOSITS)

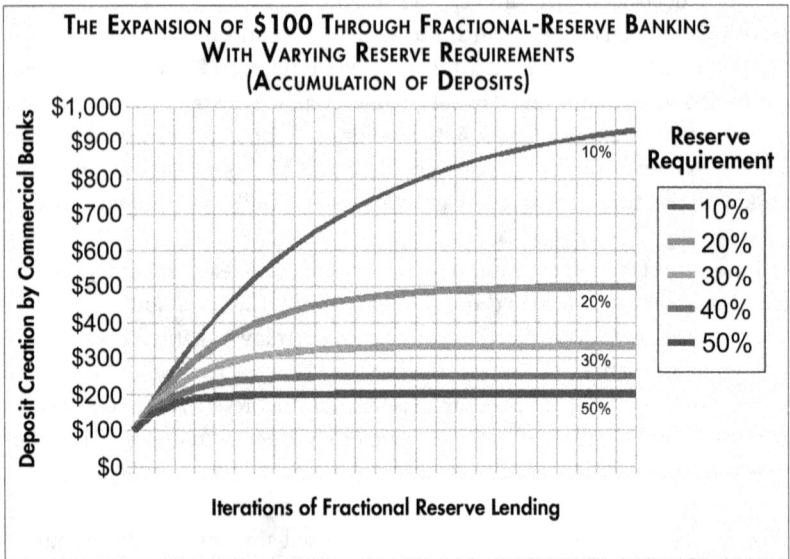

Graphical representations of deposit creation are often the easiest for people to understand. The graph above presumes that $100 of reserves are initially deposited into the banking system. The iterations of fractional-reserve lending increase moving rightward on the horizontal or x-axis as each bank embezzles reserves, lends embezzled reserves, and creates additional deposits. The total amount of deposit creation is shown on the vertical or y-axis, and it increases as one moves rightward across the x-axis. At a 50% reserve ratio, the final deposit amount is $200, double the initial $100. At a 20% reserve ratio, the final deposit amount is $500, five times the initial $100. And so forth.

The graph above is the misleading sort usually shown in economics textbooks and other conventional explanations of fractional-reserve lending. The graph is misleading because it shows a narrow reserve ratio range of 10% - 50%. It excludes the extremely low reserve ratios that prevail in the real world, and the 100% reserve ratio that would prevail in an honest banking system. Without these two critical reference points, fraudulent fractional-reserve lending seems much less harmful, and its true consequences relative to an honest money system are much harder to understand. The use of small amounts of money on the upward-rising y-axis makes the concepts easy to understand, but also prevents the gargantuan money creation that prevails in the real world from having to be revealed. On the next five pages, honest graphs that should be in textbooks and other conventional descriptions of fractional-reserve lending will be shown.

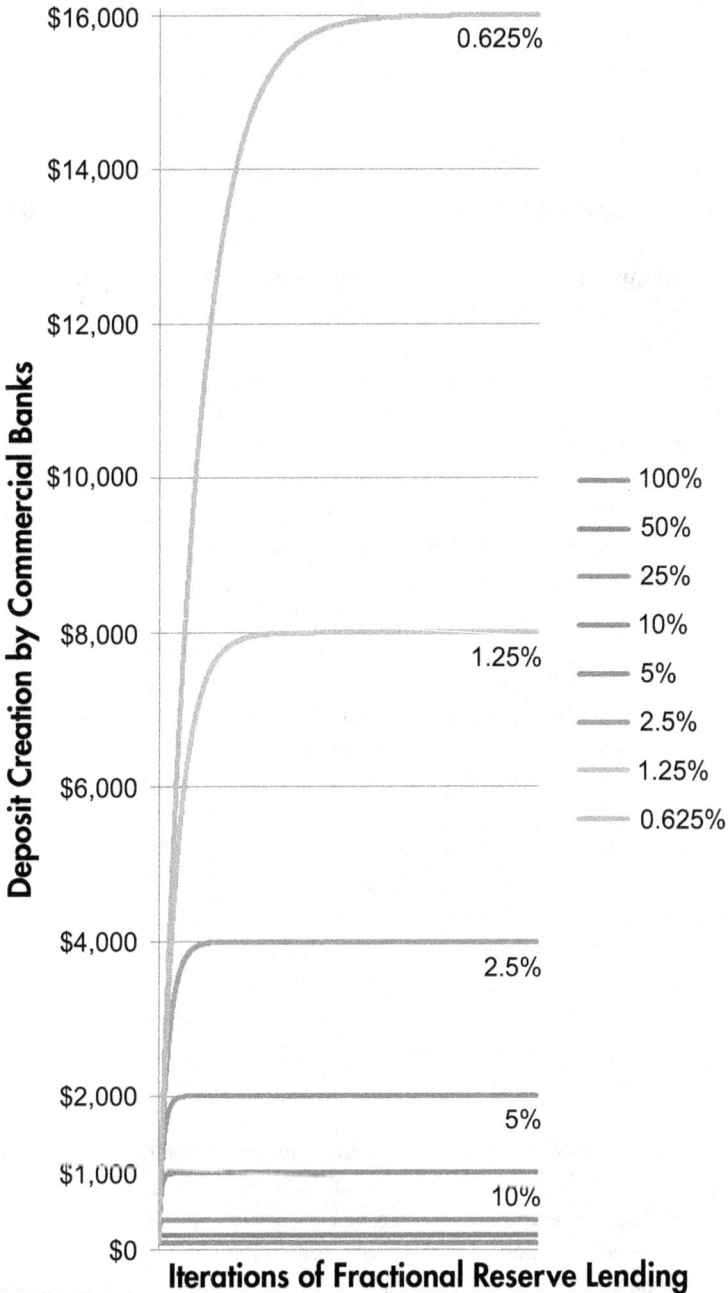

$100 of reserves initially deposited into banking system on graph above.

The graph on the previous page shows a fuller range of reserve ratios. The 100% reserve ratio that prevails in honest banking is shown; it is the perfectly-horizontal blue line on the bottom of the graph. The blue, 100% reserve ratio line doesn't increase in slope or rise because the money supply doesn't increase in quantity or rise. As shown, in an honest 100% reserve banking system, $100 of reserves deposited into the banking system result in $100 of deposits, not a penny more. People seeing the 100% reserve ratio line on the graph are much more apt to ask why such a system is not used, which is why it is omitted from most conventional descriptions of fractional-reserve lending. The low reserve ratios banks use in the real world are also included on this graph. A 0.625% reserve ratio results in $16,000 of deposits being created from an initial $100 deposit of reserves. This is the giant purple curve on the graph. In general, low reserve ratios produce the arcing curves indicative of gargantuan deposit creation, which alarms astute observers and causes them to question the desirability of fractional-reserve lending.

Conventional descriptions of fractional-reserve lending portray a 10% reserve ratio as the norm, which it is not. As we have seen, much, much lower reserve ratios actually prevail. A person taught that the reserve ratio is 10% who is shown a graph with much lower reserve ratios inevitably asks how they are attained. Answering this question requires enumeration of the many frauds outlined in this book, and these frauds are more difficult—if not impossible—to portray as honest and economically beneficial. Thus most economic textbooks and other descriptions simply pretend that reserve ratios lower than 10% don't exist, fraudulently omitting the horrifically low reserve ratios that are often the norm.

The graph on the previous page was elongated vertically, was much taller than wide. This was not done to make the area between different reserve ratio curves seem disingenuously large, or otherwise massage data, but rather to allow the curves lower on the graph to be seen separately. If the graph is not elongated, the lower curves end up being so close together that they are virtually impossible to differentiate. Even on the elongated graph, the lower three curves are very close together. This is because the gargantuan money creation at lower reserve ratios consumes most of the graph.

A graph on the following page shows a more limited range of reserve ratios so that the curves at lower reserve ratios can be viewed. On this graph, the flat, horizontal 100% reserve ratio line can be clearly differentiated from curves for lower reserve ratios which increase or rise, indicating money creation. Thus the difference between an honest 100% reserve ratio and other fraudulent less-than-100% reserve ratios can be clearly seen.

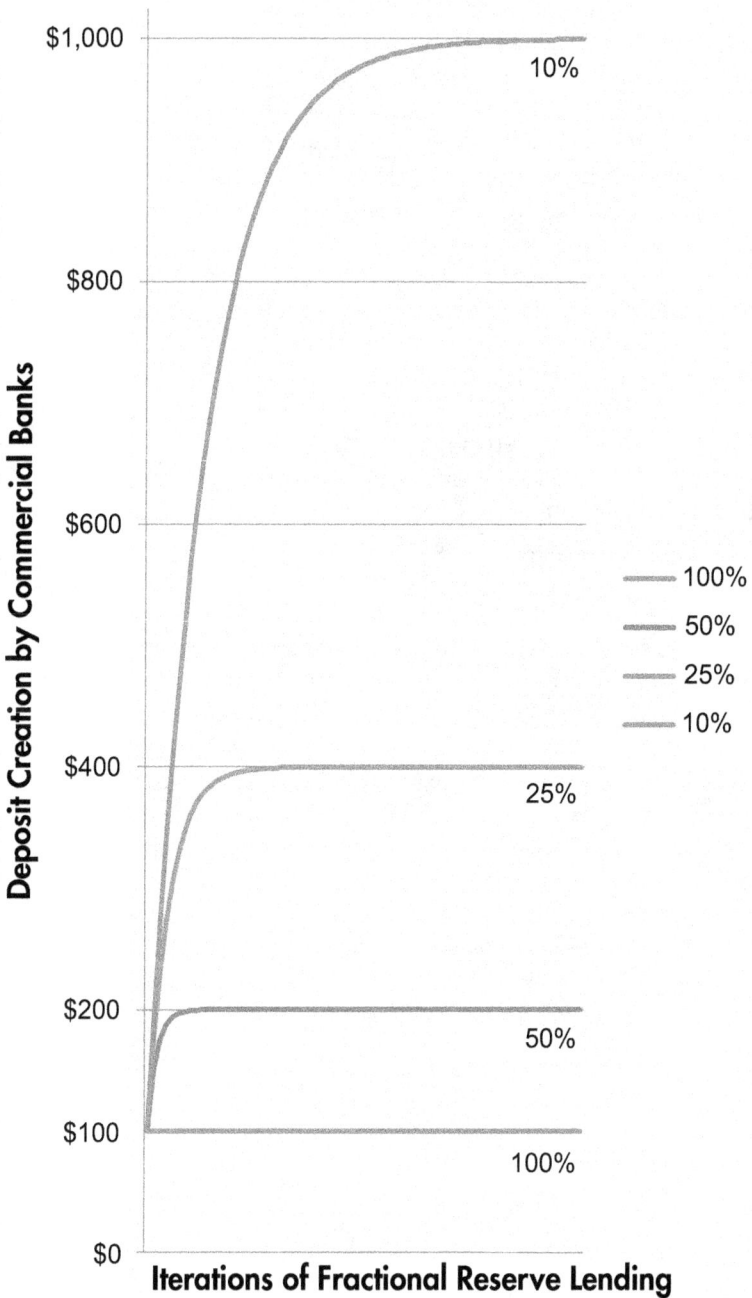

$100 of reserves initially deposited into banking system on graph above.

The graph on the following page shows a broad range of reserve ratios, 1.25% - 100%. It uses gargantuan, real-world deposit creation amounts on the y-axis. On this graph, $100,000,000,000 ($100 billion) of reserves are initially deposited into the banking system, rather than the $100 in previous examples, and total deposit creation is thus reckoned in trillions of dollars rather than thousands of dollars. Stated another way, this real-world example uses sums of money 1 billion times greater than the $100 examples. As a very rough rule, anytime you see dumbed-down descriptions of fractional-reserve lending using $100 of reserves as a baseline, multiply the amounts shown by $1 billion to obtain true real world numbers. Over time, as the money supply increases, this "rule" will become invalid and a larger multiple would be needed, but it should hold for a few years.

This graph includes one addition not on other graphs in this section, the 1.46% reserve ratio which prevailed in September 2008 just before The Bailout passed. With $100 billion of reserves injected into the banking system at this 1.46% reserve ratio, a reasonable approximation of the $102.7 billion which actually existed, $7 trillion of total deposits results. This is shown on the light blue curve on the graph which peaks out near $7 trillion.

Note the gaping difference between the flat, 100% reserve ratio line and the 1.46% reserve ratio curve, and the massive difference in money creation (or lack thereof) it shows. Few individuals learning about fractional-reserve lending in a university classroom setting, or reading about it in other conventional descriptions, are shown graphs such as the one on the following page. If they were, they would doubtless question why commercial banks are allowed to create trillions of dollars of deposits out of thin air. As emphasized repeatedly, when small money supply numbers are used, fractional-reserve lending can be made to seem reasonable, and even ethical. When horrifically huge real world deposit creation numbers are shown, the densest rube immediately begins questioning the desirability of such money creation and the system that allows it.

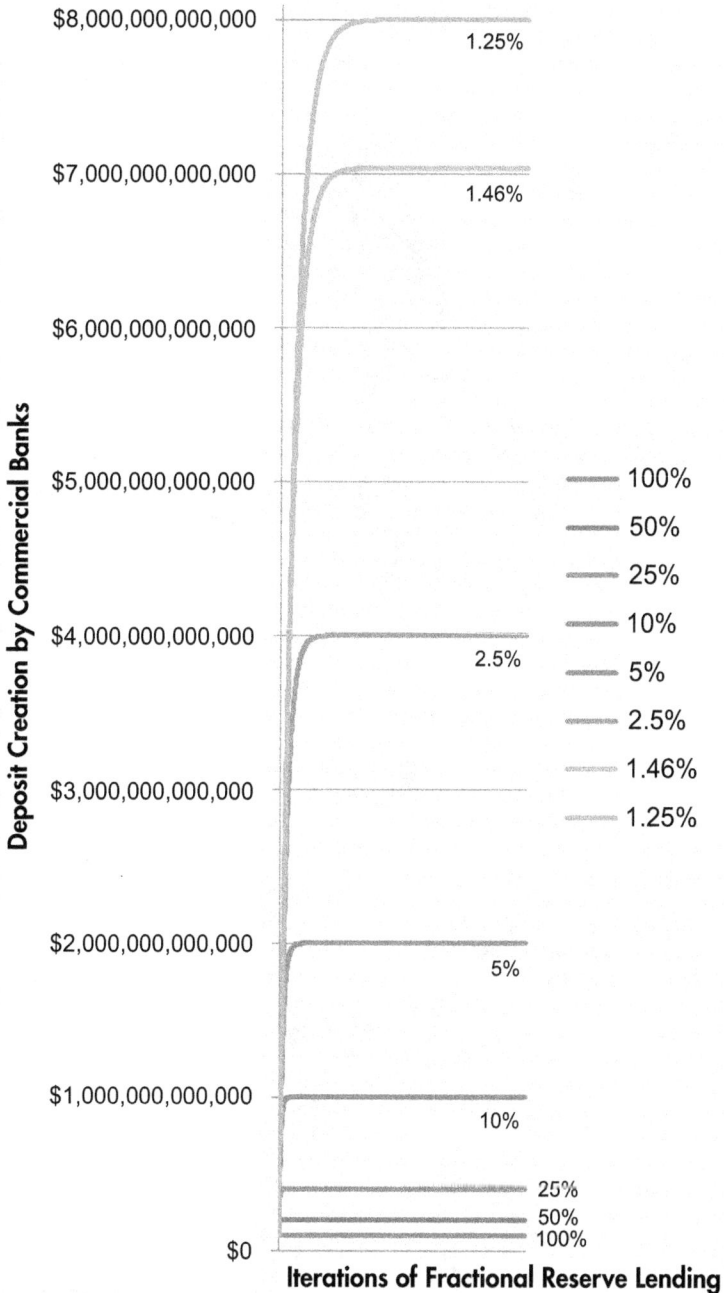

$100 billion of reserves initially deposited into banking system on graph above.

OVERVIEW OF RESERVE-REDUCING SCAMS

HONEST 100% RESERVE BANKING
All demand deposits 100% backed by reserves
No fractional-reserve lending, only demand deposits and time deposits

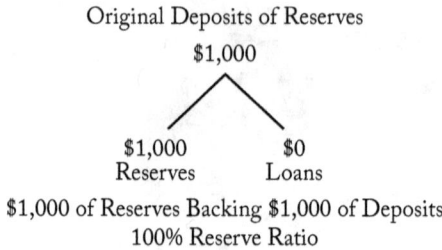

Original Deposits of Reserves
$1,000

$1,000
Reserves

$0
Loans

$1,000 of Reserves Backing $1,000 of Deposits
100% Reserve Ratio

FRAUDULENT FRACTIONAL-RESERVE BANKING
Rigid time deposit and demand deposit segregation abandoned
All deposits promised upon demand, but only a fraction backed by reserves
Same reserve ratio requirement applied to all deposits, usually 10%

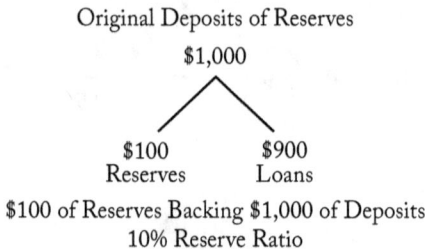

Original Deposits of Reserves
$1,000

$100
Reserves

$900
Loans

$100 of Reserves Backing $1,000 of Deposits
10% Reserve Ratio

TRANSACTION AND NON-TRANSACTION DEPOSITS
Deposits recategorized as transaction and non-transaction
Transaction = checking accounts, Non-transaction = savings accounts
Reserve ratio requirements only applied to transaction deposits
$1 of transaction deposits for every $4 of non-transaction deposits

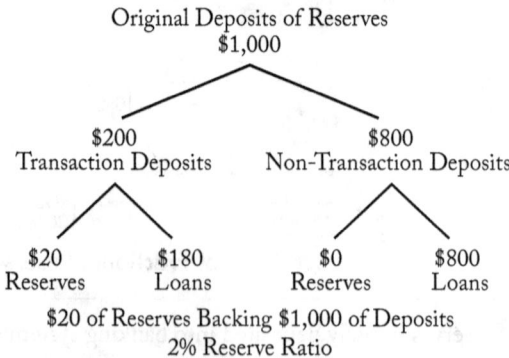

Original Deposits of Reserves
$1,000

$200
Transaction Deposits

$800
Non-Transaction Deposits

$20
Reserves

$180
Loans

$0
Reserves

$800
Loans

$20 of Reserves Backing $1,000 of Deposits
2% Reserve Ratio

RESERVE REQUIREMENT EXEMPTION AND LOW-RESERVE TRANCHE

First $11.5 million of transaction deposits exempt from reserve requirement
Next $59.5 million of transaction deposits subject to 3% reserve requirement
These are 2012 amounts, they increase regularly as the deposit supply increases
All amounts millions of dollars

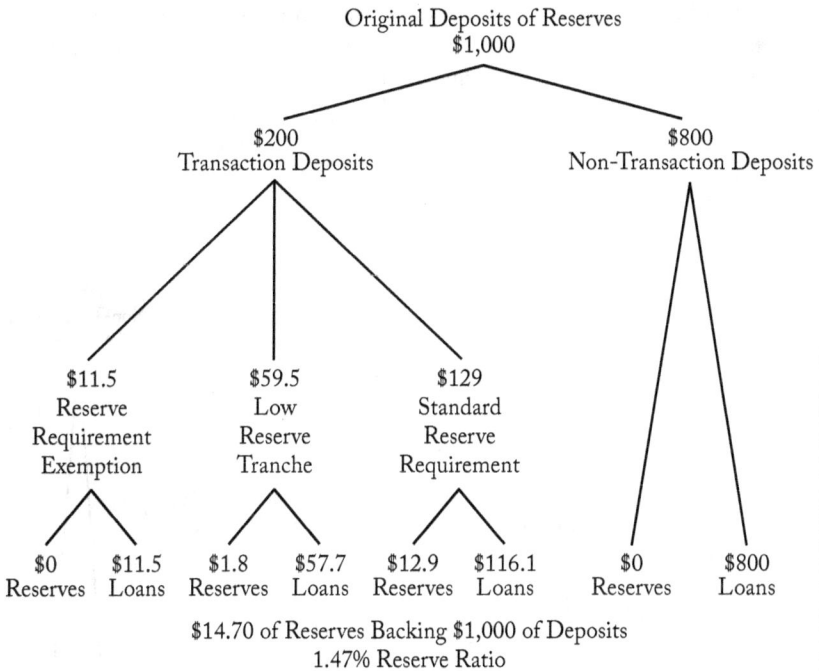

Original Deposits of Reserves
$1,000

$200
Transaction Deposits

$800
Non-Transaction Deposits

$11.5
Reserve
Requirement
Exemption

$59.5
Low
Reserve
Tranche

$129
Standard
Reserve
Requirement

| $0 Reserves | $11.5 Loans | $1.8 Reserves | $57.7 Loans | $12.9 Reserves | $116.1 Loans | $0 Reserves | $800 Loans |

$14.70 of Reserves Backing $1,000 of Deposits
1.47% Reserve Ratio

This shows a bank with $1,000 million of deposits, which is $1 billion of deposits. Transaction deposits that qualify for the Reserve Requirement Exemption are subject to a 0% statutory reserve ratio requirement. Transaction deposits that qualify for the Low-Reserve Tranche are subject to a 3% statutory reserve ratio requirement. Transaction deposits that qualify for the Standard Reserve Requirement are subject to a 10% statutory reserve ratio requirement. Non-transaction deposits are subject to a 0% statutory reserve ratio requirement. The bank's statutory reserve requirement is $14.7 million. $14.7 million of reserves back $1 billion of deposits, a 1.47% reserve ratio.

DEPOSIT RECLASSIFICATION (SWEEPS)

Transaction deposits secretly reclassified as 2 separate sub-accounts
Checking sub-account and savings sub-account created
Checking sub-account used to honor all checking account transactions
Unused funds in checking sub-account "swept" into savings sub-account
Savings sub-account classified as non-transaction, 0% reserve ratio applied
80% of transaction deposits typically swept into savings sub-accounts
Reserve ratio requirements applied to transaction accounts *after* sweeping
All amounts millions of dollars

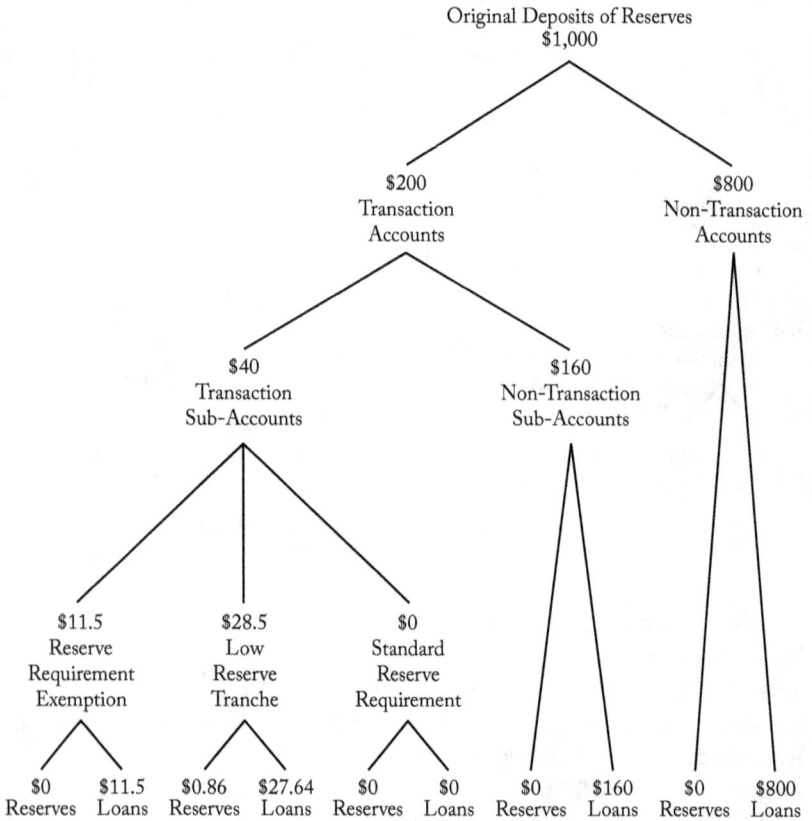

Original Deposits of Reserves
$1,000

$200
Transaction
Accounts

$800
Non-Transaction
Accounts

$40
Transaction
Sub-Accounts

$160
Non-Transaction
Sub-Accounts

$11.5
Reserve
Requirement
Exemption

$28.5
Low
Reserve
Tranche

$0
Standard
Reserve
Requirement

| $0 | $11.5 | $0.86 | $27.64 | $0 | $0 | $0 | $160 | $0 | $800 |
| Reserves | Loans | Reserves | Loans | Reserves | Loans | Reserves | Loans | Reserves | Loans |

$0.86 of Reserves Backing $1,000 of Deposits
0.86% Reserve Ratio

This shows a bank with $1,000 million of deposits, which is $1 billion of deposits. A bank with $1 billion of deposits is considered a medium-sized bank. Transaction deposits swept into non-transaction sub-accounts are subject to a 0% statutory reserve ratio requirement. The bank's statutory reserve requirement is $0.86 million, which is $860,000. $860,000 of reserves back $1 billion of deposits, a 0.86% reserve ratio.

SMALL BANKS OBTAIN MINISCULE RESERVE RATIOS WITHOUT SWEEPS
All amounts millions of dollars

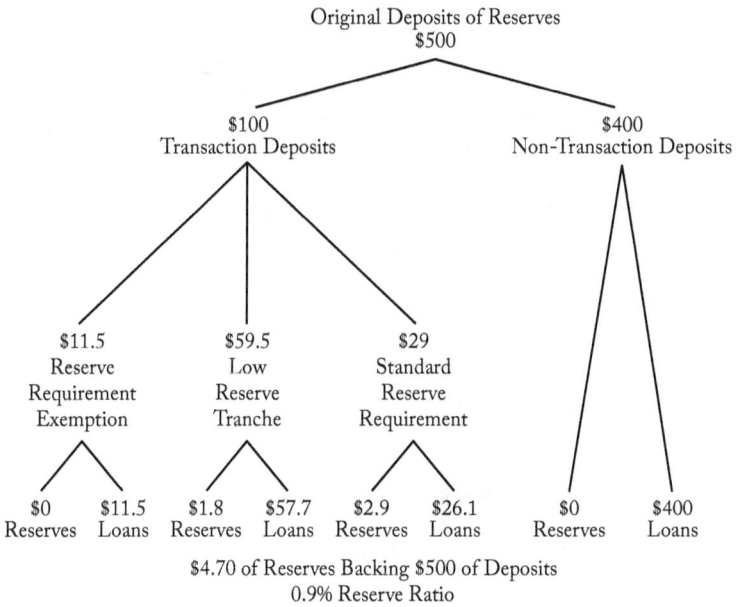

Original Deposits of Reserves
$500

$100
Transaction Deposits

$400
Non-Transaction Deposits

$11.5
Reserve
Requirement
Exemption

$59.5
Low
Reserve
Tranche

$29
Standard
Reserve
Requirement

| $0 | $11.5 | $1.8 | $57.7 | $2.9 | $26.1 | $0 | $400 |
| Reserves | Loans | Reserves | Loans | Reserves | Loans | Reserves | Loans |

$4.70 of Reserves Backing $500 of Deposits
0.9% Reserve Ratio

This shows a bank with $500 million of deposits. A bank with $500 million of deposits is considered a small bank. This small bank doesn't sweep transaction deposits. The bank's statutory reserve requirement is $4.7 million. $4.7 million of reserves back $500 million of deposits, a 0.9% reserve ratio.

LARGE BANKS CANNOT OBTAIN MINISCULE RESERVE RATIOS WITHOUT SWEEPS
All amounts millions of dollars

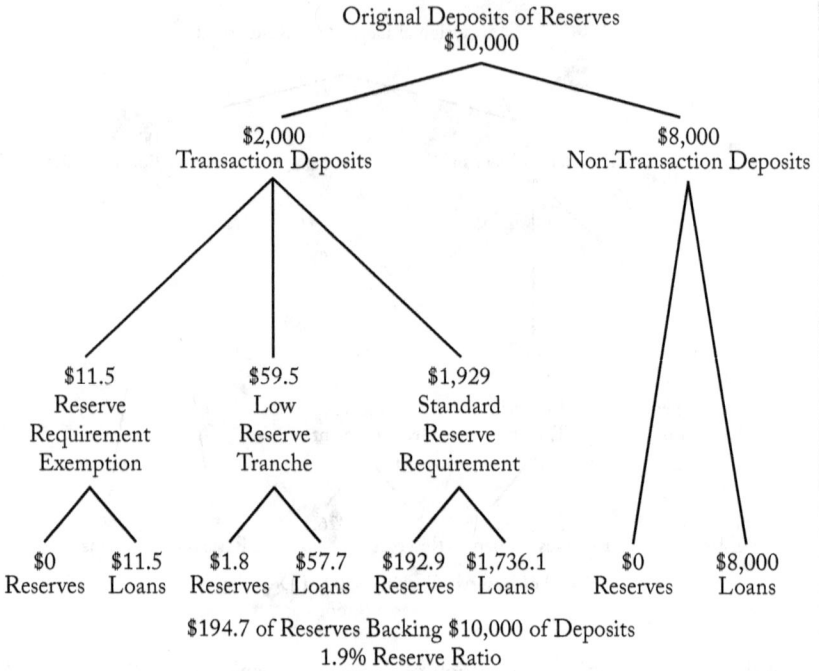

Original Deposits of Reserves
$10,000

$2,000
Transaction Deposits

$8,000
Non-Transaction Deposits

$11.5
Reserve
Requirement
Exemption

$59.5
Low
Reserve
Tranche

$1,929
Standard
Reserve
Requirement

$0 $11.5
Reserves   Loans

$1.8 $57.7
Reserves   Loans

$192.9 $1,736.1
Reserves   Loans

$0
Reserves

$8,000
Loans

$194.7 of Reserves Backing $10,000 of Deposits
1.9% Reserve Ratio

This shows a bank with $10,000 million of deposits, which is $10 billion of deposits. A bank with $10 billion of deposits is considered a large bank. This large bank doesn't sweep transaction deposits. The bank's statutory reserve requirement is $194.7 million. $194.7 million of reserves back $10 billion of deposits, a 1.9% reserve ratio.

Under normal economic circumstances in which there are no widespread depositor withdrawals (runs), banks require a 1% - 2% reserve ratio to honor all depositor withdrawals. A 1.9% statutory reserve ratio requirement forces large banks to hold more reserves than they "need."

LARGE BANKS ONLY OBTAIN MINISCULE RESERVE RATIOS WITH SWEEPS
All amounts millions of dollars

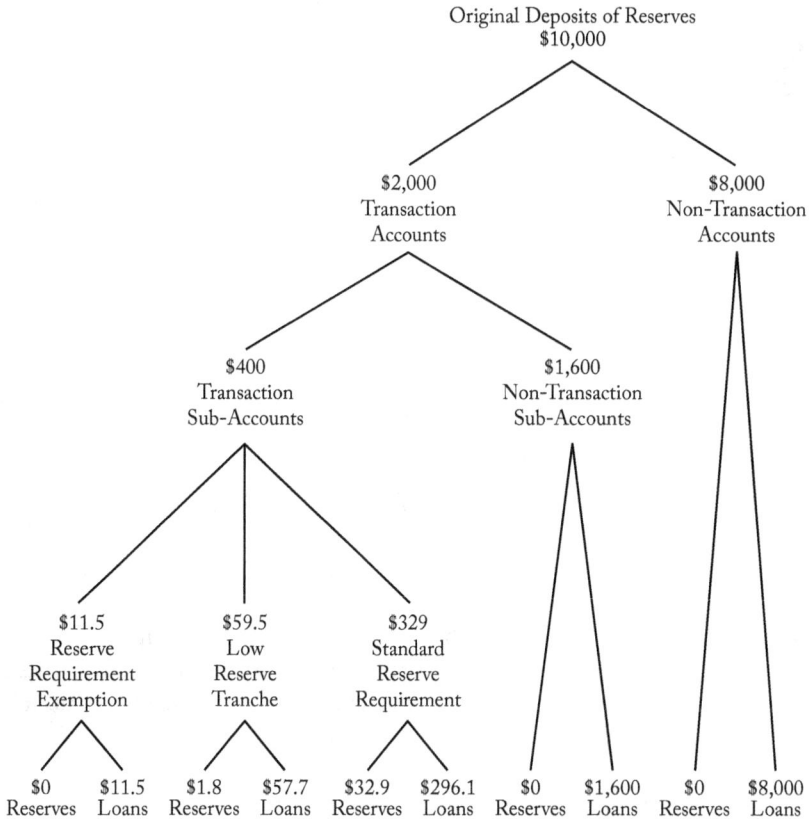

Original Deposits of Reserves
$10,000

$2,000
Transaction
Accounts

$8,000
Non-Transaction
Accounts

$400
Transaction
Sub-Accounts

$1,600
Non-Transaction
Sub-Accounts

$11.5
Reserve
Requirement
Exemption

$59.5
Low
Reserve
Tranche

$329
Standard
Reserve
Requirement

| $0 Reserves | $11.5 Loans | $1.8 Reserves | $57.7 Loans | $32.9 Reserves | $296.1 Loans | $0 Reserves | $1,600 Loans | $0 Reserves | $8,000 Loans |

$34.7 of Reserves Backing $10,000 of Deposits
0.3% Reserve Ratio

This shows a bank with $10,000 million of deposits, which is $10 billion of deposits. A bank with $10 billion of deposits is considered a large bank. This large bank sweeps 80% of transaction deposits into non-transaction sub-accounts that are subject to a 0% statutory reserve ratio requirement. The bank's statutory reserve requirement is $34.7 million. $34.7 million of reserves back $10 billion of deposits, a 0.3% reserve ratio.

Conventional descriptions of fractional-reserve lending teach Utopian 10% statutory reserve ratio requirements. More realistic statutory reserve ratio requirements are shown on these diagrams. These diagrams show how individual banks decrease statutory reserve ratio requirements. Loans in these diagrams are reserves usually transferred to other banks, resulting in additional deposit creation not shown.

PRECIPITOUS DROP IN RESERVE RATIOS CAUSED DEPRESSION v9.2006-201x

RESERVE RATIO OF U.S. BANKING SYSTEM

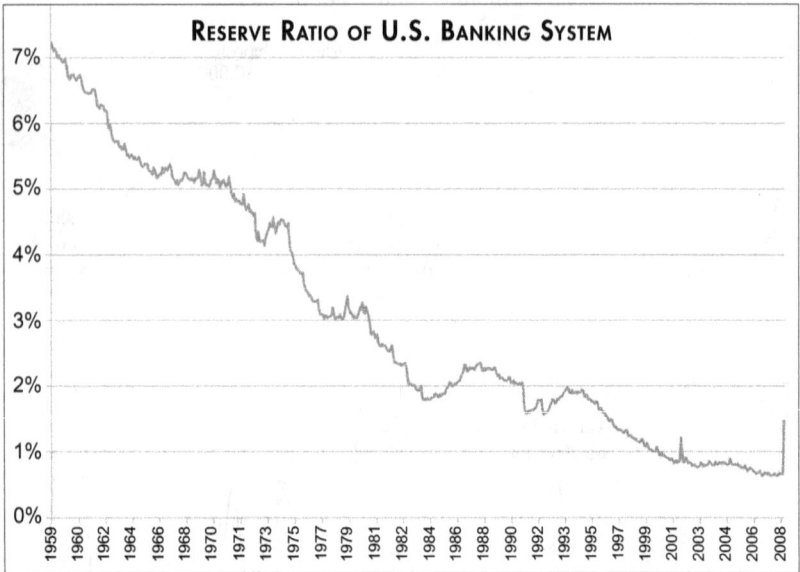

The graph above shows the decreasing reserve ratios as the numerous frauds explained were applied by commercial banks. One hardly needed Nostradamus to foresee an implosion of the U.S. banking system. In helping commercial banks lower statutory reserve ratio requirements to obscenely low levels, the Federal Reserve defaulted on its responsibility to manage the money supply of the United States and committed a crime against humanity.

The spike on the graph's right is the beginning of reserve creation by the Fed during Depression v9.2006-201x—what sheeple call The Bailout. This spike is the 1.46% reserve ratio used in examples. The author was conservative choosing this 1.46%, as the reserve ratio for the U.S. banking system did not exceed 1% for the 7 years prior to The Bailout. For the 27 months which preceded The Bailout, the reserve ratio did not exceed 0.75%, and was 0.66% when the economy finally imploded, meaning only $1 of reserves backed every $151 of deposits.

Date	Reserve Ratio	Date	Reserve Ratio	Date	Reserve Ratio
Oct 2006	0.67%	Jun 2007	0.68%	Feb 2008	0.64%
Nov 2006	0.67%	Jul 2007	0.66%	Mar 2008	0.63%
Dec 2006	0.69%	Aug 2007	0.69%	Apr 2008	0.65%
Jan 2007	0.71%	Sep 2007	0.65%	May 2008	0.68%
Feb 2007	0.67%	Oct 2007	0.64%	Jun 2008	0.66%
Mar 2007	0.63%	Nov 2007	0.64%	Jul 2008	0.66%
Apr 2007	0.65%	Dec 2007	0.65%	Aug 2008	0.66%
May 2007	0.68%	Jan 2008	0.67%	Sep 2008	1.46%

LEVERAGE

"When you combine ignorance and leverage, you get some pretty interesting results."
—Warren Buffet

Let's open Half Honest Bank with $100 in startup capital. Same 100% reserve rules as Infinite Integrity Bank, but Half Honest Bank obtains a $500 initial deposit of reserves:

Capital	Assets	Liabilities
$100	$500 (Reserves)	$500 (Deposits)
		100% Reserve Ratio

Half Honest Bank issues $400 in car loans in an honest manner, obtaining permission from depositors who convert demand deposits into time deposits:

Capital	Assets	Liabilities
$100	**$100 (Reserves)**	**$100 (Demand Deposits)**
	$400 (1 Year Loans)	**$400 (1 Year Time Deposits)**
$100	$500	$500
		100% Reserve Ratio

Auto insurance doesn't exist. A hurricane destroys most cars, and the factory which many borrowers work at. A tragedy no loan officer could foresee, but $300 of loans are nonetheless defaulted upon and must be removed from the ledger because they will no longer be paid. Half Honest Bank's updated ledger:

Capital	Assets	Liabilities
$100	$100 (Reserves)	$100 (Demand Deposits)
	$100 (1 Year Loans)	$400 (1 Year Time Deposits)
$100	**$200**	$500
		100% Reserve Ratio

Liabilities exceed assets by $300. Even if the $100 of capital is used to make up the deficit, Half Honest Bank is still $200 short. It is bank-rupt. 75% of Half Honest Bank's time depositors never get their money back, a la the goldsmith.

This is a bit of a paradox, as loans were made honestly.

The time depositor understood that their deposit would be used for a loan, but they lent money to the bank, not the borrower paying the auto loan. Half Honest Bank issued $400 of loans, but had only $100 of capital. It had $4 that might have to be paid for every $1 in its pocket—for every $1 of its capital.

This is LEVERAGE. The term derives from a lever such as a pry bar. You can't lift a 400 pound box, but with a lever 100 pounds of force can cause it to rise. In the financial world, a small amount of money can be leveraged to control a much larger sum of credit or debt. In the ledgers above, capital was LEVERAGED, used to back an amount of loans far greater than the amount of the capital. In fraudulent fractional-reserve lending, reserves are also leveraged, used to back an amount of deposits far greater than the amount of reserves.

Half Honest Bank had $400 of loans but only $100 of capital. Its loan-to-capital leverage was 4. Stated another way, Half Honest Bank's capital-to-loan ratio was 25%.

The greater the leverage, the greater the risk. If a bank's books are honest and its loan-to-capital leverage is 1, no depositor can get screwed. However, a loan-to-capital leverage of 1 isn't very profitable for investors, and many would choose a different business than banking, resulting in a shortage of credit—at least in an honest 100% reserve banking system where loan money can't simply be conjured.

Opinions about acceptable loan-to-capital leverage vary, even among the honest. In the real world, there is auto insurance. Three quarters of an economy doesn't default on loans, as in our simple example, not even after a hurricane during a Depression. And mortgages and car loans are backed by houses and cars that can be sold, allowing banks to recoup some loan money.

In a free market, banks could increase leverage as much as they want. Banks that increased leverage excessively would go rupt, and surviving banks would be those with manageable leverage. In a free market, there would be no bank Bailouts. When banks failed, depositors would lose money, and eventually flock to banks with low leverage. When all banks are committing fractional-reserve fraud, and can't be allowed to fail so as to hide and perpetuate this fraud, free market liquidation of irresponsible banks rarely occurs. Incompetent banks stay in business.

Our current fractional-reserve banking system is not a free market, and its loans are not honest, which can muddle things. This is especially true if one confuses capital and assets. Capital is the pot of "gold" where profits accrue, and is the emergency reserves used to cover defaulted loans if the bank is rupted and liquidated. Assets are reserves, as well as the loan principal, the loan itself. A responsible banker plans on some loan defaults, and keeps capital reserves to honor those defaults.

What if a bank isn't responsible? Why not open a bank with 53¢ of capital, accept $20 gajillion of deposits of reserves, and fractional-reserve lend and create and lend additional deposits until you're rich? No one would entrust deposits to a person worth 53¢, but this credibility problem aside, bank licensing laws prevent such abuses. By law, you need substantial capital to start a commercial bank, usually millions of dollars, and loans can't be more than 25 times capital. 25 is the maximum legal loan-to-capital leverage for commercial banks in America—but loans don't have to be issued honestly.

If Lotsa Leverage Bank opens for business with $100 of capital, new customers deposit $5,000 of reserves, and its statutory reserve ratio requirement is 2%, its balance sheet is:

Capital	Assets	Liabilities
$100	$100 (Reserves)	$5,000 (Deposits)
	$4,900 ("Excess" Reserves)	
$100	$5,000	$5,000
		100% Reserve Ratio

In theory Lotsa Leverage Bank can lend $4,900, but it doesn't have enough capital. The maximum loan-to-capital leverage allowed by law is approximately 25. Stated another way, the minimum capital-to-loan ratio allowed is approximately 4%. A statutory capital leverage requirement of 25 "only" allows loans equal to 25 times capital, which is $2,500 of loans. This is "all" that Lotsa Leverage Bank can lend.

To someone who works for a living, creating an amount of money equal to 25 times the amount of wealth they possess and loaning it out at interest is excessive, but to Speculatos this is restrictive. Speculatos want each dollar of capital earning profit dozens of times, not a mere dozen times.

Capital is wealth the bank owns. Reserves are wealth the bank is warehousing for depositors, which the bank possesses but doesn't own outright the way it owns capital. This is an important distinction. A bank can legitimately use capital to settle its debts, but it should not embezzle reserves and use them to settle its debts, as the reserves are owed to depositors.

In simplified ledgers shown at the beginning of this book, Fifth Fleece Bank opened with $50 of capital, accepted a deposit of $100 of reserves, and embezzled and lent $90 of reserves:

Capital	Assets	Liabilities
$50	$10 (Reserves)	$100 (Deposits)
	$90 (Loans)	
$50	$100	$100
		10% Reserve Ratio

This $50 of capital simplified learning, but is much more than "regulations" actually require. With a capital leverage of 25, First Fraud Bank only requires $3.60 of capital:

Capital	Assets	Liabilities
$3.60	$10 (Reserves)	$100 (Deposits)
	$90 (Loans)	

Capital	Assets	Liabilities
$3.60	$100	$100

10% Reserve Ratio

With interest profits from the loans added to capital, as shown in the Bailoutville chapter, the effective profit First Fraud Bank earned would have been greatly increased. The $5.40 of interest profits was added to capital. $5.40 is 10.8% of capital with $50 of capital, but is 150% of capital with $3.60 of capital. With real-world capital ratios, bank interest revenue is 14-times greater, as a percentage of capital.

The U.S. commercial banking system has two main forms of leverage, loan-to-capital leverage and deposit-to-reserve leverage. Loan-to-capital leverage is also called capital leverage. Deposit-to-reserve leverage is also called reserve leverage.

Capital leverage is a measure of the amount of loans created in excess of capital to back them. It is the ratio of loans to capital. Reserve leverage is a measure of the amount of deposits created in excess of reserves to back them. It is the ratio of deposits to reserves. Capital leverage is limited by the capital ratio or capital requirement. Reserve leverage is limited by the reserve ratio or reserve requirement.

Note that the smaller quantity is used in describing the leverage. There are more loans than capital, meaning that capital has been leveraged, has been used like a pry bar to back a larger amount of loans. Thus the proper term is capital leverage, not loan leverage. There are more deposits than reserves, meaning that reserves have been leveraged, have been used like a lever to back a larger amount of deposits. Thus the proper term is reserve leverage, not deposit leverage.

When the term leverage is used without any other descriptor, capital leverage is usually being referred to. This is because capital leverage is the only true limitation upon loan issuance and deposit creation, as will be explained, and is thus the leverage of primary concern to bankers.

Leverage and Ratios refer to two different terms that are inverses, or reciprocals. Capital Leverage is the ratio of loans to capital, but the Capital Ratio is the ratio of capital to loans. The term ratio technically refers to the result when any two numbers are divided, but is often used to refer to two numbers that when divided produce a result less than 1. In such a case, the ratio is a percentage. In the case of capital and loans at a commercial bank, loans will always exceed capital. When the larger number, the amount of loans, is divided by the smaller number, the amount of capital, the result will be larger than 1, and is called Leverage, with the smaller number, the capital, placed before Leverage. Thus the term Capital Leverage. When the smaller number, the amount of loans, is divided by the larger number, the amount of capital, the result will be less than 1, and is called a Ratio, though the smaller number is again placed before Ratio. Thus the term Capital Ratio. The Capital Leverage and Capital Ratio are different ways of describing the same mathematical reality. If Lotsa Leverage Bank has $3.60 of capital and $90 of loans, then its Capital Leverage is 25 ($90 ÷ $3.60 = 25) and its Capital Ratio is 4% ($3.60 ÷ $90 = 0.04 = 4%). The inverse or reciprocal of 25 is 1 divided by 25, or 4% (1 ÷ 25 = 0.04 = 4%). The Leverage is always the inverse of the Ratio, and vice versa, and again, they are just different ways of expressing the same basic relation.

The same principle applies to the Reserve Ratio. In the case of reserves and deposits at a fractional-reserve commercial bank, deposits will always exceed reserves. When the larger number, the amount of deposits, is divided by the smaller number, the amount of reserves, the result will be larger than 1, and is called Leverage, with the smaller number, the reserves, placed before Leverage. Thus the term Reserve Leverage. When the smaller number, the amount of reserves, is divided by the larger number, the amount of deposits, the result will be less than 1, and is called a Ratio, though the smaller number is again placed before Ratio. Thus the term Reserve Ratio. The Reserve Leverage and Reserve Ratio are different ways of describing the same mathematical reality. If Lotsa Leverage Bank has $10 of reserves and $100 of deposits, then its Reserve Leverage is 10 ($100 ÷ $10 = 10) and its Capital Ratio is 10% ($10 ÷ $100 = 0.10 = 10%). The inverse or reciprocal of 10 is 1 divided by 10, or 10% (1 ÷ 10 = 0.10 = 10%). The Leverage is always the inverse of the Ratio, and again, they are just different ways of expressing the same basic relation.

The terms Capital Leverage, Capital Ratio, Reserve Leverage, and Reserve Ratio were capitalized in the previous two paragraphs to minimize confusion, but will no longer be capitalized moving forward.

The capital ratio limits growth of the asset portion of bank balance sheets. The asset portion of bank balance sheets is primarily loans, and loans must be fractionally backed by capital. The reserve ratio limits the growth of the liability portion of bank balance sheets. The liability portion of bank balance sheets is primarily deposits, and deposits must be fractionally backed by reserves. The capital ratio and reserve ratio don't exist in a vacuum, however. They are symbiotic.

Deposits are backed by reserves and loans (promises to pay reserves in the future), and loans are in turn backed by capital. Reserves don't need backing (at least not on commercial bank ledgers) as they are literally cash. Most deposits are backed by loans rather than reserves, but if loans are defaulted, depositors can only redeem deposits for reserves by liquidating bank capital. Thus it is critical that banks maintain adequate capital, to prevent depositors from getting screwed when loans default. At a 25 loan-to-capital ratio, a bank only has enough capital to honor 4% of its loans if they default.

We have seen that the single 10% reserve ratio usually cited in descriptions of fractional-reserve lending is inaccurate, and the same is true of the single 4% capital ratio. In the real world, a complex series of rules are used to set statutory capital ratio requirements and statutory capital balance requirements of commercial banks. The world's king bank is the Bank for International Settlements (BIS). The term king bank doesn't do BIS justice. Emperor bank is more appropriate. The BIS is located in Basel, Switzerland, and will be discussed in detail in later volumes of *Bubblenomics*, but one thing it does is set capital guidelines which banks worldwide implement. These capital guidelines are called the Basel III Capital Guidelines. Basel III specifies different categories or tiers of capital, assesses the risk of a bank's loans, and uses this information to compute a statutory capital ratio requirement with a range of approximately 3% - 10%. The Basel III Capital Guidelines are almost 1,000 pages and are too complicated to summarize quickly or easily, but be aware that many commercial banks have statutory capital ratio requirements higher than 3% or 4%, though usually also less than 10%. 3% is the lowest capital ratio Basel III allows, but in 2014 Fed set a 5% or 6% minimum for many larger banks—assuming they don't cook the books. Overall, Basel III allows commercial banks to have an amount of loans equal to 10 - 33 times capital.

A commercial banker reading this description might object to presuming a capital ratio of 4% or a capital leverage of 25, and argue that a capital ratio of 8% or a capital leverage of 12.5 is more realistic. A banker rule of thumb is to assume a capital leverage of 12.5. However, capital ratios are a bit like reserve ratios in that banks apply many clever frauds to decrease them. The 8% capital ratio that was once a rule of thumb is now a fiction, and many banks obtain significantly lower capital ratios.

A commercial banker reading the descriptions of statutory reserve ratio requirements in previous chapters might have rolled their eyes. Reserves don't matter, the banker might have wanted to exclaim, because statutory reserve ratio requirements are so low as to be meaningless and banks that are short reserves can obtain massive quantities of additional reserves from the Fed Discount Window. Statutory reserve requirements don't truly limit loan creation or deposit creation, as we have seen. Statutory capital requirements limit loan creation. Limiting loan creation limits deposit creation because each newly created loan is monetized into a new deposit.

As statutory capital leverage requirements are the only true restraint on commercial bank money creation, the Fed and guv'ment are usually serious about enforcing them. If they did not do so, hyperinflation might result. If you think $7 trillion of deposits created by banks caused a huge housing bubble and econolypse, imagine how much worse it would have been if there were no statutory capital requirement, and banks created the full $16.9 trillion which statutory reserve requirements allowed. You'd need a wheelbarrow full of money to buy a Happy Meal and an M4 machine gun to keep one of the hundred million unemployed people from killing you for it.

In the real world, banks create and loan all the deposits they can, and worry about finding the reserves to back deposits after the fact if need be, via mechanisms described later. Banks can't issue loans and find capital to back them after the fact. Capital can't simply be conjured the way reserves can (until we cover investment banking and rampant re-hypothecation that is essentially fractional-reserve invest-ing). There is a Federal *Reserve* Bank which can conjure reserves for commercial banks, as we will see. There is no Federal Capital Bank which can conjure capital for commercial banks.

Leverage can involve inflation of the deposit supply or loan supply, but doesn't have to. Leverage is inflation of risk, an increase in potential payouts without an increase in wealth or resources available to pay them.

Brokers and loan officers don't own the corporations they work for. The capital being risked isn't theirs, and they don't keep interest profits on loans issued for the corporation, except maybe a tiny percentage as bonuses. Brokers and loan officers earn a living on commissions made when loans are issued or investments are sold. If you earn a commission for issuing a 30-year loan, then there isn't any more profit to be made for 30 years unless the loan is resold or refinanced. Or leverage is increased. . .

Brokers whose commissions plummet are often willing to increase leverage by any means necessary. Increasing leverage means increasing the amount of deposits or loans, usually by creating them out of thin air. One common practice is to un-derstate existing leverage through accounting fraud, and then use the low leverage as a justification for increased leverage. We're not really that leveraged, let's issue more loans or derivatives!

What if you're prosecuted for fraud? It's the mark-to-market conundrum re-visited. You didn't know you overvalued assets and understated liabilities. You are guilty of stupidity, not fraud. You play dumb, and walk.

For Speculatos making a living off fictitious paper profits, leverage is the name of the game. More leverage means more profit, but also more risk. Speculatos want the profit, but not the risk. When excessive leverage lines their pockets, Speculatos keep the money. When excessive leverage blows up in Speculatos' faces, taxpayers bail them out. Like it or hate it, that's the way the game is played, and if you want a different world, you need to change the rules.

One example during Depression v9.2006-201x is instructive. Taxpayers bailed out the Federal National Mortgage Association (Fannie Mae) and Federal Home Loan Mortgage Corporation (Freddie Mac), Government Sponsored "Enterpris-es" (GSEs) created by Franklin Delano Roosevelt's New "Deal." Fannie Fraud and Freddie Fraud escaped regulation by bribing, er funding the campaigns of, politi-cians on the following Congressional Committees: House Financial Services; Sen-ate Banking; Housing and Urban Affairs; Senate Finance; House Ways and Means; and Senate Appropriations. Fannie Fraud and Freddie Fraud executives were pros-ecuted for accounting fraud in the past, and acquitted. Bold enough in their thiev-ery that they were indicted, skilled enough at it that they walked, without politicians they "fund" proposing any reforms that would end such abuses. These crooks are experts at half-baking the books perfectly al dente, so interpretations of Fannie Fraud and Freddie Fraud debt levels vary. Taxpayers and Fed spent at least $2 trillion bailing these two GSEs out. Depending whose interpretation of the books you believe, when they failed their leverage was between 50 and 300—2 to 12 times the legal limit of 25 which commercial banks are bound by.

FRIENDLY NEIGHBORHOOD FED

"We make money the old fashioned way. We print it."

—Art J. Rolnick
Vice President and Director of Research, Minneapolis Federal Reserve Bank

Commercial bank customers write checks which are deposited at other commercial banks. To process or SETTLE these transactions, commercial banks send these checks to the Federal Reserve, the banker's bank. If a First Fraud Bank customer deposits a $100 check written by a Steal Second Bank customer, the Fed takes $100 from Steal Second Bank, and gives it to First Fraud Bank. First Fraud Bank and Steal Second Bank are required to keep a bank account with the Federal Reserve for these INTERBANK TRANSACTIONS, or payments between banks.

Let's open First Fraud Bank again:

Assets		Liabilities	
$20	(Reserves)	$200	(Transaction Deposits)
$980	(Loans)	$800	(Non-Transaction Deposits)
$1,000		$1,000	
			2% Reserve Ratio

First Fraud Bank accepts deposits of $1,000 of reserves. Deposits are classified as non-transaction deposits and transaction deposits at the 4 to 1 non-transaction deposit to transaction deposit ratio which customers usually choose. First Fraud Bank is a small bank that doesn't sweep, nor does it utilize the Low-Reserve Tranche or Reserve Requirement Exemption. First Fraud Bank applies a 0% statutory reserve ratio requirement to non-transaction deposits and a 10% statutory reserve ratio requirement to transaction deposits. Its statutory reserve requirement is $20. First Fraud Bank lends out its $980 of "excess" reserves. It has $20 of reserves backing $1,000 of deposits, a 2% reserve ratio.

Commercial banks like First Fraud Bank have two types of reserves, physical-currency reserves which are vault-cash reserves, and reserve accounts with the Federal Reserve Bank which are Fed-account reserves. First Fraud Bank's ledger is updated with vault-cash reserves and Fed-account reserves differentiated:

```
Assets                            Liabilities
   $20 Reserves                      $200 (Transaction Deposits)
      $10 (Vault-Cash Reserves)      $800 (Non-Transaction Deposits)
      $10 (Fed-Account Reserves)
   $980 (Loans)
```
_____

```
$1,000                            $1,000
                                       2% Reserve Ratio
```

On First Fraud Bank's ledger, the $20 of reserves are colored grey so that they are not counted. The indented reserve subtotals are counted. If the totals and subtotals were both counted, the same reserves would be counted twice for asset totals, which is incorrect. This nomenclature indicates that there are $20 of total reserves, $10 which are vault-cash reserves, and $10 which are Fed-account reserves.

Very roughly, the average commercial bank will keep vault-cash reserves equal to 4% - 6% of their *unswept* transaction deposits. That is, the amount of money which depositors think they have in original checking accounts, rather than the smaller amount of money which is kept in checking sub-accounts after sweeping. Vault-cash reserves equal to 5% of unswept transaction deposits is a good rough assumption. First Fraud Bank keeps vault-cash reserves equal to 5% of its $200 of transaction deposits, or $10.

Very roughly, the average commercial bank will keep Fed-account reserves equal to 1.5% - 6% of their unswept transaction deposits. Banks that don't sweep will hold a larger amount of Fed-account reserves which approaches 6% of unswept transaction deposits. Banks that sweep will hold a smaller amount of Fed-account reserves which approaches 1.5% of unswept transaction deposits, and is sometimes much lower. Banks can't decrease vault-cash reserves significantly or they will be unable to honor physical currency withdrawals by depositors. When banks sweep, reserve level decreases are primarily reductions in Fed-account reserves. This is why banks that sweep hold smaller amounts of Fed-account reserves. For a bank like First Fraud Bank that doesn't sweep, Fed-account reserves equal to 5% of unswept transaction deposits is a good rough assumption. First Fraud Bank keeps Fed-account reserves equal to 5% of its transaction deposits, or $10.

Through experience, banks have determined that these vault-cash reserve and Fed-account reserve levels are sufficient to honor depositor transactions during normal, non-bank-run economic conditions.

Though the assumptions in the paragraphs above are realistic, the example on the ledger above is oversimplified. Very few banks would have Fed-account reserves equal to vault-cash reserves. Most all banks have Fed-account reserves which are much smaller than vault-cash reserves, and a banker reading this description might point out this discrepancy. In the real world, if vault-cash reserves at a single bank were $10, then Fed-account reserves might be $5, $3, $1, or even less. If there were

$20 of total reserves, as in our simple example, then vault-cash reserves might be $15 or more, and Fed-account reserves might be $5 or less. This example assumes a 2% reserve ratio to keep math simple, rather than the 1.46% reserve ratio which prevailed in September 2008 just before The Bailout passed. With $10 of vault-cash reserves, $4.60 of Fed-account reserves would produce a 1.46% reserve ratio, which might be a better approximation. We'll nonetheless keep it simple and assume Fed-account reserves and vault-cash reserves are equal, though the reader should remain aware that this is not completely realistic.

Commercial banks used to give customers gifts like toasters for opening an account. Commercial banks open accounts at the Federal Reserve Bank. The Federal Reserve Bank gives a gift to commercial banks that open accounts, one that keeps on giving: the privilege to create deposit money via fraudulent fractional-reserve lending. For all institutions besides the Federal Reserve Bank and commercial banks, creating money is a crime.

First Fraud Bank doesn't know how many customers will demand physical-currency reserves from its vault and how many customers will write checks (or create debits) which will be sent to the Fed and create demands for Fed-account reserves. First Fraud Bank can withdraw physical-currency reserves from its Fed account if it needs more physical-currency reserves, converting Fed-account reserves into physical-currency reserves. Though a commercial bank could theoretically deposit physical-currency reserves at Fed and convert them into Fed-account reserves, this is rarely done. First Fraud Bank can take loans to the Fed Discount Window and have them monetized into Fed-account reserves, and this is the typical way that commercial banks obtain additional Fed-account reserves. Having loans monetized at the Discount Window increases the total amount of reserves that a bank holds, as the Fed literally creates reserves out of thin air. The Discount Window and interbank transactions utilizing Fed-account reserves will be described rigorously later. If you they confuse you now, don't worry.

As Fed-account reserves are simply conjured on a computer, they can be obtained much more easily than physical-currency reserves which must be printed and shipped to banks. A commercial bank can run out of Fed-account reserves and easily and instantaneously replenish them at the Fed Discount Window, but physical-currency reserves can't be easily nor instantaneously replenished. Commercial banks simply can't run out of vault-cash reserves. When depositors show up at their bank to withdraw physical-currency reserves and can't do so, panic spreads fast, and widespread bank runs rapidly materialize.

Bankers know this, and are careful to not to run out of physical-currency reserves under normal economic circumstances. It is the job of somebody very senior and very responsible to monitor both Fed-account reserve levels and vault-cash reserve levels, and make sure a bank never runs out of either type of reserves. Not a teller, a Vice President with a PhD in Finance. At larger banks there is a Reserve

Manager whose sole task is to monitor and manipulate reserve levels, and ensure that the bank maintains sufficient reserves.

Vault-cash reserves and physical-currency reserves are simply different terms for the same reserves. Physical-currency reserves are vault-cash reserves. The interchangeable use of these terms confuses some people.

First Fraud Bank's total reserves are its vault-cash reserves *and* Fed-account reserves. If First Fraud Bank deposits vault-cash reserves into its Fed account, converting vault-cash reserves into Fed-account reserves, this doesn't change its total amount of reserves. If First Fraud Bank withdraws vault-cash reserves from its Fed account, converting Fed-account reserves into vault-cash reserves, this doesn't change its total amount of reserves. Vault-cash reserves and Fed-account reserves are interchangeable, and convertible.

First Fraud Bank maintains accounts for individual depositors:

```
Assets                              Liabilities
   $20 Reserves                        $200 (Transaction Deposits)
       $10 (Vault-Cash Reserves)          $10 (William)
       $10 (Fed-Account reserves)         $30 (Robert)
   $980 (Loans)                           $60 (Mary)
                                         $100 (Other Depositors)
                                        $800 (Non-Transaction Deposits)
─────────────────────────────────────────────────────────────────
$1,000                              $1,000
                                        2% Reserve Ratio
```

This nomenclature indicates that there are $200 of total transaction deposits at Steal Second Bank, $10 which are in the account of William, $30 which are in the account of Robert, $60 which are in the account of Mary, and $100 which are in the account of other depositors.

Only a few depositors are shown. At most banks, there are tens of thousands or millions of depositors, so an actual list of depositors would be much longer.

If Mary buys bread from William and writes him a $1 check, First Fraud Bank subtracts $1 from Mary's account and adds $1 to William's account. The updated ledger after this transaction:

Assets	Liabilities
$20 Reserves	$200 (Transaction Deposits)
$10 (Vault-Cash Reserves)	$11 (William)
$10 (Fed-Account reserves)	$30 (Robert)
$980 (Loans)	$59 (Mary)
	$100 (Other Depositors)
	$800 (Non-Transaction Deposits)
$1,000	$1,000

2% Reserve Ratio

Money "changed hands," and so did a good that was bread, but to First Fraud Bank the transaction was internal bookkeeping. First Fraud Bank's total amount of deposits remained the same. Most importantly, First Fraud Bank didn't have to pay out reserves to another bank or depositor. This was an INTRABANK TRANSACTION, or payment within a bank, which did not involve any other bank.

Intra means within. Intrabank transactions occur within a single bank. Inter means between or among. Interbank transactions occur between or among multiple banks. These terms will be used frequently in later chapters, so it is important not to confuse them.

Mary pays Patricia $2 for butter, and writes her a $2 check, but Patricia banks at Steal Second Bank, not First Fraud Bank. Patricia deposits the $2 check into her Steal Second Bank account and Steal Second Bank sends this check to the Federal Reserve, the banker's bank. The Federal Reserve maintains a balance sheet for depositors, but its depositors are banks, not people:

Assets	Liabilities
$100 (T-debts)	$10 (First Fraud Bank Deposit)
	$9 (Steal Second Bank Deposit)
	$81 (Other Bank Deposits)
$100	$100

This Federal Reserve ledger is similar to commercial bank ledgers, but also different in some key ways. The Fed's assets are T-debts. The Fed can only create reserves by monetizing assets, usually debts. Usually those debts are T-debts. On the ledger above, the Fed has T-debt assets with a face value of $100, so it can only create $100 of reserves. If the Fed wanted to create additional reserves, it would need additional debt assets to monetize. Like commercial banks, Fed categorizes loans as assets because it expects them to be repaid. The T-debt is an asset to Fed because it expects guv'ment to repay the T-debt loan using tax revenues.

So a commercial bank keeps a master ledger for all its depositors, which are people or businesses. The Fed keeps a master ledger for all its depositors, which are commercial banks.

Mary's check requires First Fraud Bank to pay $2 to Steal Second Bank. The Fed processes this transaction, subtracting $2 from First Fraud Bank's account and adding $2 to Steal Second Bank's account. The Fed's updated ledger:

```
Assets                     Liabilities
$100 (T-debts)
                             $8  (First Fraud Bank Deposit)
                             $11 (Steal Second Bank Deposit)
                             $81 (Other Bank Deposits)
_____

$100                       $100
```

Money "changed hands," and so did a good that was butter, but to the Federal Reserve the transaction was internal bookkeeping. Its total deposits remained the same.

The Fed doesn't take money from Mary and give it to Patricia. Commercial banks do this. The Fed is a banker's bank. Its transactions are with banks, not you or me or other individuals. The Fed informs both banks that the check from Mary has been processed, and then each bank adjusts its depositor accounts.

Every commercial bank in America has an account at the Federal Reserve (either directly or indirectly), because every commercial bank has customers that write checks and use debit cards. The Fed performs transactions like these on commercial bank accounts roughly a half million times per day as it processes mountains of checks and debit card transactions. The Fed has a computer system called Fedwire which processes such transactions. In September 2008, Fedwire processed 11.2 million transactions, or about 522,347 per business day. These transactions totaled $69 trillion for the month, or about $3.3 trillion per day. The September 2008 totals were higher than normal because of runs on banks, but during any given month there are usually at least 9 million transactions which total more than $40 trillion, or at least 450,000 transfers per day totalling at least $2.5 trillion. If Fedwire shut down for any significant period of time, people and businesses would not be able to settle transactions and the economy would collapse.

Commercial banks can withdraw physical-currency reserves from their Fed accounts, but even if all Fed-account reserves could be completely converted into physical-currency reserves, there would not be enough physical-currency reserves to honor all deposits. In a fraudulent fractional-reserve banking system, reserves are only a fraction of the deposit supply, so it is impossible to obtain enough reserves—physical-currency or Fed-account—to honor all deposits. All commercial banks are in on the fractional-reserve scam, and understand that reserves are just a façade, especially physical-currency reserves. Commercial banks request only enough physical-currency reserves to satisfy customer demands.

A mass run on all banks, in which all depositors simultaneously try to withdraw deposits and redeem them for physical-currency reserves, would collapse the banking system and economy, as the Fed could not produce enough physical-currency reserves, or even Fed-account reserves.

In theory, Fed could easily create enough Fed-account reserves to back all deposits, as voluminous Fed-account reserves can be conjured with a mere keystroke. However, Fed must take loan assets onto its books when creating reserves, and if it did this on a large enough scale to create enough Fed-account reserves to back all deposits, so many loans would be removed from the economy that it would be irreparably disrupted and collapse.

Why not try to print enough physical-currency reserves to back every commercial-bank deposit? Impossible. Computered money can be created faster than physical money, which is why physical backing for dollars was abandoned. Speculatos want the illusion of 100% reserve backing, but the ability to conjure fortunes out of thin air on ledgers. Tethering computerized dollar blips to any physical reserve, even a worthless piece of paper, is a return to the system that Speculatos labored to destroy, and is unacceptable.

These concepts are deceptively simple, especially the idea that monetary transfers between depositors can occur without banks surrendering any reserves. When applied with rigor on a larger scale, this concept can create confusion, but it is crucial.

FRIENDLY NEIGHBORHOOD FED PICTURE PAGES

TO SKIP THE PICTURE PAGES AFTER THIS CHAPTER, PLEASE TURN TO PAGE 276

FED-ACCOUNT RESERVES VS. VAULT-CASH RESERVES

America has two forms of reserves: Fed-account reserves and vault-cash reserves. Prior to September 2008, Fed-account reserves were approximately 20% of vault-cash reserves. After The Bailout passed, Fed conjured more than a trillion dollars of reserves, causing Fed-account reserves to dwarf vault-cash reserves. This is anomalous. In healthy economic conditions, Fed-account reserves are less than vault-cash reserves, especially because sweeping decreases Fed-account reserves.

The ratio of Fed-account reserves to vault-cash reserves for the entire banking system may not be the same as the ratio of any single bank. Small banks often have few Fed-account reserves, but larger banks must maintain modest amounts because of the sheer volume of their transaction settling. When combined, differing ratios of Fed-account reserves to vault-cash reserves at many banks produce a net ratio which may be significantly different from the ratio at any single bank.

Banks keep only enough vault-cash reserves to satisfy day-to-day customer withdrawals. Decades ago, in the 1950s, 1960s, 1970s, and earlier, overall statutory reserve ratio requirements and statutory reserve requirements were much higher than they are today Banks would keep just enough vault-cash reserves to satisfy day-to-day customer demands, but would still require a large amount of additional reserves to satisfy statutory reserve requirements. They would hold these additional reserves in the form of Fed-account reserves. Thus Fed-account reserves drastically exceeded vault-cash reserves, as shown in the following graph:

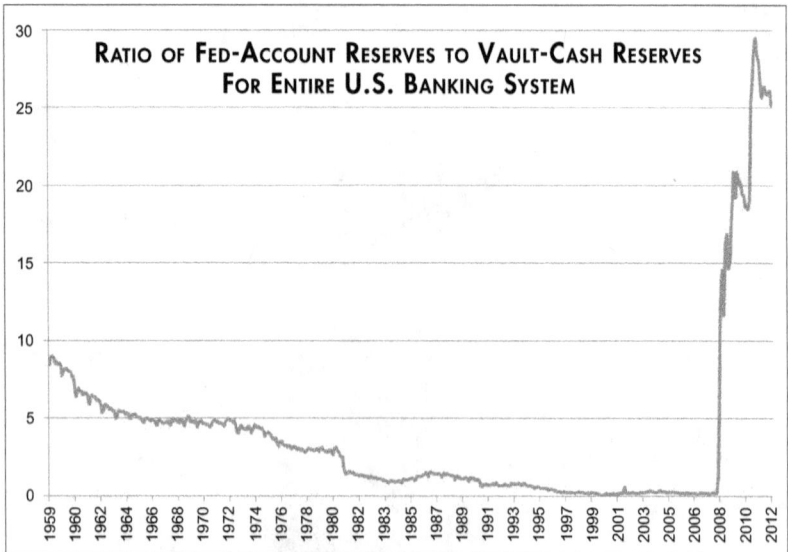

RATIO OF FED-ACCOUNT RESERVES TO VAULT-CASH RESERVES FOR ENTIRE U.S. BANKING SYSTEM

Data in the graph on the previous page is for the entire banking system. The year is shown on the x-axis. The ratio of Fed-account reserves to vault-cash reserves is shown on the y-axis. In 1959 when Fed started systematically recording this data, Fed-account reserves were 8-times vault-cash reserves. This ratio steadily decreased as statutory reserve requirements decreased. By the time the economy imploded in 2008, Fed-account reserves were 0.2-times vault-cash reserves, or 20% of vault-cash reserves. To effect The Bailout, Fed conjured more than $1 trillion of Fed-account reserves, which skyrocketed the ratio of Fed-account reserves to vault-cash reserves.

With the rightward Bailout spike removed from the graph, the downward trend prior to The Bailout is easier to observe, as shown on the graph below.

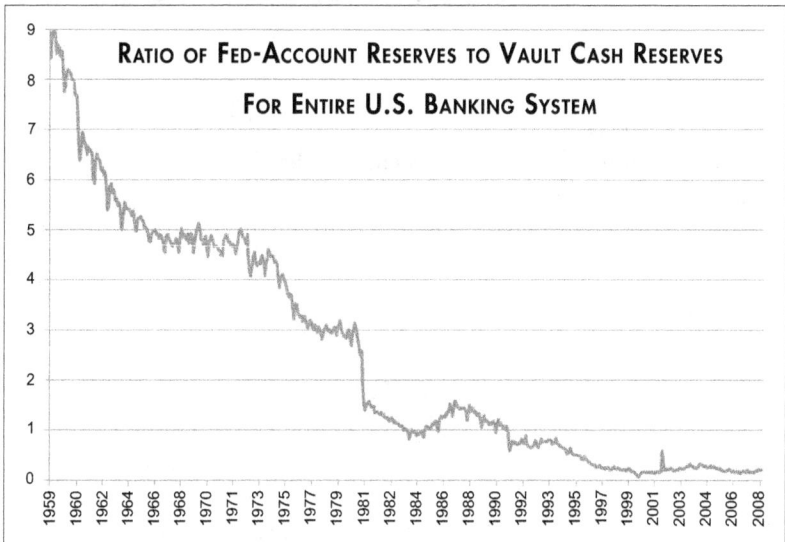

RATIO OF FED-ACCOUNT RESERVES TO VAULT CASH RESERVES
FOR ENTIRE U.S. BANKING SYSTEM

On the graph above, the spike after 1980 coincides with the Monetary Control Act, which laxened statutory reserve requirements, creating "non-transaction" deposits subject to a 0% statutory reserve ratio requirement and the 3% Low-Reserve Tranche. After sweeps were implemented in 1994, the ratio steadily decreased until it stabilized at roughly 0.2, or Fed-account reserves equal to 20% of vault-cash reserves. The small spike in late 2001 is after the 9-11 attacks, when Fed conjured reserves for banks in case panic from the attacks created bank runs.

It will probably take Fed decades to unwind The Bailout. That is, uncreate the trillions of dollars of Fed-account reserves used to bailout banks. When The Bailout is finally unwound, Fed-account reserves will probably once again be much less than vault-cash reserves.

CONJURING RESERVES

"When you or I write a check there must be sufficient funds in our account to cover that check, but when the Federal Reserve writes a check, it is creating money [reserves]."

—*I Bet You Thought*, Federal Reserve Pamphlet

"Let us assume that expansion in the money stock is desired by the Federal Reserve to achieve its policy objectives. One way the Central Bank can initiate such an expansion is through purchases of securities in the open market. Payment for the securities adds to bank reserves."

—*Modern Money Mechanics*, Federal Reserve Publication

In the previous chapter, the Federal Reserve Bank ledgers and commercial bank ledgers were shown separately. In this chapter, the Fed ledgers and commercial bank ledgers will be merged, increasing accuracy and understandability.

Guv'ment creates $100 of T-debts, and the Fed monetizes them and creates a $100 deposit for guv'ment:

```
        Federal Reserve
Assets              Liabilities
#100 (T-Debts)      #100 (Guv'ment
                          Deposit)
_____
#100                #100
```

This is the same process of monetization which commercial banks performed for their depositors, but the Fed is doing it for its depositors. The Fed doesn't have any assets that will be labelled "reserves," like a commercial bank. Fed doesn't have to embezzle reserves and lend them to create additional deposits, like a commercial bank. Rather, the Federal Reserve Bank can simply take possession of a preexisting loan or debt, place it on the asset portion of its ledger, and directly monetize it into a deposit liability, without utilizing ledger assets called "reserves."

The Fed is a banker's bank. Only banks and guv'ment can have accounts at the Fed. Guv'ment therefore can't pay people or non-bank businesses with a Fed account. Guv'ment is paid a $100 check by Fed, and deposits it at First Fraud Bank. First Fraud Bank opens a deposit account for guv'ment, just as it would for any other depositor that deposits a check:

Federal Reserve			First Fraud Bank	
Assets	Liabilities		Assets	Liabilities
$100 (T-Debts)	$100 (Guv'ment Deposit)			$100 (Guv'ment Deposit)
$100	$100		$0	$100

First Fraud Bank needs $100 of assets to honor the deposit liability it created, but has no assets. In previous examples, a commercial bank which created a deposit liability from a deposited check demanded assets from the commercial bank that issued the check. In this case, the check was issued by the Federal Reserve Bank rather than a commercial bank, so First Fraud Bank demands assets from the Federal Reserve Bank. The Federal Reserve Bank has created a deposit liability for guv'ment, and it transfers ownership of this deposit liability to First Fraud Bank:

Federal Reserve			First Fraud Bank	
Assets	Liabilities		Assets	Liabilities
$100 (T-Debts)	$100 (1st Fraud Deposit)			$100 (Guv'ment Deposit)
$100	$100		$0	$100

First Fraud Bank now has a deposit at the Federal Reserve Bank.

Commercial banks have two types of reserves, vault-cash reserves and Fed- account reserves. First Fraud Bank now has Fed-account reserves which are its deposit at the Federal Reserve Bank. First Fraud Bank enters these reserves into its ledger as an asset:

Federal Reserve			First Fraud Bank	
Assets	Liabilities		Assets	Liabilities
$100 (T-Debts)	$100 (1st Fraud Deposit) ⟵⟶		$100 (Fed Reserve Deposit)	$100 (Guv'ment Deposit)
$100	$100		$100	$100

100% Reserve Ratio

In earlier examples, $100 of reserves were initially deposited at a first bank, but the origin of these reserves was not shown. The Fed creates the $100 of reserves which are deposited at the first commercial bank. The Fed creates reserves by monetizing a debt and creating a deposit liability. *Federal Reserve Bank deposit liabilities are commercial bank reserve assets.*

Categorizing Federal Reserve Bank deposit liabilities as commercial bank reserve assets is arbitrary. This categorization exists because guv'ment passed laws which decree that Federal Reserve Bank deposit liabilities shall be commercial bank reserve assets. These laws include the Federal Reserve Act of 1913 and the Monetary Control Act of 1980. Federal Reserve Bank deposit liabilities are commercial bank reserve assets because of guv'ment decree, or fiat. Federal Reserve Bank deposit liabilities are money because the guv'ment has decreed that they are money. Federal Reserve Bank deposit liabilities are fiat money. Without the fiat—the guv'ment decree—which forces Federal Reserve Bank deposit liabilities to be accepted as money, Federal Reserve Bank deposit liabilities would be rejected as money, and a more honest money such as gold would be chosen.

The Fed's $100 First Fraud Bank deposit and First Fraud Bank's $100 Fed deposit are two separate ledger entries, but they are the same money. They are joined by arrows and enclosed by dotted lines to highlight this fact.

A depositor at First Fraud Bank can't unilaterally credit or debit their account, they must have First Fraud Bank credit or debit it. First Fraud Bank controls the balance in the depositor's account.

First Fraud Bank is a depositor at the Federal Reserve Bank. First Fraud Bank can't unilaterally credit or debit its Federal Reserve account, it must have the Federal Reserve credit or debit it. The Federal Reserve controls the balance in First Fraud Bank's account.

The Fed deposit asset shown on First Fraud Bank's ledger is the First Fraud Bank deposit liability on Fed's ledger. If Fed changes the First Fraud Bank deposit liability on its ledger, First Fraud Bank will update the Federal Reserve deposit asset on its ledger to reflect this change.

This entire process occurs on ledgers. The reserves that First Fraud Bank has on deposit at Fed are money, but they are not physical money. In this example, there is no physical money yet.

The start-up of a money system from scratch with no money initially in existence will be explained with greater rigor later. For now, if this confuses you a little, don't worry. The main thing to understand is that the same money is accounted differently on two different ledgers by two different parties. The commercial-bank deposit is a liability to the Fed because a commercial bank can demand it from the Fed, just as you or I can demand our deposit from a commercial bank. The Fed deposit is an asset to the commercial bank because the commercial bank can withdraw physical currency from the Fed account or use it to make payments to other commercial banks, just as you or I can withdraw physical currency from our commercial bank account or use it to make payments to other depositors.

This deposit duality tends to confuse people, so let's restate it. The Fed considers its deposits to be liabilities. To commercial banks, Fed deposits are assets called reserves. A commercial bank considers the deposits it creates for depositors to be liabilities. To commercial-bank depositors, commercial-bank deposits are assets called money. These dualities can be visualized better if a third ledger is added to our master ledger. This updated master ledger is shown on the left.

Assume that the deposit at First Fraud Bank is your deposit rather than guv'ments. If you kept a personal ledger, it would show your

Federal Reserve

$100	$100
Assets	Liabilities
$100 (T-Debts)	$100 (1st Fraud Deposit)

First Fraud Bank

$100	$100
Assets	liabilities
$100 (Fed Reserve Deposit)	$100 (Your Deposit)

Depositor

$100	$70
Assets	Liabilities
$100 (Your Deposit)	$50 (Mortgage)
	$20 (Food)

bank deposit as an asset, and bills you owe such as a mortgage and food as liabilities. The money you have deposited at First Fraud Bank is shown twice, once on First Fraud Bank's ledger and once on your personal ledger, but this money doesn't exist twice. The reserves that First Fraud Bank has deposited at the Federal Reserve Bank are shown twice, once on the Federal Reserve Bank's ledger and once on First Fraud Bank's ledger, but these reserves don't exist twice.

Back to the guv'ment deposit. Guv'ment had Fed monetize $100 of T-debts, and deposited the check which Fed paid it at First Fraud Bank. Guv'ment hasn't spent its deposit or issued any payments yet:

Federal Reserve		First Fraud Bank	
Assets	Liabilities	Assets	Liabilities
$100 (T-Debts)	$100 (1ˢᵗ Fraud ⟵⟶ Deposit)	$100 (Fed Reserve Deposit)	$100 (Guv'ment Deposit)
$100	$100	$100	$100
			100% Reserve Ratio

William works for guv'ment. Guv'ment writes William a $10 check. William deposits this check at First Fraud Bank. First Fraud Bank creates a $10 deposit account for William, and subtracts $10 from guv'ment's account. The updated ledgers:

Federal Reserve		First Fraud Bank	
Assets	Liabilities	Assets	Liabilities
$100 (T-Debts)	$100 (1ˢᵗ Fraud ⟵⟶ Deposit)	$100 (Fed Reserve Deposit)	$90 (Guv'ment) $10 (William)
$100	$100	$100	$100
			100% Reserve Ratio

Robert and Mary also work for guv'ment. Guv'ment writes a $30 paycheck to Robert and a $60 check to Mary. The updated ledgers:

Federal Reserve		First Fraud Bank	
Assets	Liabilities	Assets	Liabilities
$100 (T-Debts)	$100 (1ˢᵗ Fraud ⟵⟶ Deposit)	$100 (Fed Reserve Deposit)	$0 (Guv'ment) $10 (William) $30 (Robert) $60 (Mary)
$100	$100		
		$100	$100
			100% Reserve Ratio

Guv'ment, William, Robert, and Mary could write checks to one person or a million people, and as long as these people already had accounts at First Fraud Bank or deposited checks at First Fraud Bank, the process on the ledger above would simply be repeated numerous times. One large initial deposit owned by one person or entity would be broken up into many small deposits owned by several persons or entities. Deposits might be created or uncreated, and the amount of individual deposits might change, but the total amount of deposits would not change. Rather, money would be just shuffled among numerous different deposits as people and entities conducted economic transactions which are the buying &

selling of goods & services. The critical fact to First Fraud Bank is that none of these internal transactions require it to pay out reserves.

Mary buys butter from Patricia, and pays by writing a $2 check to Patricia, who deposits the $2 check at Steal Second Bank:

```
          Federal Reserve                         First Fraud Bank
Assets            Liabilities              Assets              Liabilities
$100 (T-Debts)    $100 (1ˢᵗ Fraud  ⟵————⟶ $100 (Fed Reserve   $0  (Guv'ment)
                        Deposit)                 Deposit)       $10 (William)
                                                                $30 (Robert)
$100              $100                                          $58 (Mary)⟶⟶
                                         $100                $98           │
                                                                          ↓
                                               Steal Second Bank
                                         Assets              Liabilities
                                         $0 (Reserves)       $2 (Patricia)⟵
                                         $0                  $2
                                                             100% Reserve Ratio
```

To keep this book from becoming absurdly long, and even more boring, rudimentary steps shown many times will now be grouped. $2 was subtracted from Mary's account, and $2 was added to an account created for Patricia by Steal Second Bank.

You have seen all this before, but not with the Fed ledger also shown. Steal Second Bank presents Mary's $2 check to the Federal Reserve. The Federal Reserve processes the check. It subtracts $2 from First Fraud Bank's account, creates a new account for Steal Second Bank, and adds $2 to this account:

```
          Federal Reserve                         First Fraud Bank
Assets            Liabilities              Assets              Liabilities
$100 (T-Debts)    $98 (1ˢᵗ Fraud   ⟵————⟶ $98 (Reserves)      $0  (Guv'ment)
                       Deposit)                                $10 (William)
                  $2  (Steal 2ⁿᵈ                               $30 (Robert)
                       Deposit)                                $58 (Mary)
$100              $100                      $98                 $98
                                               Steal Second Bank
                                         Assets              Liabilities
                                         $2 (Reserves)       $2 (Patricia)
                                         $2                  $2
                                                             100% Reserve Ratio
```

First Fraud Bank's account balance at the Federal Reserve Bank has decreased from $100 to $98, so First Fraud Bank subtracted this amount from its reserve assets. Steal Second Bank's account balance at the Federal Reserve Bank has increased from $0 to $2, so Steal Second Bank added this amount to its reserve assets.

In the real world, Steal Second Bank must raise capital and be licensed by guv'ment before opening a Federal Reserve Bank account. Opening a Federal Reserve Bank account is much harder than opening an account at a commercial bank, and is usually not done quickly or easily. This is because opening a Federal Reserve Bank account is part of the process of opening a bank, and guv'ment doesn't let just anyone become a banker with the power to create money. Steal Second

Bank would have already opened a Federal Reserve Bank account, even if the account balance was zero.

As more entries are added to these ledgers and they become more crowded, names in parenthesis will be shortened. Banks have only two types of reserves, vault-cash reserves and Fed-account reserves. On commercial bank ledgers, "reserves" are Fed-account reserves. Any reserves shown on commercial bank ledgers opposite Fed ledgers should be presumed to be Fed-account reserves, unless they are explicitly labelled cash, cash reserves, currency, or vault cash. Crowded ledgers also make it impossible to outline paired entries with a dotted-line box, but arrows connecting these entries will still be included. These arrows indicate two ledger entries that are a single amount of money.

Steal Second Bank created a $2 deposit for Patricia when she deposited a check, but might not allow Patricia to spend her $2 deposit until $2 of reserves have been paid by First Fraud Bank to back the deposit. For miniscule transactions, commercial banks usually credit depositor accounts before reserves are paid, especially if the depositor has good credit and has never deposited checks which bounce. Transactions which are miniscule to commercial banks are often large to depositors, but for 4-or-5 figure transactions or larger, commercial banks usually confirm reserve transfers before allowing depositors access to funds.

The simple transaction-settling concept shown on these ledgers could be extrapolated to the entire economy. Hundreds of millions of people and entities (businesses, governments, nonprofit organizations, etc.) would buy & sell goods & services, writing checks to each other to settle these economic transactions, or utilizing debit cards which create non-physical, computerized checks. Commercial banks would credit and debit hundreds of millions of depositor accounts as these transactions occurred. In some cases, new depositor accounts would be created or uncreated, but the total balance in all depositor accounts would not increase—not yet anyway.

In many cases, checks would be written by depositors at one commercial bank to depositors at another commercial bank. The Federal Reserve Bank would process these transactions by subtracting funds from the account of the commercial bank whose depositor wrote the check and adding funds to the account of the commercial bank whose depositor deposited the check.

After many checks are written, the ledger for the entire economy might be:

```
        Federal Reserve                          First Fraud Bank
Assets              Liabilities          Assets              Liabilities
$100 (T-Debts)      $10 (1st      ⟸  ⟹  $10 (Reserves)      $10 (Deposits)
                         Fraud
                         Deposit)        $10                 $10
                    $40 (Steal
                         2nd
                         Deposit)                    Steal Second Bank
                    $20 (3rd
                         Thievery        Assets              Liabilities
                         Deposit)        $40 (Reserves)      $40 (Deposits)
                    $30 (4th
                         Filch           $40                 $40
                         Deposit)
$100                $100                            Third Thievery Bank

                                         Assets              Liabilities
                                         $20 (Reserves)      $20 (Deposits)

                                         $20                 $20


                                                   Fourth Filch Bank

                                         Assets              Liabilities
                                         $30 (Reserves)      $30 (Deposits)

                                         $30                 $30
                                                   100% Reserve Ratio
```

As Federal Reserve Bank deposit liabilities are commercial bank reserve assets, the Fed is shuffling reserves back and forth among commercial banks when it credits or debits their Fed accounts. Fed shuffles reserves back and forth among commercial banks to settle transactions among depositors at commercial banks. Settling transactions among commercial-bank depositors thus causes the reserve levels of commercial banks to fluctuate. This is a critical observation.

Commercial-bank depositors pay each other with commercial-bank deposits. Commercial-bank deposits function as money for depositors with accounts at commercial banks. That is, commercial-bank deposits are the medium of exchange which commercial-bank depositors use to settle transactions. No depositor with an account at a commercial bank can create the deposits they use to settle transactions. If depositors with accounts at commercial banks could create commercial-bank deposits which are money to them, every depositor would simply create commercial-bank deposits and hyperinflation would result.

Commercial banks settle transactions for their depositors using commercial-bank deposits, but commercial banks don't settle transactions among themselves using commercial-bank deposits. Commercial banks pay each other with Federal-Reserve-Bank deposits. Federal-Reserve-Bank deposits function as money for commercial banks with accounts at the Federal Reserve Bank. That is, Federal-Reserve-Bank deposits are the medium of exchange which Federal-Reserve-Bank depositors (commercial banks) use to settle economic transactions. No commercial bank with an account at the Federal Reserve Bank can create the reserves they use to settle transactions. If commercial banks with accounts at the Federal Reserve Bank could create reserves which are money to them, every commercial bank would simply create reserves and hyperinflation would result.

Federal-Reserve-Bank deposits and commercial-bank deposits are not independent and unrelated. Rather, they are interdependent. While Federal-Reserve-Bank deposits (reserves) and commercial-bank deposits (deposits) both function as money, reserves are the more fundamental form of money. Federal-Reserve-Bank deposits (reserves) back commercial-bank deposits (deposits). Reserves back deposits. Deposits are redeemed for reserves.

It is easy to grow confused. Remember goldsmiths. Reserves are like gold and deposits are like the paper promissory notes which goldsmiths circulated. With goldsmith bankers, someone has to dig gold up for there to be reserves, and if anyone digs up gold and deposits it at the goldsmith bank the supply of reserves increases. With cybersmith bankers, only the Central Bank can create reserves. In the United States, the Central Bank is the Federal Reserve Bank.

As we will see later, under the monetary system that America's Founding Fathers created, gold was reserves, anyone could mine gold, bring it to a U.S. mint, have coins that were legal money minted from the gold, spend those gold coins, and thereby circulate reserves which are money. Thus we the people controlled the supply of reserves, and a democracy of money resulted. This power was taken from we the people (along with our gold, as shown in *Bubblenomics*), and transferred to the Federal Reserve Bank. The Federal Reserve Bank has a monopoly on reserve creation. It is the only entity in America that is allowed to create reserves. Fed creates paper-dollar-bill reserves and computer-ledger reserves, neither of which is a commodity like gold. This is a tyrannical system in dire need of reform, but the question of what to replace it with is extremely contentious, and we have much ground to cover before this question can be answered thoroughly and intelligently. As noted in *Bubblenomics*, deciding what form reserves should take and who should be able to create them is perhaps the most important decision a civilization makes. If a civilization chooses the wrong physical or non-physical form for reserves, or entrusts the power to create reserves to the wrong parties, it is doomed. Much more on this concept later, for now it is something to keep in mind.

Goldsmiths held gold reserves and created paper promissory notes which exceeded gold reserves. Cybersmiths hold Fed reserves and create deposits which exceed Fed reserves. Medieval bankers issued paper promissory notes which could be redeemed for gold reserves. Modern commercial bankers issue computerized promissory notes called deposits which can be redeemed for Fed reserves.

A medieval depositor simply brought gold reserves to a goldsmith to deposit reserves, but this reserve-depositing process is more circuitous with non-physical, computerized Fed reserves. The Fed doesn't dig up gold reserves or accept deposits of gold reserves, it creates reserves by monetizing a debt and creating a deposit liability which is reserves. Being non-physical, these reserves can't be spent the way gold reserves could. For non-physical ledger reserves to function as money, everyone must be made to accept a ledger entry as money. For everyone to accept a ledger entry as money, everyone must be given an entry on the ledger, and be able to use this ledger entry to buy & sell goods & services, issue payments and receive payments. This ledger entry is called a bank account.

Being a banker's bank, the Federal Reserve Bank can't open bank accounts for individuals or entities that are not banks or guv'ment (an exception because it licenses commercial banks, creates the Central Bank, and gives it a monopoly on reserve creation). The Federal Reserve must utilize an intermediary or middleman which maintains a ledger entry for individuals. Commercial banks are this intermediary. When the Fed creates ledger-entry money for guv'ment, guv'ment transfers this ledger-entry money to a commercial bank, which allows guv'ment to pay individuals or entities by transferring ledger-entry money to their commercial bank accounts.

Thus Fed reserves are not brought to commercial banks the way gold was brought to a goldsmith bank. Rather, reserves are created by Fed on its ledger, credited to guv'ment, and transferred to commercial banks by guv'ment so that guv'ment can use reserves to pay non-bank entities. The Fed creates reserves, gives the reserves to a commercial bank, and tells the commercial bank that the reserves belong to guv'ment, which is free to spend them as it wishes. The commercial bank then creates a deposit for guv'ment which is backed by the Fed's reserves in the same way that a goldsmith's promissory note was backed by gold.

In theory, the Fed could simply create ledger entries for hundreds of millions of individuals and businesses, and there would be no need for commercial banks. However, this is a hassle that the Fed isn't interested in—especially because commercial banks must assess the credit worthiness of individuals and entities and the value of collateral to issue loans. The Fed properly views this as the purview of private banks, not the Central Bank. Speculatos would never let the Fed directly issue loans regardless, as Speculatos earn profit off commercial bank loans, and Central Banks such as the Federal Reserve are created to Bailout commercial banks. Central Banks Bailout commercial banks by conjuring reserves for commercial banks that have lie-abilities exposed and face demands for reserves they have promised depositors but don't possess.

Though unrealistic, this analogue of the Fed as the only bank in existence and the sole creator of all deposits can help those who are confused. The Fed could simply create reserves, and then create a deposit account for guv'ment which is a claim to those reserves. Guv'ment would pay workers and contractors by having the Fed transfer deposit credits from guv'ment's account to the accounts of workers and contractors. These depositors would have a claim to Fed-account reserves in the same way a medieval worker paid a paper promissory note had a claim to gold reserves.

Again, this one-bank system would be completely unacceptable to Speculatos because it only involves the reshuffling of preexisting reserves, rather than the creation of exorbitant amounts of deposits whose quantity drastically exceeds reserves. This one-bank system is a 100% reserve system. There are no Speculatos creating and lending an amount of deposits equal to 68 times reserves or more and earning obscene profits via loan interest payments.

Depositors with accounts at commercial banks worry about running out of commercial-bank deposits. If depositors with accounts at commercial banks pay out too many commercial-bank deposits to other depositors, they run out of commercial-bank deposits and are insolvent.

Commercial banks with accounts at the Federal Reserve Bank worry about running out of Federal-Reserve-Bank deposits. If commercial banks with accounts at the Federal Reserve Bank pay out too many Federal-Reserve-Bank deposits, they run out of Federal-Reserve-Bank deposits and are insolvent.

In this chapter's ledgers, every deposit was 100% backed by reserves. All banks could always honor all reserve demands from depositors or other banks. No bank worried about a reserve shortage because no bank had a reserve shortage. Despite the computer font, the commercial bank portion of banking system was honest—until fractional-reserve lending proceeds:

```
        Federal Reserve                              First Fraud Bank
Assets              Liabilities              Assets              Liabilities
$100 (T-Debts)      $10 (1st                 $10 (Reserves)      $680 (Deposits)
                         Fraud               $670 (Loans)
                         Deposit)            ─────────────────────────────────
                    $40 (Steal               $680                $680
                         2nd
                         Deposit)                 Steal Second Bank
                    $20 (3rd                 Assets              Liabilities
                         Thievery            $40 (Reserves)      $2,720 (Deposits)
                         Deposit)            $2,680 (Loans)
                    $30 (4th                 ─────────────────────────────────
                         Filch               $2,720              $2,720
                         Deposit)
─────────────────────────────────                Third Thievery Bank
$100                $100                     Assets              Liabilities
                                             $20 (Reserves)      $1,360 (Deposits)
                                             $1,340 (Loans)
                                             ─────────────────────────────────
                                             $1,360              $1,360

                                                 Fourth Filch Bank
                                             Assets              Liabilities
                                             $30 (Reserves)      $2,040 (Deposits)
                                             $2,010 (Loans)
                                             ─────────────────────────────────
                                             $2,040              $2,040
                                                          1.46% Reserve Ratio
```

These commercial bank ledgers utilize the 1.46% reserve ratio which prevailed in September 2008 just before The Bailout. On these ledgers, the Federal Reserve Bank creates $100 of reserves that are injected into the economy by being deposited at commercial banks. Commercial banks then create an amount of deposits equal to 68 times reserves, or $6,800. $100 of reserves backing $6,800 of deposits is a 1.46% reserve ratio. Different commercial banks would have different reserve ratios because they utilize different sweep rates and different percentages of their deposits qualify for the Low-Reserve Tranche and Reserve Requirement Exemption, but this oversimplified example assumes that each commercial bank has a 1.46% reserve ratio. Each commercial bank holds an amount of reserves equal to

1.46% of its deposits, or creates an amount of deposits equal to 68 times the amount of reserves it holds.

The ledger for the entire banking system would be:

Federal Reserve		First Fraud Bank	
Assets	Liabilities	Assets	Liabilities
♦100 (T-Debts)	♦100 (Commercial ⟵⟶	♦100 (Reserves)	♦6,800 (Deposits)
	Bank Deposits)	♦6,700 (Loans)	
♦100	♦100	♦6,800	♦6,800
			1.46% Reserve Ratio

We are concerned with the larger ledger on the previous page which shows individual commercial banks. Once each commercial bank embezzles reserves, issues loans, and creates deposits which drastically exceed reserves, commercial banks no longer have the ability to honor all deposits, and paying out reserves becomes problematic or even impossible. We have covered the simple situation in which a depositor walks into First Fraud Bank and demands reserves. If depositors demand an amount of reserves which exceed First Fraud Bank's $10 of reserves, then First Fraud Bank is rupted. When a First Fraud Bank depositor writes a check to a depositor at Steal Second Bank, the demand for reserves comes from Steal Second Bank rather than a depositor, but First Fraud Bank is still rupted if it doesn't have enough reserves to honor the demand.

First Fraud Bank is rupted if depositors with $680 of deposits write checks to other commercial banks which exceed $10. Steal Second Bank is rupted if depositors with $2,720 of deposits write checks to other commercial banks which exceed $40. Third Thievery Bank is rupted if depositors with $1,360 of deposits write checks to other banks which exceed $20. Fourth Filch Bank is rupted if depositors with $2,040 of deposits write checks to other banks which exceed $30...

Commercial-bank depositors can control what they spend, and can only become insolvent if they spend excessively. A commercial bank can't control what its depositors will spend, and can become insolvent if its depositors write too many checks to other banks.

A 1.46% reserve ratio hardly seems large enough to honor all reserve demands. Depositors write checks to other banks which exceed 1.46% of total deposits. Don't they?

Yes, they do. In September 2008 just before The Bailout passed, $7.05 trillion of bank deposits were backed by $102 billion of reserves, yet there were an average of 522,347 billion Fedwire transfers per day totalling $3.3 trillion. $3.3 trillion of transfers means $3.3 trillion of depositor transactions settled each day. When these depositor transactions are settled, reserves are often paid out by commercial banks. As we will see later, not all Fedwire transactions represent real commerce, but rather are transactions for Repurchase Agreements and Discount Window loans that provide reserves to banks that are short reserves. Nonetheless, with such huge volumes of reserve transfers taking place, many commercial banks have their lie-abilities exposed and are seemingly rupted.

THREE-BANK MONTE

"Approximately 7,300 depository institutions are eligible to initiate or receive funds transfers over Fedwire. Use of Fedwire, however, is highly skewed. 67 participants account for 80 percent of the volume of payments, and 23 participants account for 80 percent of the value of payments."

—Board of Governors of the Federal Reserve System Website

When buying & selling goods & services, commercial-bank depositors transfer deposits to other commercial banks, creating flows of reserves between commercial banks. Balancing these reserve flows is a key to keeping a fractional-reserve system functioning.

First Fraud Bank and Steal Second Bank each have $10 of reserves but issue $680 of deposits:

```
      Federal Reserve                          First Fraud Bank
Assets           Liabilities            Assets              Liabilities
$20 (T-Debts)    $10 (1ˢᵗ Fraud)  ◄───► $10 (Reserves)     $680 (Deposits)
                 $10 (Steal 2ⁿᵈ)  ◄─    $670 (Loans)
─────────────    ──────────────         ──────────────      ──────────────
$20              $20                     $680                $680

                                              Steal Second Bank
                                        Assets              Liabilities
                                    ◄   $10 (Reserves)     $680 (Deposits)
                                        $670 (Loans)
                                        ──────────────      ──────────────
                                        $680                $680
                                                            1.46% Reserve Ratio
```

Frank has a $50 deposit at First Fraud Bank. Steve has a $50 deposit at Steal Second Bank. If Frank writes Steve a $5 check, then First Fraud Bank must give Steal Second Bank $5 of reserves. The Federal Reserve Bank transfers the reserves when processing Frank's check.

Here are the ledgers. The commercial-bank deposits are processed first. First Fraud Bank subtracts $5 from its deposits, and Steal Second Bank adds $5 to its deposits:

```
      Federal Reserve                          First Fraud Bank
Assets           Liabilities            Assets              Liabilities
$20 (T-Debts)    $10 (1ˢᵗ Fraud)  ◄───► $10 (Reserves)     $675 (Deposits)
                 $10 (Steal 2ⁿᵈ)  ◄─    $670 (Loans)
─────────────    ──────────────         ──────────────      ──────────────
$20              $20                     $680                $675

                                              Steal Second Bank
                                        Assets              Liabilities
                                    ◄   $10 (Reserves)     $685 (Deposits)
                                        $670 (Loans)
                                        ──────────────      ──────────────
                                        $680                $685
                                                            1.46% Reserve Ratio
```

Steve might not have access to the additional $5 yet, depending upon the funds availability policy of First Fraud Bank, but the funds have been posted to his account.

Steal Second Bank demands a reserve payment from First Fraud Bank by presenting Frank's check to the Federal Reserve Bank for processing. On the Federal Reserve Bank's ledger, $5 is subtracted from First Fraud Bank's account and $5 is added to Steal Second Bank's account. First Fraud Bank and Steal Second Bank update their reserves to reflect the Federal Reserve Bank's changes:

```
        Federal Reserve                          First Fraud Bank
Assets              Liabilities          Assets              Liabilities
$20 (T-Debts)        $5 (1ˢᵗ Fraud) ⟵        $5 (Reserves)      $675 (Deposits)
                    $15 (Steal 2ⁿᵈ)  ⟶    $670 (Loans)
─────────────────────────────────      ─────────────────────────────────
$20                 $20                    $675                $675

                                               Steal Second Bank
                                         Assets              Liabilities
                                          $15 (Reserves)      $685 (Deposits)
                                         $670 (Loans)
                                         ─────────────────────────────────
                                         $685                $685
                                                         1.46% Reserve Ratio
```

Prior to processing the check, First Fraud Bank and Steal Second Bank both had $10 of reserves backing $680 of deposits, a 1.46% reserve ratio. First Fraud Bank now has $5 of reserves backing $675 of deposits, a 0.7% reserve ratio. Steal Second Bank now has $15 of reserves backing $685 of deposits, a 2.2% reserve ratio. First Fraud Bank's reserve ratio decreased. Steal Second Bank's reserve ratio increased.

If First Fraud Bank's statutory reserve ratio requirement was greater than 0.7%, it would now have an illegal reserve shortage. First Fraud Bank would have to decrease deposits or increase reserves, in ways which will be explained later. Remember, there is no fixed statutory reserve ratio requirement for any commercial bank, as all commercial banks obtain different reductions in statutory reserve ratio requirements from the Reserve Requirement Exemption, Low-Reserve Tranche, and sweeping. Each commercial bank will therefore have a different overall statutory reserve ratio requirement.

The decreased reserve levels that result when depositor transactions are processed are another reason that commercial banks sweep accounts. First Fraud Bank's reserves decreased, but did not slip below the 0.6% statutory reserve ratio requirement, meaning First Fraud Bank is not required by law to obtain additional reserves. First Fraud Bank's reserves did slip below the level typically required to honor depositor withdrawals, meaning the next reserve payout may rupt it. First Fraud Bank's buffer against illegally low reserve levels is also eroded, and even a small additional reserve payout will probably decrease its reserve levels below the 0.6% statutory reserve ratio requirement.

Steal Second Bank has "excess" reserves, and can create additional deposits by issuing additional loans. Steal Second Bank is styling. . . Until Steve the Steal Second Bank depositor writes Frank the First Fraud Bank depositor a $30 check:

```
        Federal Reserve                              First Fraud Bank
Assets            Liabilities                 Assets            Liabilities
$20 (T-Debts)     $35 (1ˢᵗ Fraud)  ◄────────►  $35 (Reserves)   $705 (Deposits)
                  -$15 (Steal 2ⁿᵈ)            $670 (Loans)
────────────────────────────────            ──────────────────────────────────
$20               $20                         $705              $705

                                                    Steal Second Bank
                                             Assets            Liabilities
                                             -$15 (Reserves)   $655 (Deposits)
                                             $670 (Loans)
                                            ──────────────────────────────────
                                             $655              $655
                                                        1.46% Reserve Ratio
```

Individual steps in the transaction settling process will no longer be shown. Steal Second Bank subtracted $30 from its deposits, and First Fraud Bank added $30 to its deposits. First Fraud Bank demanded a reserve payment from Steal Second Bank by presenting Steve's check to the Federal Reserve Bank for settling. On the Federal Reserve Bank's ledger, $30 is subtracted from Steal Second Bank's account and $30 is added First Fraud Bank's account. First Fraud Bank and Steal Second Bank updated their reserves to reflect the Federal Reserve Bank's changes.

There is an obvious problem on these ledgers. Steal Second Bank only had $15 of reserves, but owed $30 of reserves, so now has -$15 reserves. That is, negative $15 of reserves. Steal Second Bank has a negative reserve level and is rupted.

A banker reading this example would roll their eyes. Total reserves in the banking system were $20. $30 is 2.2% of the $1,360 deposit supply. In the actual U.S. banking system in September 2008, the deposit supply was $7.05 trillion. 2.2% of $7.05 trillion is $156 billion. No one would ever write a single $156 billion check, not even the U.S. guv'ment, the largest single entity in the economy.

That example was a little unfair, but not totally unfair. It highlights the fundamental problem that exists in a fraudulent fractional-reserve banking system in which deposits dwarf reserves. There are not enough reserves to honor deposits—whether demanded in physical currency or paid to another bank.

So Steal Second Bank is rupted. Or is it? What if Frank writes a $30 check back to Steve? Or some other First Fraud Bank depositor writes a $30 check to a Steal Second Bank depositor? Say Felicia the First Fraud Bank depositor writes a $30 check to Selena the Steal Second Bank depositor.

If Felicia writes Selena a $30 check and Steve writes Frank a $30 check, then First Fraud Bank owes Steal Second Bank $30 of reserves and Steal Second Bank owes First Fraud Bank $30 of reserves. The two reserve payments effectively cancel, and the net result is that neither bank owes the other any reserves. The deposits within commercial banks will have shifted to different accounts, but the total amount of deposits has not changed, nor have the net reserve levels held by each bank.

If Bank of America depositors pay $1 billion to Citibank depositors and Citibank depositors pay $1 billion to Bank of America depositors, then the amounts cancel, and neither Bank of America nor Citibank owes the other reserves.

If reserve flows between banks cancel out, there is no net reserve drain which exposes lie-abilities. If reserve flows between banks don't cancel out, there is a net reserve drain which can expose lie-abilities.

This principle is called NETTING. It is also called TRANSACTION NET-TING, PAYMENT NETTING, or SETTLEMENT NETTING. When multiple transactions among multiple parties are summed and cancellations are factored out, the resulting or net transaction is much smaller. Netting transactions decreases liability and risk for each party. A huge portion of commercial banks' lie-ability exposure is negated because of reserve payment netting.

Netting applies to direct deposits and direct withdrawals. If Bank of America depositors pay $10 billion of direct withdrawals to Citibank depositors and Citibank depositors pay $10 billion of direct withdrawals to Bank of America depositors, then the amounts cancel, and neither Bank of America nor Citibank owes the other reserves. If businesses with Bank of America accounts pay $10 billion of direct deposits to employees with Citibank accounts, and businesses with Citibank accounts pay $10 billion of direct deposits to employees with Bank of America accounts, then the amounts cancel, and neither Bank of America nor Citibank owes the other reserves.

Direct deposits and direct withdrawals which are scheduled at regular intervals allow exact prediction of a significant percentage of the economic transactions in an economy, and thus exact prediction of a significant percentage of banks' lie-ability exposure or lack thereof. If a Bank of America depositor with a 30-year Citibank mortgage pays $1,500 to Citibank on the 1st of each month, and a Citibank depositor with a 30-year Bank of America mortgage pays $1,500 to Bank of America on the 1st of each month, then the reserve payments cancel, and neither bank has lie-abilities exposed.

In this case of mortgage payments made to commercial banks, accounts of depositors have been decreased by the amount of the mortgage payments. Deposits that depositors work to obtain, which claim goods & services, have been transferred to Citibank and Bank of America, which simply conjured these deposits out of thin air. Citibank and Bank of America are hustling stupid depositors who don't know that loans are simply created out of thin air. The Fed is also involved, so the hustle is basically a Three-Bank Monte.

Reserve flow cancellation allows more rapid loan issuance and deposit creation. Here are the ledgers before First Fraud Bank or Steal Second Bank have issued any loans or created any lie-abilities:

```
        Federal Reserve                                      First Fraud Bank
Assets              Liabilities                     Assets              Liabilities
$20 (T-Debts)       $10 (1st Fraud)  ←————————→     $10 (Reserves)      $10 (Deposits)
                    $10 (Steal 2nd)                 ———————             ———————
—————               —————                           $10                 $10
$20                 $20

                                                        Steal Second Bank
                                                    Assets              Liabilities
                                                    $10 (Reserves)      $10 (Deposits)
                                                    ———————             ———————
                                                    $10                 $10
                                                              100% Reserve Ratio
```

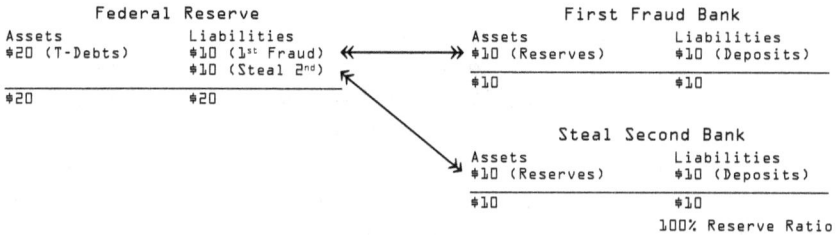

Initially, the reserve supply equals the deposit supply, meaning there is a 100% reserve ratio and all deposits can be honored. When First Fraud Bank issues a loan check, and that check is deposited at another bank, First Fraud Bank must pay reserves to that bank to honor the check. If First Fraud Bank only has $10 of reserves, it would seem that it can only issue a $10 loan check. If it issues a loan check larger than $10, it will be asked to pay out an amount of reserves which exceeds the amount of reserves that it possesses, and will be rupted.

This limitation is the reason it takes so many iterations of deposit creation to reach the maximum total deposit creation—in theory anyway. When First Fraud Bank accepts $10 of reserves, it is chomping at the bit to create $670 of additional deposits, lend them out, and start earning interest on its $10 of reserves 67 separate times. First Fraud Bank wants to decrease its reserve ratio and loan itself up as rapidly as possible.

Suppose First Fraud Bank knew that a borrower it issued a loan to was going to deposit a loan check at Steal Second Bank. First Fraud bank would know this because borrowers list their bank on loan applications. The home, car, or other item the borrower is purchasing with the loan check also has an owner whose bank is known. If First Fraud Bank knew that a check deposited from Steal Second Bank would offset its loan check, then the reserve flows between First Fraud Bank and Steal Second Bank would cancel out, and First Fraud Bank could issue a larger loan check.

In theory, First Fraud Bank and Steal Second Bank could both create a $670 loan check with only $10 of reserves, so long as each bank's loan check was deposited at the other bank. Both banks could loan themselves up in one shot, rather than enduring multiple iterations of money creation.

In theory anyway. In practice, in September 2008 just before The Bailout passed, there were $102 billion of reserves, not $20, and $6.9 trillion of deposits could be created rather than $1,340. Two banks can't each issue a $3.5 trillion loan check to instantly loan themselves and the banking system up. No one wants a loan that big—or at least has sound enough credit to obtain a loan that big.

In the real economy, banks issue hundreds of millions loans which are small relative to the deposit supply, not just a few big loans which are a huge percentage of the deposit supply. In the real economy, there are thousands of banks (depository institutions), not just 3 or 4 as in our examples. With so many loans and banks, forecasting where loan checks will end up being deposited is impractical. However, banks realize that a significant percentage of all reserve payments cancel, and know that most payments won't require a full reserve payout. This allows banks to lend much more aggressively and loan themselves up more rapidly. In our example, First Fraud Bank couldn't issue a single $670 loan if it only had $10 of reserves, but it might issue $20, $30, or $40 loans, depending upon what percentage of its transactions usually cancel and don't require reserve payouts. Issuing $10 loans, it would take First Fraud Bank 67 iterations to loan itself up, but $20, $30, or $40 loans would only take 34, 22, and 17 iterations, respectively. This is a huge difference.

To increase the amount of its loans, First Fraud Bank needs another bank to do the same, so that reserve payments cancel. First Fraud Bank needs a conspirator or many conspirators if it is going to run the fractional-reserve scam with optimal efficiency and create loanable deposits out of thin air as fast as possible.

Even that example is oversimplified, as banks usually have millions or billions of dollars of reserves but issue mortgages which are hundreds of thousands of dollars, and car loans, student loans, and credit card loans which are much smaller. In the real world, banks know their amount of reserves, estimate their reserve ratio and deposit multiplier, and determine the total amount of deposits they can create from a given level of reserves. They then begin creating and lending deposits as rapidly and aggressively as possible. Aside from finding borrowers, the limiting factor is how fast other banks are also creating and lending deposits, and the degree of reserve flow cancellation which will occur. Under normal, healthy economic conditions, if banks find qualified borrowers they create deposits out of thin air and lend them, and worry about finding reserves to back the deposit later—especially if the loan is something lucrative like a mortgage that will generate an income stream for the bank for 30 years.

Withdrawing reserves from the banking system as a whole is different than withdrawing reserves from one bank and transferring those reserves to another bank. Reserves withdrawn from a bank and not deposited at another bank can't be cancelled out by a reciprocal reserve flow. Widespread reserve withdrawals from banks as a whole quickly expose fractional-reserve lie-abilities and rupt all banks.

Even if reserve withdrawals don't exceed a commercial bank's reserves and can be honored, withdrawing reserves plummets reserve ratios. If $10 of reserves back $680 of deposits and $5 of deposits are redeemed for reserves, then reserves have been decreased by 50% ($10 to $5) but deposits have only been decreased by 0.5% ($680 to $675). Each $1 of reserves backed $68 of deposits before the withdrawal, but each $1 of reserves backs $135 of deposits after the withdrawal. Normal transaction activity will now rupt the bank unless it can decrease deposits or increase reserves.

Individual banks which face withdrawals can decrease deposits or increase reserves, but when many banks face withdrawals and are forced to attempt the feat, the Federal Reserve must step in and issue massive Bailouts by creating reserves that banks use to honor lie-abilities. This saves banks and allows them to continue their profitable fraud, but consigns the economy to stagnation. Again, the mechanism by which reserve creation stifles economic recovery will be described later.

Withdrawing reserves from a bank and using them to pay a person or business doesn't usually decrease total reserves in the banking system, as the person or business paid reserves usually redeposits the reserves at another bank. One exception is physical cash reserves which are withdrawn from banks and physically stashed under mattresses, in non-bank safes, etc. Another exception is reserves withdrawn from a U.S. bank and transferred out of America. When reserves are withdrawn from a U.S. bank and deposited at a foreign bank, there is a contraction of the reserve supply in the American banking system.

A massive $550 billion wave of withdrawals occurred in a very short period of time in September 2008. The collapse of the U.S. housing market made many depositors nervous, and they wanted to transfer their reserves to safer overseas economies which had not inflated a housing bubble. Depositors attempted to withdraw more than $550 billion of reserves from a U.S. banking system which only had $102 billion of reserves, which meant there was a $448 billion reserve shortage. A $448 billion reserve shortage is not a trivial problem. If unremedied, it is a civilization-collapsing kind of problem, and that is not hyperbole. This run on U.S. banks worsened Depression v9.2006-201x, almost destroyed America, and is the reason that The Bailout was passed.

Banks can fractional-reserve lend within themselves. William deposits $100 at First Fraud Bank. First Fraud Bank has a 2% statutory reserve ratio requirement. We assume a 2% reserve ratio rather than a 1.46% reserve ratio to keep the math simple. First Fraud Bank keeps $2 of reserves to honor statutory reserve requirements, embezzles $98 of "excess" reserves, and issues a $98 loan check to Steve. Steve uses the loan check to buy Mary's house, and gives the check to Mary:

Assets	Liabilities
$2 (Reserves)	$100 (William)
$98 ("Excess" Reserves)	$98 (Mary's Loan Check)
$98 (Steve's Loan)	
$198	$198
	100% Reserve Ratio

Mary deposits her loan check at First Fraud Bank rather than at a different bank. First Fraud Bank creates a new deposit for Mary. First Fraud Bank normally pays out reserves to another bank to honor a deposit which that bank created to "cash" the loan check, but in this case First Fraud Bank created the deposit so no other bank asks for reserves to honor the check. First Fraud Bank gets to keep its reserves:

```
Assets                              Liabilities
  $2 (Reserves)                      $100 (William)
 $98 (Steve's Loan)
 $98 (Reserves)                       $98 (Mary)
```
___
```
$198                                $198
                                        51% Reserve Ratio
```

First Fraud Bank maintains its 2% statutory reserve ratio requirement by setting aside $1.96 of reserves to back Mary's $98 deposit. First Fraud Bank has $96.04 of "excess" reserves:

```
Assets                              Liabilities
  $2.00 (Reserves)                   $100 (William)
 $98.00 (Steve's Loan)
  $1.96 (Reserves)                    $98 (Mary)
 $96.04 ("Excess" Reserves)
```
___
```
$198.00                             $198
                                        51% Reserve Ratio
```

First Fraud Bank would combine reserves and deposits on its books, as it views the total reserves of all depositors as a pool which can be used to honor withdrawal demands of any single depositor:

```
Assets                              Liabilities
  $3.96 (Reserves)                   $198 (Deposits)
 $96.04 ("Excess" Reserves)
 $98.00 (Loans)
```
___
```
$198.00                             $198
                                        51% Reserve Ratio
```

The deposit creation has taken place within First Fraud Bank, rather than at another bank. Mary's loan payment to First Fraud Bank is an internal bookkeeping transaction to First Fraud Bank and there is no reserve drain to another bank.

When First Fraud Bank paid reserves to another bank to honor its loan check, that bank had "excess" reserves and issued another loan. Here First Fraud Bank has "excess" reserves, not some other bank, so it can now issue another loan. If that loan check is also deposited at First Fraud Bank, First Fraud Bank once again "cashes" the check by creating a new deposit, sets aside a small amount of reserves to back the new deposit, and can issue another loan with its remaining reserves. If that loan check is also deposited at First Fraud Bank, it once again "cashes" the check by creating a new deposit, sets aside a small amount of reserves to back the new deposit, and can issue another loan...

Having every loan check deposited at the bank which created it is ideal for banks, as no reserves have to be paid out. This is similar to the situation in which two depositors at the same bank pay each other. The difference is that in this case a new deposit has been created.

If a borrower with a First Fraud Bank account asks First Fraud Bank for a loan check which will be paid to a First Fraud Bank customer and thus deposited at First Fraud Bank, then First Fraud Bank could issue a check which far exceeds its "excess" reserves because it knows there will be no massive reserve drain. As the new depositor spends their money and writes checks to depositors at other banks there will be reserve drains, but there will be no massive, initial reserve drain from the entire check being deposited at another bank.

The first determination a commercial bank makes about a potential borrower, besides an assessment of their trustworthiness and ability to repay a loan, is whether or not they will be depositing a loan check at another bank. First Fraud Bank offers extremely-low interest rates to large corporate and business borrowers with First Fraud Bank accounts who will spend much of their loan money at other businesses with First Fraud Bank accounts. This is portrayed as loyalty to customers, which it is to some degree, but the primary rationale is that such loans don't require immediate payouts of reserves, and have lower-than-normal reserve payouts as loan funds are spent.

Most Speculatos own corporations in addition to banks. Speculatos create a bank, have their corporations and families keep accounts at the bank, and then use the bank to create money out of thin air and issue low-interest loans to their corporations and families. Without a bank, $1 of corporate earnings can only be used to buy $1 of goods & services. With a bank, $1 of corporate earnings can be leveraged to issue $67 of loans, say $47 to sheeple in the community, $20 to the Speculato corporation. Speculato corporations use their gaggle of loan money to crush competitors, buy competitors they can't crush, and expand. Companies like Standard Oil used this tactic extensively. Most businesses competing with Speculato corporations are not in cahoots with a bank, can't conjure money, and therefore don't stand a chance. There is no angle that Speculatos have not thought of. They enrich themselves every step of the way, in every manner conceivable.

Every bank would love to be the only bank, for then there could be no reserve payments to other banks. The only lie-ability exposure would be depositor withdrawals of physical-currency reserves, which are limited under normal economic conditions. Few people pay their mortgages or car loans with physical-currency reserves, after all. They use non-physical payment methods such as checks, debit cards, direct withdrawals, etc.

Larger banks have an advantage because more of their transactions will be internal, a la William and Mary. If half the residents, businesses and borrowers in the country have First Fraud Bank accounts, a significant percentage of all economic transactions will be internal to First Fraud Bank. First Fraud Bank's reserve drains are decreased.

In normal business, consolidation is driven by a desire for greater economies of scale and larger profit. This is true of banking, but consolidation is critical in banking for a far more important structural reason: larger banks have a greater percentage of transactions that are internal, which limits reserve payouts and lie-ability exposure.

Fewer banks have less reserve flow imbalances. If customers at First Fraud Bank are writing checks to customers at 14,000 other banks, First Fraud Bank must rely on reciprocal reserve flows from each of those 14,000 banks to limit reserve drains. If customers at First Fraud Bank are writing checks to customers at 6,000 other banks, First Fraud Bank must rely on reciprocal reserve flows from 6,000 banks, a much smaller number of banks. When the number of banks is decreased, the chance of reserve flow imbalances is decreased. Speculatos therefore want a small number of larger banks, rather than a large number of smaller banks.

It is no accident that in 2008 America's 5 largest commercial banks held more than 32% of deposits, 25 commercial banks held 53% of deposits, and 50 commercial banks held 59% of deposits. In 2011, America's 5 largest commercial banks held 38% of deposits, 25 commercial banks held 59% of deposits, and 50 commercial banks held 66% of deposits. In just three years, America's largest 50 banks amassed an additional 7% of total deposits, or about $575 billion of deposits.

The long-term consolidation trend is starker. In 1984, the 10 largest commercial banks held 15% of deposits, in 2008 they held 40% of deposits, and in 2011 they held 47% of deposits. Since 1984, the 10 largest commercial banks amassed an additional 32% of total deposits, or about $2.6 trillion of total deposits (based on 2011 U.S. bank deposit figures).

There were 14,507 commercial banks in America in 1984 and 6,296 commercial banks in America in 2011, a decrease of 8,211 banks or 57%. That is 8,211 commercial banks which the remaining commercial banks don't have to worry about paying reserves to or receiving reciprocal reserve payments from.

Fedwire transfers $3.3 trillion per day, but 80% or $2.6 trillion of these transfers originate from just 23 banks. A significant portion of the outgoing reserve payments from one of these banks will usually be balanced by incoming reserve payments from another one of these banks. This netting on a massive scale is how commercial banks with $102 billion of reserves can honor $3.3 trillion of daily transactions without being rupted. Commercial banks also obtain massive loans of conjured reserves from the Fed to eliminate Daylight Overdrafts and Overnight Overdrafts in their Fed accounts, and also obtain loans of preexisting reserves via financial instruments called Repurchase Agreements, but let's not get ahead of ourselves.

In general, commercial banks want most depositor transactions to involve non-physical, digital money because such transactions don't require the payout of physical reserves. With non-physical, digital transactions, reserve shortages which do arise can be instantly alleviated with computer-blip reserve loans rather than pesky physical-currency reserves, and the Fed can always conjure massive quantities of digital reserves to save banks. Obtaining massive quantities of physical-currency reserves is much more problematic for banks.

You may be confused. Let's summarize: First Fraud Bank customers write checks to Steal Second Bank customers, and vice versa, creating back and forth reserve streams which cancel. If First Fraud Bank customers write large numbers of checks to Steal Second Bank customers, and no Steal Second Bank customers write checks to First Fraud Bank customers, a reserve drain from First Fraud Bank to Steal Second Bank occurs. First Fraud Bank never has enough reserves to weather monstrous reserve payouts, nor does any other commercial bank, because their reserves are always a small fraction of deposits. Banks rely on the perpetual streams of reserves flowing between them to cancel, limiting lie-ability exposure. The reserve streams never cancel totally, but if huge differences are eliminated, paltry reserves (and Fed loans of newly conjured reserves) can cover reserve drains that occur. This allows commercial banks to create an amount of deposits equal to 68 times reserves, and earn interest on each $1 of reserves 67 separate times without ever having their scam exposed.

Our banking system is a Great Pyramid of frauds in which banks endlessly juggle lie-ability hot potatoes. With hundreds of millions of people and entities buying & selling, reserve streams always become unbalanced occasionally. When this happens, lie-abilities are exposed and banks fail, dragging the economy down with them. The solution is never to prevent banks from creating lie-ability hot potatoes, but for sheeple to accept Bailout blisters for the greater good.

Quite a shell game, isn't it? Like the Three-Card Monte street hustlers perform, but with the entire economy.

THREE-BANK MONTE PICTURE PAGES

TO SKIP THE PICTURE PAGES AFTER THIS CHAPTER, PLEASE TURN TO PAGE 300

EACH COMMERCIAL BANK'S DEPOSITS ARE A UNIQUE FORM OF MONEY

Sheeple think of checks and deposits at commercial banks as a single money that is dollars, but this is incorrect. Each commercial bank creating deposits actually issues its own money. Though this checkbook and deposit money is denominated in dollars, is reckoned using the measure of value called the dollars, it is not dollars. Checkbook and deposit money that commercial banks issue is denominated in dollars and can be redeemed for dollars, but is not literally dollars, which is a critical distinction.

To see how commercial banks issue their own money, we'll use Robinson Crusoe economics, as we did in *Bubblenomics*. Crusoe economics uses simplified situations to illustrate basic principles. Crusoeville has one goldsmith named Greedy who circulates paper promissory notes. Suppose a second goldsmith named Grubber begins circulating paper promissory notes. There are now three forms of money: gold, Greedy promissory notes, and Grubber promissory notes. As Greedy promissory notes and Grubber promissory notes can both be redeemed for an ounce of gold, they seem like the same money to sheeple, even though they are not.

Greedy and Grubber know how the fractional-reserve-banking scam works because they both run it. They know that paper promissory notes are not fully backed by gold, and that either bank can be rupted in an instant if depositors demand gold. When Greedy is presented Grubber paper promissory notes, he promptly presents them to Grubber and redeems for gold to minimize his risk. Grubber does the same when presented with Greedy paper promissory notes.

Greedy and Grubber each trust themselves to run the scam, but someone else running the scam may get too greedy, issue too many promissory notes, make depositors suspicious, and be bank-rupted by a bank run. Even careful goldsmiths are sometimes unlucky and face runs. If this happens, any paper promissory notes from the rupted bank which were not redeemed for gold are worthless. Ignorant sheeple happily accept this risk, but not goldsmiths. When presented paper promissory notes from another goldsmith, goldsmiths demand gold payment immediately. They redeem worthless paper promissory notes for gold immediately, converting the intrinsically worthless paper promissory notes into a commodity of intrinsic value immediately.

As always, substitute ledger reserves for gold and commercial-bank deposits for paper promissory notes, and you have our modern banking system. The deposits issued by each bank seem the same to sheeple, but each commercial bank creating deposits is actually issuing its own money. All commercial-bank deposits (money) use the same monetary unit (the dollar) and are backed by the same type of reserves (Federal Reserve reserves), but that doesn't change the fact that each bank is essentially issuing its own money.

Each commercial bank's money (deposits) are backed only by the amount of reserves the commercial bank holds, which means the chance of not being able to redeem a deposit for reserves varies bank to bank. Commercial bankers understand the scam, know that deposits are backed by paltry reserves, and demand reserve payments anytime they are presented a deposit issued by another commercial bank. Like goldsmiths who demanded gold payment immediately when presented a promissory note from another goldsmith, cybersmiths demand reserve payments immediately when presented a promissory note from another cybersmith.

In a more absolute sense, reserves are money, and bank deposits are just promises to provide reserve money upon demand. In a literal, absolute sense, commercial-bank deposits are not money. However, commercial-bank deposits which are promises to redeem reserve money function as a medium of exchange. Sheeple accept commercial-bank deposits as payments instead of reserves, so commercial-bank deposits effectively function as money.

Though goldsmiths demanded gold payment immediately when presented paper promissory notes from other goldsmiths, and cybersmiths demand reserve payments immediately when presented deposit promissory notes from other cybersmiths, the entire banking system is predicated upon depositors never being smart enough to make this same demand. The fraudulent fractional-reserve banking system is predicated upon the fact that depositors will view commercial-bank deposits as money rather than viewing reserves as money, and will have so much faith in the integrity of commercial-bank deposits that they rarely demand reserves. This is why reserves are almost never mentioned in discussions of money & banking that are disseminated to sheeple. Goldsmiths and cybersmiths are hypocritical, but also audacious and clever. They convince sheeple to trust deposit promissory notes that they themselves don't trust.

Poof Goes the Money Supply

"In numerous years following the [Civil] War, the Federal Government ran a heavy [budget] surplus. It could not pay off its debt, retire its securities, because to do so meant there would be no bonds to back the national bank notes. To pay off the debt was to destroy the money supply."

—John Kenneth Galbraith

"Neither the banker nor the borrower ordinarily realize that a loan just completed is putting into circulation that much new money, or 'inflating the currency' by the amount of the loan. Neither the banker nor the borrower ordinarily realize that he [or she] is starting an endless chain of successive transactions which will continue as long as this credit substitute for money remains in circulation. When a bank loan is paid, someone draws on one of these deposits to pay it, and of course so much of that deposit goes out of existence, and a train of successive transactions which would otherwise have been made with that portion of that deposit ceases."

—Irving Fisher

Every commercial bank loan is issued by creating money. Every commercial bank loan is literally conjured money created out of thin air. When commercial bank loans are repaid and loan principal is decreased or extinguished, the money created for loans is uncreated or extinguished. This chapter will describe this process by which money is unconjured back into thin air. It will show how paying off loans causes money to be destroyed or uncreated.

First Fraud Bank accepts a $100 deposit of reserves, applies a 10% statutory reserve ratio requirement, keeps $10 of reserves to back the $100 deposit, and issues a $90 loan to John Q. Debtor which he deposits at Steal Second Bank. Steal Second Bank creates a $90 deposit for John Q. Debtor, demands $90 of reserves from First Fraud Bank to back the $90 deposit, and First Fraud Bank pays the $90 of demanded reserves. The ledgers at the end of this process:

```
                    First Fraud Bank
     Assets                    Liabilities
      $10 (Reserves)            $100 (Deposits)
      $90 (Loan)
     ─────────────────────────────────────────
      $100                      $100

                    Steal Second Bank
     Assets                    Liabilities
      $90 (Reserves)            $90 (John Q. Debtor)
     ─────────────────────────────────────────
      $90                       $90

                              53% Reserve Ratio
```

Total deposits are $190. This is the money supply. The deposit supply which is the money supply was initially $100, but increased to $190 when First Fraud Bank monetized a loan.

The Debtor has to make monthly loan payments to First Fraud Bank. Assume loan payments are $10 per month and that all $10 is principal, no interest is paid.

John Q. Debtor spent his $90 of loan money at A Business and has no money. A Business is a Steal Second Bank depositor. John Q. Debtor bought goods & services from A Business by writing checks to A Business. Steal Second Bank processed these checks by debiting John Q. Debtor's account, and crediting the account of A Business. As these transactions were completely internal to Steal Second Bank, it didn't have to pay reserves to any other bank. Thus the net result was that John Q. Debtor's deposit was transferred to A Business:

```
                    First Fraud Bank
     Assets                    Liabilities
      $10 (Reserves)            $100 (Deposit)
      $90 (Loan)
     ─────────────────────────────────────────
      $100                      $100

                    Steal Second Bank
     Assets                    Liabilities
      $90 (Reserves)            $90 (Deposits)
                                 $90 (A Business)
                                 $0 (John Q. Debtor)
     ─────────────────────────────────────────
      $90                       $90

                              53% Reserve Ratio
```

On Steal Second Bank's ledger, deposit totals are colored grey so that they are not counted. The indented deposit subtotals are counted. If the totals and subtotals were both counted, the same deposits would be counted twice for liability totals, which is incorrect. This nomenclature indicates that there are $90 of total deposits at Steal Second Bank, $90 which are in the account of A Business, and $0 which are in the account of John Q. Debtor.

John Q. Debtor can't create money out of thin air like banks, he must obtain money for loan payments from the existing supply of money. John Q. Debtor must work and produce a good or service which someone will trade money for. Say that someone is A Business. John Q. Debtor goes to work for A Business and they write him a paycheck for $10. Steal Second Bank processes this check by transferring $10 from the account of A Business to the account of John Q. Debtor:

```
              First Fraud Bank
   Assets                 Liabilities
    $10 (Reserves)         $100 (Deposit)
    $90 (Loan)
   ─────────────────────────────────────
    $100                   $100


              Steal Second Bank
   Assets                 Liabilities
    $90 (Reserves)         $90 (Deposits)
                           $80 (A Business)
                           $10 (John Q. Debtor)
   ─────────────────────────────────────
    $90                    $90
```

53% Reserve Ratio

John Q. Debtor now has money for his loan payment. He makes his loan payment by writing a $10 check to First Fraud Bank. On First Fraud Bank's ledger deposits increase by $10, on Steal Second Bank's ledger deposits decrease by $10:

```
              First Fraud Bank
   Assets                 Liabilities
    $10 (Reserves)         $100 (Deposit)
    $90 (Loan)              $10 (Loan Payment) ◄◄
   ─────────────────────────────────────
    $100                   $110


              Steal Second Bank
   Assets                 Liabilities
    $90 (Reserves)         $80 (A Business)
                           $10 (John Q. Debtor) ►►
   ─────────────────────────────────────
    $90                    $80
```

53% Reserve Ratio

As mentioned, steps will be consolidated on ledgers. John Q. Debtor's $10 deposit at Steal Second Bank is colored grey to indicate that it has been transferred to First Fraud Bank. The loan payment liability on First Fraud Bank's ledger is a deposit.

First Fraud Bank demands $10 of assets from Steal Second Bank to back the $10 deposit liability it has incurred. Steal Second Bank transfers $10 of reserves to First Fraud Bank:

```
                    First Fraud Bank
        Assets                    Liabilities
         $10 (Reserves)            $100 (Deposit)
         $90 (Loan)
      ≫ ─── $10 (Reserves)              $10 (Loan Payment)
      ─────────────────────────────────────────────────
        $110                       $110


                    Steal Second Bank
        Assets                    Liabilities
         $80 (Reserves)            $80 (Deposits)
      ≪ ─── $10 (Reserves)
      ─────────────────────────────────────────────────
        $80                        $80

                                    53% Reserve Ratio
```

The $10 of reserves at Steal Second Bank are colored grey to indicate that they have been transferred to First Fraud Bank. As $10 of loan principal has been paid, First Fraud Bank subtracts $10 from the loan balance:

```
                    First Fraud Bank
        Assets                    Liabilities
         $20 (Reserves)            $100 (Deposit)
         $80 (Loan)                 $10 (Loan Payment)
      ─────────────────────────────────────────────────
        $100                       $110


                    Steal Second Bank
        Assets                    Liabilities
         $80 (Reserves)            $80 (Deposits)
      ─────────────────────────────────────────────────
        $80                        $80

                                    53% Reserve Ratio
```

What about the $10 loan payment deposit which First Fraud Bank possesses? Can First Fraud Bank keep this deposit and spend it?

No.

First Fraud Bank's liabilities exceed its assets, which is not allowed. First Fraud Bank's liabilities total $110 and its assets total $100. First Fraud Bank's liabilities exceed its assets by $10. First Fraud Bank must decrease its liabilities by $10 or increase its assets by $10, or it is rupted. A $90 deposit liability was originally created out of thin air by First Fraud Bank when it monetized the loan. This $90 deposit liability was literally the loan money. Now that $10 of the loan has been paid off, $10 of deposit liabilities must be unmonetized. The deposit liabilities created solely to facilitate the loan must be uncreated. The $10 loan payment is subtracted from First Fraud Bank's ledger and is not added to any other ledger:

First Fraud Bank

Assets	Liabilities
$20 (Reserves)	$100 (Deposits)
$80 (Loan)	
$100	$100

Steal Second Bank

Assets	Liabilities
$80 (Reserves)	$80 (Deposits)
$80	$80

56% Reserve Ratio

Total deposits are $180. This is the money supply. The money supply has decreased or contracted from $190 to $180, by $10. Money was uncomputered. The fractional-reserve lending process was reversed.

The reserve ratio of the banking system increased from 53% to 56% when deposit money was uncomputered. More deposits can now be honored. This is because the amount of deposits which exceed reserves decreased. Lie-abilities decreased.

If John Q. Debtor made 8 more $10 payments, the entire loan would have been uncomputered. All the money that was created for the loan would have been uncreated. The monetized loan would have been completely unmonetized.

In the real economy there are thousands of banks, and oceans of loan payments moving to and from them. The commercial-bank deposits used to make loan payments can take a long and winding path and come from any bank, but the principle outlined above nonetheless holds. Principal payments on fractional-reserve loans are subtracted from a commercial-bank deposit somewhere. The commercial bank which receives the payment doesn't keep the deposit, but rather uncreates it. As the total of all commercial-bank deposits is the money supply, a decrease in commercial bank deposits is a decrease in the money supply. Paying off the principal on a monetized loan therefore decreases the money supply.

Those with advanced banking knowledge would correct the statement above, and note that the money supply is circulating currency plus commercial-bank deposits. This more advanced definition of the money supply will be explained in *Bubblenomics 3* in the *Currency* chapter.

First Fraud Bank has a 10% statutory reserve ratio requirement so must hold $10 of reserves to back its $100 of deposits. First Fraud Bank was paid $10 of reserves by Steal Second Bank, so now has $20 of reserves. $10 of these reserves must back the $100 deposit, $10 of these reserves can be recategorized as "excess" reserves:

First Fraud Bank

Assets	Liabilities
$10 (Reserves)	$100 (Deposit)
$80 (Loan)	
$10 ("Excess" Reserves)	
$100	$100

Steal Second Bank

Assets	Liabilities
$80 (Reserves)	$80 (Deposits)
$80	$80

56% Reserve Ratio

First Fraud Bank can use its $10 of "excess" reserves to issue another $10 loan. If it does, $10 of loan money is computered, the deposit supply once again increases to $190, and there is no net reduction in the money supply.

The Fed's ledgers were not shown in these examples to simplify learning, but the Fed would have processed loan payments between commercial banks. It would have performed the reserve transfers between First Fraud Bank and Steal Second Bank.

Most depositors don't pay off entire loans with one lump sum payment. If they could afford to do so, they wouldn't need loans. There are a few depositors with enough money to pay off loans with one lump sum payment. These depositors sometimes purchase loans. Commercial banks sometimes sell loans they have created to these depositors.

First Fraud Bank has $1 billion of deposits and a 2% statutory reserve ratio requirement. It keeps $20 million in reserve and issues $980 million of loans to individuals and businesses who deposit their loan checks at Steal Second Bank, which also has a 2% statutory reserve ratio requirement:

First Fraud Bank

Assets	Liabilities
$20,000,000 (Reserves)	$1,000,000,000 (Deposits)
$980,000,000 (Loans)	
$1,000,000,000	$1,000,000,000

Steal Second Bank

Assets	Liabilities
$19,600,000 (Reserves)	$980,000,000 (Deposits)
$960,400,000 ("Excess" Reserves)	
$980,000,000	$980,000,000

50.51% Reserve Ratio

Total deposits are $1,980 million ($1.98 billion). This is the money supply. The deposit supply which is the money supply was initially $1,000 million ($1 billion), but increased to $1,980 million when First Fraud Bank monetized loans.

One of Steal Second Bank's depositors is a very rich investor with a $100 million deposit. Call him Soros. Soros buys mortgages. One of First Fraud Bank's loans is a $1,000,000 mortgage for a mansion:

First Fraud Bank

Assets	Liabilities
$20,000,000 (Reserves)	$1,000,000,000 (Deposits)
$980,000,000 (Loans)	
$1,000,000 (Mortgage)	
$979,000,000 (Loans)	
$1,000,000,000	$1,000,000,000

Steal Second Bank

Assets	Liabilities
$19,600,000 (Reserves)	$980,000,000 (Deposits)
$960,400,000 ("Excess" Reserves)	$100,000,000 (Soros)
	$880,000,000 (Deposits)
$980,000,000	$980,000,000

50.51% Reserve Ratio

On these ledgers, the loan and deposit totals are colored grey so that they are not counted. The indented loan and deposit subtotals are counted. If the totals and subtotals were both counted, the same loans and deposits would be counted twice for asset and liability totals, which is incorrect. This nomenclature indicates that there are $980 million of total deposits at Steal Second Bank, $100 million in Soros' account, $880 million in other depositors' accounts. This nomenclature also indicates that there are $980 million of total loans at First Fraud Bank, a $1 million mortgage, and $979 million of other loans.

First Fraud Bank decides to sell its $1,000,000 mortgage. Why would it do this? A $1 million mortgage pays a lot of interest and is profitable, isn't it? Assuming the borrower actually pays the mortgage, yes, it is very profitable. For now, assume the borrower pays the mortgage. Why sell the mortgage then?

Banks earn lucrative fees issuing or ORIGINATING loans. Bank executives and officers are paid bonuses in addition to their salaries for originating loans. First Fraud Bank is loaned up. It can't issue additional loans unless it waits for loans to be paid off and for "excess" reserves to increase, which is a gradual process. If First Fraud sells a loan, it immediately frees up a significant amount of reserves, and can then issue another loan which generates additional origination fees and pays a percentage of those origination fees to executives, loan officers, and mortgage brokers.

If First Fraud Bank bank sells a loan and issues another loan, it still has a profitable loan on its books which is paying interest, but it has earned origination fees on two loans, the loan which is on its books, and the loan which it sold to investors and which is off its books. First Fraud Bank can originate and sell loans indefinitely, as long as it can find an investor to buy each loan it sells, and a borrower to go into debt for each new loan is originates. During the housing bubble, banks paid out tens of billions of dollars in originating fees to employees and executives.

So First Fraud Bank wants to sell its $1 million mortgage. Soros agrees to buy the mortgage for $1 million. In the real world, Soros would demand a discount and would only purchase the mortgage if he could pay less than $1,000,000, but we'll ignore discounting for now and assume he pays full price. Soros writes a $1,000,000 check to First Fraud Bank:

First Fraud Bank

Assets	Liabilities
$20,000,000 (Reserves)	$1,000,000,000 (Deposits)
$980,000,000 (Loans)	
$1,000,000 (Mortgage)	$1,000,000 (Soros
$979,000,000 (Loans	Payment)
$1,000,000,000	$1,001,000,000

Steal Second Bank

Assets	Liabilities
$19,600,000 (Reserves)	$979,000,000 (Deposits)
$960,400,000 ("Excess"	$99,000,000 (Soros)
Reserves)	$1,000,000 (Soros)
	$880,000,000 (Deposits)
$980,000,000	$979,000,000

50.51% Reserve Ratio

On these ledgers, Soros' deposit is divided into a $99 million deposit he is not paying out, and a $1 million deposit he is buying the loan with. Soros' $1 million Steal Second Bank deposit has been colored grey to indicate that it has been transferred to First Fraud Bank.

First Fraud Bank demands $1 million of assets from Steal Second Bank to back the $1 million deposit liability it has incurred. Steal Second Bank transfers $1 million of reserves to First Fraud Bank:

First Fraud Bank

Assets	Liabilities
$20,000,000 (Reserves)	$1,000,000,000 (Deposits)
$980,000,000 (Loans)	
$1,000,000 (Mortgage)	$1,000,000 (Soros
$979,000,000 (Loans)	Payment)
$1,000,000 (Reserves)	
$1,001,000,000	$1,001,000,000

Steal Second Bank

Assets	Liabilities
$19,600,000 (Reserves)	$979,000,000 (Deposits)
$959,400,000 ("Excess" Reserves)	$99,000,000 (Soros)
	$880,000,000 (Deposits)
$1,000,000 ("Excess" Reserves)	
$979,000,000	$979,000,000

50.51% Reserve Ratio

Don't let the big numbers and sub-accounts confuse you. This is the same reserve-payment process we have seen many times.

First Fraud Bank gives Soros the $1 million mortgage that he purchased. The loan has not been paid off. The borrower must still make payments to Soros or Soros can sue the borrower and foreclose on the mansion.

The loan is no longer First Fraud Bank's concern, so it removes the loan from its ledger. It also combines reserves on its ledger, adding the $1 million of reserves paid by Steal Second Bank to the $20 million of reserves it previously possessed:

First Fraud Bank

Assets	Liabilities
$21,000,000 (Reserves)	$1,000,000,000 (Deposits)
$979,000,000 (Loans)	$1,000,000 (Soros Payment)
$1,000,000,000	$1,001,000,000

Steal Second Bank

Assets	Liabilities
$19,600,000 (Reserves)	$979,000,000 (Deposits)
$959,400,000 ("Excess" Reserves)	$99,000,000 (Soros)
	$880,000,000 (Deposits)
$979,000,000	$979,000,000

50.51% Reserve Ratio

What about the $1 million payment from Soros which First Fraud Bank possesses? Can First Fraud Bank keep this and spend it?

No.

First Fraud Bank's liabilities exceed its assets, which is not allowed. First Fraud Bank must decrease its liabilities by $1 million or increase its assets by $1 million or it is rupted. A $1 million deposit liability was originally created out of thin air by First Fraud Bank when it monetized a loan. This $1 million deposit liability was literally the loan money. Now that the $1 million loan is no longer on First Fraud Bank's ledger, the loan must be unmonetized. The deposit liability created solely to facilitate the loan must be uncreated. The $1 million payment from Soros is subtracted from First Fraud Bank's ledger and is not added to any other ledger:

First Fraud Bank

Assets	Liabilities
$21,000,000 (Reserves)	$1,000,000,000 (Deposits)
$979,000,000 (Loans)	
───────────────	───────────────
$1,000,000,000	$1,000,000,000

Steal Second Bank

Assets	Liabilities
$19,600,000 (Reserves)	$979,000,000 (Deposits)
$959,400,000 ("Excess"	$99,000,000 (Soros)
Reserves)	$880,000,000 (Deposits)
───────────────	───────────────
$979,000,000	$979,000,000

50.53% Reserve Ratio

Total deposits are $1,979 million. This is the money supply. The money supply has decreased or contracted from $1,980 million to $1,979 million, by $1 million. Money was uncomputered. The fractional-reserve lending process was reversed.

The reserve ratio of the banking system increased from 50.51% to 50.53% when deposit money was uncomputered. More deposits can now be honored. This is because the amount of deposits which exceed reserves decreased. Lie-abilities decreased.

First Fraud Bank has a 2% reserve ratio, so is legally required to keep $20 million of reserves to back its $1 billion of deposits. First Fraud Bank was paid $1 million of reserves by Steal Second Bank, so now has $21 million of reserves. $20 million of these reserves back the $1 billion of deposits, $1 million of these reserves are recategorized as "excess" reserves:

First Fraud Bank

Assets		Liabilities
$20,000,000	(Reserves)	$1,000,000,000 (Deposits)
$979,000,000	(Loans)	
$1,000,000	("Excess" Reserves)	
$1,000,000,000		$1,000,000,000

Steal Second Bank

Assets		Liabilities
$19,580,000	(Reserves)	$979,000,000 (Deposits)
$959,420,000	("Excess" Reserves)	$99,000,000 (Soros)
		$880,000,000 (Deposits)
$979,000,000		$979,000,000

50.53% Reserve Ratio

Selling the mortgage increased First Fraud Bank's reserves, giving it "excess" reserves which can be used to issue another $1 million loan.

As Steal Second Bank's deposits decreased by $1 million, from $980 million to $979 million, it decreased its reserves and increased its "excess" reserves. It recategorized $20,000 of reserves as "excess" reserves. Steal Second Bank has a 2% reserve ratio, so is legally required to keep $19.58 million of reserves to back its $979 million of deposits. Its remaining $959.42 million of reserves are "excess" reserves which can be used to issue a $959.42 million loan.

If First Fraud Bank was short reserves, it could have sold the $1 million loan to obtain reserves. This is the other reason banks usually sell loans. In healthy or "boom" economies, banks sell loans so that they can issue more loans and earn additional originating fees. In unhealthy or "bust" economies, banks face runs, don't have the reserves which depositors demand, and frantically begin selling loans trying to obtain reserves. More on this later.

In the first example in this chapter with the $100 initial deposit of reserves, deposit money was only uncreated when the loan was repaid. Selling a loan and uncreating money often confuses people, as the loan still exists. The loan still exists, but it exists outside the banking system rather than on banks' books, which is a critical distinction.

Any two parties can create a loan, but they can't create money for the loan. For an honest loan to occur, someone must have surrendered the money loaned, meaning preexisting money is used for the loan. Only banks can issue loans by creating the money for loans.

A loan outside the banking system can be issued and paid off by two commercial-bank depositors who simply write checks to each other, as they do when buying or selling an apple or an orange. A lender writes a borrower a check which is a loan, and a borrower writes a lender checks which are loan payments. Any two parties can also buy or sell a loan in the same way they sell an apple or orange. A loan buyer can write a loan seller a check, and the loan seller simply gives him the loan contract. That loan contract requires a borrower to write loan payment checks to whoever owns it. None of these transactions involve the creation or uncreation of money, but rather the transferal of preexisting money among various parties who are issuing loans, paying loans, buying loans, and selling loans.

A commercial bank doesn't keep every good & service being bought and sold by its depositors on its ledgers. When two commercial-bank depositors sell each other an apple or orange, the commercial bank doesn't keep the apple or orange on its books. When two commercial-bank depositors sell each other a loan, the commercial bank doesn't need to keep the loan on its books. Commercial bank ledgers only contain loans which were monetized (excepting borrowings by commercial banks, which would needlessly complicate this discussion and can be ignored).

When a monetized loan is paid off, the deposit liability created for the loan is uncreated. Once a commercial bank sells a loan, the loan payments are no longer made directly to the commercial bank. Loan principal payments made directly to the commercial bank are the mechanism by which loan money is uncomputered. If a commercial bank creates a deposit for a loan but doesn't uncreate that deposit when its sells the loan and removes the loan from its books, then the deposit created for the loan never gets uncreated. Thus a bank selling a loan uncomputers the deposit created for the loan when it sells the loan.

There are two types of loans: monetized loans and non-monetized loans. Monetized loans are fraudulent loans which are issued by creating the money for the loan out of thin air. Non-monetized loans are honest loans which are issued without creating money for the loan out of thin air. Non-monetized loans are issued with preexisting money which someone surrenders. When a commercial bank sells a monetized loan to any party besides another bank, it is essentially converting that loan into a non-monetized loan, which means the monetization is undone, and the money created for the loan is uncreated.

Uncreating money is harder than creating money because banks must obtain money to uncreate. When a bank sells a loan, the money which it uncreates is the money paid by the purchaser of the loan. The purchaser has replenished the deposit money which the bank created, lent to the borrower, and has not been repaid yet. The bank uncreates the money paid by the loan purchaser rather than the loan principal payments made by the borrower.

The bank doesn't care whose deposit is uncomputered, so long as some deposit is uncomputered. The bank is merely concerned with decreasing deposit liabilities by the same amount that it is decreasing loan assets. The bank can't uncreate the deposit of someone who did not buy the loan, as that someone would complain that their deposit money was stolen. Later we will see that interest paid on loans is placed in a deposit liability account that the bank owns, and that this deposit can be debited to uncomputer money, but for now the simple example of a normal depositor buying the loan and having their deposit uncomputered will suffice.

Though the steps of loan creation and deposit creation on commercial bank ledgers were shown separately, they are properly viewed as a single step. A loan asset & deposit liability are created together. No borrower signs a loan which is an agreement to repay money without being paid money, and no lender pays a borrower money without an loan agreement which obligates the borrower to repay that money. The uncreation (or removal) of a loan asset from a bank's books and the uncreation of deposit liabilities created for that loan are also properly viewed as a single step. Loan & money uncreation is the yang to the yin of loan & money creation.

A commercial bank can't uncreate a loan without uncreating a deposit, because then liabilities exceed assets, and the bank is rupt. The loan was an asset. The money created for the loan was a liability. If the bank uncreates the asset but not the liability, then liabilities exceed assets, which is not allowed. Thus a commercial bank can't sell a loan to a party outside the banking system without simultaneously uncomputering an amount of deposits equal to the face value of the loan.

The only exception is if the commercial bank has amassed assets which exceed liabilities. This is usually done by investing interest profits from loans. Banks take interest profits and lend them out for additional loans, or buy preexisting loans. If a commercial bank has assets which exceed liabilities, it can sell some assets without liabilities exceeding assets. This exception will be covered in a later chapter, so if this paragraph confused you, don't worry.

Uncomputering money makes sense on the ledgers, but in the real world still seems absurd. Uncomputering money is like seeing a pig fly. You know Porky has the power, but no matter how many times you watch him take off, it seems unnatural.

Dollars are computer accounting entries. People think of dollars as physical pieces of paper, but that isn't accurate. Physical paper dollars are less than 10% of the money supply, computered dollars are more than 90% of the money supply. These percentages will vary as mountains of money are computered and uncomputered, but in general, the amount of ledger money in circulation far exceeds physical money. Computer ledgers are the new printing presses. Most dollars are digital blips like the dots Pacman eats, nothing more.

It bears repeating that the total dollar supply isn't just physical dollars, but physical dollars and digital "checkbook" ledger money which banks computer. Or uncomputer. . .

Inflation is increasing the supply of money as if inflating a balloon, by creating money out of thin air. DEFLATION is decreasing the supply of money as if uninflating or deflating a balloon, by uncreating money out of thin air. Inflation is computering money, deflation is uncomputering money. Deflation is the yang to the yin of inflation.

Hyperinflation is a rapid increase in the money supply, HYPERDEFLATION is a rapid decrease in the money supply. Hyperinflation devastates an economy, and so does hyperdeflation. Hyperinflation is caused by the Federal Reserve rapidly creating mountains of reserves, and commercial banks creating an amount of deposits equal to 68 times reserves (or more) via fraudulent fractional-reserve lending. Hyperdeflation is caused by massive, widespread bank runs in which legions of depositors demand reserves which banks have promised them but simultaneously embezzled and lent out, and therefore don't possess. As banks frantically sell loans to obtain the reserves needed to honor withdrawal demands, monstrous sums of deposit money are uncomputed, deflating the money supply with extreme rapidity. Picture the money uncreation diagrams earlier in this chapter with hundreds of billions of dollars rather than hundreds of dollars, and you begin to get the picture.

You'll never hear the mainstream media mention hyperdeflation. Ever. Candid descriptions of hyperdeflation would wise sheeple up in a hurry. Imagine turning on the national news, and hearing a trusted news anchor say, "Commercial banks sold more than $100 billion of loans today to honor depositor withdrawals, uncreating the $100 billion which was created for those loans, and creating a cascading wave of money uncreation." Tens of millions of Americans would stop what they were doing, do a double take, glance at each other with confusion, and then commit themselves to understanding why banks can create and uncreate loan money.

Hyperdeflation occurred during Depression v8.1929-1942. Hyperdeflation also occurred during Depression v9.2006-201x, but was hidden from the public.

Suddenly ceasing inflation of the money supply caused Crusoeville's Depression, and uncomputering dollars caused America's Depressions. When massive amounts of money are uncomputed, prices of goods & services must decrease to adjust to the decreased supply of money, but as in Crusoeville, few people know the money supply has decreased. Without access to bank computers, how could they know? Sheeple pay the same old prices, but there is now less money.

If there are 10 apples and $10, each apple costs $1. If the money supply is decreased to $6, but prices stay at $1 an apple because no one knows the supply of money has decreased, then only 6 apples are purchased. There is not enough money to buy all apples at current prices. 4 apples go unsold and 40% of apple sellers go bankrupt, creating a Depression.

Deflation can create Depressions. And has. Hyperdeflation can completely collapse an economy and reduce it to bronze-age barter. It can destroy a civilization which has been duped into accepting fraudulent fractional-reserve banking. That may seem like an exaggeration. It is not. During Depression v9.2006-201x, it almost happened.

Imagine a $7.05 trillion money supply which was decreased by $550 billion, or 7%, in just a few hours or days by systemic bank runs. Almost instantaneously, there is not enough money to purchase 7% of the goods & services in the economy, and the hyperdeflation process snowballs. Depositors withdraw reserves, banks sell loans to obtain those reserves, selling loans causes uncomputering of deposits that is literally a decrease in the money supply, a decrease in the money supply causes more goods & services to go unsold, which causes more panic which causes more depositors to withdraw reserves...

The entire economy becomes a sadistic game of musical chairs because deposits exceed reserves, and there are not enough reserves to honor all deposits. Widespread demands for reserves cause massive amounts of deposits to be uncomputered as banks sell loans to obtain reserves, hyperdeflating the money supply. If the accelerating bank runs are not stopped, trillions of dollars are uncomputered in just a few days as ever-increasing amounts of lie-abilities are exposed. As the money supply decreases and can't claim all goods & serves at inaccurate, unadjusted prices, hordes of goods & services in the economy go unsold. Prices free fall until merchants must sell goods & services for less than they cost, bankrupting them, thereby increasing panic and demands for reserves, which accelerates the hyperdeflation further. Soon there is soon not enough money in circulation to conduct trade, and the economy collapses...

Preventing this hyperdeflationary econolypse—which can only occur under a corrupt banking system in which deposits exceed reserves—is the true story of The Bailout that passed in September 2008. Again, more on this later.

Someone must incur more debt as yours is paid off, or the money supply will deflate and induce a Depression. To avoid recessions and Depressions, the supply of money must remain stable. For the supply of money to remain stable, someone must always be in debt.

This is because money is debt. Most of the money supply is computered dollars, but dollars are only computered when loans are "monetized." Every computered dollar is a monetized debt, and later we'll see that the same is true of every physical dollar. The entire money supply is debt! If every monetized debt were paid off, the entire money supply would vanish!

Contrast this system with one in which money is a physical commodity like gold. Or a 100% reserve ledger-money banking system. In both these honest money systems, loan money can't be cyclically computered or uncomputered, created or uncreated. No money-destruction paradox is possible.

Every dollar is created to monetize a debt, but every debt need not utilize monetization. As explained, honest loans can be made from preexisting money, without monetization, and such loans can be paid off without decreasing the money supply. Unfortunately, honest loans are only a small percentage of total loans. Most loans are monetized, and if all monetized loans were paid off, there would be no money left in circulation.

If every dollar is debt, then every dollar is earning interest. For who? Bankers. In September 2008 when The Bailout passed, there was roughly $13.5 trillion in existence. Each one of these dollars was conjured out of thin air by, and earns interest for, the banker parasites who rule the world.

This debt paradox is difficult to wrap your brain around, and for some, difficult to believe. Though counter intuitive and absurd, it is unfortunately true, and represents a mind-boggling tragedy.

Poof Goes the Money Supply Picture Pages

To skip the picture pages after this chapter, please turn to page 323

PAYING OFF DEBT CONTRACTS THE MONEY SUPPLY INDUCING A DEPRESSION

Money Supply	Loan Principal Payment	Apples	Apple Price	Unsold Apples if Prices Don't Adjust
$100	$1	100	$1.00	0
$99	$1	100	$0.99	1
$98	$1	100	$0.98	2
$97	$1	100	$0.97	3
$96	$1	100	$0.96	4
$95	$1	100	$0.95	5
$94	$1	100	$0.94	6
$93	$1	100	$0.93	7
$92	$1	100	$0.92	8

Assume a Crusoeville economy in which no money exists. You obtain a $100 mortgage from First Fraud Bank, which creates it out of thin air. This is the only money in existence. The oversimplified loan payment is $2 per month. $1 of each loan payment goes to principal, $1 to interest. The bank keeps the interest payments and spends them into the economy, obtaining real goods & services even though it is producing no honest goods & services. The bank uncomputers principal payments, deflating (decreasing) the money supply.

There are 100 apples in the economy. When $100 is created, the price of apples equalizes at $1 per apple. As your loan principal payments are uncomputered, the money supply decreases. If people knew the money supply was deflating, they could adjust prices. People don't know the money supply is deflating, so don't decrease prices. At incorrect old prices, there is not enough money to buy all apples. After your first payment there is $99 and 100 apples, 1 apple goes unsold. After your second payment there is $98 and 100 apples, 2 apples go unsold. After your third payment there is $97 and 100 apples, 3 apples go unsold...

Depressions are nothing more than this simple principle applied on a massive scale, economy-wide. If the money supply deflates 1% and price don't adjust, 1% of goods go unsold, and 1% of businesses eventually go rupt.

Oversimplified? Yes. The correlation isn't this exact, especially once complex real-world variations like money velocity and non-transaction account fluctuations are factored in. Inaccurate? No. Hell no. This table shows why it is impossible for sheeple to get out of debt under the current money system. Paying off debt deflates the money supply, inducing a Depression.

MONETARY DEFLATION VS. PRICE DEFLATION

Just as there is monetary inflation and price inflation, there is monetary deflation and price deflation. Monetary inflation generally causes price inflation, and we have seen Speculatos muddle this causality. Speculatos play the same game with monetary deflation and price deflation, and demonize commodity money like gold by failing to differentiate monetary deflation and price deflation.

Monetary deflation is a decrease in the money supply.

Price deflation is a decrease in prices.

Price deflation can be good or bad. Price deflation caused by monetary deflation is bad; suddenly and unexpectedly deflating the money supply renders price signals inaccurate, forcing prices to decrease to adjust to the decreased supply of money, and bankrupting businesses that must suddenly sell goods for less than cost. Price deflation caused by increases in productivity or output is good; this good price deflation results when the output of goods grows faster than the money supply.

Let's use Crusoeville economics to demonstrate the difference between good price deflation and bad price deflation. $100 and 100 apples, apples cost $1. Monetary hyperdeflation occurs, $30 is uncomputered or otherwise removed from the economy, and there is suddenly $70 and 100 apples. People don't know money was uncomputered, so they don't adjust apple prices, they keep apple prices constant at $1 per apple. $70 buys 70 apples, 30 apples go unsold. Until prices correct, there is not enough money to purchase all apples in the economy, and 30% of apples go unsold, which is devastating. A 30% deflation of the money supply caused Depression v8.1929-1942. Prices eventually decrease to adjust to the decreased supply of money, settling at an equilibrium price where all money purchases all goods & services in the economy; in this case, apple prices eventually plummet to 70¢. $70 and 100 apples, for the supply of money to purchase all apples, they must cost 70¢. Except it costs 90¢ to produce an apple, meaning that all businesses selling them for 70¢ lose money and eventually go broke, and people who used to work producing apples lose their jobs. Monetary deflation has caused price deflation, and ravaged the economy.

The worst thing a leader could do if faced with monetary hyperdeflation would be to try and prevent prices from adjusting downward and decreasing; only when prices adjust to the decreased supply of money can all goods & services in the economy be sold again. FDR faced a hyperdeflation during the Great Depression, and prevented prices from adjusting by legally decreeing minimum prices. FDR thought that price hyperdeflation during the Great Depression was caused by excessive competition and capitalism. He thought businesses were "overcompeting" so much that they were driving prices too low. FDR did not realize that price hyperdeflation was actually caused by monetary hyperdeflation. FDR's stupidity exacerbated Depression v8.1929-1942 greatly. Had FDR allowed the free market to set new equilibrium prices and liquidate malinvestment in the process, Depression v8.1929-1942 might have been Depression v8.1929-1935. By failing to understand rudimentary economics, FDR transformed a plain old Depression into a "Great" one, causing tens of millions of Americans to suffer for another half-decade needlessly—and that half decade might have been a decade or more if America hadn't entered World War II.

Some historians now believe that America allowed Japan to sneak attack Pearl Harbor in December 1941 to facilitate America's entry into World War II. World War II ended the Great Depression, not FDR or his New "Deal." If FDR had understood basic undergraduate economics, Depression v8.1929-1935 would have been over long before World War II. Sometimes the truth is sick, but the sick truth is that American leaders were grateful for World War II on one level because it resuscitated the American economy. If the Great Depression had been over for half a decade in 1941, America might not have let the Pearl Harbor attack happen. Regardless, Americans enjoying economic prosperity would have been much less agreeable to fighting World War II. A speculative point, but not a totally absurd one.

Back to Crusoeville and good price deflation. $100 and 100 apples, apples cost $1. Mild monetary inflation occurs, the money supply increases to $101. An automated apple picker is invented, allowing less workers to pick the same old amount of apples, and more workers to labor planting apple trees. Apple production increases to 102 apples. There is now $101 and 102 apples, apples cost 99¢. Price deflation has occurred despite monetary inflation because innovation and productivity enhancements increased apple production. This is good price deflation.

Good price deflation is typical under commodity money systems such as the gold standard or silver standard. Historically, the money supply increased almost every year under a gold standard as more gold was mined, but it increased at a very gradual rate. The supply of goods & services increased faster than the supply of gold money, and the prices of goods & services therefore gradually decreased. Gradually is the key word. Markets can adjust to modest changes in the supply of money or goods & services without devastation resulting.

In the 1800s, prior to systemic guv'ment meddling with the money supply, good price deflation was usually the norm. As technology increased productivity, goods became cheaper to produce in ever larger quantities. Massive monetary inflation didn't pilfer all this additional production, so prices of goods steadily decreased. The same old wages bought more and more goods & services year after year, which is the exact opposite of our corrupt money system in which prices increase year after year and the same old wages buy less goods & services year after year.

In *Bubblenomics*, we noted that a loaf of bread was 7.7¢ in 1931 and $1 bought 13 loaves of bread at that time. $1 buried in 1931 and dug up today would only buy 1 loaf of bread, meaning monetary inflation had stolen 92% of the dollar's purchasing power, or 12 of the 13 loaves of bread. If we had kept honest money and perpetuated the good kind of price deflation, the price of bread would have decreased, and $1 buried in 1931 would buy 15 or 16 loaves of bread today.

In an honest money system, saved money would buy more goods & services in the future, meaning there would be more incentive to save and invest. Honest money encourages savings naturally because of the good price deflation it creates. The savings and frugality encouraged by this honest money system is the exact opposite of the rabid, heedless consumption of America today, which is financed by absurd amounts of debt. With honest money, America could not have mortgaged its future to the hilt.

Computers are an example of good price deflation. The price of computing power has steadily decreased as innovative computer manufacturers cram more transistors into ever smaller microchips and microprocessors. Computers have experienced relentless price deflation, but no one would argue that decreasing computer prices are bad. Strong, sustainable growth in real economic output is good, not harmful.

Speculatos muddle monetary inflation and price inflation by using the generic descriptor "inflation" to describe both. They engage in a similar charade by using the term "deflation" to describe both monetary deflation and price deflation. All modern Depressions were and are caused by massive monetary deflation. That is, hyperdeflation. Commodity money has a mild deflationary bias because its supply grows slowly relative to the supply of goods & services. Speculatos often criticize commodity money as being deflationary, implying that it causes the bad kind of price deflation which results from monetary deflation. Monetary deflation and monetary inflation are both difficult with precious metal money because it physically exists; no one would think of destroying huge amounts of gold, nor has anyone invented an easy way to conjure massive quantities of gold. Though there are occasional deflations in commodity money systems when the commodity which is money is transferred out of an economy and decreased in supply, monetary inflation and monetary deflation are only rampant in corrupt money systems in which fortunes can be created or destroyed on ledgers at the whim of Speculatos. By failing to distinguish between good price deflation caused by productivity increases, and bad price deflation caused by sudden contractions of the money supply, Speculatos are able to demonize honest commodity money that prevents monetary hyperinflation and monetary hyperdeflation.

GOLD RESERVES ALONE DO NOT PREVENT INFLATION & DEFLATION

Even commodity reserves such as gold don't protect against inflation and deflation if fraudulent fractional-reserve banking is allowed. In a system of fractional-reserve banking, banks can accept deposits of gold reserves and still engage in rampant deposit creation, conjuring promises to redeem gold reserves that exceed the supply of gold reserves. When lie-abilities are exposed and banks face widespread demands for gold reserves they don't possess, gold reserves can't be conjured in massive quantities the way Fed-account reserves can be. The system then implodes, unless it is saved by an FDR-esque gold seizure that provides banks the gold reserves they need to honor deposits.

Many "gold bugs" argue that a "gold standard" which utilizes gold reserves would minimize inflation and deflation and prevent Depressions, and should be the primary monetary reform. This is only half true. Gold reserves limit reserve inflation, the creation of gaggles of reserves out of thin air. However, if commercial banks create deposits which dwarf the supply of gold reserves, then inflation and deflation of these deposits results, Depressions still result, and the economic stability provided by gold reserves is subverted. Gold bugs recognize the need to limit inflation of the reserve supply, but often fail to recognize the need for a 100% reserve banking system which prevents commercial banks from creating deposits in excess of reserves. An honest money system limits inflation of both the reserve supply and the commercial-bank deposit supply. Any reform that limits only one of these forms of inflation is illusory, and will fail.

Speculatos oppose the gold standard, or any system of gold reserves, because it prevents Central Banks from creating massive amounts of ledger reserves. Massive amounts of ledger reserves are needed to Bailout commercial banks that practice fraudulent fractional-reserve lending and have lie-abilities exposed. Speculatos therefore champion a "gold fetters" doctrine which argues that gold fetters or shackles the economy, preventing inflation of the reserve supply that can be used to counter deflation of the commercial-bank deposit supply. This argument is absurd and counter intuitive, but Speculatos focused on the need to counter deflation rather than the need eliminate the inflation that causes deflation. By doing so, they were able to distort the perception of a gold-reserve system that helps prevent Depressions and demonize it as a cause of Depressions. In academia, gold reserves are no longer viewed as beneficial, but rather as fetters or shackles which had to be removed. And were removed. Unfetter the economy! Unshackle it! Emancipate it from the tyranny of gold! Don't eliminate rampant inflation of commercial-bank deposit money, eliminate constraints on rampant inflation of reserve money needed to Bailout commercial banks that rampantly inflate deposit money! The term "gold fetters" is shrewd propaganda which distorted the perception of gold. The gold fetters concept will be explained rigorously later, as will the historical backdrop of the Great Depression under which it arose.

In general, gold reserves are not as perfect as "gold bugs" think, and it may be inevitable and even desirable that all reserves become non-physical computer blips. There may also be some need for a central bank, as there are certain advantages to a central bank and unified currency. Having acknowledged all this, there is still a profound need for inviolate limitations on inflation of the money supply, which can only be implemented by limiting creation of reserves and limiting creation of commercial bank deposits leveraged from reserves.

THE SUPERHIGHWAY TO SERFDOM

"The ordinary man is passive. Within a narrow circle, home life, and perhaps the trade unions or local politics, he feels himself master of his fate. But otherwise he simply lies down and lets things happen to him."

—George Orwell

"The few who understand the system will either be so interested in its profits or be so dependent upon its favours that there will be no opposition from that class, while on the other hand, the great body of people, mentally incapable of comprehending the tremendous advantage that capital derives from the system, will bear its burdens without complaint, and perhaps without even suspecting that the system is inimical to their interests."

—Widely distributed anti-banking quotation misattributed to the Rothschilds

Under feudalism, Lords owned assets like land. Serfs worked land and gave most of what they produced to Lords. Our world is drowning in debt, and sheeple labor endlessly to service that debt, resulting in debt serfdom.

A lot has been covered, let's stop a moment, catch our breath, and summarize, so that the totality of this debt serfdom can be appreciated.

Money creation occurs *only* through debt creation. If there is no debt, there is no money. To increase the money supply, debt must increase. Money is debt.

The financial infrastructure of America and most every nation on Earth is debt based. Every nation in the world is in debt. Every government in the world is in debt. Every corporation in the world is in debt. Most every human on Earth is in debt. In debt to whom? To Central Banks, commercial banks, investment banks, and supranational banks such as the World Bank and International Monetary Fund.

Decreasing monetized debt decreases the money supply. Decreasing the money supply causes Depressions. If the U.S. guv'ment paid off its debt, the resulting monetary deflation would collapse the economy. If sheeple paid off their debt, the resulting monetary deflation would collapse the economy. Debt can't be eliminated without destroying the money supply, and as destroying the money supply collapses the economy and causes a Depression, debt can't be eliminated, or even sharply decreased. A system that tethers money to debt not only encourages debt, it enslaves with debt that can't be eradicated.

Money is debt. Debt requires interest payments. Money thus requires interest payments. Every circulating dollar both physical and digital is debt which requires interest payments. Every euro, pound, yen, yuan, franc, krona, won, krone, peso, and rupee is also debt which requires payment of interest. With only a few exceptions, most money used by most nations and humans on Earth is debt which requires interest payments.

Interest payments to whom? To Central Banks, commercial banks, investment banks, and supranational banks such as the World Bank and International Monetary Fund. Who owns, controls, or profits off Central Banks, commercial banks, investment banks, and supranational banks such as the World Bank and International Monetary Fund? Speculatos.

As the money supply increases, so does the debt supply. Speculatos increase the money supply and debt supply far faster than population or economic output increase. Overall debt thus increases massively in real terms. As time passes, everyone has more debt, and pays more interest on that debt. Many loan payments are via indirect means, such as taxes which pay guv'ment debt, or higher prices which pay corporate debt. Regardless, the long-term consequence is that ever larger percentages of a society's resources are allocated for interest payments to bankers.

This debt serfdom makes it virtually impossible for sheeple to accumulate wealth. Americans in previous generations understood that property and land were wealth, and strived to own property and land which were passed along generation after generation without debt burden. Today most Americans owe ever-larger debts on ever-smaller pieces of land. Most Americans today think they "own" their home even though it is mortgaged. The net worth of most Americans—and humans—when all their debt is factored in is virtually nil. Most Americans—and humans—die having labored their entire life paying debts yet owning almost nothing.

Medieval serfs agreed to a term of bondage which required them to work for Lords, and were aware of their servitude. Modern serfs signing loans agree to a term of bondage which requires them to work for banking Lords, but are unaware of their servitude. Modern serfs are unaware of their bondage and servitude because the debt serfdom which bankers have instituted is clandestine. Everyone knows there is debt, but only a few privileged initiates understand the money creation which accompanies debt. Only Lords understand that money has been transmuted into an insidious debt-bondage mechanism which is used to enslave serfs via interest tithes.

Technological advancement gives an illusion of wealth increase, but the real wages and standard of living of serfs stagnate and decrease as ever-increasing inflation taxes and interest tithes are levied. If technology were factored out and serfs reckoned their wages in real terms which accounted for monetary inflation and interest tithes, they would realize that they are growing much, much poorer.

Our world has two classes of people, Lords who create debt by creating money, and serfs who must labor to obtain money to pay that debt. As serfs labor for money, money they use to pay loans can be used to purchase their labor. A banker paid interest on a conjured loan by a laboring serf can use that money to buy the labor of that serf. Serfs thus pay debt with their labor, allowing fractional-reserve bankers to siphon a percentage of the labor of the entire human race without producing any honest goods & services.

John Q. Debtor is a typical American who makes $50,000 a year, has a $200,000 30-year mortgage at 5% interest, and pays 20% of his income for all taxes. A conservative estimate, as the average mortgage is $300,000 financed in the 6% range, average income is $45,000, and the average American pays more than 30% of their income for all taxes. We presume lower debt and tax levels, and higher income levels, than most Americans have.

Debtor will pay interest on his mortgage roughly equal to the face value: $200,000. After the taxman takes 20%, Debtor has $40,000 per year to spend. $200,000 of interest is 5 years of Debtor's after-tax income. If Debtor starts working at age 18 and retires at 65, he works 48 years. 5 of those 48 years is 10% of them. Speculatos siphon 10% of Debtor's lifetime wages by conjuring mortgage money out of thin air.

What if Debtor's mortgage is 6% rather than 5%? $231,000 of interest, 6 years of his life, 13% of his lifetime after tax income. A 7% mortgage? $275,000 of interest, 7 years of his life, 15% of his lifetime income. A $300,000 mortgage at 5%? 8 years of his life, 17% of his lifetime income.

In September 2008 just before The Bailout passed, lenders held $11.25 trillion in outstanding mortgage debt. If all these mortgages are 30-year mortgages at 5% interest, Speculatos receive roughly $11.25 trillion of interest payments over the life of the mortgages. If there are 10,000 Speculatos, this is $1.125 billion for each. Much of the $11.25 trillion of interest payments is spent running banks and paying other expenses, but what remains is still a massive fortune, even if all mortgages are not paid.

There are roughly 50 million home mortgages in America. In most families both spouses work, but presume one person per mortgage. When the interest payments made on mortgages are converted into labor equivalents, Speculatos obtain the labor of 50 million Americans for roughly 5 years of their life, or 10% of their working years.

That's just mortgages. What about car loans? Student loans? Credit cards? More than a billion credit cards exist just in America, with balances totaling $2.5 trillion. More than 3 cards for every man, woman and child in America. The average American household has $10,000 in credit card debt. Many are "revolvers" who only pay minimum payments. $18.1 billion in late fees were assessed to these debt serfs in 2007 alone. Late fees on top of ruinous interest, assessed by bankers lending money created out of thin air.

Assume a credit card with a $10,000 balance and a 12% interest rate. This is conservative. Millions of debt serfs would be ecstatic to have only $10,000 in credit card debt, and would love to convert all their 20% (or higher) cards to a "mere" 12%. Assume a minimum payment only, which optimistically pays just the interest. This is optimistic because banks structure minimum payments so that they don't pay off any of the loan principal and only cover part of the interest owed; unpaid interest is added to the outstanding balance on the card each month, increasing the balance perpetually. On our $10,000 12% credit card, we owe $100 a month just in interest (using oversimplified calculations). This seems trivial, until you sum it up over decades with millions of people. Enough crumbs make a cake. $2.5 trillion of credit cards at 12% interest is $25 billion of interest per month. Imagine you could create $2.5 trillion out of thin air and earn $25 billion a month on it! Not all credit card debt is conjured, but much of it is, so this data is rough though still reasonably accurate.

Mortgages are paid off, but not most credit cards. If John Q. Debtor holds a $10,000 credit card for the 48 years of his working life and only pays interest, he gives Speculato 1.5 years of labor. Including the mortgage, 6.5 years of labor, or 14% of his lifetime labor.

Many sheeple have mortgages, car loans, and credit card debt. To pay just the interest on these loans, they labor for Speculatos a decade or more of their lives. That is, 25% or more of their working lives. This doesn't include interest on the federal debt, interest on state and local government debt, or interest on business and corporate debt which people pay in the form of higher prices or higher taxes.

If every dollar was monetized for a 5% loan, then each year bankers receive interest payments equal to 5% of the total money supply. In September 2008 the M3 dollar supply was roughly $13.5 trillion, and 5% interest on $13.5 trillion for a single year would be $675 billion. In 2008, U.S. Gross Domestic Product, the total of all goods & services produced in America that year, was $13.2 trillion. $675 billion is 5.11% of $13.2 trillion. Very roughly, 5.11% of the output of the entire American economy, 5.11% of the annual labor of more than 300 million Americans, was siphoned by Speculatos producing nothing.

Some economists might balk at using the M3 money supply for such a calculation, as it includes money circulating outside America. Fine. We'll use more conservative M2 money supply data. The M2 money supply approximates the amount of money circulating inside the United States. In September 2008, M2 was $7.74 trillion. Imagine being able to create $7.74 trillion out of thin air, lend it out, and charge interest on it. Lent at 5%, this is $387 billion of interest payments per year.

The total output of the U.S. economy (GDP) in 2008 was $13.2 trillion, $387 billion is 3% of $13.2 trillion. There are 300 million Americans, very roughly, 3% of GDP is the annual labor of 3% of them, or 9 million Americans. A small cabal of bankers with the power to create money out of thin air produced nothing yet confiscated the annual labor of 9 million Americans.

Again, these rough estimates don't include bank operating costs which are a significant expense, and are not completely accurate for a number of other reasons, but they give a general sense of the big-picture price of fraudulent fractional-reserve lending. Fractional-reserve lending is taught with small numbers which make learning easier, but as always, it is important to see the appalling results when it is applied on an economy-wide scale.

Speculatos engineer similar wealth confiscation in every nation on Earth that utilizes fraudulent fractional-reserve banking. This is most every nation on Earth. As noted in *Bubblenomics*, the implementation of this fraudulent fractional-reserve banking system worldwide, along with central banks that provide the bailouts which support it, is the most significant historical development of the last several centuries. Speculatos abused this fraudulent banking system to conjure fortunes and fund both sides of every major war of the last several centuries, engineering these conflicts for profit with total disregard for the destruction and loss of life that resulted. Fraudulent banking was also used to engineer the clandestine subjugation of most of the human race, and created banking pharaohs that will never be overthrown because sheeple don't even know they exist.

The total output of the world economy (GDP) in 2008 was $61 trillion. If Speculato wealth confiscation rates throughout the rest of the world were similar to those in America, then 3% of $61 trillion was confiscated by Speculatos, which is $1.8 trillion. Very, very roughly, this is how much Speculatos pilfered from the entire human race in 2008 just via fractional-reserve lending. There were 6.7 billion people on Earth in 2008, very roughly, 3% of world GDP is the annual labor of 3% of them, or 201 million people. A small cabal of bankers with the power to create money out of thin air produced nothing yet confiscated the annual labor of 201 million humans. Again, this is a brute-force estimate, but even if significant error is conceded, it is nonetheless appallingly large. A significant portion of this confiscated wealth is amassed by a few hundred Speculato family dynasties which become fabulously wealthier.

Assassinations and other extra-legal tactics utilized by Speculatos seem less ridiculous when their massive profit is understood. If you had access to this fraudulent, fractional-reserve gravy train and someone tried to eliminate it, is it really so absurd to think that you might allocate a few million of your $1.8 trillion of annual income to harass the reformer? Or simply hire an assassin to kill them? You may not be capable of such evil behavior, but sociopathic Speculatos are.

Have you ever been on a descending flight, vectored over a residential area, and peered down like some god at thousands of houses? Imagine how triumphant Speculatos feel during such a flight—on their private jet of course. To Speculatos, each house contains a stupid serf toiling to enrich them, paying a mortgage, car loan, and other loans, all conjured out of thin air. Speculatos on such descents smile with immense satisfaction as they envision an entire world filled with stupid serfs, all ignorantly slaving away paying conjured debts. How smug and invincible would you feel if you had successfully implemented our banking & money system and enslaved the entire world with it? If billions of stupid brutes toiled to enrich you with absolutely no sense that they were doing so? As Frederic Morton once observed, Speculatos conquered the world more thoroughly, more cunningly, and more lastingly than any Alexander or Caesar, and they did so publicly yet secretly, using a corrupt banking & money system, and debt.

Speculatos view sheeple as dumb oxen, mere livestock that exist to labor and be slaughtered for their benefit. This is obviously not the author's view, and he realizes how offensive it is, but as we conclude this book, it is imperative that we confront the evil which underlies all the complex banking theory.

Our evil money & banking system did not spontaneously manifest, but rather was created by evil people. Evil people purposely conceived and implemented our evil money & banking system as a way to steal. Evil people perpetuate our evil money & banking system with evil actions that include lying and murder. Many people have a dogmatic inability to accept that the elite can be this sociopathic and monstrous. The elite can be this evil, and they often are. The unwillingness of sheeple to face this curdling truth is a fundamental barrier to reform.

On one level, people choose debt freely and deserve what they get, but on another level, the system is designed to perpetuate it and enslave sheeple with it. Sheeple are raised in a system that keeps them ignorant of money mechanics, glorifies materialism, conditions them to believe what they own is who they are, and then offers easy credit. Establishment economists shrug off trillion dollar federal deficits, and tell people a nation's budget isn't like a household budget, that trade and budget deficits are actually a national blessing. It all leads to comfort with debt, the sense that it is an intrinsic part of modern life, and impossible to avoid. By the time most sheeple ponder the desirability of debt, they are locked and loaded for life with a mortgage, car loan, and credit cards, and often a family they must support, and there is no escape.

The second quote at the beginning of this chapter is often attributed to the Rothschilds. Though not written by them, it is an excellent encapsulation of the thinking of Speculatos, and is included to emphasize that things are not always what they seem. Fraudulent fractional-reserve lending can be perpetuated only by maintaining widespread ignorance, by making our corrupt money system seem like anything but what it is.

The ultimate purpose of a fractional-reserve banking system is to turn sheeple into hamsters that toil relentlessly. A corrupt money system creates an inescapable interest treadmill that enriches parasitic Speculatos. This treadmill is perpetuated via a system of inextinguishable debts which sheeple don't deduce. The labor allocated to Speculatos via interest payments on money conjured out of thin air is staggering, and it is preposterous to call this wealth transfer anything but feudalism. Sadly, the great body of people, mentally incapable of comprehending the tremendous advantage that Speculatos derive from fractional-reserve feudalism, bear its burdens without complaint, without even suspecting that the system is inimical to their interests.

BUBBLENOMICS 3

It is not enough to say that banks create and uncreate money and condemn this practice as evil. For the evil of the fractional-reserve, Federal-Reserve system to be understood to a degree that will lead to reform, people must be shown a vivisection of its complex machinations. Performing this vivisection is a time consuming and lengthy process, so *Bubblenomics* will be serialized into multiple volumes. A full conclusion will be provided at the end of the final volume of *Bubblenomics*, but for now two problems with our banking system have been identified, fractional-reserve lending which allows commercial banks to create deposits which exceed reserves, and central banks such as the Federal Reserve with a monopoly on reserve creation.

Maintaining 100% reserve backing for demand deposits and requiring all lent demand deposits to be converted to time deposits is a simple yet monumental principle. Abandoning this principle and implementing fraudulent fractional-reserve lending is the root cause of most every war and financial crisis in history, and a significant portion of all human suffering.

Fraudulent fractional-reserve banking must be abolished. A private cabal of bankers should not have the power to create money while everyone else works for money. Honest 100% reserve banking eliminates this tyranny. Under an honest 100% reserve banking system, commercial banks can redistribute preexisting reserves, but can't create deposits in excess of reserves. Under an honest 100% reserve banking system, commercial banks create loans but not money.

There is still the question of who should have the power to create reserves, what quantity of reserves should exist, and what form reserves should take. This is a more difficult and complex problem than fractional-reserve lending. To abolish fractional-reserve lending but allow rampant inflation of reserves it to swan dive from the frying pan into the fire.

Before reforms which slay the fractional-reserve, Federal-Reserve kraken can be discussed meaningfully, we must examine a large number of additional frauds. This crusade will continue in *Bubblenomics 3*. People may be too stupid and lazy to ever learn the truth, as Speculatos claim and hope. But you have to try.

LR
May 2016

For information about *Bubblenomics 3*, and the novel The *Founding Fathers Return*, in which George Washington, Thomas Jefferson, and Benjamin Franklin are suddenly and mysteriously transported to present-day America, please visit Lawrence on the web at LawrenceRowe.com.

AFTERWORD

"What country can preserve it's liberties if their rulers are not warned from time to time that their people preserve the spirit of resistance? ... The tree of liberty must be refreshed from time to time with the blood of patriots & tyrants. It is it's natural manure."

—Thomas Jefferson

When I began researching our money & banking system, I assumed it would be easy to understand. I figured I would read a few books which would clearly enumerate its operation, and obtain a working knowledge rapidly. I had no intention of writing a non-fiction book, especially not one about economics, banking, or money.

Unfortunately, there were no books which provided a truly comprehensive summary of our banking & money system, especially not any which were scientifically rigorous yet easy to understand. I read book after book after book, and found the same superficial summaries regurgitated, often with the same elementary misconceptions and errors. I called experts, especially at the Federal Reserve and commercial banks, and found that they all used the same obfuscatory and deceptive academic language, usually without being cognizant of it. This language obscures what is actually happening under the hood of the banking system, and is meant to dupe and confuse those who are not banking initiates, mystifying the system so its corrupt nature is not understood.

I eventually had to read a number of horrifically boring academic papers and textbooks, including those which bankers learn from at universities and professional certification associations such as the American Bankers Association. These books and papers explained what was happening under the hood of the banking system in precise and unambiguous terms, though they utilized mathematics most people are incapable of understanding.

There was one glaring absence in formal academic texts. The ultimate moral, political, and socioeconomic consequences of our money & banking system were either misrepresented or ignored. Academic texts seemed to encourage initiates to manipulate and utilize the system without contemplating its morality. This was disconcerting, as the immorality of the system is the most glaring aspect to people outside academia who learn about it for the first time.

When I finally understood how our money & banking system operates, I was appalled, not just by the fact that it was fundamentally evil, but by the simplicity of the fraud it perpetrated. I had expected something more complex.

I realized that someone needed to write a book which explained our money system, not just superficially, but in detail, without the rudimentary errors in most non-academic books on the subject. Insiders laugh at most non-academic money & banking books because of their galling errors. I wanted a book which an insider could not debunk as being inaccurate. A book which any person, even one with no formal education, could understand. A book which explained the nuts and bolts of the system rigorously, so that it could not be dismissed as superficial summaries often are. A book which made the evil nature of our money & banking system apparent.

There was no such book. So I wrote it. I sacrificed dearly to do so. This book may not be enthralling, but anyone who reads it will have a clear understanding of why our banking & money system is evil and needs reform.

Until humanity reforms its money & banking system, solutions to its most vexing problems will remain elusive. Persistent atrocities such as poverty, war, and Depressions will never be eradicated without money & banking reform.

Evil people never give up power voluntarily. Evil people live like Pharaohs on the ill-gotten gains pilfered using our evil money & banking system. These evil people will never voluntarily surrender the power to conjure money. We the People will have to take this power from these evil people. Human civilization may have to undergo violent convulsions to eradicate its evil money & banking system.

Money & banking reform may not be implemented in our time. Reform is possible today, but only if people decide to educate and empower themselves, which they may not do. Reform also requires courage, and most Americans have become complacent. Disheartening, but true.

I have at least left a resource which future scholars can utilize to rapidly educate themselves about our money & banking system, without enduring the hassle I did. In a more enlightened and courageous time, perhaps this treatise can help provide the education that must precede reform, demystifying our banking & money system for neophytes. Only when the operational principles of our money & banking system are understood by all people, rather than a small cabal of insiders, will reform be possible, allowing a saner, more just world.

In some future era, the general populace may be more educated, moral, and motivated and muster the wisdom and the courage to undertake the daunting task of money & banking reform. It is my fervent hope that this happens. I hope that humanity will one day become more focused upon realizing its potential, making life, liberty, and the pursuit of happiness a birthright for all humans rather than just a privileged few that live in developed nations or control nations.

LR
May 2016

ENJOY THE BOOK?

Please leave a review

LawrenceRowe.com/reviews

LAWRENCE ROWE
Author of THE FOUNDING FATHERS RETURN

Please visit LawrenceRowe.com to learn more about *Bubblenomics*.

INDEX OF PICTURE PAGES

MASTER'S IN BUBBLENOMICS

FRIENDLY NEIGHBORHOOD FED

THREE-BANK MONTE

POOF GOES THE MONEY SUPPLY

Index of Website Hyperlinks

This index provides hyperlinks to primary sources, especially Federal Reserve policies, regulations, data, and statistical releases. These hyperlinks are ordered according to usefulness and relevance. Some links may become deprecated over time and may no longer function. Many images of webpages in this book can also be clicked on to view the original webpages. If more Americans accessed these primary sources and understood them, our nation would be better off.

Main Website of Board of Governors of Federal Reserve System
http://www.federalreserve.gov

Federal Reserve Data Releases
http://www.federalreserve.gov/econresdata/statisticsdata.htm

Current Federal Reserve Release H.3
Aggregate Reserves of Depository Institutions and Monetary Base
http://www.federalreserve.gov/releases/h3/current/

Current Federal Reserve Release H.6
Money Stock Measures
http://www.federalreserve.gov/releases/h6/current/

Current Federal Reserve Release H.8
Assets & Liabilities of U.S. Commercial Banks
http://www.federalreserve.gov/releases/h8/current/

Federal Reserve Policy Tools
http://www.federalreserve.gov/monetarypolicy/policytools.htm

Federal Reserve Statutory Reserve Ratio Requirements
http://www.federalreserve.gov/monetarypolicy/reservereq.htm

Federal Reserve Sweeps Data
http://research.stlouisfed.org/aggreg/swdata.html

Federal Reserve Branches
http://www.federalreserve.gov/otherfrb.htm

Federal Reserve Bank Services
https://www.frbservices.org/

FDIC

https://www.fdic.gov/

FFIEC

http://www.ffiec.gov/

FFIEC Call Report Search Page

https://cdr.ffiec.gov/public/ManageFacsimiles.aspx

BIBLIOGRAPHY

A Brief History of Deposit Insurance in the United States: Prepared for the International Conference on Deposit Insurance. (1998). Washington, DC: Federal Deposit Insurance Corporation. Retrieved from https://www.fdic.gov/bank/historical/brief/brhist.pdf

Anderson, R. G., & Rasche, R. H. (2001). *Retail Sweeps Programs and Bank Reserves, 1994 - 1999.* Federal Reserve Bank of St. Louis Review, 83(1), 51-72. Retrieved from https://research.stlouisfed.org/publications/review/01/0101ra.pdf

2013 Federal Reserve Payments Study. (2014). New York, NY: The Federal Reserve System. Retrieved from http://www.frbservices.org/files/communications/pdf/general/2013_fed_res_paymt_study_detailed_rpt.pdf

Federal Reserve Account Management Guide. (2016). New York, NY: Federal Reserve Bank Services. Retrieved from https://www.frbservices.org/files/regulations/pdf/amg_0116.pdf

The Federal Reserve System: Purposes & Functions. (2005). Washington, DC: Board of Governors of the Federal Reserve System. Retrieved from http://www.federalreserve.gov/pf/pdf/pf_complete.pdf

Feinman, J., Deschler, J., & Hinkelmann, C. (1993). *Reserve Requirements: History, Current Practice, and Potential Reform.* Federal Reserve Bulletin, 78(6), 569-589. Retrieved from http://www.federalreserve.gov/monetarypolicy/0693lead.pdf

Fisher, I. (1933). *The Debt Deflation Theory of Great Depressions.* Retrieved from https://fraser.stlouisfed.org/scribd/?title_id=3596&filepath=/docs/meltzer/fisdeb33.pdf#scribd-open

Fisher, I. (1935). *100% Money: Designed to Keep Checking Banks 100% Liquid, To Prevent Inflation and Deflation, Largely to Cure or Prevent Depressions, and To Wipe Out Much of the National Debt.* New York, NY: Adelphi.

Friedman, D.H. (1977). *I Bet You Thought.* New York, NY: Federal Reserve Bank of New York. Retrieved from http://files.eric.ed.gov/fulltext/ED175743.pdf

Gonczy, A. M. (1992). *Modern Money Mechanics: A Workbook on Bank Reserves and Deposit Expansion.* Chicago, IL: Federal Reserve Bank of Chicago. Retrieved from https://upload.wikimedia.org/wikipedia/commons/4/4a/Modern_Money_Mechanics.pdf

Guide to the Federal Reserve's Payment System Risk Policy on Intraday Credit. (2012). Washington, DC: Board of Governors of the Federal Reserve System. Retrieved from http://www.federalreserve.gov/paymentsystems/files/psr_guide.pdf

Nuri, V.Z. (2002). *Fractional Reserve Banking as Economic Parasitism.* Retrieved from http://econwpa.repec.org/eps/mac/papers/0203/0203005.pdf

Payment Systems in the United States. (2003). Basel, Switzerland: Bank for International Settlements. Retrieved from http://www.bis.org/cpmi/paysys/unitedstatescomp.pdf

Reserve Maintenance Manual. (2013). Washington, DC: Board of Governors of the Federal Reserve System. Retrieved from http://www.federalreserve.gov/monetarypolicy/files/reserve-maintenance-manual.pdf

VanHoose, D., & Sellon, Jr., G. (1989). *Daylight Overdrafts, Payments System Risk, and Public Policy.* Federal Reserve Bank of Kansas City Economic Review, 74(8), 9-29. Retrieved from http://www.kansascityfed.org/publicat/econrev/econrevarchive/1989/3-4q89vanh.pdf

SIGN UP FOR LAWRENCE ROWE'S NEWSLETTER
Sneak Previews • Exclusives • Special Offers

LawrenceRowe.com/signup

Some men would be great in any time.

THE
FOUNDING
FATHERS
RETURN

A Novel

LAWRENCE ROWE

Please visit LawrenceRowe.com
to learn more about *The Founding Fathers Return*.

THE FOUNDING FATHERS RETURN

A Novel